LIVING WITHIN
LIMITS

LIVING WITHIN LIMITS

Ecology, Economics, and Population Taboos

GARRETT HARDIN

OXFORD UNIVERSITY PRESS
New York   Oxford

Oxford University Press

Oxford   New York
Athens   Auckland   Bangkok   Bombay
Calcutta   Cape Town   Dar es Salaam   Delhi
Florence   Hong Kong   Istanbul   Karachi
Kuala Lumpur   Madras   Madrid   Melbourne
Mexico City   Nairobi   Paris   Singapore
Taipei   Tokyo   Toronto

and associated companies in
Berlin   Ibadan

Library of Congress Cataloging-in-Publication Data
Hardin, Garrett James, 1915–
Living within limits : ecology, economics, and population taboos /
by Garrett Hardin.
p. cm.   Includes bibliographical references and index.
ISBN 0-19-507811-X
ISBN 0-19-509385-2 (Pbk.)
1. Birth control.   2. Population.   I. Title.
HQ766.7.H35   1993
304.6′66—dc20   92-24250

1 3 5 7 9 10 8 6 4 2

Printed in the United States of America

I teach only two things: the cause of human sorrow
and the way to become free of it

THE BUDDHA

Acknowledgments

The writing of this book has been greatly facilitated by the material aid extended by the Ecumenical Fellowship, the Laurel Foundation, and the Pioneer Fund. I am also very grateful for long continued encouragement from Charles T. Munger, Cordelia S. May, John H. Tanton, and Harry F. Weyher. Valuable comments on the manuscript were contributed by John Rohe and Hugh H. Iltis. My wife, Jane, has judiciously mixed encouragement with criticism, while putting up with an author in the house for more years than bear telling.

Santa Barbara, California   G. H.
November 1992

Contents

I

ENTANGLING ALLIANCES

1

The Challenge of Limits

A funny thing happened on the way to the second nationwide Earth Day in 1990. Twenty years earlier the first Earth Day had been saluted with much talk about population problems. At that time world population stood at 3.6 billion. But when the second Earth Day rolled around, the topic of population was almost completely ignored. Was that because world population had stopped growing? Hardly: in the intervening two decades it had increased 47 percent to an estimated 5.3 billion— an increase of 1.7 billion (more than six times the present population of the United States).

Common sense tells us that the per capita share of environmental riches must decrease as population numbers increase, and waste disposal necessarily becomes an ever greater problem. Of course common sense is sometimes wrong. But if that is so in this instance, the celebrants of the 1990 Earth Day should have been shouting, "We've found the secret of perpetual growth!" A few incurable optimists did defend this position, but most people lumped their claims with those of the flat earthers, ignoring both. The celebrants were generally silent about the 47 percent increase in population. Why?

The answer comes in two parts, the first being historical. It is now known that the planners of Earth Day 1990 were under economic pressure to leave population out of the picture. When directors of philanthropic foundations and business concerns were solicited for financial support they let it be known that they would not look kindly on a population emphasis. Money talks, silence can be bought. (Why the bankrollers shied at population will become clear later.)

The second aspect of the answer is more subtle. It has long been recognized that some of our most deeply held views are not neat, precise propositions but broadly "global" attitudes that act as the gatekeepers of the mind, letting in only those propositions that do not challenge the dominant picture of reality. Germans call such gatekeeper attitudes *Weltanschauungen,* an impressive mouthful that is quite adequately translated as "worldviews." For all but the last few hundred years of human history the dominant worldview was a limited view: resources were limited, human nature was fixed, and spending beyond one's income was a sin. This essentially conservative perception prevailed until about 1600.

Then science and technology shook the foundations. One presumed limit after another was shown to be, in part, false. Age-old justifications for conservative, thrifty action were questioned. In our century the new spirit was deftly captured in the advertisement of an airline: "Fly now, pay later!" Since man, an optimistic ani-

3

mal, usually presumes that "we" will be richer later, conservatism was redefined as living on credit cards. In the public mind the limited worldview was replaced by a limitless worldview. The new orientation was intoxicating.

An effective gatekeeper of the mind does not call attention to itself. It actuates a psychological mechanism called a *taboo*. This South Sea island word was introduced into the English language by Captain Cook in 1777. That population discussions have been significantly hemmed in by taboo from Cook's time to the present can be easily demonstrated. Ten years before the English word was created, the Scottish economist Sir James Steuart, after attributing poverty to overpopulation, ended by confessing: "How to propose a remedy for this inconveniency, without laying some restraint upon marriage; how to lay a restraint upon marriage without shocking the spirit of the times, I own I cannot find out; so I leave every one to conjecture." Thomas Robert Malthus, who really got the population debate off the ground in 1798, was only a year old when Steuart thus bowed to the power of taboo.

The population taboo, while far from absolute, is still with us, as is illustrated by two examples from among many. In 1980 *Newsweek* published a 2,600-word essay on "Vanishing Forests," in which not a single word was said about the role of population growth in causing worldwide deforestation. In 1989 *The New Yorker* published a 26,000-word extract of an environmentalist book *The End of Nature* which included only seventy-nine guarded words on population.

An element of behavior that is transferred from one culture to another is likely to suffer a sea change. So it has been with taboo. Pacific islanders apparently have no hesitancy in explicitly giving taboo as a reason for stopping a discussion. By contrast, Westerners, with their cherished tradition of free speech and open discussion, would be embarrassed to say (for instance), "We will not discuss population because it is under a taboo." Instead, they change the subject. Hundreds of articles are written every year about the pathological effects of overpopulation—traffic congestion, deforestation, loss of species, soil erosion, and air pollution—without any mention of population growth as an essential cause.

In the United States in the middle of the 1980s the practical issue of population control became entangled with the moral issue of abortion. This is somewhat puzzling because there is no *necessary* connection between the two. Limiting population growth is easier to achieve when abortion is readily available, but population control is quite possible in a nation that prohibits abortion. A thorough political history of this entanglement is yet to be written, but it is safe to say that, beginning about 1980, abortion became a red herring that was deliberately dragged across the path of nearly every discussion of population. Since abortion, a tabooed topic only three decades earlier, was still regarded as indecent by millions of Americans, the topic of population control got tarred with the same brush.

But this has been a late development. In the first century after Malthus resistance to discussing population control came from other sources, principally from the social pioneers who were reshaping European culture into a more humane one. Reformers who were trying to persuade society to deal compassionately with children, women, and poor people often considered population a distraction.

Earlier, the principal supporters of population studies had been economists. Malthus, the first British professor of economics (then called "political economy"), pioneered in emphasizing the connection between economics and population.

John Stuart Mill kept the connection alive in the 1850s, but by the centennial of Steuart's statement the subject of population had virtually disappeared from the discipline of economics. Now, after yet another century, the topic is still missing from most economics textbooks.

Marxists have confidently asserted that the advance of technology, coupled with distributional justice, would automatically solve all problems mistakenly labeled "population." A similar conclusion was reached in the capitalist world, where the spirit of laissez-faire was invoked to generate a theory of automatic (and nearly painless) population regulation. The theory of "benign demographic transition" and the "child survival hypothesis" (to be discussed later) have, in effect, told people "Not to worry!" So ambiguous is statistical evidence that both of these optimistic theories of automatic population control survived nearly half a century before being abandoned by professionals. (They still persist on college campuses and in the popular press.)

The "Don't worry" theories of population control amount to a reaffirmation of the religious idea of Providence. Professional publicists know there is always a good living to be made by catering to the public's craving for optimistic reports. Such behavior finds no justification in the attitude of the Buddha, expressed five centuries before Christ: "I teach only two things: the cause of human sorrow and the way to become free of it." The present work, though written by a non-Buddhist, proceeds along the Buddhist path—first to reveal the causes of human sorrow in population matters and then to uncover promising ways to free ourselves of the sorrow.

Hearing the Buddha's statement today many people think, "How depressing! Why accept such a pessimistic outlook on life?" But they are wrong: it is not a pessimistic view if we reword it in terms that are more familiar to our science-based society. Reworded: "Here's something that isn't working right. I want to fix it, but before I can do that I have to know exactly why it doesn't work right." One who looks for causes before seeking remedies should not be condemned as a pessimist. In general, a great deal of looking for causes must precede the finding of remedies.

A great source of shared sorrow comes to us these days from an environment that has been badly mistreated for many centuries. Describing and looking for remedies to this sorrow is the obligation of ecology. Though the science of ecology was named more than a century ago, the public scarcely became aware of it until Rachel Carson's *Silent Spring* was published in 1962. Since then an avalanche of discouraging reports on the environment has engulfed the public.

Broadly stated, most ecological problems reduce to the single problem of balancing supply and demand. That may sound simple enough, but the two words *supply* and *demand* stand for utterly disparate things. Supply is strictly limited, though we often cannot state the limits with any precision. Demand, however, is essentially unlimited, because the word implies *demands made by human beings*. There is no intrinsic limit to the demands that can be made by people. The natural tendency to produce an imbalance between supply and demand is the source of Buddhistic "sorrow." Preventing, or at least minimizing, this sorrow requires solving the population problem. Such was Malthus's view; and such must ours be.

Two centuries of intermittent wrestling with population problems have produced useful insights about the reality and nature of limits, the meaning of progress, the properties of exponential growth, the utility of usury, scale effects, and the consequences of diminishing returns. Enlightenment has come from many quarters, not least from the engineering theory of controls. Journalists hanker after simple, one-paragraph answers to the threat of overpopulation: unfortunately there is no persuasive brief answer. However I think we can now see the *form* that acceptable answers must take. These are summarized in the concluding chapter.

Four centuries of sedation by the delusion of limitlessness have left humanity floundering in a wilderness of rhetoric. The history of population theories is a history of wishful thinking. By myriads of ruses hucksters have tried to divert attention from the conservation principles of science, implying that to accept the reality of limits is to become a pessimist.

But scientists are not saddened by conservation laws. Instead they agree with an aphorism attributed to Hegel: "Freedom is the recognition of necessity." From this it must be inferred that some day political conservatism will once again be defined as contented living within limits. The limitless world view will have to be abandoned. Before we can accept this necessity we must rid ourselves of many illusions that have in the past supported unworkable theories of population growth. To these we now turn our attention.

2

Overpopulation: Escape to the Stars?

"Why worry about too many people on earth when we have the whole universe to expand into? Europe solved its population problems earlier by shipping the excess off to the New World: why can't we continue this process? Already our space programs have pointed the way." This possibility is constantly raised in public meetings and should be taken seriously. So long as there is a glimmer of hope in sidestepping the problem of overpopulation by escaping to the stars, many people will refuse to grapple with the problem of adjusting to earthly limits.

The Dream of Extraterrestrial Migration

In the 1950s a Monsignor Irving A. DeBlanc deplored "an often expressed idea that birth control is the only answer to problems created by a fast-growing world population." Instead of trying to curb population growth, said DeBlanc, we should welcome it and make plans to ship off the excess. Thus we could continue humanity's millennia-old tradition of moving to a new home after making a mess of our old one.

We can grant that DeBlanc's intentions were good. They fitted in with his value system: he was the director of the National Catholic Welfare Conference's Family Life Bureau, an organization committed to encouraging large families. Their publicity was addressed principally to Roman Catholics.

Some Catholics endorse space migration because the church hierarchy opposes artificial methods of birth control. But we must not forget that science itself has become something of a religion to millions of people. The marvels of technology have brought many people to an uncritical worship of a god called "Progress," which is sometimes equated with perpetual growth. If this means that the control of population growth is immoral there remains only migration to the stars to correct for overpopulation on earth. Thus can theistic and atheistic religions meet at the crossroads of conception.

In 1958, four years after the founding of NASA—the National Aeronautics and Space Administration—its congressional guardian, the Science and Astronautics Committee, supported the idea of space migration as an ultimate solution to the problem of a "bursting population." The hired technical staff of NASA no doubt thought poorly of proposals like DeBlanc's; but when an agency is fighting for the space that counts—space at the public trough—its administrators are in no hurry to correct statements that increase the size of their budget.

How stands the supply of inhabitable planets? Are they *practically* available to us earthlings? Early in this century it was thought that Mars and Venus were possible sites for human life. Not long after NASA was founded it became irrefutably clear that no other planet revolving around our sun is suitable for our kind of life. We now know that a human being on the surface of Venus would have to breathe air that is 96 percent carbon dioxide, at a temperature hot enough to melt lead, laboring under an atmospheric pressure equivalent to the hydraulic pressure half a mile down in our oceans. (It is thought that Venus has already been subjected to a devastating "greenhouse effect" of the sort that now worries us here on earth.)

As for Mars—that old war-horse of science fiction—living on the red planet would be about like living on a Mount Everest that was twice as high. The air of Mars contains only traces of water; its pressure is only 1 percent of our atmospheric pressure at sea level; and the temperature, day and night, is below zero degrees Fahrenheit. So when we talk about celestial migration, we are really considering only interstellar migration, migration toward stars other than our sun—stars that are *presumed* to have planets of their own. It is further *presumed* that, among the hypothesized planets, a few may be as favorable for life as the earth is. (We are not interested in finding another Venus or Mars.)

Numeracy: A Commonsense Approach

In recent years Americans have come to recognize that the fruit of education must include not only literacy, but numeracy—the ability to handle numbers creatively. Scientists and technicians need to be fully numerate, of course. This fact need not frighten the nonprofessional citizen because (fortunately) a great deal of meaning can be extracted from numbers by simple common sense. A passage from the life of that interesting eighteenth-century character Samuel Johnson illustrates the point. Though his life revolved around words—he was the compiler of a famous dictionary—he had an astute feeling for the right way to deal with numbers, as this passage from Boswell's *Life of Johnson* shows:

Johnson: "Were I a country gentleman, I should not be very hospitable, I should not have crowds in my house."

Boswell: "Sir, Alexander Dick tells me that he remembers a thousand people in a year to dine at his house: that is reckoning each person as one each time he dines there."

Johnson: "That, Sir, is about three a day."

Boswell: "How your statement lessens the idea."

Johnson: "That, Sir, is the good of counting. It brings everything to a certainty, which before floated in the mind indefinitely."

Boswell failed to extract the best meaning from the numerical report because he simply "froze" on the big number, "a thousand." Dr. Johnson, however, did not panic but proceeded to compare the proffered number with another that was well known and relevant to the situation, namely the number of days in a year.

There is a general point to be made here. No number is inherently "big" or "little"; it is only in comparison with other numbers that it takes on the attribute of size. Any comparison may help somewhat, for example, showing that all the people who broke their New Year's resolutions, if lying end to end, would stretch from here to—where? Timbuctoo? But a truly relevant number is better. Don't panic (like Boswell); but (like Johnson) look for a relevant comparison.

Also, don't bother about a precise number if a rough approximation will do the job. A modern admirer of Dr. Johnson, intoxicated by the power of a hand calculator, might divide 1,000 by 365 and announce that the average number of guests per day was 2.739726027. But why bother with such precision? A rough "three a day" is precise enough.

Overpopulation Is More Than a Scientific Problem

An oft-repeated query takes this form: "Since man has succeeded in landing on the moon, why can't we——?" The blank is filled in with the speaker's favorite "wanna have." The implication is that the second problem is like the first and cannot possibly be so difficult, technically.

Landing on the moon was a great technical triumph. It was also a political accomplishment. In 1961 President Kennedy and the Congress committed the nation to complete this program by the end of the decade. Only eight years later, in 1969, the first astronaut set foot on the moon. To put this achievement in perspective note the following: from 1919 (when rocket pioneer Robert Hutchings Goddard published *A Method of Reaching Extreme Altitudes*) to 1969 was precisely half a century. What amazing technological progress to make in so short a time!

Unfortunately the really difficult part of dealing with overpopulation is not technical; it is something else. The problem is one of understanding and controlling human behavior. These are formidable problems. Four times half a century has passed since Thomas Robert Malthus awakened the world to the "population problem" in 1798. Population analysts have achieved no triumph comparable to the landing of men on the moon. Space travel and population control are utterly different sorts of "problems." For the solution of the first we look for Newtons; for the second, Buddhas. We need to see why.

Extraterrestrial Migration: Some Relevant Scientific Details

Distance

Beyond the sun the nearest star is Alpha Centauri, at 4.3 light-years distance. (A "light-year" is a measure of distance, not time: it is the distance that light travels in one year.) Alpha Centauri is 25 million million miles distant from the earth. (That's not a typo: "million million" is correct—"quadrillion," if you prefer.)

Transit Time

To escape the earth, a spaceship must exceed a velocity of 25,000 miles per hour. At 25,000 mph it would take a spaceship 1,000 million hours to get to Alpha Centauri—that adds up to 114,000 years in transit. It is intimidating to think of designing a self-sustaining human colony that could govern itself successfully for more than a hundred thousand years. More speed is needed.

Even at the speed of light a journey to Alpha Centauri would take over four years, but there are good physical reasons for thinking this speed cannot be approached very closely. Sebastian von Hoerner thinks that 3 percent of the speed of light is the best we could hope for. That's some 22 million mph. At that speed it would take 140 years to go from earth to Alpha Centauri. The trip would require about five generations of human time. One might argue that future advances in technology should reduce the time of transit; but on the other hand, suppose that none of the presumed planets of Alpha Centauri were suitable for human life? In that case our Spaceship Mayflower would have to "set sail" again, for perhaps another five generations, before its passengers could even *hope* to find a new earth to set foot on.

Energy

Don't suppose that spacehip Mayflower could, like the earth, be made self-sustaining by ordinary agriculture. Sunlight could keep green plants on such a ship growing for only the first few months of the trip. Long before the craft got as far away as Neptune there would be too little sunlight for photosynthesis; and everyone knows how dim the distant stars are. In the dark, plants use oxygen, just as animals do all the time. Long before Neptune was passed the plants would be competing with people for oxygen. Since Alpha Centauri is the nearest star, that means that most of the 140 years of the voyage would take place in starlight only. Very romantic no doubt, but not very nourishing. To regenerate oxygen on board energy would be required. From what source could the colonists get enough energy for five generations of living in the dark?

Freeman Dyson has suggested that the travelers could throw hydrogen bombs, one by one, out the back end of the ship, capturing perhaps 10 percent of the energy with a shield between the ship and the explosion. (Obviously a few engineering details need to be worked out before our spacehip can take off!) The mobile colony would need a safe method of storing and using energy for 140 years.

Cost

In recent years we have had enough experience with inflation to have little confidence in the estimated dollar costs of far-out dream projects. Dyson has proposed a way of looking at the problem that bypasses the confusion caused by inflation. The savings and donations used by our ancestors to pay for the trip on the historic Mayflower to the New World can be expressed in human years of effort required to accumulate the necessary capital. Dyson figures it required 7.5 years of one person's labor to pay the cost of one family's passage in the Mayflower that brought the Pilgrims to North America. For the historic trip of the Mormons from Illinois to Utah in the nineteenth century he reckons the cost at 2.5 human years per family. For one of the most thoroughly worked out plans of a space colony he estimates a cost of 1,500 human years per family. If we assume that a family is four people, that means 375 human years of work per person sent off on the space voyage.

When we express the cost of a trip in the fundamental terms of human years of work it is obvious that it would be a rare passenger who could finance his own trip. A person working 50 years of his life (from age 15 to 65) can turn out only 50 human years of work, and he consumes most of this sum in the process of living. It is not easy to say how much of it he can save, but it is certainly not much. So each hypothetical emigrant on a spaceship would have to be subsidized by a large community of people who stayed behind. This scientific fact obviously calls for some generosity in the political system.

Though dollars are a less fundamental measure than human years of work, a little perspective can be gained by roughly expressing the cost in dollars. Consider a nuclear submarine. This is a very elaborate piece of machinery, but it surely is not nearly as complicated as a spaceship capable of making a 140-year trip to the stars. A typical nuclear submarine costs $1 billion and carries 140 sailors. The boarding cost per sailor works out at $7,000,000 (and we neglect the running expenses, which are considerable). If each sailor had to buy his position on the sub (as British gentlemen in the nineteenth century had to buy their commissions in officers' corps), could an ordinary man hope to make enough money to pay his embarkation fee before he became too old to be accepted on board? It is hard to see how an average man could save more than $10,000 a year from an ordinary job. At that optimistic rate of savings it would take him 700 years to accumulate the capital sum needed for his embarkation fee.

Human Population: Growth Outruns Solutions

For interstellar migration to prevent an increase of population on earth, people would have to be exported as fast as the world's population is increasing. (Worse: if we agree that the world is already overpopulated, people would have to be shipped off faster than this. But let us take a sunny view of things and ignore the possibility that the earth is already overpopulated.)

During 1961, the year that President Kennedy committed the United States to going to the moon, the *increase* of the world's population was *64 million.*

During the years 1969 to 1972 a dozen Americans set foot on the surface of the moon, as part of the Apollo project (now discontinued). In the last year of that effort world population increased by *76 million.*

The rate of global population increase was 2.1 percent per year in 1961. It remained steady for awhile, and then began falling slowly, reaching a post-Apollo low of 1.7 percent in the year 1979, where it seems to have stayed for ten years, until 1989 when it ominously rose again to 1.8 percent. Though the percentage rate was less in 1989 than in 1961, the base on which that rate operated was greater, so the absolute annual increase in world population in 1989 was at a new high of *94 million.*

Time after time the press, addicted to optimism, reports that "Population growth is slowing." This is both true and false, depending on the interpretation of the sentence. "Optimistic" opinion makers ask us to focus on the decrease in the *percentage rate,* a process that can be typographically represented in this way:

$$2.1\% \rightarrow {\scriptstyle 1.7\%}$$

But focusing the typography on the *absolute rate* gives a different picture:

$$\text{\scriptsize 64 million} \rightarrow \text{\small 79 million} \rightarrow \text{\large 93 million}$$

The absolute rate of increase has increased every year since the end of World War II. It is the absolute increase, rather than the relative rate, that stresses the environment. It is a sad aspect of American life that so many opinion makers are unable to appreciate the distinction between relative and absolute rates. Or perhaps—compulsive optimists that they are—they are unwilling to face facts.

By 1989 the daily increase of world population was 258,000. The accumulated increase, from 1961 to 1989, amounted to more than 2.2 billion. It should be noted that the increase during a single generation in the last half of the twentieth century was greater than the entire world population at the time World War II began. During the 28 years in which world population increased by 2.2 billion people, NASA managed to put twelve men on the moon, three at a time, for a few hours. The threesomes were never remotely close to constituting a self-sustaining colony. (And our moon is only one one-hundred-millionth as far away as Alpha Centauri.)

One could continue playing with numbers, but dreams and reality are so far apart that a further refining of the figures is not worth the effort. Moreover, numerical analyses of the interstellar migration problem are rendered irrelevant by human and political facts yet to be considered. Beyond the entertaining numbers lies a simple logical principle that trivializes precise numerical analysis.

Life on Board the Spaceship Mayflower

Whatever else one might say of our spaceship, its mass is certainly finite. Every pound incorporated into its structure, or put on board as passengers or cargo, costs a small fortune. The ship cannot gain significantly in mass by sweeping up interstellar dust as it hurtles through space. The vacuum of space is emptier than the best vacuum we can achieve in the laboratory. True, at its great speed, the craft will encounter many micrometeorites, but they will almost all be truly *micro.* (Those that are *macro,* say an ounce or more in mass, would constitute a serious threat to the vessel. Striking the spaceship at 25,000 mph an ounce of matter could wreak tremendous damage, the repair of which would deplete some of the precious supplies of the ship.) For 140 years the space pilgrims would have to live on an absolutely rigid budget. The limitations of this budget must be strongly impressed on them before they take off. The wayfarers would have to succeed where our democratic legislatures usually fail: they would have to live within their budget.

Obviously the inhabitants of the new Mayflower could not be a random sample of the earth's population. Nowhere would this be more apparent than in their reproductive behavior. Since their supplies and living areas are indubitably limited, an increase in the population of the colony would be intolerable. The concept of individual reproductive rights would have to be renounced before the emigrants came aboard. (Note that the earth also is a limited spaceship, but this fact is not obvious until we think through the problems of the spaceship Mayflower.)

Qualifying for Embarkation

A numerate analysis of all the factors involved in the economy of a spaceship leads to the conclusion that solving overpopulation on earth by this means is highly improbable, even with the most sanguine predictions of the future of technology. But discouraging as this analysis may be it is actually optimistic as compared with an analysis that goes beyond numbers.

Picture the day when our spaceship starts to load up for its trip to the stars. Would-be emigrants have been presented with a pamphlet that describes the necessary restrictions to human freedom on board the vessel. They have been told that they must read this pamphlet ahead of time. At the door stands the embarkation officer. Of each candidate he asks:

"Do you swear to accept the absolute control over your reproduction by the spaceship community for the duration of the trip?"

If a candidate says, "I do," the officer responds: "Then you may climb aboard."

But notice what happens when a candidate says, "No, I absolutely reject the control of my reproduction by any community whatsoever. Reproduction is a fundamental human right that must not be given up for any reason on earth—or off the earth, for that matter."

In that case the embarkation officer has only one response: "Sorry, buddy! Turn around and rejoin the community into which you were born. People with ideals like yours cannot be tolerated on board an interstellar spaceship."

Limits that are ambiguous on the spacecraft we call "earth" would be precise and beyond doubt on spaceship Mayflower. Unlimited reproduction would clearly be an antisocial act. Multiplied sufficiently, a swarm of spaceships could purify the earth of acceptors of reproduction control. They would leave behind only rejectors—who would perpetuate the very problem of overbreeding that led to this failed "cure" of the population problem. Acceptors would be removed from spaceship earth, though *their* behavior creates no need for spaceships to leave this planet.

Reductio ad Paradoxum

Euclidean geometry boasts a subtle and powerful analytical technique called the *reductio ad absurdum*. A question is settled once and for all if it can be shown that the assumptions of the problem lead to a logical absurdity. Assumptions may, for instance, lead to the conclusion that *A* both *is,* and *is not,* equal to *B.* This is an absurdity, so no more analysis is needed. Whoever thinks a different answer is justified must first show that there is something wrong with the *reductio* itself.

The extraterrestrial-migration-as-a-solution-to-overpopulation proposal has just been demolished by what we can call a *reductio ad paradoxum.* The proposed solution is ruled out of court not by fancy mathematics but by political reality: the choosing of people as candidates for such migration selects those whose ideals make the extravagant solution unnecesary, while leaving on earth the very ones whose ideals have created the problem in the past and will continue to do so in the future. The "solution" selects for its own failure.

This disproof of interstellar migration as a practical expedient was first published in the *Journal of Heredity* in 1959. The history of the reception of this paper is of interest. The essay had two distinct parts: the numerical analysis and the logical analysis. The conclusion was widely noticed in the popular press, but only the numerical analysis was reported. Yet the logical analysis is clearly the decisive part. Why this selectivity in reporting?

As a favorable comment one can say that the emphasis on numbers in the press is evidence that the public is at last making progress in thinking with numbers. Number crunching has become fashionable. No one wants to reverse this progress: but the widespread reluctance to embrace logic is disquieting.

Perhaps the refusal to pay attention to the reductio ad paradoxum bespeaks an admirable love of fair play? As long as analysis is restricted to estimates of numbers, there is room for differences of opinion. Arguments can continue. (In fact, they *will* continue, for arguing is a form of sociability.) Acceptance of the validity and sovereign power of the reductio ad paradoxum puts an end to the social game of arguing.

Some readers may regard the space and the time devoted to demolishing the spaceship solution as excessive. But in following the path of the Buddha we must uncover the reasons for sorrow before we can find a way to free ourselves from it. Those who are familiar with the practice of psychoanalysis will recognize that it too has a Buddhist orientation.

Three Approaches to Reality

There is no royal road to the solution of problems, but it helps to have a checklist of viewpoints to use in the process of discovery. Implicit in the analysis of the interstellar migration proposal were three approaches that we can call *literacy, numeracy,* and *ecolacy.* Rather than try to give these words polished definitions let us develop their meanings through examples.

Literacy

The original meaning refers only to the management of printed material, but it will help to consider "literacy" as including the mastery of spoken words as well. At the literate level, population problems are often attacked with verbal weapons: *human rights, responsibilities, duties, obligations, sanctity of life, will to live, need, altruism, global village, unity of mankind.* The weapons are powerful motivators, but the combined use of more than one often creates a contradiction. On board a spaceship Mayflower the unbridled exercise of the "right to reproduce" by a few will ultimately nullify the "right to life" for the whole colony. How are conflicting rights to be reconciled? Obviously only through making them quantitative—numerate— and adopting numerical standards of allocation. Innumerate rhetoric is not powerful enough to enable us to beat our way out of a morass of rights.

Numeracy

This word appears to have been coined in the 1950s. It refers to the practice and art of using numbers to resolve problems. If the wage earner of a family is killed at work through the fault of his employer, what monetary recompense is due his family? Those who are allergic to numeracy may claim, "You can't put a price on life." This statement leads to one of two inferences: (a) "Life is infinitely valuable," or (b) "Life has no monetary value." Neither results in acceptable action. The first fails because no employer can pay an infinite amount of money; the second fails because the payment of zero dollars is not acceptable to the dependents of the victim. The employer would reject the first; injured parties, the second. Rhetorically it is easy to *say* that life and money are incommensurable; in real life, justice demands that we somehow commensurate the incommensurable.

Rhetorically almost any space activity can be justified by such terms as *manifest destiny, the next frontier, man's insatiable curiosity, our religious obligation to have dominion over everything,* and so on. But when we learn the numerate price of some of these "obligations" we may have second thoughts. The price of the exploration of far space by living human beings is exorbitant: before we leap we need to think—and *think numerately.*

Ecolacy

This word is derived from *ecology,* which is itself a term that is not easy to define. The name of most disciplines is restrictive, defining a small area of concern. Ecology is an extensive science, one that attempts to take account of all the factors that are influential in a given situation: environmental factors such as heat, light, moisture, and chemicals; biotic factors such as predators, parasites, and disease; and the role of human beings in augmenting or diminishing other factors as time passes. It is not easy to define ecology in a way that is both neat and useful. Suffice it to say that an ecologist tries to see the whole picture. Since he runs great risks, an ecologist is likely to make great mistakes; but narrow answers are not enough.

The ecological thinker is haunted by the consequences of time. He is not satisfied with a plan that looks good *at first:* he wants to know what will happen over the course of a long period if the plan is put into operation. Medical personnel became keenly aware of the ecological point of view when the antibiotic penicillin was introduced. Since it was expensive in the early days, doctors understandably tried to make scarce supplies go a long way by using minimal doses. The result was ecologically predictable: the use of minimal doses for lethal infections selected for the most resistant individual bacteria, which soon became the dominant types in hospitals, with a resultant loss of human life. Once the ecology of natural selection was understood by the medical community new strategies were devised. Either a massive dose of the antibiotic was used, or none at all. Alternatively physicians tried to fool the "bugs" by changing rapidly from one antibiotic to another, thus hoping to outrun the evolution of resistance to specific antibiotics.

The sequence *literacy—numeracy—ecolacy* mirrors the order in which these approaches have been given names, but the history of their use is not quite so simple. No doubt words were used before numbers; but, in a primitive way, the ecolate view may be older than either of the other two. What sophisticated people interpret as unintelligent conservatism on the part of "primitive" people generally springs from an "instinctive" nonverbal recognition of the complexity of life. Civilized people now face the problem of regaining something of the primitive "holistic" view of the world without abandoning the limited but powerful tools of formal analysis. As they make this advance, limits will play a larger part in their thinking. As they see the forest more clearly they will less often be distracted by the trees.

Seldom does a single attitude lead to the best answer to a problem. It is wise to challenge each proposed alteration with this checklist of questions:

The literate question: "What are the right words?"

The numerate question: "What are the relevant numbers?"

The ecolate question: "And then what?"

3

Uneasy Litter Mates:
Population and Progress

In the fifth century B.C., Herodotus reported that there had been a time when a person could walk across North Africa from the Atlantic to the Indian Ocean and be always in the shade of trees. No more: the land was well on the way to becoming the desert we know today. Herodotus generalized: "Man stalks across the landscape, and deserts follow in his footsteps." In the tenth century A.D., a Samanid prince identified four earthly paradises: the regions of Samarkand, southern Persia, southern Iraq, and Damascus.[1] No one who has visited any of these sites now would dream of calling it a paradise. They have been cursed with wars, but warfare is only a secondary cause of their degradation.

Throughout history human exploitation of the earth has produced this progression: *colonize—destroy—move on.* When the Pollyannas write history they focus only on the first of these three actions, the desirable effects of which were most evident during the rapid colonization of the New World. In 1845 a now obscure American journalist coined a deathless phrase when he spoke of "the fulfillment of our manifest destiny to overspread the continent allotted by Providence."[2] "Manifest destiny" is one of those catchphrases we love. We would not welcome the words of a journalist who identified colonization as but a prelude to destruction and abandonment.

The restless "moving on" of the human species has depended on always having fresh land to move to. Optimists are not easily frightened by the results, of course: as late as 1980 one Pollyanna brightly explained how all turned out for the best in this best of all possible worlds: "Each year deserts the world over engulf an area the size of Massachusetts. A great deal of land lost is agricultural . . . . Fortunately, however, land is always being replaced or coming under cultivation to make up for land lost."[3] An ecologist—ever guided by the question "And then what?"—would insist on a clarification of the above quotation: Does "always" mean "forever"? If so, it implies that there are no limits to earthly space. It is not surprising that ecologists are not the most popular of people in a growth-oriented economy.

Whenever territorial expansion finally comes to an end, the human population will be reduced to living on the limited resources of the earth. Problems of the allocation of limited resources then become central in human affairs. It was natural for Malthus, the economist, to see population growth as intensifying these problems.

17

Malthus: Out of Revolution, Conservatism

In writing *An Essay on the Principle of Population,* Malthus[4] was less than completely original in his views—a fact Karl Marx relished emphasizing decades later. Several predecessors had clearly stated some of the important elements of Malthusian theory, but in their day the attention of the public was directed elsewhere.

The first sentence of the preface tells how Malthus came to write it: "The following *Essay* owes its origin to a conversation with a friend, on the subject of Mr. Godwin's essay on 'Avarice and Profusion.'" The friend was his father. Stereotype has it that the parent-versus-child relation translates politically into one of conservative versus radical. In this family the politics were reversed. Daniel, the father, was a friend and disciple of Rousseau's. (In fact, the French philosopher was a house guest of the Malthus family on a visit to England.) Young Malthus thought Rousseau and his father were wrong in their view of the human future.

Daniel Malthus was no more radical than many another Englishman in his admiration of things French and his belief that the French Revolution signaled a great advance in human history. The revolution was seen as a continuation of the emancipation of the human spirit that had begun with the revolt of the English colonies in America two decades earlier. Happily turning sequence into trend (which is half-brother to "destiny"), some political pundits wondered if perhaps the English people were not the next on destiny"s list of those to be freed from the shackles of entrenched, unearned power. It was a heady time. Wordsworth recalled the atmosphere, after the French Terror had brought about English disillusionment with the revolution:

> Bliss was it in that dawn to be alive,
> But to be young was very Heaven! . . .
> When Reason seemed the most to assert her rights
> When most intent on making herself
> A prime enchantress . . .[5]

Wordsworth was twenty-three when the revolution took place. The poet Coleridge was twenty-one; the essayist Hazlitt, fifteen. The literary crowd was the backbone of the English supporters of the French Revolution. The backbone began to crumple when the Terror took over.

Robert Malthus moved onto a stage that had been set by others, specifically (as his title page tells us) by "the speculations of Mr. Godwin, M. Condorcet, and other writers." In the literal sense of the word, Malthus's essay is *reactionary,* but the word is not here to be taken in a pejorative sense. Arguing with his father, thirty-two-year-old Robert so neatly skewered the utopias of the Englishman Godwin and the Frenchman Condorcet that the delighted parent urged him to publish his remarks, which he did. (Whether his father ever changed his opinion is not clear: he died two years later.)

The son's argument can be put simply: since distress moves people to limit the number of their children, a utopia that, by hypothesis, did away with all hardships and anxiety would be self-defeating because the unhampered reproduction of the happy people would produce overpopulation, thus creating new distress. Distress is the point at which equilibrium occurs—not happiness, as Godwin and Condorcet supposed. (Details of Malthus's argument are postponed to Chapter 11.)

Godwin: The Work

In 1793, while enthusiasm for what was taking place on the other side of the Channel was still glowing, William Godwin (thirty-seven years old) published a two-volume work that furnished the literati an attention-grabbing paean to anarchy, *Enquiry Concerning Political Justice.* As Alexander Gray says, "it is difficult for us today," nearly two centuries after the event, "to appreciate the horror with which, on its appearance, Godwin's *Political Justice* was viewed by the respectable classes."[6] However something of this revulsion is imaginable if, looking at the judgments assembled in Box 3-1,[7] you ask yourself this question: "Which of these ideals would I like to inculcate in a child of my own?" It may be objected that the statements are taken out of context; but that, of course, is precisely the way the average reader takes the bons mots of any popular book.

Perhaps the best summary of Godwin's 270,000 words was his advice to "obey no man."[8] Godwin's message was not welcomed by the wealthy and powerful.

Box 3-1. Shocking Sentiments of William Godwin.

On property. [Man] has no right of option in the disposal of anything which may fall into his hands. Every shilling of his property, and even every, the minutest, exertion of his powers have received their destination from the decrees of justice. He is only the steward.

Of promises. Promises are, absolutely considered, an evil, and stand in opposition to the genuine and wholesome exercise of an intellectual nature.

On cooperation. Everything that is usually understood by the term cooperation is, in some degree, an evil.

Of gratitude. [I]f by gratitude we understand a sentiment of preference which I entertain towards another, upon the ground of my having been the subject of his benefits, [then gratitude] is no part either of justice or virtue.

On obedience to the law. Few things can be more absurd than to talk of our having promised obedience to the laws. If the laws depend upon promises for their execution, why are they accompanied with sanctions? . . . There is but one power to which I can yield a heart-felt obedience, the decision of my own understanding, the dictate of my own conscience.

On war. The utmost benevolence ought to be practised towards our enemies. We should refrain from the unnecessary destruction of a single life, and afford every humane accommodation to the unfortunate.

On work. It seems by no means impossible that the labor of every twentieth man in the community would be sufficient to supply the rest all the absolute necessaries of life. If then this labor, instead of being performed by so small a number, were amicably divided among the whole, it would occupy the twentieth part of every man's time . . . . It follows that half an hour a day employed in manual labor by every member of the community would sufficiently supply the whole with necessaries.

Utopia at last. The men therefore whom we are supposing to exist, when the earth shall refuse itself to a more extended population, will probably cease to propagate. The whole will be a people of men, and not of children. Generation will not succeed generation, nor truth have, in a certain degree, to recommence her career every thirty years. Other improvements may be expected to keep pace with those of health and longevity. There will be no war, no crimes, no administration of justice, as it is called, and no government. Beside this, there will be neither disease, anguish, melancholy, nor resentment. Every man will seek, with ineffable ardor, the good of all.

There was some talk of having the book suppressed; but its price was so high—three guineas—that it was argued there was no need to suppress it. However, in spite of its price, it had a wide readership and, for better or worse, an influence (through derivative literature) that persists to the present time. Many of the ideals espoused by Godwin are still embraced by people who refuse to discuss population.

When an American who has lived through the campus disorders of the 1960s looks over the subjects in Box 3-1 he is likely to experience a feeling of déjà vu. Godwin urges his readers to "neither trust in nor give" promises, cooperation, or gratitude. By rejecting law, war, and cooperation with older people, the newly saved are to show their disdain for what was formerly called "the settled order." (In the 1960s it was called "the Establishment" or "the System.") And the *Enquiry* sees nothing admirable about a society based on respect for hard work. (Sound familiar?)

Godwin: The Man

The emphasis of the present work is on ideas—their structure, their interaction, their history, and their power to affect history. Personalities will, for the most part, be ignored. But there are times when exceptions are in order, and this is one of them. The two men against whose ideas Malthus reacted had uncommonly interesting personal histories. Malthus's own history, by contrast, was uncommonly dull.

What sort of man was William Godwin? One might reasonably suspect that the extreme position he took was a reaction against his early mentors—as indeed it was. His father was a Calvinist minister of the most rigid sort. For our Oedipus only one road seemed open, and William took it. Against the Calvinist view that all evil comes from within, the son declared that individual men and women are inherently good: it is human institutions that are the source of the evil. We should banish institutions, said Godwin. Marriage is an institution, so out with it! When William met Mary Wollstonecraft he discovered a soul with kindred views. While writing *A Vindication of the Rights of Woman,* she had lived, unmarried, with an American naval officer by whom she had a child. Wollstonecraft and Godwin were plainly made for each other.

In our own century, in the early days of the sex revolution, some young couples indulged in the game of "Let's not get married, but pretend we have." Ironically, Mary and William found themselves forced by their ideals to play the opposite game. When Mary became pregnant the couple realized that their child would suffer real civil disadvantages if it was born a bastard, so they got married. But because both were embarrassingly on record as being opposed to marriage for the most principled of reasons, they could hardly hold their heads up in public—*their* public— if they were known to be married; so they kept their legal union a secret as long as they could. Their game was, "Let's get married, but pretend we're living in sin." (Pride produces paradoxes.)

It was unquestionably a happy marriage, perhaps because biology stepped in to see to it that it did not last too long. The fond mother contracted childbed fever and died two weeks after the birth—a common enough occurrence in the days before Semmelweis and Pasteur. Godwin was left with young Mary.

The widower felt keenly his inadequacy as a single parent, but he found no way out of his predicament until the initiative was taken by a widow, a Mrs. Clairmont. While he was sitting on his little balcony of an evening a clarion voice floated over to him from a neighboring apartment: "Is it possible that I behold the immortal Godwin?" William was hooked. The second marriage was not a happy one for Mary, who was six years old when it took place. The stepdaughter got out of the home as soon as she could—how, we shall see presently.

Godwin supported his family by writing, which was no better paid an occupation then than it is now. He was a wretched manager: the money he touched vaporized. He was perpetually in debt, and to some of the best people in England. Few were the men of letters who had not kissed many guineas goodbye as they disappeared into the Godwin household. Even the solid industrialist Josiah Wedgwood, son of the founder of the famous pottery works and fond uncle of young Charles Darwin, "lent" Godwin large sums.[9] Francis Place, a pioneer fighter for birth control and himself a successful businessman, estimated that Godwin muddled away 1,500 pounds a year over a ten-year period, "notwithstanding he had for the last four or five years paid no rent for the house he lived in, which was worth 200 pounds a year."[10] "To thine own self be true," advised Polonius in *Hamlet;* Godwin was scrupulously true to the shocking ideals he had expressed in *Political Justice.*

No account of the Godwin family is complete without mention of the elopement of Mary and Shelley. Godwin, remember, was opposed to the institution of marriage. But when adolescent Mary, unhappy with her position as a stepdaughter, ran off with the married poet Percy Bysshe Shelley, Godwin was beside himself. Hoist with his own petard! He berated the young plutocrat, moderating his reproaches only after wealthy Percy coughed up large sums of money.

A year and a half after the elopement, Mary gave birth to a son, and before another year had passed Shelley's wife had committed suicide. The elopers married. We hear of Mary Shelley once more when she wrote *Frankenstein.* Though the high Brahmins of literature may disagree, one could argue that the wife's best-known novel has had more enduring influence than all the husband's much-praised poetry.

As for Mary's father, he continued to be, as one Victorian commentator epitomized him, "the prince of spongers," borrowing his way to the end of a long life. Unhappily for Godwin, his influence declined after the publication of Malthus's work. He tried his hand at annihilating Malthus some two decades later, but not even his best friends credited him with a kill. A suitable tombstone for this revolutionary might well read:

WILLIAM GODWIN
1756–1836
Father of the Author of Frankenstein
and Irritant That Produced Malthus

Condorcet: Courage in Extremis

Marie Jean Antoine Nicholas de Caritat, Marquis de Condorcet, was both a nobleman and a man of learning. It is never easy to combine the two careers: the intrusive and frequent demands of social life disrupt the sustained effort required for original

thinking. Nevertheless Condorcet managed to make himself into a passable mathematician. He dearly wanted to be a member of the French Academy, but his family
thought that "le titre et métier de savant" was beneath the dignity of a nobleman.
Finally they relented and permitted the Academy to make Condorcet a member.[11]

Condorcet was nobility's ugly duckling in another way: as the revolution
approached he found himself in sympathy with the proletariat. Being a fellow traveler to a revolution is apt to be more dangerous than opposing it; the Parisian lawyer
Pierre Vergniaud said before being guillotined in 1793, "the revolution eats its children." When fair-minded Condorcet proposed that Louis XVI be imprisoned
rather than beheaded, he aroused the suspicions of his bloodthirsty compatriots.
Recognizing the danger of his situation, he went into hiding.

His family had to be taken care of. His marriage, like that of many of the nobility, had been one of convenience, but he had grown to love his wife, Sophie, who
was now reduced to selling underclothes in a women's shop.

At this juncture Condorcet wrote, "I shall perish like Socrates and Sidney, for I
have served my country."[12] Then what would happen to his daughter? As the scion
of a convicted criminal she could not inherit the paternal property. A divorce could
change the situation in the child's favor. At this point we encounter a new variation
on the marriage theme. Whereas Godwin and his paramour married for the love of
their child, Condorcet and Sophie divorced for the same reason.

Now ensued months of hiding and writing. Lying low in the modest home of
an artist's widow he scribbled away on a work that, when finished, comprised some
68,000 words, just one-quarter the length of Godwin's treatise. Starting work in
July 1793, Condorcet completed his book (in rough form, it is true) in a mere nine
months. Then, in March 1794, hearing rumors that the Jacobins were hot on his
trail, and not wanting to endanger his hostess, he left his hiding place to look for

---

Box 3-2. Condorcet: The Dream of a Condemned Man.

How admirably calculated is this picture of the human race, freed from all these chains,
secure from the domination of chance, as from that of the enemies of its progress, and
advancing with firm and sure steps towards the attainment of truth, virtue, and happiness,
to present to the philosopher a spectacle which shall console him for the errors, the crimes,
the injustice, with which the earth is still polluted, and whose victim he often is! It is in the
contemplation of this picture that he receives the reward of his efforts towards the progress
of reason and the defense of liberty. He dares then to link these with the eternal chain of
human destiny; and thereby he finds virtue's true recompense, the joy of having performed a lasting service, which no fatality can ever destroy by restoring the evils of prejudice and slavery. This contemplation is for him a place of refuge, whither the memory
of his persecutors cannot follow, where, living in imagination with man restored to his
rights and his natural dignity, he forgets him whom greed, fear, or envy torment and corrupt; there it is that he exists in truth with his kin, in an elysium which his reason has been
able to create for him, and which his love for humanity enhances with the purest enjoyments.

[Here ends the book.]

Sketch for an Historical Picture of the Progress of the Human Mind, 1795.

another. Legend has it that he was recognized as a person not used to taking care of himself when he stopped in a bistro for a bite to eat. He ordered an omelette. "How many eggs?" the proprietor asked. "A dozen," answered the noble mathematician, thus revealing his unfamiliarity with the numbers of the household. He soon found himself in the prison of Bourg-La-Reine. The next day he was dead. Whether he voluntarily took poison, or was killed by others, was never found out: but does it matter? One way or another, a revolution eats its children.[13]

Esquisse d'un tableau historique des progrès de l'esprit humain was published the year after the author's death. The English translation came out the same year. It is a compact work, filled with enthusiasm. Considering the circumstances of its writing, the concluding paragraph, given in Box 3-2, can truly be called noble.

The Idea of Progress

It is not easy to develop an awareness of the large ideas that frame our unconscious pictures of reality. To help render the unconscious conscious, the physicist-turned-philosopher Thomas Kuhn popularized the term *paradigm*.[14] This Greek word for "pattern" refers to something more global and less focused than "theory" or "hypothesis." Whether it is the best word may be debated, but it can help us understand human history. As we pursue this goal we will be guided by one paradigm after another. Three great historical paradigms have been identified and labeled. These are the golden age, the endless cycle, and the idea of progress.

The golden age paradigm presumes a wonderful world that once was but never more shall be (or shall be only after we have won our way to it through acts of virtue). This view is incorporated in the myth of the Garden of Eden. Somewhat different is the endless cycle paradigm, which sees unremitting repetitions in history with little enduring advance: *Plus ça change, plus c'est la même chose.*

Both of these paradigms come down to us from ancient times. They were named long after they were born. Both must have been products of a gerontocracy, a society ruled by its elders. It is natural for the old to feel that things have gone to hell in a handbasket since the good old days; or that every improvement is followed by its deterioration. Are these conclusions the legitimate products of experience, or are they merely by-products of the speaker's hormonal changes? Where is one to find an age-free arbiter to judge?

Finally there is the idea of progress, born of a figurative extension of a spatial concept into the realm of historic time. This idea also has ancient roots, but it did not become influential until the eighteenth century. By that time the age composition of European populations was shifting in favor of the young, and the rate of technological change was accelerating. In the past two hundred years the idea of progress has become the ruling paradigm of Western society. It has penetrated every corner of our life; and it is intimately connected with theories of population dynamics. The classic account of the development of this concept was given in 1932 by the English historian J. B. Bury in *The Idea of Progress*.[15] There is now a large literature on the subject.

The idea of progress made a significant upward thrust into people's consciousness when Condorcet's book was published. In some respects his dreams were not so different from Godwin's: "Our hopes regarding the future state of humanity can be reduced to these three important points: the destruction of inequality between nations; the progress of equality within one and the same nation; and, finally, the real perfecting of mankind."[16]

Condorcet's argument, however, put less emphasis on political and moral aspects of the change. He divided the history of mankind into ten epochs, of which the first nine were complete and the tenth was just beginning. The epochs were characterized by the invention and development of material things: bow and arrow, animal husbandry, the tools of agriculture, manufacturing, and so on.

There is something schizophrenic about progress as promoted by Condorcet. The title of his book refers to something that is certainly nonmaterial, "the human mind" *(esprit);* and he bravely announces that "nature has assigned no limit to the perfecting of the human faculties." But he buttresses his argument with material examples—inventions, for instance. During the succeeding century the emphasis of the idea of progress shifted from matters of the spirit (Condorcet's emphasis) to more material matters. Now when people say, "You can't stop progress!" they generally mean "You can't stop *material* progress." We should not wonder at this change of emphasis: the shift, as it affected the psychology of consumers, created new opportunities for all those who are in the business of *selling* material things. Extracting profits from the sale of ideas is more difficult.

Condorcet was the supreme optimist. As mankind approached perfection there would be an increase in both the human population and in per capita wealth and income. But, he asked,

> must there not come a time when . . . the increase in the number of men surpassing that of their means, there shall result necessarily, if not a continual decrease in prosperity and in population, if not a truly retrograde course, at least a sort of oscillation between the good and the bad? And will not this oscillation, in societies arrived at this point, be a constant source of almost periodic calamities? Will it not mark the point where all further improvement shall become impossible, and in the limits of perfectibility of the human race, which it shall reach in the course of the ages, and which it can never pass? . . .
>
> But, supposing that this time should actually come, there would result nothing alarming, either to the happiness of the human race or to its indefinite perfectibility; if we suppose that prior to this time the progress of reason shall have advanced on a par with that of the sciences and the arts . . . men will know then that, if they have obligations towards beings who are yet to come into the world, they do not consist in giving to them existence only, but happiness. . . . There could, then, be a limit to the possible means of subsistence, and, in consequence, to the greatest possible population, without there resulting that premature destruction, so contrary to nature and to the social prosperity, of a portion of the beings who have received life.

As we become acquainted with Malthus's writings we will see that his conclusions are objectively not very different from those of Condorcet. The sharpest difference is in emphasis. No matter how frankly Condorcet admitted the dangers of population growth he always managed to give an optimistic "spin" to his rhetoric. Malthus, on the other hand, generally managed to accentuate the negative.

Condorcet and his followers have had more influence on the climate of opinion in our time than has Malthus. Optimism is more attractive than pessimism. In history, causation is a tricky concept but it seems most likely that the idea of progress has had immensely constructive effects on the development of our world. Confident that there are no limits, our movers and shakers have managed to find ways around *apparent* limits. (Their success leaves unanswered the question as to whether some limits are real and inescapable.)

What of Progress in the Future?

Our increasing anxiety about the depletion (of material wealth) and the increase of pollution (by material wastes) makes us wonder whether we are not at last approaching "the limits of perfectibility" of our materialistic world. Though not decisive, the present trend is clear enough to make some of us have second thoughts about our much-vaunted "progress."

Even if material progress is throttled down we need not give up hope of further improvement in the overall conditions of life. The inventory of possibilities is immensely enlarged if we reinstate Condorcet's original emphasis on the human mind (*esprit*—"spirit"), which may indeed be possessed of "indefinite perfectibility." ("Indefinite" is not the same thing as "infinite," though it is often read as such.) We need to re-establish the pristine meaning of the idea of historical progress, calling attention to inadequately exploited potentialities in the nonmaterial realm. Such is one of the goals of this book. But before much advancement can be made toward this objective we need to dismantle many delusions about the characteristics and consequences of human population growth that have grown up in the protective shadow of the insufficiently examined idea of progress.

4

Population Theory: Academia's Stepchild

"Every year Malthus is proven wrong and is buried—only to spring to life again before the year is out. If he is so wrong, why can't we forget him? If he is right, how does he happen to be so fertile a subject for criticism?"

I wrote those words in the 1960s in an introduction to an anthology of essays on population.[1] How naive I was! I supposed that the voices that were then sounding the alarm about population growth would at last get the public's attention. And so they did for about a decade during which environmentalists made common cause with populationists. But some of the most influential of the environmental activists viewed population as a dangerous and unwanted diversion from what they conceived to be humanity's true problems.[2] Their stifling of public concern for population problems was reinforced during the Reagan years by self-styled "supply-side economists." Soon the predominent population message broadcast by both the political left and the political right was "Not to worry!"

In 1968 ZPG, Inc., was founded to promote zero population growth as an ideal both for the United States and for the world. Its membership was confined mostly to 350 chapters on college campuses. Twenty-one years later, in 1989, the number had shrunk to just nine.[3] Though Paul Ehrlich's *The Population Bomb* was a bestseller in 1968, worrying about population growth did not become a growth industry.

Malthusians saw population growth as a "root cause" of inflation, unemployment, pollution, congestion, unwanted immigration, influxes of heartrending refugees, trade wars, drug wars, and terrorism. Each of these pathologies has many causes; anti-Malthusians belittled population. Common economic experience made it hard to believe that a population gain of 2 to 4 percent per year (which characterizes poor countries) could be serious; the less than one percent annual growth rate found in rich countries seemed even more trifling. Students of population, however, pointed out that the *average* gain in world population during the past million years has been less than 0.002 percent per year. That "small" rate of increase, operating over a million years, has produced our present five billion people, not a "small" number by any standard. When it comes to rates of increase that are continued indefinitely, no rate that exceeds zero by the most minute amount can be regarded as small.

The first edition of Malthus's essay has very few numbers in it. Subsequent editions, more defensive in tone, include ever more numerical data. But, using numbers or not, Malthus struck many people as a heartless man. Karl Marx identified him as the "principal enemy of the people," while Pierre-Joseph Proudhon called him "a political assassin," and Pierre Leroux asserted that "Malthusians propose an annual massacre of the innocent."[4] The vilification continues to this day.

Such an *argumentum ad hominem* carries little logical weight, but "a decent respect to the opinions of mankind"—and womankind—requires that all the evidence bearing on Malthus's character be presented. History records Malthus's vigorous opposition to a "Poor Law" that had reduced free workers to pauperdom. Moreover, as William Petersen tells us,

> [H]e is less well known as the advocate of free universal education, free medical aid to the poor, state assistance to emigrants, and even direct relief to families of more than six children, or as the opponent of using minors in cottage industry, and of free trade when it benefited the traders but not the public. The advocacy of free education for all was especially significant and, for his day, most unusual. Malthus did not see the gap between the social classes as innate; it could be bridged by the development of a sense of responsibility among the common people. And the upper classes were not automatically right by reason of their social position; if they did not fulfill their duty toward the lower classes and assist them in becoming self-reliant, they were thereby censurable.[5]

Malthus evidently found the accusation of hard-heartedness painful to bear. In 1806, eight years after his first publication, he complained that his critics

> proceed upon the very strange supposition that the *ultimate* object of my work is to check population, as if anything could be more desirable than the most rapid increase of population, *unaccompanied* by vice and misery. But of course my ultimate object is to diminish vice and misery, and any checks to population which may have been suggested, are solely as means to accomplish this end.[6]

"It is," Malthus said, "an utter misconception of my argument to infer that I am an enemy to population. I am only an enemy to vice and misery, and consequently to that *unfavorable proportion* between population and food which produces these evils."[7] And more explicitly: "In the desirableness of a great and efficient population, I do not differ from the warmest advocates of increase."[8]

Thus unjustly, "Malthusian" now often stands for attitudes that were objectionable to Malthus himself. It has been said that one of the minor tragedies of life is that an author never escapes his first edition. It was all too easy for readers with conflicting biases to misread Malthus's first edition. His claim that he was not an anti-people person was made in the appendix to the third edition. But what critic of a first edition bothers to read the third? And who reads appendixes?

Malthus Refuted?

Reading his *Essay on Population* one can justifiably infer that Malthus thought that England was already fully stocked with people; any further increase in population would bring about a corresponding decrease in prosperity. What, in fact, did happen in England after 1798, the year the *Essay* was first published?

In 1817, in the fifth edition, Malthus admitted that the census of 1811 "showed a greatly accelerated rate of progress, and a greatly improved healthiness of the people." So: as the English population increased after 1798, misery actually decreased. This was not at all what Malthus had expected. Yet the author clung to his theory to the end of his life (in 1834), though empirical facts continued to go against him. Malthus was indeed a stubborn man.

Improvements in living conditions were not confined to England. The most convincing evidence of progress is found in the diet of European peoples before and after the publication of Malthus's essay. A diet that includes some meat is nutritionally better and more expensive than a wholly vegetarian diet. Before 1800 Europeans consumed only half a pound of meat per person per year, their diet being almost wholly coarse bread and potatoes. By 1850 the meat portion had risen to 100 pounds per capita per year.[9] During the nineteenth century the average life expectancy rose from twenty-eight to fifty years, principally as a result of a dramatic fall in infant mortality, while the average height of adult Europeans increased by six inches. Understandably, the vigor and productivity of the workers also increased greatly, and with these personal gains came increases in the gross national product of the nations in which diets had improved. Better food produced a larger population of stronger people who earned larger incomes, which financed a still better diet, which . . . and so on and on. Truly, a "virtuous circle" had been set in place.

Population changes in several regions are shown in Box 4-1. During the 180 years that ended in 1980 the population of England, Scotland, and Wales increased almost six times; of the world, five times; and of the United States, forty-five times. Accompanying this explosive growth was a great increase in material well-being, the greatest occurring in the United States, where population growth was also greatest. A most un-Malthusian result! From facts like these some critics derived the counter-Malthusian conclusion: the more children, the better—forever. For more than a hundred years Malthusians have been fighting a rear guard action against such optimism.

Population Growth, Destroyer of Dreams

Are we then to conclude that "bigger is better" in all respects, at every level of population? Before we sign on with the chamber of commerce, we should look around for contrary effects of population growth. We need a simple example to epitomize what happens when population increases.

Look up into the sky! What do we *not* see? We do *not* see a heaven swarming

Box 4-1. Population Growth Since Malthus's Essay.

Region	Population numbers in millions (rounded)		Approximate factor of increase
	1800	1980	
United Kingdom	10	56	6
The world	906	4,414	5
United States	5	227	45

with airplanes. What is the significance of this? And what does it have to do with the size of the population?

Recently a flying enthusiast plaintively asked, in a letter to a popular magazine, what was happening to recreational flying in the United States.[10] From 1980 to 1985, while the population was increasing by 5 percent, the number of nonmilitary pilot licenses declined by 14 percent. "What," the writer asks, "has happened to the dream of Icarus, of Leonardo . . . ?"

Long before writing was invented men must have dreamed of flying through the air like a bird. The Greek myth of Icarus grew out of this primordial longing. While Columbus was busy discovering a new world to the west, Leonardo da Vinci was trying to devise a way to fly over the old one. When men finally succeeded in producing planes that could stay aloft, intoxicated futurists painted pictures of a world pulsating with aircraft. In the 1920s and 1930s the covers of *Popular Science* and *Popular Mechanics* again and again depicted such a scene. The air pullulated with gaggles of "personal airplanes." The two-car garage of Everyman's home was to be augmented by the two-plane hangar.[11]

The brave new world of aviation was not to be. The personal plane that was to have become the aerial equivalent of the personal jalopy never materialized. The sale of single-engine planes declined from a annual high of 17,811 in 1978 to about 1,000 in 1987—down a whacking 94 percent.[12] There is no reason to think that their sales will ever recover. The bubble has popped: the future is past.

Why? True to a tradition of his tribe, our letter writer knew the answer: it was all the fault of lawyers and the government. With its multitudinous regulations Washington took the fun out of flying, while legal actions brought by lawyers, together with the cost of liability insurance, made flying prohibitively expensive. The engineers did their duty by the future: it was bureaucrats and lawyers who were to blame for the collapse of the dream.

There's some merit in this complaint, but it does not do justice to a fundamental factor that rules out the possibility of unlimited numbers of personal flying machines: overpopulation. It's easy for one person—me—to imagine myself as Leonardo flying through the air, because this intoxicating vision has only me in it. The dream is in the singular. But the science fiction of the magazine covers is a very plural dream: thousands—no, millions—of ordinary people were supposed to fly at the same time. (Nothing less would do, for there must be no nasty elitism in the world of tomorrow!)

Limitations of space have forced us to give up the dream of personal airplanes. Not space in the abstract, but practical space. Sure, if I want to fly from Santa Barbara to Fresno, the cylinder of space extending from these two cities out to the Pleiades seems, by human standards, to be infinite. But the most important space is take-off and landing space, which has reference to a point, not a volume. The practical space in which personal airplanes must take off, fly, and land is dangerously limited.

If population growth is not contained, and if a constant fraction of the population insists on flying airplanes, then sooner or later collisions between aircraft must become so common that the dream of an unlimited number of personal airplanes has to be abandoned. In truth, we reached that point some time ago. "Bigger is better"? Not if the demand variable (created by population) has the potential of growing bigger without limit, while the supply variable (space), is severely constrained.[13] If I want to fly to Fresno I don't want to have to land at an airport in Sacramento and then take slow surface transportation back to Fresno.

Technological optimists don't give up easily. They dream of sophisticated electronic equipment that would make it possible to place untold thousands of planes in the corridors between two cities. This dream presumes that each plane would be subject to rigid central control over its path and speed. Without trying to assess the probability of success in producing a computerized air traffic control system that would work flawlessly—for accidents would be unacceptable—we should ask what such an achievement would do for the dreams of Leonardo? What the true Leonardo dreams of is flitting about as effortlessly as a swallow, uncontrolled by directives emanating from a central political authority. This dream bubble has been popped by an *argumentum ad paradoxum:* the overpopulation that produces the need for flight to escape freeway congestion also produces the aerial congestion that negates the blessings of innovative technology.

With this example before us we cannot but wonder: as our population continues to grow, what other amenities that we enjoy today (or dream about for tomorrow) will we have to give up before tomorrow comes?

To be fair we must admit that there is another side to the coin. A larger population sometimes opens up desirable new opportunities. A country as small as Monaco cannot manufacture an automobile at a reasonable price; and only a very large nation can afford the extensive infrastructure required to send human beings to the moon. Where is the balance of good and bad resulting from population growth? Can we correctly estimate, in advance, the net gain or loss flowing from an innovation? And can we control the growth of population? At what cost?

"Truth" in Information-Mutable Sciences

The list of subjects recognized as science runs from anthropology through astronomy, botany, chemistry, economics, psychology, and sociology to zoology. That's a wide gamut, and it is generally recognized that the assemblage can be sorted into at least two groups. But what should the groups be called? Traditionally some of the sciences (notably physics) have been called "exact"; but what does that leave for the rest? "Inexact sciences"? Seldom is anyone so rude as to use that term in public. But what is the difference between physics, say, and sociology?

In recent decades academic disciplines have been divided into "natural sciences" and "behavioral sciences." There is a curious lack of parallelism in these terms. The second group includes sociology, but no one is willing to call this an "unnatural science." The adjective "behavioral" refers only to human behavior, which enters into sociology in a way that it does not in physics or chemistry. Some examples can clarify the distinction.

After making arduous measurements and calculations an astronomer predicts that there will be a total eclipse of the sun on 24 August 2007, giving the exact path it will follow on the globe. Whether his prediction is correct or not, the publication of it will have absolutely no effect on the path of the eclipse on 24 August 2007. Astronomy is an *information-stable science.*

For contrast, consider Alfred Kinsey's pioneering studies of human sexual behavior in the United States. Although we do not know for sure, the extensive publicity given these studies in 1948 probably influenced American sex behavior in the years thereafter. A sociological study like Kinsey's can be said to be part of an *information-mutable science.* Although the figures turned up in sociology are not as exact as those of astronomy, this difference is probably less important than the effect that published figures have on future measurements themselves.

Many natural scientists have difficulty in understanding the distinction just made, though John Q. Public grasps it easily. Information mutability suggests that certain special instances of freedom of speech and freedom of inquiry need to be re-examined. (Maybe not changed, but at least examined.) In Canada the province of British Columbia used to have a law that stated: "No person, corporation, or organization shall, after the issue of the writ for an election, take any straw vote which will, prior to the election, distinguish the political opinions of the voters in any electoral district."[14] The rationale for this injunction is found in the well-known sociological phenomena of "underdog effect" and "bandwagon effect." Which effect (if either) will be called forth by publicity given to pre-voting polls is indeterminate, but many lovers of democracy feel there is something unfair about the effects that polling has on voting. Such apparently was the belief of the electorate in British Columbia in 1960, when the restriction on freedom to poll was passed. (But in 1982 the legislature repealed the law.)[15]

Though America has never had such a law, government bureaus act with considerable restraint. The Bureau of the Census *might* include in its decennial census questions about the sex habits of householders, but it doesn't. Even the information it does gather often creates a storm when it is published. If a comparison of two successive censuses of River City reveals that its population is in a declining phase, the River City Chamber of Commerce may blow its top when the data get out. The chamber correctly assumes that knowledge of a decline may dissuade new industries from settling in River City.

Tempests over publicity versus suppression cannot be entirely avoided if the Bureau is to do its work, but some potentially troublesome reports can be nipped in the bud. In both 1980 and 1990 the Bureau refused to determine whether the aliens it counted were illegal or legal residents, though it was under considerable pressure to make this determination. (It was subjected to even more effective counterpressure by political organizations that did not want the truth to be known.) Because demography is an information-mutable science, no fact should be assumed a priori to be neutral. This means that some of the most significant investigations in demography must be carried out by organizations beyond the reach of the government—the NGOs they are called, the nongovernmental organizations.

A Specialty with No Licensed Experts

Some of our most enduring problems are ones for which there are no licensed experts. If this seems a shocking statement, note that two of the greatest unsolved problems of our time are the threat of atomic annihilation and the threat of overpopulation. For neither problem is there a cadre of experts who are legally or morally licensed to give authoritative answers.

Consider the first question: "Can we survive an all-out thermonuclear war?"

Those who know most about the physical potentials of nuclear explosives are not united in their answers. Physicists of great competence hold opposing views. The late Albert Einstein assured us that civilization cannot survive a thermonuclear war. Just as confidently the physicist Edward Teller says that such a war is survivable, and he has devoted the latter part of his life to a search for technology that will permit a nation (ours, of course) to wage and win an atomic war. Which expert are we to believe? And are all the experts addressing the same problem?

Perhaps we should take a poll of all highly trained physicists? It is probable that the results would show that the majority of them agree with Einstein; but, even if this were so, would that settle the issue? The majority is not necessarily right. After all, there was a time when most experts thought the world was flat. Moreover, as Marshall McLuhan said, "An expert is a man who doesn't make the slightest error on the road to the Grand Illusion."

When there is unremitting disagreement among experts, it is difficult to know what sort of expertise is relevant. Differences between physicists on the nuclear war question derive less from differences as to the facts of physics than from uncertainties about human reactions. How will people react to overwhelming threats and crushing disasters? Can we control the human propensity to make mistakes in the construction and operation of complex control systems? Can we lay out an exhaustive strategy for responding effectively to enemy threats? Mathematics, logic, psychology, and the principles of political science—these disciplines, and more, must be called upon to deal with "the threat of the atom." A knowledge of pure physics is not enough. Physicists *as such* cannot completely evaluate the threat of thermonuclear war. Human beings are involved in both the deploying and the taming of the atom. This means that the core problems lie in the behavioral sciences— which, as we have just seen, are not "exact" or information-stable sciences, but information-mutable sciences. When there are no recognized experts, the distinction between authorities and laymen loses much of its meaning. We then have to rely on common sense and intuition as we evaluate the evaluators.

Turning to population we wonder whom we should consult about the future. We think first of demographers because, etymologically, demography consists of the "writings about people" (Gr. *demos,* "people"). In practice, demography is mostly restricted to the counting of people. But given points on a graph corresponding to past counts of people it is only human to hope that the curve connecting past points might successfully predict the future.

Unfortunately experiences in predicting the future have not been very happy. Reviewing a small sample of past failures is a salutary exercise. Paul Demeny has pointed out that "in 1945, Frank Notestein, then the most eminent figure among American demographers, foresaw a year 2000 population of some 3 billion."[16] The population of the world is now expected to be twice that when the new century rolls around. In 1933 statisticians on President Hoover's Research Committee on Social Trends thought that the population of the United States would probably stabilize below 150 million. It is now 255 million, fully 69 percent greater, and still growing. Thirteen years later the U.S. Bureau of the Census was willing to raise the 1990 population prediction only to 165 million, a number that was surpassed by the year 1960. Many such instances led Joseph S. Davis to conclude that "the very term 'population trend' is deceptive and dangerous."[17]

That was said in 1952, and in a few more years the majority of the demographers found themselves fighting a battle against the journalists. The demographers pointed out that all their future-referenced figures were merely the result of continuing a curve that connected the population figures of the past on into the future; but the future is obviously not an item of *knowledge* until it arrives. What we give you, said the demographers, are projections (of past curves), not predictions.

The warning had little effect, of course: the projections of demographers were happily converted to predictions in the press, no matter how carefully demographers hedged their statements. One very successful journalist recently even eliminated the middle man and became his own ebullient demographer, confidently predicting populations a hundred years ahead. He backs up his predictions with impressive statistics, which Michael Teitelbaum bluntly called "GIGO trash"— "Garbage In, Garbage Out."[18]

It is wise and proper that trained demographers should hesitate to make any projections for fear they will be taken as predictions, but it is also understandable that the eminent demographer, Nathan Keyfitz of Harvard, should view the result with some misgiving. Demography has, he says, "withdrawn even from its borders and left a no-man's land which other disciplines have infiltrated."[19] Some of the solidest parts of demography act principally as a handmaiden to business, telling clients the age and economic circumstances of potential customers, both now and in the near future (that is, in the next five years). We need demographers just as we need accountants: both deal with records of the past, which, in the hands of a few gifted analysts, may be used to expose possible futures.

The inadequacies of projections are easily seen when we look at prophecies made in the 1930s, the years of a worldwide economic depression. It was almost universally agreed that population growth was coming to an end, both here and in the world at large. Only the final figures were controversial. Quite a few prophets were predicting the possibility of a world war ahead (from which they might have predicted a postwar pronatal psychology). But who could foresee the consequences of the antibiotics to come? (The sulfa drugs gave only the merest hint of the potency of penicillin and the like.) The fantastic power of DDT to kill mosquitoes and thus, for a time, diminish malaria, one of the great diseases of the world, was also yet to be appreciated.

There is no way that mere statistical projection can predict particular technological changes like these. Our best efforts should be bent toward understanding the fundamental elements involved in setting the limits of the world, guarding as best we can against errors bred by too little imagination.

Why Take a Census?

The ancients tended passively to accept the world as it is. We moderns love to define the unsatisfactory aspects of life as "problems" that we intend to "conquer." Thus it comes about that we speak of the "population problem" whenever we are distressed to find that life is not as pleasant as we would like it to be. In tackling the population problem, how important is it to have precise numbers? Do Americans, for instance, need to know the precise number of people living in the United States?

The American government being a *representative* democracy, our forefathers quite naturally assumed that it was essential that the number of citizens represented by each congressman be counted. "The actual enumeration," says Article I, Section 2 of the U.S. Constitution, "shall be made . . . every . . . ten years, in such manner as [the Congress] shall by law direct."

That was written in 1787, long before the development of scientific sampling methods, so of course the Congress specified that a census be taken. (Censuses are mentioned in the Bible.) At first blush one might suppose that the "total count" produced by a census would be more reliable than the result of sampling, but this is not necessarily the case. The greater the freedom of movement in society the harder it is to get all the citizens to stand still to be counted. The probable error of the U.S. census is not known with any exactitude, but professionals think the undercount of the first census (1790) may have been 2.5 percent of the population reported. It is believed that the undercount of the 1980 census was 1.4 percent. If so, that means that the reported figure (226,545,805) was too low by more than three million people. (3,171,641 people, if you insist on quoting your pocket calculator).

The error in world population figures is unknown, but it is bound to be much greater. If it is as much as 5 percent (which is not unlikely), the world population for mid-1989, reported by the United Nations as 5.321 billion, may have been as little as 5.055 billion or as much as 5.587 billion. (That would make the uncertainty plus or minus 266 million—more than the population of the United States at the time.) Newspapers made a great to-do about reaching the 5-billion mark on a certain date, but we don't know within many months the exact time when world population surpassed five billion. But—does it matter?

As far as the United States is concerned, having gotten in the habit of taking a decennial census we may never stop, though a great deal of money could be saved if sampling were substituted for the census. The cost of the 1990 census was over $2 billion, or slightly more than $8 per person. A scientific sampling method could yield equally reliable results at a cost of perhaps $50 million. We should note that the Netherlands stopped taking censuses after 1971. The Dutch government believes it can get a good enough handle on the numbers by keeping track of births, deaths, immigration, and emigration. The population of the Netherlands is probably known more accurately without a census than is the population of the United States with one.

Hedgehogs and Foxes in Population Studies

In 1953 the philosopher Isaiah Berlin caught the attention of the learned community with a characterization of two contrasting types of intellects. His small book, *The Hedgehog and the Fox,* begins thus: "There is a line among the fragments of the Greek poet Archilochus which says: 'The fox knows many things, but the hedgehog knows one big thing.'"[20] After pointing out that "scholars have differed about the correct interpretation of these dark words," Berlin uses the images to distinguish between professional historians and men of letters.

No single interpretation of Archilocus's "dark words" should be taken as gospel.

I choose to employ the fable to distinguish between empiricists and theoreticians in the unending pursuit of knowledge—between investigators who glory in pursuing many little things while exhibiting a minimal interest in theory, and those who seek the "big things" that explain a wealth of little things.

It is now widely believed (and, I think, correctly believed) that the survival of a nation under modern competitive conditions depends on broadening the electorate's competency in numerate matters. Numeracy is a virtue; but like all virtues the praise of it can be carried too far. The study of populations naturally generates a mountain of statistics that may be fun to fiddle with. Playing fox with statistics may be more comforting than being a hedgehog looking for the few big generalizations that make sense of the all-too-numerous little facts of demography.

Differences between "exact" and "inexact" sciences are not always obvious in publications. Any good public library makes possible a comparison between the *Handbook of Chemistry and Physics* and the United Nations' *Demographic Yearbook*. Both are filled with tens of thousands of figures; but the accuracy of the two is utterly different.

A single example will show the extreme which accuracy sometimes reaches in the exact sciences. Physical theory tells us that "Dirac's number" is 1.00115965246, with an uncertainty of only 1 part in 50 billion. To visualize the uncertainty, imagine the distance between Los Angeles and New York (2,451 miles) being measured by placing hairs side by side for the whole extent. (The thickness of an average human hair is only 80 microns, or roughly one three-hundredths of an inch.) The distance between the two cities is 50 billion hair-widths. Were Dirac's number to be set equal to this distance, the uncertainty of the number would be only one hair-width![21] This figure has been checked by many independent investigators.

The contrast offered by the *Demographic Yearbook* could hardly be greater. Most of the recorded figures have not been checked by independent investigators. The stated population of a nation is whatever figure is sent to the United Nations by the officials of that country. There is often a strong suspicion that the ruling power of a nation wants, for political reasons, to exaggerate (or to minimize) the size of the population. The United Nations is not licensed to meddle with the figures sent it through official channels. As for the aggregate population of the entire world, do national exaggerations and minimizations substantially cancel each other out? No one knows. The end result is that there is, at all times, a considerable but unknown uncertainty in the published figures; and there is no assurance that the relative error stays the same from one yearbook to the next.

In demography, trends are of the greatest interest; but trustworthy trends presuppose reliable figures. Furthermore, a trend in human affairs is not like a vector in physics: it can change unexpectedly. In part this is because demography is an information-mutable science. When truth is mutable, accuracy to one part in 50 billion—or even one part in 1,000—would be pointless. Archilocus's hedgehogs are more needed than foxes.

Many important human measures are difficult to define. "Literacy" is an example. If a person can write his name, should he be counted as one of the literate? Will literacy determinations in one country be comparable in accuracy to those in another? In the end we must agree with René Dubos: "Trend is not destiny." Predictions in the behavioral sciences are inherently risky. Yet international cooperation depends on the nations reaching some sort of agreement in their predictions of the future course of population growth and the resource needs created by population growth.

From Bucharest to Mexico City

Whenever nations get together in an attempt to solve their mutual problems it is certain that the product of their meetings will be rich in words and poor in numerical accuracy and ecological wisdom. This has been repeatedly illustrated in the history of the League of Nations (founded in 1919) and the United Nations (founded in 1945). Nearly a century's record has produced little to be optimistic about; but it has produced a little.

Lately, for instance, progress has been made in putting together a "Law of the Sea" to govern international fishing activities. As it becomes increasingly more difficult to deny the consequences of overfishing, further progress will no doubt be made. In this, as in all matters that require agreement among sovereign powers, the greater the suffering that follows from failure to agree, the faster will be the progress in reaching and enforcing agreements. *No progress without pain.* Probably most people regard this as a pessimistic conclusion, but it can easily be reworded into an optimistic mode: *Severe pain generates its own corrective, progress.* (It's astonishing what one can do with words!)

Does population growth necessarily create suffering and pain? Opinions differ: power and status create biases in reporting. Hunger, disease, deforestation, and loss of soil are the most disturbing consequences of overpopulation. At any given moment millions of human beings are suffering from these conditions. No precise figure can be given for how many, because the answer depends on definitions, and on data coming from remote areas that are difficult and unpleasant to survey. Poverty is a matter of definition. By World Health Organization standards it is likely that, at any given moment, as many as a thousand million human beings are suffering from malnutrition if not starvation. Almost always, the people who suffer the most are the least observed by reporters. Well-fed, healthy reporters seldom seek assignment to distant and miserable areas of malnutrition and starvation.

Moreover, well-fed government officials have a vested interest in bending the truth to minimize the possibility of a revolution in the system that supports them. They understand very well that the published results of surveys can affect how miserable people feel. Officials may flatly deny the existence of distress in those parts of the world for which they are responsible. Alternatively, they may admit the suffering but deny the role of population in causing it, pouncing on other factors as scapegoats.

Such scapegoating took place at the first United Nations conference on population in Bucharest in 1974. The head of China's delegation used both denial and scapegoating to steer the conference away from thoughts of population control. "Population is not a problem under socialism," he said, and then went on to serve up some tempting scapegoats. "The primary way of solving the population problem," he said, "lies in combating the aggression and plunder of the imperialists, colonialists and neo-colonialists, and particularly the superpowers."[22] His analysis was warmly welcomed by other delegates from the Third World. In the richer world it was also welcomed by the Vatican and the intellectual descendants of William Godwin.

The leader of the Indian delegation contributed the most memorable phrase of the conference: "Development is the best contraceptive." Operationally this translates into: "Instead of demanding that we poor countries control our populations, you rich countries should give us money for erecting factories, building dams, and eliminating poverty." In retrospect it looks as though the Indian delegation was just grandstanding at Bucharest, because two years later the central government of India issued the following statement for internal consumption:

> If the future of the nation is to be secured . . . the population problem will have to be treated as a top national priority. . . . It is clear that simply to wait for education and economic development to bring about a drop in fertility is not a practical solution. The very increase in population makes economic development slow and more difficult of achievement. The time factor is so pressing, and the population growth so formidable, that we have to get out of the vicious circle through direct assault upon this problem as a national commitment. . . . Where [an Indian] state legislature, in the exercise of its own powers, decides that the time is ripe and it is necessary to pass legislation for compulsory sterilization, it may do so.

Individual Indian states did not grasp the power offered them, but voluntary sterilization continued to be encouraged. In the last six months of 1976 over six million people were sterilized in India. The number is impressive, until one looks behind it. Five years earlier, at a sterilization fair in the state of Gujarat (the birthplace of Mahatma Gandhi), nearly a quarter of a million men were vasectomized in one month's time; but—a questionnaire revealed that they had already had an average of 4.3 living children before they consented to the operation. Such a fertility rate doubles the population in less than a generation. In a culture like India's the population effect of voluntary sterilization, commendable though it be, is less than spectacular.

It is fair to say that in 1974 China, the most populous country in the world, made a shambles of the international population conference. Just ten years later the United States, the richest country in the world, took over China's destructive role at the second U.N. conference on population in Mexico City, repeating India's slogan, "Development is the best contraceptive."

There's an old saying that "politics makes strange bedfellows." So also do unconsciously shared ideologies. At first glance, the ideologies of China and the United States seemed (in 1984) to be very different: Marxism in China, capitalism in the United States. However, the common and unconsciously shared ideology of the two was (and is) a deep faith in technological progress. Holders of the reins of power in both nations believe that technology can solve all problems.

Yet faith in technology is highly selective. Technology that attacks the demand end of the demand-and-supply equation is not generally approved of. Communists denigrated contraception in 1974, capitalists rejected abortion in 1984. Both rejections stemmed in part from a childlike belief that technology can increase supply without limit. If there is no limit to supply, why risk squelching demand, that great engine of material growth? Those who worship at the shrine of technological progress are so committed to encouraging demand that they will even dismiss well-established scientific truths. For example, when plans were being made in Stockholm for the 1974 World Population Conference in Bucharest, "as each new perpetual-motion-machine solution was propounded," to furnish the world with unlimited supplies of energy, one of the scientists would simply point out that it violated the second law of thermodynamics. Finally, in frustration, one of the economists blurted out, "Who knows what the second law of thermodynamics will be like in a hundred years?"[23]

During early development each human being is at first a bit of a fox (in Isaiah Berlin's terms), taking in a great grab bag of little facts. "Making sense of the world" requires that we metamorphose later into something of a hedgehog as we grope for the large ideas that will free us from memorizing so many little ones. This change is especially desirable in ecology, which can so easily become an unmanageable mass of little facts. Sanity in the face of complexity requires that we find the simple, basic fall-back positions that make sense of the world. How thinkers have managed to do this needs now to be explained.

5

Default Status:
Making Sense of the World

"There are three kinds of lies," said Benjamin Disraeli, Queen Victoria's favorite prime minister: "lies, damned lies and statistics." Scientists are inclined to argue with this, holding that statistics (properly used) are one of the glories of the scientific method. But since statistics are often *not* properly used it must be admitted that Disraeli had a point. As used, statistics are often a sort of black magic, accompanied by a disparagement of common sense. That won't do. As the logician Willard Van Orman Quine has said: "Science itself is a continuation of common sense. The scientist is indistinguishable from the common man in his sense of evidence, except that the scientist is more careful."[1]

The physicist John Platt agrees in minimizing the distance between science and common sense: "It may surprise many people to know that the chain of new scientific reasoning in a whole research study is frequently less complex than an everyday business decision or a crossword puzzle or a game of chess. It would have a salutary effect on our attitudes if for twenty-four hours we could cross out the words 'science' and 'scientist' wherever they appear and put in their place the words 'man reasoning.'"[2]

Stereotypes of scientists often imply that being scientific means having a perpetually open mind. Not so. A claim that lies too far outside the accepted view of things is often completely ignored by the scientific community. For instance, half a century ago the writer of a letter to the British journal *Nature* claimed that the average gestation period of different animals, from rabbits to cows, was an integral multiple of the number pi (3.14159 . . .). The evidence was ample, the statistical agreement was good.[3] But, to this day, the scientific community has ignored this claim. No understandable reason was proposed for the association of the two phenomena, and no one has been able to imagine any. It is just too ridiculous. Evidently the scientific mind is not completely open. To what extent is it closed, and how is this partial closure justified? Since population inquiries are beset by statistics, we need to understand the accepted limits of scientific inquiry.

Law and the Default Status

John Smith is charged with the commission of a crime. Guilty, or not guilty? If you have no closer contact with the evidence than is available in the newspaper you may find it easy to reach a conclusion. But if you are put on a jury charged with carefully weighing all the evidence you soon realize how hard it is to reach a doubt-free verdict. The evidence is contradictory, the story confused. You realize that you cannot be *absolutely sure* of anything. But you are duty-bound to reach some sort of conclusion . . . guilty or not guilty—what do you say?

What you say depends on where you live. Evidence that leads to one conclusion in England or the United States leads to another in countries that follow Napoleonic law. In the United States, in default of absolute knowledge, you base your conclusion on this premise, "Innocent until proven guilty." In France the judge follows the rule, "Guilty until proven innocent." The difference in these two *default positions* can make a great difference in the judgment reached.

We are not concerned here with appraising the justice of the two legal systems. The essential point is this: one default position or the other must be embraced, for the most practical of reasons. No good can come of demanding absolute proof. The default position reveals where men of common sense, in a certain jurisdiction, have agreed to place *the burden of proof.* It is the *denial* of the default position that must bear the burden of proof.

Perpetual Motion Machines and Default Doctrine

Because energy is needed to support all life, population problems are inextricably tied in with the properties of energy. Scientists routinely reject, *without examination,* any claims to have found a source of unlimited energy. To many laymen this behavior seems arrogant and narrow-minded. The basic issues can be made clear by a brief account of the historical development of the scientific approach.

The nineteenth century was preeminently a century of invention. Amateur inventors, lured by the successes of men like Edison, bombarded the U.S. Patent Office with clever and outlandish proposals. Among the most enduring proposals were those of perpetual-motion machines. Examination of these applications finally exhausted the patience of the office, which decreed that no more perpetual motion applications would be accepted unless accompanied by a working model. That put a stop to most of the applications.[4]

The bureaucratic gag was challenged in the autumn of 1917 when an amateur inventor petitioned the Congress to investigate his marvelous scheme for producing unlimited energy. Because America had entered World War I just six months earlier, it was easy to get a hearing for the proposal. The House voted 234 to 14 to have a commission of five scientists investigate the claim.

The commission returned an entirely negative report. It turned out that the inventor had thought that one could get free energy from a massive rotating flywheel. He had not bothered to factor in the energy needed to start the flywheel turning. The patent was denied. The next year the Patent Office announced that it would not even look at future perpetual motion applications, with or without models. In 1930 all of the old application files were burned.

The press criticized scientists who scoffed at the invention: aren't scientists supposed to be open-minded? Does not science progress by examining *every* possibility? The answer to the second question is *no.* As for being open-minded, how much open-mindedness can we afford? This virtue, like all others, needs to be quantified.

A spirited defence of the closed-mindedness of scientists was given a decade later by the British astrophysicist, Arthur Eddington, in a discussion of the second law of thermodynamics. Since there are frictional losses of energy in every machine, to move forever a machine must be able to generate energy out of nothing. The second law says this cannot be done. This law is the fundamental basis for the rejection of all perpetual-motion machines. Eddington defended the law in these words:

> The second law of thermodynamics holds, I think, the supreme position among the laws of Nature. If someone points out to you that your pet theory of the universe is in disagreement with Maxwell's equations—then so much the worse for Maxwell's equations. If it is found to be contradicted by observation—well, these experimentalists do bungle things sometimes. But if your theory is found to be against the second law of thermodynamics I can give you no hope; there is nothing for it but to collapse in deepest humiliation.[5]

If the lack of an open mind shocks you, ask what would happen if scientists had completely open minds? Consider the consequences if this default position were adopted: "Each new proposal advanced will be assumed to be true until it is proven false." The number of ambitious but poorly trained dreamers must greatly exceed the number of well-trained scientists. The scientific community would soon be overwhelmed by unworkable proposals, and the advance of science would be greatly retarded.

Proposals-on-trial should be treated differently from citizens-on-trial. In the latter case we are keenly aware of how *we* would feel if the Anglo-Saxon default assumption ("innocent until proven guilty") were abandoned. It is our psychological *identification* with the accused that makes us enshrine this default position in our criminal law. But in the case of a scientific proposal it is an idea that is on trial, not a human being. An idea has no feelings to be hurt if we find it "guilty." It has no civil rights. We put the burden of proof on any proposal that contradicts common sense.

Since an understanding of the ways of science is far from universal, even in circles labeled "educated," we are not surprised to learn that as late as the 1980s a U.S. district judge, faced with a suit against the Patent Office by a perpetual motion inventor, sought the advice of an expert. He found someone he thought the perfect consultant—a former patent commissioner, electrical engineer and lawyer. The expert ruled in favor of the inventor, and presented the court with a $13,000 bill for his advice.[6] In the opinion of the vast majority of scientists the value of this expert's advice was less than zero. Any competent physicist could have given the right advice at essentially no cost, using no more than a minute of his time.

If scientists had "world enough and time," they might investigate each and every claim. But the world is finite, and time will not stop for fruitless inquisitions. Most scientists, most of the time, take the risk of missing something good by refusing to invest any of their limited time in the examination of far-out claims.[7] When it comes to proposals that necessitate the abandonment of scientific principles previously identified as "basic," the default position imposed on the new proposal must be "false, until proven otherwise."

If an inventor of a supposed perpetual motion machine doesn't like the default position imposed against him he can thumb his nose at the world by constructing his machine and reaping riches "beyond the dreams of avarice" from the sale of the energy it produces. Such an empirical proof would finally compel those narrow-minded scientists to re-examine their theories! Of course, without patent protection the inventor might not be able to prevent others from also benefiting financially. But the invention of a real perpetual motion machine would surely be rewarded with a Nobel prize.

The Language of Science

Science is not *about* words, but it must be explained *with* words—which are never wholly satisfactory. The most fundamental propositions of science have been given a variety of labels over the centuries. "Eternal truths" and "self-evident propositions" are some of the older names, now viewed with disfavor. In the nineteenth century there was much talk of the "Laws" of science (with a very capital *L*). In the twentieth century the *L* went to lower case status, with all that the change implies.

But this didn't satisfy the mathematical physicist E. T. Whittaker.[8] He felt that the really basic elements of science should be given a strong name: "postulates of impotence." (See Box 5-1.) Such a postulate, he said, "is not the direct result of an experiment"; rather "it is the assertion of a conviction of the mind, that all attempts to do a certain thing, however made, are bound to fail."

It is hardly to be expected that the passage in Box 5-1 will ever be quoted in a popular science magazine. Writers engaged in "selling" science don't like to mention *impossibilities, failure,* or *impotence.* These terms suggest a self-confessed helplessness that seems unworthy of a creative and open mind. Moreover the last of the three italicized terms, because of its personal and medical connotations, is likely to make at least half the audience feel queasy.[9] It is no wonder that in half a century's time Whittaker's proposal, though not attacked by professionals, has not

---

Box 5-1. E. T. Whittaker on Postulates of Impotence: The Default Position.

[Consider the following statements:] "It is impossible to derive mechanical effect from any portion of matter by cooling it below the temperature of the coldest of the surrounding objects"; or the postulate of Relativity, "It is impossible to detect a uniform translatory motion, which is possessed by a system as a whole, by observations of phenomena taking place wholly within the system"; or the postulate (which plays an important part in the explanation of homopolar bonds in chemistry) that "It is impossible at any instant to assert that a particular electron is identical with some particular electron which had been observed at an earlier instant"; or the postulate of Imperfect Definition in quantum mechanics, "It is impossible to measure precisely the momentum of a particle at the same time as a precise measurement of its position is made." Each of these statements, which I propose to call *Postulates of Impotence,* asserts the impossibility of achieving something, even though there may be an infinite number of ways of trying to achieve it. A postulate of impotence is not the direct result of an experiment, or of any finite number of experiments; it does not mention any measurement, or any numerical relation or analytical equation; it is the assertion of a conviction of the mind, that all attempts to do a certain thing, however made, are bound to fail.

"Some Disputed Questions in the Philosophy of the Physical Sciences," 1942.

been publicized among the laity. Not being acquainted with Whittaker's insight, the general public has trouble understanding the reasons for scientific decisions.

Evidently the word *impotence* is not very acceptable; neither are *inconceivable, unthinkable,* or *impossible.* Rhetorically, all are too strong, too negative for general acceptance. What is needed is a word that indicates great reluctance to go off on a wild goose chase—but not an absolute refusal to do so. The scientific mind is not closed: it is merely well guarded by a conscientious and seldom sleeping gatekeeper. Fortunately recent development in the literature of computer programming has furnished the term that is needed: *default status.*

The default status is automatically assigned to the position that common sense would take. This "resting" position is most economic of time.[10] As the term is used by scientists, it is important to note that, "Unlike its normal English usage, default carries no pejorative connotation."[11] Assigning default status to a scientific proposition does not free it forever from examination: it merely announces, in firm tones, that the *burden of proof* falls on all assertions to the contrary. The scientific mind is not forever closed. Default status is a great conservator of effort.

I think it is more than that (but here I skate on the thin ice we call "metaphysics"). Psychologically, the default status carries a greater weight than the softer words, "rejection of burden of proof." We hint at the stature of "default status" by quoting Whittaker's judgment that such an assignment asserts "*a conviction of the mind* [italics added] that all attempts to do a certain thing, however made, are bound to fail." This is a strong statement. It asserts our willingness to circumscribe the freedom of rational investigation. "Freedom" is an intoxicating word but, as John Silber says, "Unlimited freedom is an oxymoron, for there can be no freedom unless we observe the limits that make freedom possible."[12] However hazardous voluntarily accepted limits may appear to philosophers of science, the fact is that the intelligent circumscription of scientific investigation, consciously or unconsciously made, has served science well for many centuries of progress.

Epicurus Throws Down the Gauntlet

The full flowering of science is a very recent thing, historically speaking. But its roots extend backward in time to well before the birth of Christ. So long as those who meditated on the world supposed that things appeared without material or understandable causes—that maggots were spontaneously generated from filth, that druids or fairies or pixies or gods frequently intervened in the affairs of the men—for so long was science seriously handicapped. A great and essential scientific step was taken in the third century B.C., when a remarkable man verbalized one of the most basic default positions. This was the Stoic philosopher Epicurus (341–270 B.C.), who said, "Nothing is created out of that which does not exist: for if it were, everything would be created out of everything with no need of seeds. And again, if that which disappears were destroyed into that which did not exist, all things would have perished, since that into which they were dissolved would not exist."[13]

Epicurus did not *prove* his thesis; indeed, a negative cannot be proved. Epicurus's statement must have arisen, as Whittaker said later, from "a conviction of the mind." In defense of Epicurus's position it can be pointed out that every apparent counterexample over the centuries has evaporated when it was subjected to close scrutiny. Science, perhaps the most impressive of all human intellectual edifices, has been built on the default foundation laid down by Epicurus.

In ancient times the most extended presentation of the Epicurean view was given by the Roman Lucretius, an exact contemporary of Julius Caesar, in his long poem, *On the Nature of Things.* It is doubtful if this had much influence on the development of thought for the next thousand years: in the chaos and declining prosperity that followed the fall of Rome most Europeans "had other fish to fry."

Perpetual Motion, a Sort of "Original Sin" in Science

Perpetual motion is an anti-Epicurean notion. Derek Price argues that it was probable, though not certain, that the pursuit of perpetual motion did not become a "growth industry" until after 1088 A.D., when "some medieval traveler . . . made a visit to the circle of Su Sung" in China. At this place there was exhibited a marvelous water clock that seemed to run forever without any motive force being required to replenish the elevated water supply. "How was the traveler to know that each night there came a band of men to turn the pump handles and force the tons of water from the bottom sump to the upper reservoir, thus winding the clock for another day of apparently powerless activity?"[14]

Such may have been the historical origin of what Price calls "the chimera of perpetual motion machines . . . one of the most severe mechanical delusions of mankind." The delusion was not put to rest until the late nineteenth century when explicit statements of the conservation of matter and energy were advanced by physicists and accepted by scientists in general. It should be noted that a comparable advance was made in biology at about the same time when Pasteur (and others) demolished the supposed evidence for the spontaneous generation of living organisms. Modern public health theory is based on, and committed to, the belief that Epicurus was right: there is indeed a "need of seeds," for disease germs to appear in this world of ours.

The "conviction of the mind" that limits are real, now firmly established in the natural sciences, has still to be made an integral part of orthodox economics. As late as 1981 George Gilder, in his best-seller, *Wealth and Poverty,* said that "The United States must overcome the materialistic fallacy: the illusion that resources and capital are essentially things which can run out, rather than products of the human will and imagination which in freedom are inexhaustible."[15] Translation: "Wishing will make it so."

Six years later at a small closed conference two economists told the environmentalists what was wrong with their Epicurean position. Said one: "The notion that there are limits that can't be taken care of by capital has to be rejected." (Does that mean that capital is unlimited?) Said another: "I think the burden of proof is on your side to show that there are limits and where the limits are."[16] Shifting the burden of proof is tactically shrewd: but would economists agree that the burden of proof must be placed on the axiom, "There's no such thing as a free lunch"?

Fortunately for the future progress of economics the wind is shifting. The standard ("neoclassical") system of economics assumes perpetual growth in a world of no limits. "Thus," said economist Allen Kneese in 1988, "the neoclassical system is, in effect, a perpetual motion machine."[17] The conclusion that follows from this was explicitly laid out by Underwood and King: "The fact that there are no known exceptions to the laws of thermodynamics should be incorporated into the axiomatic foundation of economics."[18] But it will no doubt be some time before economics is completely purged of the covert perpetual motion machines that have afflicted it from the time of Malthus to the present.

Amplitude of the Scientific Default Status

It is convenient to introduce the idea of default status with the legal principle of "innocent until proven guilty." The example misleads, however, if it is supposed that the default status in science is as tentative and narrow of application as the legal default status. When, at the outset of a trial, we assign innocence to the accused we by no means presume that all accused persons are truly innocent. Taking many court trials together it may be that the majority of the accused are, in fact, guilty. The presumption of innocence is made *as a matter of method,* not as a matter of fact.

In science the default position is chosen not only as a matter of method; it is also justifiable as a distillation from facts. An example from physical chemistry shows the nature of a scientific default position. The real number system is surely a well-established position. From this one would assume that 50 units plus 50 units would give 100 units. Yet when 50 milliliters of pure alcohol is added to 50 milliliters of water the result is 97 milliliters of alcoholic solution. What has happened? Has 3 milliliters of matter been destroyed, contrary to one's Epicurean assumptions? No: if one makes the measurements *in weight* one finds that 50 grams of alcohol added to 50 grams of water yields 100 grams of the mixture. Matter has not been destroyed. Apparently the two different kinds of molecules pack together in an odd way. In reacting to a surprising result like this scientists do not give up the traditional default position without making a heroic effort to give Epicurean conservation assumptions a chance. A scientist who behaved otherwise would soon make a fool of himself.

Of course a really solid contradictory instance, obtained by many different workers in many different ways, will cause a default position to be abandoned. But a law like the law of gravity is not a mere methodological convenience. We have many reasons to believe it true, and none to doubt it.

Yet—and this is Whittaker's point—if we apply the most rigorous meaning to *proof,* we cannot prove the statement of a default principle of science to be true. We are sure that "all attempts to do a certain thing"—the contrary of the default statement—"are bound to fail." Why are we so sure? For two sorts of reasons.

First: no contrary instances have yet been found, though many attempts have been made, in some cases over many centuries of time. Second: the default statement is but one strand in an intellectual fabric that *makes sense,* whereas all other variants do not. Speaking in general, Whittaker bases such statements on "a conviction of the mind." Epicurus, using the particular instance of the conservation of matter, says that a world in which matter is not conserved does not make sense. If there were continual creation, the world would ultimately become impacted with matter, probably lethally so. Contrariwise, if matter were continually destroyed would not the world ultimately disappear entirely? But here we are! (And Epicurus had no intimation of what we now know to be true, that the world has had literally billions of years to vanish or become utterly impacted. But here it is.)

Is that physics? No; not exactly. Is it "metaphysics"? Perhaps; but we cannot do without such thinking, so we should not let ourselves be disturbed by the belittling quotation marks around the word "metaphysics." The human mind has its convictions that logic knows not of.

Population theory is based on a few, but very powerful, convictions of the mind. These have not been easy to get accepted because they conflict with the very human urge to take an "optimistic" view of things. Since the increase in the human population depends on resources, we need to take a closer look at what passes for optimism and pessimism in the area of resource availability.

6

The Ambivalent Triumph of Optimism

To increase—even to live—human populations require exploitable resources. Concern for the future of our children makes us wonder how long resources will last. Attitudes toward conservation depend largely on information furnished by the press, radio, and television. How good is this information? Mostly it is not very good. We don't have to probe the shoddier representatives of the press to illustrate the fine art of warping attitudes. A single example from a quality source will do.

How much petroleum is there in the world? This is not a simple question. Do we want to know the total amount of petroleum *resources,* both discovered and undiscovered? This is obviously debatable. A more useful base on which to lay plans for the near future is what is called *proved reserves,* which is defined as the supply "that can be economically produced with current technology at today's prices."

Before proceeding further it would be well to call attention to the confusibility of the terms *resources* and *reserves.* A creative writer who turned out a novel in which the two principal characters were named Jean Robinson and Jan Robertson would be criticized for causing needless confusion. Unfortunately the analysts of the real world frequently burden the public with terms that, though definitively different, scarcely differ to the eye and ear. Such are *resources* and *reserves.* These terms have been used for so long that they can hardly be jettisoned now. When a feeling of imminent confusion sweeps over the reader, he is urged to review the definitions in the preceding paragraph.

Even for reserves there is no precise and stable figure. A new technology may lower the cost of taking oil out of the ground. A rise in price will cause the ledger entry for some underground oil to be moved from the category of economically unrecoverable to that of economically recoverable. The scarcity that causes the price to rise "brings oil out of the ground," in the words of optimistic economists. Scarcity, in the mind of some economists, creates more oil. (Geologists know better.)

The price of oil is very sensitive to proved reserves, but decidedly insensitive to estimates of ultimate resources. (This difference tells us a great deal about human nature.) The official figure for proved reserves varies over time. Usually the estimate goes up a bit. Sometimes more than a bit—a fact almost invariably taken as an excuse for new expressions of optimism. Let's see how the Wall Street Journal treated one of these upward shifts in "proved reserves."

A headline on page 34 of the Journal for 9 February 1988 reads:

WORLD OIL RESERVES ROSE 27% IN YEAR
AS PRODUCER NATIONS BOOSTED ESTIMATES

The first two paragraphs of the 900-word report continue the optimistic note:

> The world oil glut has suddenly got bigger, postponing the day of any severe short-
> ages into the next century.
> Based on authoritative new estimates, proved international oil reserves
> increased spectacularly within the past year—as much as 190 billion barrels, or
> 27%, despite the drilling downturn. That's enough new oil to satisfy global needs
> for an additional nine years, based on current use of 20 billion barrels annually.

What impression is left on the mind of the reader? He probably thinks that the
human race found 190 billion barrels of oil during the past year, whereas the brutal
fact is that the world used up and lost 20 billion barrels of oil during the year. The
"finding" referred to occurred in account books kept by the Oil and Gas Journal,
where 190 billion barrels were moved from the column for total (and unknown) oil
resources to the column for oil *reserves.* In some fields of human endeavor this sort
of wizardry is called "creative accounting." What was created in this case was not
oil but numerals in ledgers. (In international espionage this would be called "dis-
information.")

Yet the reporter says that "the supply increases puncture the widely held theory
that the world is using up oil reserves faster than they are being replaced." That's
not quite right. The theory that is truly widely held by the knowledgeable is this: the
world's oil *resources* are being used up faster than they are being replaced. Of that
there is no shadow of doubt. At the very least, petroleum is being destroyed a million times faster than it is being synthesized by today's geological processes. It took
hundreds of millions of years for nature to produce the present supply. It seems
almost certain that we will have run through the economically recoverable reserves
before the two hundredth anniversary of the Drake discovery well of 1859.

By the year 2059, will all the oil have been "used up"? No: there will still be oil
in the ground at that time—billions of barrels of it. So long as petroleum is used
primarily as a fuel, it is not the money price of oil but its energy price that will ultimately determine when the industry stops pumping. Assuming rationality prevails,
that will be the day when the energy content of a barrel of oil "produced" will be
less than the amount of energy that must be used to get the next barrel from the
ground to the point of use. (A complete accounting must include the energy used
in manufacturing the needed drilling equipment, in drilling the wells, in pumping
the oil, and in refining, transporting, and distributing it.) If we act rationally—a
preposterous assumption, perhaps—we will stop using oil when it takes 1,000 calories of energy to obtain a quantity of oil that yields only 999 calories. We will be
damned fools if we authorize government subsidies to "producers" to pump fuel
oil beyond that point.

It is surprising how many hard-headed businessmen live in a world of illusions
created by deceptive words. The financial world habitually speaks of the yearly
"production" of oil. But the unvarnished truth is this: *we human beings have never
produced so much as a single barrel of petroleum.* We merely extract oil from the

ground and then destroy it. Only nature produces it—and at a very slow rate. Yet an oil analyst for Morgan Stanley & Company says that in the light of the latest figures it is "difficult to argue that running out of oil should be mankind's principal concern."

But what does the word "mankind" imply? (Forget, for the moment, the sexist issue.) Surely the word implies not only extension in space but also extension in time. "Mankind" extends backward farther than the beginning of agriculture, some ten thousand years ago; and forward (if we can avoid nuclear destruction) many tens of thousands of years. By contrast, the forward horizon of money managers (like those at Morgan Stanley) is seldom as much as ten years away. To survive indefinitely in good shape a nation must take as its advisers people who can see farther than investment bankers.

So where did this 27 percent "increase" in oil come from? An accompanying table in the newspaper shows that the increase claimed for four areas of the world was two percent or less during the year. Only two areas claimed a greater increase: the western hemisphere (22 percent) and the Middle East (41 percent). The Middle East is especially interesting.

Abu Dhabi *tripled* the estimates of its reserves, making them nearly twice the reserves claimed by the United States. And Iran doubled its estimated reserves, the government justifying its accounting by saying that the new figures "came from the highest authority—in the name of God."

The *Journal* article that began on such a positive note did not inform its readers of the true source of the revised figures until the last three paragraphs. This was consistent with a tradition of journalism that calls for putting the major emphasis in the first paragraph, while consigning qualifications to the end of an article. Space limitations often force the makeup man to cut off the tail of a piece at the last minute. If this article had been cut from 900 words to 700, the reader would not have learned of the hanky-panky taking place in oil accounting in the Mid-East. A more disturbing thought: perhaps the original article was 1,200 words long? In which case, what essential information was confined to the 300 words no reader ever saw?

It is not the *policy* of good newspapers to distort the news; but the *rules* of journalism often have that effect. Rule 1: Catch the reader's attention with the leading sentence. Rule 2: Optimism attracts more readers than pessimism. Rule 3: If a last minute cut must be made, chop off the tail. No matter how objective a journalist may be, these rules, acting together, create an optimistic bias in newspaper reports.

Headline writers also contribute to the distortion of the news. The headline is often written under great pressure of time. A headline writer is almost certain *not* to look at the tail of the article. The content of the first few sentences determines the thrust of the headline.

Had a scientist been given the task of writing the headline for the article on oil reserves, the result would have been something like the following:

THE WORLD NOW POORER BY
TWENTY BILLION BARRELS OF OIL
BUT IMAGINATIVE ACCOUNTING
"CREATES" GREAT INCREASE IN MID-EAST

Why did Abu Dhabi and Iran go on such a binge of creative accounting? Therein lies the real story, but the reporter missed it. And it is doubtful if many readers suspected a different story. Too many readers in our part of the world have been brainwashed in optimism.

It Pays to be Optimistic—No Matter What

One would like to believe that truth will win out in the end, that unjustified optimism will be unmasked, that realism (called "pessimism" by some) will finally prevail. But this may not happen. Faith in the ultimate victory of truth comes naturally to scientists—and to many others in our science-infected society. We love to recall John Milton's stirring words in the *Areopagitica:* "Though all the winds of doctrine were let loose to play upon the earth, so Truth be in the field, we do injuriously by licencing and prohibiting to misdoubt her strength. Let her and Falsehood grapple: who ever knew Truth put to the worse in a free and open encounter?"

Noble and comforting these words may be, but they are only words. How strong are the "winds of doctrine"? If the wealth of vested interest accelerates one wind to gale force while the opposing wind is but a gentle zephyr is it so certain that "Truth" will prevail? Or, if it will do so "in the long run," how long is *long?*

We need to place oil resources in the framework of human ecology. The optimist may assume that petroleum supplies will last forever; the pessimist says, *not so.* In the long run, of course, the pessimist is bound to be right. Certainly by the year 2059 petroleum will be a curiosity, too expensive to use as a source of energy (though as a source of ready-made exotic chemicals it may still be worth pumping out of the ground). The "end of oil" (as fuel) may even come a good many decades before 2059; but come it will. What happens in the meantime to the fortunes of optimist and pessimist as they let their expectations guide their actions?

In the near term—five or ten years—the optimist who uses oil as if it would never be exhausted will prosper. But the pessimist who refrains from using this cheap, convenient, and extinction-fated resource will be at a disadvantage competing with the optimist. "Truth," competing with "Falsehood," will actually be "put to the worse in a free and open encounter" *in the near term.* Perhaps for several decades the optimist will win out—getting richer, earning more prestige in the community, marrying better, and perhaps having more children than the pessimist. Several decades is the better part of a person's working life.

The pessimist expects that the decrease in the total amount of oil will drive the price up, but for a long time his expectation may be falsified. A small price rise may stimulate a great deal of exploration, resulting in the finding of more oil. A large rise in price will stimulate a search for economies in the use of oil, which, if successful, will lower the demand and drive down the price. Thus is the pessimist made to look foolish—in the short run.[1]

The optimist is frequently praised as a citizen who stimulates "development" in the community, while the pessimist ("wrong," time after time) is taunted with cries of "Chicken Little!" Following every prediction but the last, the sky does *not* fall: this is the millstone that hangs around the neck of every publicity-seeking pessimist. In the extended historical period from 1859 to 2059 (or whenever the practical supply of fuel oil finally does come to an end), optimists prosper in every decade but the last. This fact of life explains why a respected management consultant has put the matter this way: "An entrepreneur is an optimist by definition."[2] Only at the end of an era do surviving pessimists have a chance to be recognized by their fellow citizens as being (finally) right, but it is not likely that they will then be praised for their foresight. (Anyway, most of the pessimists may be dead by the time they are proven right.)

The favorable treatment of optimists in a capitalistic, commercial society meshes well with the facts of biology. Consider what animal behaviorists have learned about chickens. You can't find a more impressive example of machismo incarnate than a strutting, brilliantly colored rooster. Apparently hens think so too: quantitative studies show that flamboyant roosters do most of the "treading." When the behavior and coloring of roosters is toned down by hormone injections, hens become less responsive sexually. Sexual selection favors machismo—which, in Darwinian terms, is why roosters behave the way they do.[3]

It is not too much to classify what we call "optimism" in the human species as a form of machismo (which need not be confined to one sex). Most of us, most of the time, find that consorting with optimists is more fun than hanging around with pessimists. Statistically speaking, optimists must have an advantage over pessimists in many lines of human activity, including reproduction. If so, natural selection must, in general, favor optimistic personalities over pessimistic ones. Publicists who bias their reports to the optimistic side are merely "doin' what comes naturally." Nature takes care of her own.

Can Optimism Be Overdone?

Social forces select in favor of adaptive changes in a business firm, but finally the firm goes bankrupt, becomes extinct. Why? Because the healthy optimism that caused a firm to prosper in its youth may finally become the excessive optimism that sinks the company in old age. One business consultant described the reactions of a "mature" business concern thus: "When things are going well, the average businessman assumes they will continue to go well. When a problem arises, he assumes it will go away quickly by itself. By the time he wakes up to the fact that he really has a problem, it's often too late to do anything about it."[4] Dinosaurs become extinct; businesses go bankrupt; nothing lasts forever.

One can argue that bankruptcies wouldn't occur if businessmen only had enough foresight. True; but this "iffy" statement gets us nowhere. More important is the fact that *bankruptcy serves a social purpose:* it selectively eliminates the less competent business concerns, leaving their social function (whatever it is) in the hands of the more competent. It may be difficult for creditors and shareholders of a defunct concern to view bankruptcy with complacency, but a society that prevents bankruptcy soon gets into trouble. One of the weaknesses of a socialist state is precisely that it lacks an efficient equivalent of bankruptcy. Without such a mechanism, inefficiency flourishes and waste snowballs.

Overoptimism is tolerable in the world of private capitalism precisely because capitalism is a "profit *and* loss" system. The error of too much optimism at the level of a firm can be corrected before it does irreparable damage to society as a whole. What is learned from the error of one firm can make society as a whole stronger.

But overoptimism among those who are in political control of the total system of society has other consequences. A totalitarian dictator in control of the Office of Public Information can hide, for a while, a substantive failure. But when public knowledge catches up with reality, a nearly mortally wounded society may find itself being shoved aside by other societies.

When Lyndon B. Johnson was president of the United States, one of his esteemed advisers was the political scientist W. W. Rostow, a man of unquenchable technological optimism. Asked about the consequences of all-out thermonuclear war, he brightly opined that one of the benefits of a nuclear leveling of Manhattan Island would be this: the first phase of urban renewal would thus be accomplished at no cost to the United States Treasury.[5] To recast an old saying, with optimists like this, who needs pessimists? (We will hear more of Rostow later.)

The social value of optimism at the level of firms-within-a-nation is different from its value when the nation is the unit of selection. This is an example of what is called the *scale effect,* of which we will find many instances as we continue inquiring into the complexities of population. Many stupid actions taken by society could be avoided if more people were acutely aware of scale effects. Whenever the scale is shifted upward, one should always be alert for possible contradictions of the conventional wisdom that served so well when the unit was smaller. Optimism that is of survival value at the level of the firm may be fatal at the level of the nation as a whole. Failure of the electorate to appreciate scale effects can put the survival of a democratic nation in jeopardy. When all the candidates for president sound like gung-ho business promoters, what chance is there for reality thinking to prevail? When all politicians are hucksters of unqualified optimism, what hope is there for that open encounter of truth and falsehood that Milton praised? Unlimited optimism is a dangerous drug.

Beyond Optimism

Few characteristics more surely mark the true professional than his ability to distrust the tools he works with. Among the scholar's tools not the least hazardous are words. Because multitudes happily use words without worrying about them, it does not follow that a single word stands for a single thing—or indeed for anything at all. More: a person who thinks long and intensively about a subject often becomes convinced that he is working with things for which there are no words. At that point he may coin new words (which may or may not help).

The Latin words *maximum* and *minimum* had existed for many centuries when the philosopher Leibniz felt the need for another word to indicate "the maximum good" (which could be either the maximum of a good thing or the minimum of a bad one). So, in 1710, he coined the word *optimum* to stand for this concept.

Leibniz needed the new term to give rhetorical punch to his contention that ours "is the best of all possible worlds," a view that was satirized by Voltaire in 1758 in his sprightly novelette *Candide.* In 1737, some Jesuits tried to damn Leibniz's sunny view by labeling it "optimism." Then, as now, the suffix *-ism* was often added with pejorative intent. (Consider the words *racism* and *sexism* in our own time: they certainly are not complimentary terms.) "Optimism," however, has grown away from its uncomplimentary origin and is now deemed desirable by most people.

After Leibniz it was inevitable that the opposing term *pessimism* would soon be coined. The *Oxford English Dictionary* cites the poet Coleridge as the earliest user. This was in 1794—just in time, one might say, to be applied to Malthus's famous essay on population (1798), which most people regard as supremely pessimistic. In true Buddhist fashion Malthus uncovered some of the causes of human sorrow, and tried to show that there are ways to become free of it. But few of those who damn Malthus have ever read extensively in his works. Trained as a minister in the Church of England, Malthus became an economist through self-education. After his death, the essayist Carlyle (in 1849) called economics "the Dismal Science." And many people today think of the population portion of economics as the utterly dismal science.

Suppose the words *optimism* and *pessimism* had never been coined: would we be worse off? Words are convenient handles for dealing with facts; but the handles sometimes cause us to miss seeing the factual complexities to which they are attached. Every use of a classificatory term is an exercise in prejudice—an act of *prejudgment.* To recognize this you have only to listen to an argument in which the discussants bombard one another with the words *racism, fascism, communism, sexism, ethnocentrism,* and *bigotry.* Substantive issues are shortchanged in the excitement of hurling verbal spitballs.

Is population a dismal subject? Are the substantive facts of population pessimistic? Much depends on what you regard as the essential Malthusian doctrine. The title of Malthus's book is *An Essay on the Principle of Population,* but he never bothered to tell us what *the* principle is. His silence has generated confusion ever since.

It is widely held that Malthusianism—note the pejorative *-ism*—leads to some such conclusion as this: "The growth of population will ultimately lead to universal disaster for the human race." If that is a true and inescapable extraction from the facts, then the Malthusian theory is definitely gloomy.

A more defensible summary of population theory, however, would be something like the following: Disaster is a natural outcome of perpetual population growth, but disaster can be forestalled if society can find the will to put an end to population growth. Such a statement is only provisionally gloomy—in which case one might just as well say that it is provisionally cheerful.

Before we can discover the needed corrective measures we must change our image of the world we live in, making it correspond more closely to reality. For too long our "instinctive" reactions have presumed an uncrowded frontier that is forever open. Now that the wide open frontier is no more, we must make our behavior fit the reality of a limited earth. Continued population growth will produce an increasingly more crowded world. "Spaceship earth" is more than a metaphor.

7

Cowboy Economics versus
Spaceship Ecology

Europe-focused histories present the world as it appeared to Europeans and to the cultures derived from that continent. It is said that the New World was discovered in 1492—a statement that would have surprised the Aztecs had they heard it. Adopting for the moment the Eurocentric point of view, we note that whereas before 1492 there were about 24 acres of Europe per European, afterward there were some 120 acres of land per European.[1] The fivefold increase presumes the legitimacy of property gained by conquest. This sudden wealth led to what W. P. Webb called an "age of exuberance." No wonder, as Catton and Riley remarked, "Opportunities thereafter seemed limitless . . . [and] it is not surprising that an optimistic belief in 'progress' developed."[2] The age of exuberance has lasted for over four centuries, but seems to be drawing to a close as the sixth century looms on the horizon.

An Uncommon Sense of "Conservative"

Epicurus proclaimed two important default positions: (1) nothing can be created out of nothing, and (2) no existing thing can be converted into nothingness. These are universally accepted by natural scientists, who view them as *conservative* statements since they refer to the conservation of things. Are economists conservative, in this sense?

The record is mixed. Economists demand that their helpers, the accountants, balance their books exactly; and an economist is likely to tell his beginning students that "There's no such thing as a free lunch." But before the course is far advanced the conservative sense of this incantation seems often to be forgotten. The man-made complexities of the world of finance make it difficult to recognize the underlying conservation of true wealth.

Scientists have had an easier time dealing with matter and energy. By 1879 the conservation of these entities had been well established in the natural sciences, but in that year the "single taxer" Henry George (1839–1897) defiantly proclaimed non-conservation in the social sciences[3] (see Box 7-1). Real estate developers and commercial promoters in general still sing George's song. (There's irony in this fact because George was intent on removing the profits from real estate speculation.)

Box 7-1. Henry George on Limitless Progress.

I assert that in any given state of civilization a greater number of people can collectively be provided for than a smaller. I assert that the injustice of society, not the niggardliness of nature, is the cause of the want and misery which the current theory attributes to over-population. I assert that the new mouths which an increasing population calls into existence require no more food than the old ones, while the hands they bring with them can in the natural order of things produce more. I assert that, other things being equal, the greater the population, the greater the comfort which an equitable distribution of wealth would give to each individual. I assert that in a state of equality the natural increase of population would constantly tend to make every individual richer instead of poorer.

Progress and Poverty, 1879.

The outlandishness of George's nonconservative claim was easier to defend in the nineteenth century. The benefits of economies of scale in manufacturing were becoming increasingly more evident, while *dis*economies of scale were much less evident. The means of harvesting nature's riches were steadily being improved by scientific and technological advances. Blaming poverty on inequitable political systems, while ignoring the changing ratio of population to resources, has continued to be the practice of political liberals from George's time to the present.

Conservatives in political matters do not often speak of inequities but they do support political liberals in downgrading the importance of the population-to-resources ratio. Bluntly put, political conservatives are *not* conservative in the Epicurean sense. Though they are anxious to conserve the riches and power of the present generation of the rich, they are relatively indifferent to the conservation of today's environmental riches for generations yet to come. They are ardent in their defense of time-honored customs, no matter how pathological the consequences.

Conservatives in the Epicurean sense, who might be called *ecological conservatives,* hope to replace an exploitative economy with a sustainable one, one that passes on to our children the wealth, diversity, and beauty of the natural world. Few of these found a position in the Reagan administration, which was composed almost entirely of pure political conservatives.

One of President Reagan's more shocking appointments was of James Watt as secretary of the Interior. The overriding goal of the Interior Department should be the conservation of natural resources for posterity. James Watt repudiated this ideal. In both words and deeds he showed that he was driven by a determination to *use up all resources as fast as possible.* As a fundamentalist Christian he justified his improvidence on the grounds that the Day of Judgment was at hand. Since the world was scheduled to be destroyed shortly, Watt could see no reason for not dissipating the nation's riches as fast as possible. Operating by this philosophy, Watt diminished the wild resources of the country in many ways that could not be remedied later. The only good coming from his regime was this: before he was forced out of office, public reaction to his well-publicized atrocities had more than doubled the membership of the leading environmental organizations.

Siamese Twins: Ecology and Economics

By virtue of their word roots, economics and ecology are sister sciences. The Greek root *oikos* means household. Ecology should be the science (*-logy*) of the household, while economics (*-nomics*) should be the discipline that deals with its numerical aspects. Logically, economics should be a branch of ecology, but that is not how the academic relationship has developed. (Vested interests are more effective than logic in determining the divisions of academia.)

Over thousands of years intellectual specialties have crystallized, one by one, out of the mother-liquor of *philosophy,* a term that originally meant no more than a generalized love of wisdom. Invariably each new crystal has grown for awhile before being named. Aristotle, Oresme, Gresham, and Hume had much to say about the subject matter of economics, but not under that name; and economic facts were generally mixed with other matters. The discipline "economics" was not so named until about half a century after Adam Smith died in 1790. As for the subject matter, Malthus was the first Englishman to become a professor of what we now call economics.

Ecology crystallized out later. The term was coined in the 1860s by Ernst Haeckel, the biologist who introduced Darwin's work to the Germans.[4] Ecology developed slowly and was scarcely known outside the academic world until the publication of Rachel Carson's classic *Silent Spring* in 1962.

Ecology and economics are both concerned with the behavior of populations of organisms. Ecology deals with the behavior of plants and animals (which may or may not include the human animal); economics confines its attention to the behavior of the human animal only, and to only certain kinds of behavior at that. Though population studies have been central concerns of ecology from the beginning to the present day, economics has, curiously, abandoned population. After Malthus, the last major economics textbook to emphasize population matters was John Stuart Mill's *Principles of Political Economy,* published in 1848. Thereafter the subjects of economics and population underwent a prolonged and mostly wordless divorce; by the twentieth century the topic of population was reduced to few and insubstantial paragraphs in the major textbooks of economics. At the present time some texts do not even list the word *population* in the index.

The major ways in which ecology and economics differ is in their attitudes toward (a) limits, (b) discounting the future, and (c) dealing with irreversible changes. The logical affinity of the two subject areas calls for cooperation in investigating such subjects as human population. Given enough good will and sufficient effort on the part of both economists and ecologists, it should be possible to bring the two disciplines together again. A beginning was made in 1988 with the formation of an International Society for Ecological Economics, and the founding of the journal *Ecological Economics.* Making sense of human population problems certainly requires insights from both specialties.

'Production" as a Scientific Problem

The instant popularity of *Silent Spring* moved ecology out of academia and into the market place. Within a very short time something like open warfare developed between businessmen and economists on the one hand and ecologists and environmentalists on the other. Ecologists, like other natural scientists, accept Epicurean conservation as the default position of all analysis. Rhetorically this means that there is little or no true production in the world, merely alterations of various sorts among the different forms of matter and energy. In economics, by contrast, the word "production" has something of a mystic quality. Accounting problems *seem* simple if one never questions the apparent production of something out of nothing (or the apparent evaporation of unwanted things into nothingness).

The Epicurean spirit was reintroduced into European science in 1773 by a now-obscure Italian named Pietro Verri, when he ruled creation out of the court of scientific inquiry: "All the phenomena of the universe, whether they are produced by the hand of man or by the universal laws of physics, are not to be conceived of as an actual *creation* but only as a modification of existing materials."[5] Economists are moving toward the Epicurus-Verri position, but they still have a way to go. Many economists are not explicitly anticonservative, only implicitly so—which may be worse, since implicit commitments are harder to unmask.

Cowboy Economics

In a country as rich in resources and as underpopulated as the United States was during the nineteenth century, truly wasteful behavior was seldom so labeled. Economic buccaneers grabbed what they wanted from the environment, littering the landscape with what they didn't want. This behavior could be defended as an economizing of human effort. Hungry Kit Carson would shoot a buffalo and eat only the tongue, leaving the rest of the carcass to spoil. Had he dismembered the animal and smoked the excess meat to preserve it, he would have been worse off for having wasted precious time.

But times have changed, and buffalo are rare. Four years after *Silent Spring* the economist Kenneth Boulding attracted wide attention with his analysis of economic systems into two varieties, the first of which he called "cowboy economics" (see Box 7-2).[6] As a result of the immense growth of the human population (unmatched by a corresponding increase in the area or volume of the spaceship earth on which we live), we now need to replace happy-go-lucky cowboy economics with a freedom-restricting regime that Boulding calls "spaceship economics."

Scientific papers that present a fundamentally new point of view are sometimes ignored for awhile. The idea of a spaceship economy (though not under that name) was first spelled out by Boulding in two technical papers in 1945 and 1949. So far as Boulding could tell, these earlier articles "produced no response whatever" among his fellow economists.[7] It was only after the publication of *Silent Spring* that the originality and wisdom of his contribution came to be widely appreciated.

The resources of typography can be exploited to make Boulding's insight obvious. Using different kinds of type to mirror the emphases implicit in cowboy economics we can write:

$$\textit{Hazy Resources} \quad \rightarrow \quad \text{Production} \quad \rightarrow \quad \textit{Throwaway Wastes}$$

A cowboy economist is keenly aware of the things produced, but—in the language economists like to use—only "marginally" aware of resources used up and

---

Box 7-2. Kenneth E. Boulding on Economics: Cowboy versus Spaceman.

The closed earth of the future requires economic principles which are somewhat different from those of the open earth of the past. For the sake of picturesqueness, I am tempted to call the open economy the "cowboy economy," the cowboy being symbolic of the illimitable plains and also associated with reckless, exploitative, romantic, and violent behavior, which is characteristic of open societies. The closed economy of the future might similarly be called the "spaceman economy," in which the earth has become a single spaceship, without unlimited reservoirs of anything, either for extraction or for pollution, and in which, therefore, man must find his place in a cyclical ecological system which is capable of continuous reproduction of material form even though it cannot escape having inputs of energy. . . . In the cowboy economy, consumption is regarded as a good thing and production likewise; and the success of the economy is measured by the amount of the throughput from the "factors of production," a part of which, at any rate, is extracted from the reservoirs of raw materials and noneconomic objects, and another part of which is output into the reservoirs of pollution. If there are infinite reservoirs from which material can be obtained and into which effluvia can be deposited, then the throughput is at least a plausible measure of the success of the economy. . . .

In the spaceman economy, throughput is by no means a desideratum, and is indeed to be regarded as something to be minimized rather than maximized. The essential measure of the success of the economy is not production and consumption at all, but the nature, extent, quality, and complexity of the total capital stock, including in this the state of the human bodies and minds included in the system. In the spaceman economy, what we are primarily concerned with is stock maintenance, and any technological change which results in the maintenance of a given total stock with a lessened throughput (that is, less production and consumption) is clearly a gain. This idea that both production and consumption are bad things rather than good things is very strange to economists, who have been obsessed with the income-flow concepts. . . .

"The Economics of the Coming Spaceship Earth," 1966.

---

wastes generated. It can be easily understood why the cowboy economist's production function is not frankly labeled as such in economic literature. Such a truthful acknowledgment of bias would expose the discipline to ridicule.

The bias of the cowboy economist's production function was increased during World War II by the invention of a statistic called the gross national product (GNP). This aggregating measure includes all payments received for products sold and services rendered—the "goods" of economic life—but it ignores the "bads" that may accompany economic activity. If a beautiful and awe-inspiring forest is destroyed to make way for agriculture, the *cost* of destruction is part of the GNP, but the *values* of the forest destroyed are ignored. The so-called "reclamation" of a primeval estuary (which has always been a wetland) is dealt with in a similarly biased way. The cost of filling in the wetland is added to the GNP, as is also the sale of this land to someone who builds a factory on it. No account is taken of the loss of breeding area for fish and crustaceans. An ecologist would be inclined to augment the statistic of the GNP with a GND—"gross national destruction."

Moreover, whenever action is taken to correct the undesirable effects of "progress," the costs of corrective actions enter into the accounting procedure in a perverse way: they are added into the total sum of "goods," though the correction may not even succeed in returning the system to the status quo ante "progress." For instance, if the cost of medically treating people who suffer from respiratory diseases caused by the mining of coal is $3 billion, then that $3 billion is included in the GNP, though clearly the money spent on medicine cannot be spent on other things that would yield positive pleasure to consumers. And the uncorrected residual pain suffered by the miners receives no economic accounting whatsoever in the GNP. Very little sagacity is required to realize that gross pollution coupled with a generous support of socialized medicine could ultimately send a nation with the highest GNP in the world into the poor house. (And no doubt the costs of building and running the poor house would be added to the GNP!)

However comforting a half-blind production function may be to cowboy economists it is not admissible in a discipline that aims to become a science. To merit the name of science a discipline must be firmly grounded in conservation principles. Whoever it was who coined the folksy saying, "There's no such thing as a free lunch," brought the academic discipline of economics closer to the Epicurean vision of reality.

Spaceship Ecology

Naturally those who became rich living on the subsidies of nature resented it when ecologists and environmentalists expanded the application of the "no free lunch" doctrine to include the environment in which the human species lives and has its being. But gradually the economic fraternity is following Boulding's lead as they set about substituting the broad view of spaceship ecology for the narrower view of cowboy economics.

Ecologists see economics as a fractional specialty within the broader discipline of ecology. (Few economists agree—which is understandable.) There is always the danger that ecologists will have just as inadequate a view of the production function as economists used to have, though with the opposite emphasis:

$$\text{Source} \ \rightarrow \ \text{\small Production} \ \rightarrow \ \text{Sink}$$

Narrow-minded economists emphasize "production" and virtually ignore what happens to the *source* of nature's resources, as well as to nature's *sink,* which has to absorb the unwanted, so-called "by-products" of production. Equally narrow-minded environmentalists loudly deplore the exhaustion of the sources and the pollution of the sinks while giving scant credit to the human agents who practice the difficult art of shaping potential wealth into actual human wealth—"production," as economists call it.

The sins of these two narrow-minded groups spring from the widespread human failing to appreciate fully the difficulties of the other fellow's job. Since the literature of environmentalism is produced by men and women who are skilled with words but, in general, are without experience in economic production, society's entrepreneurs generally receive too little credit for the very real contributions they make to everyone's welfare. It is therefore interesting to read, in Box 7-3, the testimony of one of the literati on the art of the entrepreneur.[8]

Box 7-3. A Wordsmith Tells His Experiences as a Businessman.

[Speaking of himself in the third person, Theodore H. White tells how he organized] a small publishing enterprise to publish each year a new kind of diary, spacing each full week on two open-spread pages, to be called an "Executive Desk Diary," of the kind now common. The idea took root, became a company which still exists. But what appalled White was the exertion a business person had to put into the execution of even the simplest idea, like diary publishing. He had to find the right kind of paper at the right price; the paper had to be erasable, for people constantly erase and rescratch diary notes. Then the paper must be moved to the printer, from the printer to bindery, from bindery to warehousing, from warehousing to sales people.

White came away from a year of exploring such publishing with an increased respect for the small entrepreneur who creates a business where none had existed before. Businessmen brought things together: steel to construction sites, coal to ore, oil to port, book to bookstores. If they did it well, businessmen could make two and two add up not to four, but to five, six or even more. This quirk of the business system, he decided, is what irritates most intellectuals, who believe that invariably two and two must be four, as four and four must become eight, and if they do not, then someone cheated.

In Search of History, 1978.

Theodore H. White was a career journalist-historian who happened, rather by accident, to find himself for a brief time engaged in a commercial enterprise. He discovered that making money by supplying society with something for which there is a demand is far from easy. His testimony is convincing because it is the testimony of a "reluctant witness," surely the most trustworthy kind of evidence. Note that White, in the closing sentence, expresses an anti-Epicurean sentiment, implying that something can be created out of nothing. Of course matter and energy must have been conserved; what was not conserved was information—the organization of matter into a desk calendar. A keen appreciation of difficulties like White's understandably make businessmen annoyed with the criticisms of Epicurean environmentalists.

A truly *general* form of the production function under the accounting rules of a society that has adopted spaceship ecology must give *equal* emphasis to *source, production,* and *sink.* The result is this:

Source (resources) $\rightarrow$ Production (alterations) $\rightarrow$ Sink (pollution thereof)

At different stages in the exploitation of nature by the human species the relative importance of the three elements of the ecological-economic production function differ. In assaying their relative importance, cowboy economics may be good enough for a sparsely populated world, but in our heavily populated world nothing less than true "spaceship economics"—ecological economics—will suffice to make life livable for us, for our children, and for our children's children.

8

Growth: Real and Spurious

One of the Rothschilds is credited with saying that "Compound interest is the eighth wonder of the world." How so? Because interest makes money *grow,* supposedly *without limit.* Ecologists regard the claim as arrant nonsense, for it implies a denial of Epicurean conservation.

Like putative records of lifeless money in savings banks, real populations of living organisms grow by compound interest, but this biological reality does not move scientists to reverence. Biologists know that the growth of animals or plants does not violate conservation principles; biological growth merely involves the transfer of matter from the nonliving world to the living. Though new arrangements of matter—new chemical molecules—are created, the quantity of matter/energy remains the same.

Before delving deeper into population theory (the topic of the next chapter) we need to see what scientific sense can be made of growth phenomena in the world of finance. In developing the argument there will be quite a bit of manipulation of numbers, but no great precision in numbers is called for. The conclusions reached will be *robust,* a curious academic word that means that the illustrative data can be varied over quite a wide range of values without affecting the *practical* conclusions.

Growing Rich by Sitting Tight

To accept compound interest at face value is to be confronted with an apparent creation of wealth. A bank account earning 5 percent compound interest per year doubles in value every 14 years. Let us indicate the initial deposit by D and time (in units of 14 years) by t. (For instance, when the number of years is 28, $t = 2$.) The value of the account at the end of time t is given by a simple equation:

$$\text{Value} = D \times 2^t$$

Since time (t) is written as an exponent of the number 2 we speak of this as an exponential equation and say that the value of the account grows *exponentially.* (There are other ways of representing the growth function, but they too involve exponents.)[1]

Figure 8-1 is a graph of the exponential growth of a bank account that draws compound interest. Note that the curve becomes ever steeper with the passage of time. This is not the sort of thing we expect of natural processes, which run down

61

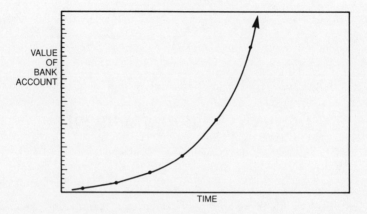

VALUE
OF
BANK
ACCOUNT

TIME

Figure 8-1. The value of a bank account that draws compound interest, showing the nature of exponential growth. With the passage of time the curve rises ever more steeply.

after awhile. After a few decades of living the strength of human muscles diminishes, memory becomes less reliable, and vigor fades. By contrast a bank account, growing exponentially, increases at the same *relative* rate (say, 5 percent per annum) year after year, and at an ever-increasing *absolute* rate. (One year's 5 percent increase of $100 is $5; by the time the account has grown to $1,000 a year's increase is $50.) No wonder Mr. Rothschild said that compound interest (exponential growth) was a thing to marvel at.

In the early years of a savings account the increase may not justify making the sacrifice of locking money away instead of spending it. As time goes on, however, the rewards for self-denial become greater. By influencing the distribution of rewards in society, compound interest selectively confers power on those who are capable of postponing gratification. Compound interest favors people who take the long view. (Sometimes the ones who are favored are merely those who were lucky enough to have had ancestors who took the long view.) Postponement of gratification is rewarded: does this mean that the longer the postponement the better? Let's see what happens when the time involved is great.

In chapter 27 of the book of Matthew we are told that when Judas regretted betraying Jesus for thirty pieces of silver, he brought the money to the chief priests saying, "I have sinned," and cast down the pieces of silver as he left the temple. At that point the booty became the priests' problem. They decided that since the coins were "the price of blood" they should not be added to the holy treasury. "And," verse 7 tells us, "they took counsel, and bought with them the potter's field, to bury strangers in."

Not a bad solution to an embarrassing problem. But suppose some rambling Rothschild had persuaded the priests that they should "make their money grow" so the temple would be able to do more good at a later date? Had this happened, Matthew 27 might have been written along the following lines:

> Taking counsel with certain wise men called economists, the priests converted the
> thirty pieces of silver into gold, which they used to open up an account in the Peo-

ple's Perpetual Gold Bank of Jerusalem, saying, "Let this wealth purify itself by quietly drawing interest at 5 percent per year for two thousand years. Then let both principal and interest be withdrawn from the bank and divided among all the people then living who regret the death of Jesus."

Gold and silver fluctuate in price. Let's suppose that the original thirty pieces of silver were equivalent to two grams of gold, which the priests deposited in the bank. That's about one-fourteenth the weight that could be carried in a one-ounce letter. Not much, you may say: but watch the account grow!

Presumably those who regret the death of Jesus would include both Jews and Christians, who comprise about 20 percent of the world's people. (Statistics on religious affiliation are not very reliable.) For simplicity, let's assume that the population of the earth has fallen back to five billion by Regretters' Pay Day, 2026 A.D. That would produce about one billion claimants to the account. On that wondrous day, how much would each beneficiary receive from the People's Perpetual Gold Bank?

At 5 percent compound interest the total sum would, in two thousand years, grow to the equivalent of 4.78×10^{42} grams of gold. How great a mass is that?

The earth has a mass of only 5.983×10^{27} grams. Very little of that mass is gold, but let's suppose that it all could, by the magic of nuclear chemistry, be converted into gold. To pay off the beneficiaries, the Jerusalem bank would have to remove from its vaults 8×10^{14} solid gold earths. (That's 800 trillion earths made of solid gold.) With a billion petitioners to be paid, *each one* should receive 800,000 solid gold earths. If advance news of the payoffs persuaded *all* the earth's people suddenly to regret the death of Jesus, every man, woman, and child would be entitled to only (!) 160,000 earth-masses of gold. Where are the vaults that could store so great a quantity? Not on this earth, certainly.

The Gift of Graphing

According to an ancient Chinese proverb, "A picture is worth a thousand words." Whether this is true or not depends on what you are trying to accomplish with the picture. Some pictures are superbly adapted to the mobilization of passion. Colored pictures are good; moving colored pictures are better; and sound-augmented, moving, colored pictures are the most effective of all.

Pictures are splendid for dealing with the surface of things; but when we want to get to the deeper reality a picture may mislead us. For instance: a picture of a man shooting an elephant may make us indignantly try to stop the shooting of elephants everywhere. But what if the elephant threatened with shooting is so unfortunate as to live in a region where there are too many elephants for the food supply? Which is the crueler experience for an elephant—being shot and dying instantly or dying slowly of starvation? A picture neither asks nor answers the deeper question.

Realistic pictures are often *ambiguous*—or, in Latin, "driving (our thoughts) both ways." (The man photographed shooting an elephant might be a heartless sadist or he might be a tender-hearted animal lover.) Advertisers, publicists, and rabble-rousers love pictures precisely because they discourage critical thinking.

Advocates are seldom disturbed by the fact that a picture worth a thousand words may require 10,000 words to validate it.

There is another kind of picture that pays less attention to the surface of things as it plunges to a deeper reality. This is the graph. Dealing with the problem of an interest-bearing bank account a graph comes closer to picturing reality than a photograph can. (How could a camera depict 800,000 earth-masses of gold?) Where processes taking place over time are concerned, a static photograph is not as good as a graph (like Figure 8-1). Though in fact static, a graph can be a visual metaphor for change.[2]

Humanity has not always had graphs at its disposal. The acceptance of this advance, like all social change, suffers from inertia. Millions of people have not yet learned to make use of graphs in thinking about processes. In our day gadgetry is more quickly accepted than ideas. It took only a decade for society to make room for xerography, video recorders, and word processors. The acceptance of intellectual concepts is generally slower. For instance: in the seventh century a bundle of mathematical ideas from India—so-called Arabic numerals, plus zero, plus negative numbers—migrated into the Western world. Not until the seventeenth century were these inventions widely accepted—*a thousand years' delay.*

The idea of graphing, closely related to mathematics, also took a lot of getting used to. Graphs were unknown to the ancients. The origins are obscure, but graphing seems to have been first brought to a recognizably modern form by Nicholas Oresme (circa 1325–1382), bishop, economist, and scientist. Mathematicians and natural scientists adopted graphing early, but scholars in other disciplines did so more slowly. More than four centuries after Oresme's discovery Malthus did not use a single graph. (The job of explaining population dynamics would have been made much easier if he had.) Economists in general did not take up graphing until well into the nineteenth century—*five hundred years' delay.*

Today's financial journals use graphs lavishly; general newspapers, sparingly; and literary quarterlies not at all. Producers of the third class of publications seem to be literate only; other publishers are also numerate.[3] Those who write what they hope will be popular accounts of science face a dilemma. Undoubtedly graphs can make exposition clearer and more powerful, but the final copy has to pass inspection by the gatekeepers of the written word, who are generally nonnumerate literary critics. The gatekeepers are likely to rebel at being asked to broaden their education in a direction they have sedulously avoided most of their lives. To save face, they give the numerate or graph-rich book an unfavorable review. Thus is the fissure between the two cultures perpetuated.[4]

The propagation of knowledge is roiled by conflicting interests. A writer wants to be read, but he wants also to be understood; the critic wants to save face; the potential reader wants an easy education. The balance of interests usually counsels leaving out the math and the graphs *for the present.* But the prudent present has a nasty way of extending itself into cowardly centuries. Should writers not, at their financial peril, now and then give some weight to the *long-run* interests of society?

In the technological future a nation in which graphing is second nature among the majority of its citizens will unquestionably have an advantage over nations controlled by mere words and questionable photographs.[5]

Exponential Growth: Out of This World

When we became aware of the magnitude of the hypothetical bank account maintained in the People's Perpetual Gold Bank of Jerusalem we asked: where are the vaults that could store so great a quantity of gold? To which the answer was, "Certainly not on earth." It follows from this that Figure 8-1 needs revision; by simply ending the upward sweeping line below the upper border of the enclosing frame that graph is, at best, silent as to the reach of money-at-interest. Figure 8-2 comes closer to graphing reality.

Since we cannot possibly find billions of earth-masses of gold in or on the earth to satisfy the demands of long continued compound interest, we must—contradicting Mr. Rothschild—say that compound interest is not one of the wonders *of* the world; it is a wonder *out of this world.* That is why the line in our revised presentation, Figure 8-2, breaks through the confining rectangle of the figure as it soars off "towards infinity."

This violation of the tradition of graph-printing needs to be justified. Why has the reader never seen a graph like Figure 8-2 before? One reason is that reproducing such an iconoclastic figure in a book presents special problems for the publisher. (It is only human to take the easy way out.) But I think there is a deeper reason: Freudian *denial.* Two centuries ago there was a widespread belief in providence, an extra-terrestrial force that somehow (sometimes) took care of the human species. We no longer hear much of providence, but the hunger to be taken care of remains. The interest on capital—*usury,* to use the older, more inclusive term—seems to be a providential caretaker (of the lender at least). Mathematics and graphs that imply an adverse criticism of money-at-interest are apt to be ignored, that is, denied.

Fertile Absurdities as a Probe for Truth

Substantive wealth such as gold does not increase with the passage of time, contrary to expectations created in our minds by the institution of money-at-interest. This point was made above by creating a scenario with an absurd ending: a worldly bank account worth 800 trillion solid gold earths. Denial defends its position: "That's an absurdity! Therefore I will pay no attention to the logical point you have just made."

Reason responds: Like it or not, the conclusion is logically true. If the scenario was an absurdity, it was a *fertile absurdity,* an attention-getting way of showing the idiocy of the assumptions. The ability of numeracy to uncover fertile absurdities is one of the reasons for importing numeracy into expository writing.

Unfortunately a device that compels attention may also sidetrack it. We see this in public reactions to the work of a humorist like Art Buchwald. Now and then he discusses an injustice about which he feels keenly, but even then he uses a light, bantering touch. This is a necessary concession to the typical reader, who does not want his equanimity disturbed. The technique of the humorist is necessarily ambivalent. He needs humor to get past the reader's defences; but then he runs the risk that his audience may say, "Oh, he's just being funny!"

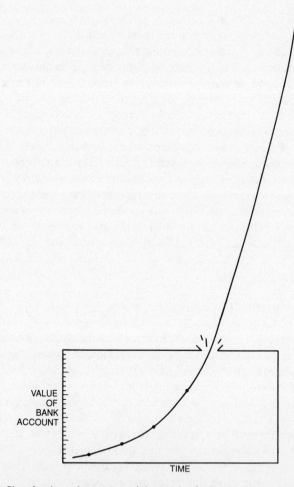

Figure 8-2. Showing how the exponential growth of a bank account at compound interest will, if indefinitely continued, break through all limits.

A fertile absurdity relies on monstrous figures to get attention, but their very monstrosity may cause the conclusion to be dismissed. At a second stage we need to show that the conclusion does not depend on the magnitude of the figures. Nor does it depend on precise figures: the conclusion is, as we have said before, *robust.* Even the slightest increase in the paper value of money-at-interest creates an intellectual problem; for, in human experience, there is no spontaneous generation of matter. So let us suppose that the priests, having second thoughts about the safety of their funds, told the manager of the gold bank that they wanted to close out their account a year after Christ was crucified.

"Certainly," says the manager, "Here are your two grams of gold."

"But," protests a priest, "you promised us that you would pay 5 percent interest. Where's the additional tenth of a gram of gold?"

"What additional tenth of a gram are you talking about? We put your gold in the safe and there it stayed for 365 days. That's what I have just taken out and returned to you. Are you telling me that gold can have pups? Gold doesn't breed. It just sits. Take your two grams and scram!"

Dead matter does not breed. ("Breeding" does take place in some atomic reactors, but, though the term has a certain aptness, the breeding in a reactor is quite another phenomenon, and has no bearing on the points made here.) It is a great wonder that the human mind should ever have conceived such a thing as compound interest, unthinkingly assuming that interest is capable of compelling dead matter—gold or whatever—to breed like rabbits.

Aristotle knew better: "Money is sterile," he said. Yet during the past thousand years we have built a civilization on the seldom questioned assumption that money is fertile. "Make your money work for you!" bankers say—meaning, "Make it breed for you." At this late date millions of people believe in the fertility of money with an ardor seldom accorded to traditional religious doctrines.

Interlude: Economic Delusions Breed Tragedy at Versailles

World War I was brought to an end by the Treaty of Versailles. At the peace meeting of national leaders one of the advisers to the British government was John Maynard Keynes, then thirty-five years old. In a vindictive mood the Allies, particularly France, were determined to make Germany pay dearly for being solely responsible (as they saw it) for the ruinous war just ended. They imposed overwhelming reparations on the defeated nation.

Keynes, one of the best economists of his day, knew that the reparations were utterly unrealistic. Germany possessed no such wealth, nor could any believable economic growth keep up with the interest being earned on the unpaid balance. Keynes calculated that by 1936, if the accumulated unpaid reparations earned 5 percent compound interest per year, the grand total still owed by Germany would be 50 percent more than the initial reparations assessed.[6] Versailles had put Germany on a perpetual treadmill. The result of the so-called peace treaty would, he wrote his father, be the "devastation of Europe." As a matter of principle he then resigned his post as a government advisor and returned home to put his thoughts into a small book.

The result, published in 1919, was *The Economic Consequences of the Peace,* surely one of the greatest polemical works ever written. "If," said Keynes, "the European Civil War is to end with France and Italy abusing their momentary victorious power to destroy Germany and Austria-Hungary now prostrate, they invite their own destruction. . . ."[7] It took the rest of the British citizenry almost two decades to appreciate the truth of this remark.

The People's Perpetual Gold Bank of Jerusalem presented earlier was an absurdity created for pedagogical reasons. The Treaty of Versailles was an unconscious but equal absurdity, created by men tragically unaware of the catastrophe they had set in train. Germany made some attempts at paying the reparations, but the task was hopeless. France felt cheated, and in 1923 she set up a military occupation of the Ruhr, the steel-making region of Germany. France's idea was to collect payments "in kind" at the source—in freshly made steel. But collection on the scale called for by the treaty would never end: German workers would become slaves in fact, if not in name. The Germans rebelled, and all work stopped in the Ruhr.

Inflation was already rampant in Germany, and by November the economy had collapsed. The government repudiated the old mark, creating a new rentenmark. The economy started up again, France was left whistling for her "just desserts," and the army of occupation eventually marched back home.

Anything else? Oh, yes: the consensus of historians is that all this disorder contributed significantly to creating conditions that favored the rise of Adolf Hitler. Causation is never absolutely certain in history but it is a plausible hypothesis that the Treaty of Versailles was a major factor in causing World War II.

Two mutually reinforcing morals can be drawn from this experience. The first: vengeance can be dangerous, even fatal, for the avenger. The second: actions that rest on untruth lead to disaster. The reparations that were demanded of Germany were beyond her ability to pay; augmented by interest payments the sum grew exponentially "out of this world." But the victors wanted payment *in* this world. An exponential increase in wealth that might, without danger, have been presumed at a low level became impossible at the level called for by the treaty. The treaty was an absurdity, but not a useful one, for it bred disaster.

Default Positions in Economics

Throughout time, but particularly in the past century and a half, the progress of science has been buffeted by two crosscurrents. On the one hand, new scientific discoveries make a mockery of old statements of impossibility. As a result, many non-scientists (but few scientists) think that *anything we can dream of we can have* (sooner or later). Cornucopists point out that there was a time when humankind could not fly or see through solid matter or identify a particular human being by the examination of a single hair follicle. Now "we" (only a few of us, actually) can do all these things, and more. Maybe tomorrow someone will invent an antigravity machine or find a way to travel faster than the speed of light. Who is to say what is forever impossible? The "Who is to say?" of the cornucopists opens the mind's door to all conceivabilities.

On the other hand, beginning in the middle of the nineteenth century a quite different intuition arose among scientists, being strongest among the most capable professionals. This was the belief that there is a small number of very broad impossibilities within whose confines possibilities have their being. The impossibilities are commonly expressed as "conservation laws," which refer to elements that are so fundamental that neither creation nor destruction affects them. Conservation laws define the default positions of science and place the burden of proof on those who deny these positions. "No free lunch" is a major default position of economics.

Many nonscientists, nurtured on science fiction, which they take too seriously, are repelled by the thought of impossibilities. This is not the view of scientists. Their gut feeling is that "only if some things are impossible can other things be."[8] (If 2 + 2 could equal either 3, 4, or 5, a trustworthy arithmetic would be impossible.) Scientists believe ultimately in real limits, however difficult it may be to nail them down in words that will be forever valid.

Games People Play: Usury

The sixteenth-century essayist Michel de Montaigne lived out his life before the great acceleration in scientific progress began. In a largely prescientific world it is only common sense to hold, as Montaigne did, that "No man profiteth but by the loss of others." If a man who deposits two grams of gold in a savings bank later collects 2.1 grams it can only be because someone (the banker, perhaps) is now 0.1 gram of gold the poorer. Material wealth is "conserved," as physicists say. In the mid-twentieth century such transactions were labeled "zero-sum games." We can visualize what happens in a zero-sum transaction between two people, say Tom and Jerry. (The left side of the equation below represents the situation *before,* while the situation *after* is on the right.)

$$\text{(before)} \qquad \text{(after)}$$
$$\text{Tom} + \text{Jerry} = (\text{Tom} + 3) + (\text{Jerry} - 3)$$

As Montaigne might express the change, "It was Jerry's loss of 3 units of wealth that gave Tom his profit of 3 units." A modern scientist would say: "In the universe defined by Tom + Jerry, the units are *conserved.*" Perhaps this becomes more obvious when we rewrite the equation in the following form:

$$(\text{Tom} + 3) + (\text{Jerry} - 3) = (\text{Tom} + \text{Jerry}) + 0$$

Now we see where the name "zero-sum game" comes from. Wealth, in a two-member, Montaignesque, system, is conserved. The sum of personal gains is matched by the sum of personal losses. In the transaction, the whole system gains exactly *zero.* A winner may view the result as no more than he deserves, while the loser may complain, "Unfair!" But what say the bystanders?

However various the religions of the world are, most of them try to imbue their followers with a love of fair play. In a nongrowing society (with unavoidable "frictional" losses due to decay, and so on) there are more human losers than human winners. (There are more paupers than millionaires.) In such a world, taking the part of the losers is a promising path to political power. With personal and institutional power to gain it is no wonder that, early on, religious leaders condemned the lending of money at interest, no matter how small. They called the practice "usury." For a long time after the death of Christ usury had no defenders in the

Christian community. There is no documented reason to think that primeval religious leaders had a profound understanding of the ultimate consequences of exponential growth. Love of fair play was sufficient reason for condemning a usurious banking system.

Nature is Added to the Game

It was not until the thirteenth century that Christian leaders began to find a justification for charging "moderate" interest. At this point usury was redefined as the charging of "excessive" interest. Anyone who distinguishes between "normal" and "excessive" in deciding what is permissible and what is forbidden is practicing what Joseph Fletcher calls "situation ethics."[9] (Note that the Ten Commandments, and most traditional religious-ethical proscriptions, are not stated in situational terms. This is their fatal weakness.) For simplicity, and to avoid arguments about the point at which interest begins to be "excessive," the rest of this discussion will use the old-fashioned term "usury" for *all* positive rates of interest.

Usury was first permitted on a tribalistic basis: it was permissible for Jews to charge Gentiles interest, and for Gentiles to charge Jews. Even today, devout Moslems who refuse to exact interest from fellow religionists are quite willing to invest their oil revenues in interest-bearing financial instruments of the non-Moslem world. In such an arrangement the conscience of the lender is spared by an inbuilt discrimination made between *brothers* and *others*. The parochialism of *Us* versus *Them* is older than catholicity. Loyalty to *Us* forbids profiting from losses imposed on brothers; losses sustained by *Others* can be accepted with cheerful indifference.[10] With the passage of time the sheer growth of population makes it easier to view almost all people as "others." Once that shift is made, it is easy to accept universalized usury.

Why should a borrower consent to the charging of usury? The motivations of borrowers and lenders are significantly different. The lender hopes to increase his wealth (though of course he will have to wait awhile for the gain). The borrower on the other hand wants his pleasure now. Perhaps he wants a new sofa. The psychological gain from early comfort may more than balance the loss caused by working longer hours to discharge the accumulating debt. The interest extracted from the borrower is the cost he pays for his impatience.

There is another reason why usury has become more popular since the thirteenth century. With the passage of the centuries "nature" has increasingly been dealt into the game of human life. In its simplest form, the game now has three participants. As a representative transaction consider the following case. Tom borrows a sum of money from Jerry, which he uses to buy some mining equipment. With this equipment he digs ore out of the ground and sells it for enough money to pay off his debt plus interest, with a profit left over for himself. A first attempt to represent the results of this enterprise produces the following equation:

$$\text{(before)} \qquad\qquad\qquad \text{(after)}$$
$$\text{Tom} + \text{Jerry} + \text{nature} = (\text{Tom} + 4) + (\text{Jerry} + 2) + \text{nature}$$

The numbers arbitrarily entered into the equation above make the point that when nature is dealt into the game, both Tom and Jerry may benefit. Envy may make Jerry resent the fact that Tom's gain is greater than his, but Jerry cannot maintain that he has been cheated out of some of his wealth. Tom, of course, can claim that the reward for vigorous activity should be greater than the reward for merely passively collecting interest.

The true situation is far more complex than our equation indicates. Metal may be extracted from the ore that is mined, and the product may be fashioned into machinery for making useful things that simplify the lives of multitudes of people not formally engaged in the initial enterprise. They gain from the "trickle-down effect" of human enterprise.

In a narrow economic frame of reference, conservation *appears* not to be observed in our equation; such an appearance is always suspect. In a true Epicurean spirit we must balance the production equation so that it is an honest zero-sum game. For a long time human beings were either unaware of the role of nature in the increase in human well-being, or they thought of it as a providencelike entity that bestowed blessings-without-loss on humanity. In the late twentieth century the movement labeled "environmentalism" has corrected the historical errors in this way:

(before) (after)

$$\text{Tom} + \text{Jerry} + \text{Nature} = (\text{Tom} + 4) + (\text{Jerry} + 2) + (\text{Nature} - 6)$$

Thus can we formally depict the environmentalist's version of the game of life as a zero-sum game. The numbers, however, are figurative. The stated loss of (-6) suffered by nature may take many forms: loss of soil, pollution of ground water, and extinction of species are only a few of the many possible, which are seldom measured or estimated until the losses begin to hurt.

A Difference Between Economics and Ecology

Serious mistakes can be made by analysts who have difficulty seeing some of the players in the game. In the past, economists have often been blind to nature. The following example serves to illustrate the point.

The economist Peter Bauer, in an essay on Malaya (Malaysia) spoke of the "largely empty and economically backward Malaya of the nineteenth century."[11] A paragraph later Bauer again put forward the image of "emptiness" when he referred to the "hitherto empty jungle." A biologist with even the slightest experience in the field finds this imputation of emptiness nothing short of astounding. Charles Darwin would never have applied the adjective "empty" to a tropical jungle. Writing home from Brazil in 1832, he spoke ecstatically of his experiences "wandering in the sublime forests . . . surrounded by views more gorgeous than even Claude [Lorrain] ever imagined."[12] The complexity and beauty of tropical ecosystems has been a source of endless wonder to biologists from Darwin's day to the present time. It is plausibly estimated that more than half of the world's 20 to 30 million species of plants and animals live there. "Backward Malaya in the nineteenth century" had many species of plants and animals that were wiped out by the commercial "development" of the twentieth century—"empty" indeed!

Bauer's ignorance of the tropics did not spring from a simple lack of experience. Born in Budapest, he spent most of his life in European cities (principally London), but he did have a few months' exposure to Malaysia. But when out of the city he evidently observed with city-grown eyes. To shock economists as Bauer has shocked ecologists, an animal-loving biologist would have to describe the center of New York City in some such words as these: "Except for Central Park, Manhattan is virtually an empty island."[13]

Global economics must be enriched to include nature in the equations that show the exchanges taking place among human beings. As used by economists, the exchange equation takes this form:

$$\text{Tom} + \text{Jerry} = (\text{Tom} + a) + (\text{Jerry} + b)$$

If $a - b = 0$, the equation is balanced; this is a zero-sum game.

If $a - b =$ a positive number, the game is a positive-sum game and an economist has no hesitation in saying that "wealth has been created." This, of course, contradicts the economist's usual claim that there are no free lunches.

Following World War II the rich countries of the world, for complex reasons we need not go into here, dedicated some of their wealth to the "development" of the poor countries of the world. Unfortunately, enthusiasm outran knowledge. Agencies like the World Bank, with many billions of dollars at their disposal, were advised almost entirely by ecology-ignorant, city-bred economists like P. T. Bauer. The results have, not surprisingly, been all too often unfortunate for the objects of their interventions, the poor people themselves. If an environment is perceived as "empty" until the developmental economist rides up on his white horse, God help the environment![14] (And God help the poor!)

Ecologists, like other scientists, regard the assertion that wealth has been created as evidence of a serious defect in the plus-sum equation, precisely because it violates conservation. Ecologists insist on putting nature into the picture:

$$\text{Tom} + \text{Jerry} + \text{nature} = (\text{Tom} + a) + (\text{Jerry} + b) + \{\text{nature} - (a + b)\}$$

What people have taken from nature, nature has lost. Thus is conservation observed when economics is wedded to ecology.

Naturally those who have been trained in traditional economics take exception to the new equation. They fear that acknowledging the contributions of nature to human wealth may lead to demands that we curb the rate at which we appropriate nature's wealth. Their main objections are two. The first is the classic one voiced two centuries ago by the American artist John Trumbull in response to the demand that he do something for posterity: "What has posterity done for me?" There is no easy answer to this question, but it should be noted that if this cynical view had been that of all our ancestors, most of us wouldn't be here today.

The second objection to the conservation of nature's wealth is most often heard from types who glory in being "hard-headed." They ask: "Which is more important—dickie-birds or human beings?"

The implied choice is fraudulent. When dickie-birds are sacrificed something of value is removed from human life. In the terrible days after the Chinese revolution of 1949 the poverty was so great that the people killed almost all the birds and ate them. Understandably, each person decided that his life was more important than the lives of the birds around him. What they were blind to was the total ecosystem of which both human beings and birds were but parts. Killing insect-eating birds subsequently caused an increase in the number of insect pests that competed with people for food. The Chinese learned the hard way that dickie-birds do matter.

Though they did not know it, the Chinese were choosing between two worlds: {a world with human beings *plus* birds} and {a world with human beings *minus* birds.} Even if we grant the hypothesis that the number of human beings would be greater in the second case it is not a foregone conclusion which world we should strive for. Is the total value of human life greatest when the quantity of *human* lives is greatest, if the *quality* of life is poorer for all individuals? The answer is not obvious.

The policy choice is *not* {man *or* nature}, but {man *with* nature} versus {man without nature}. City dwellers whose experience with natural things is minimal may express no interest in nature; but those whose experience has given them an appreciation of the enrichment of human life by other kinds of life will grant the wisdom of opposing the uncontrolled destruction of natural wealth. Conservation of the environment in this generation enriches the lives of subsequent generations.

When "nature" is left out of a written equation, the *before and after* change looks like the magical creation of wealth. Since human beings are involved in this magic, economists (and others) who are satisfied with nature-free equations develop a dangerous hubris about the potency of our species. The hubris is built into the GNP (gross national product), a statistic that has, since 1942, been quoted every day in financial reports. While taking account of the exchanges of money between the Toms and Jerrys of the nation, the GNP is blind to what happens to natural resources. All the exchanges of money incident to pumping oil out of the ground and burning it in automobiles increase the GNP, but the fact that the oil, once burned, is lost forever to the wealth of the nation receives no notice in the GNP. Similarly the loss of healthy, breathable air is not noted—except for the *increase* in GNP caused by the money that is spent for pollution control equipment on automobiles as well as the hospital bills attributable to auto-generated smog. The inconsistencies of GNP-based economics have been caustically noted by Robert Repetto (Box 8-1).[15]

Conventional economic thinking has been dominated by the GNP for half a century. It is easy to see why the entrance of ecological thinking into economic thinking in the 1960s was so vigorously opposed. People do not give up delusions easily: an increase in GNP sometimes stands for a loss in income. Only now are some insight-

---

Box 8-1. Devastating Defects of the GNP.

If toxic substances leak from a dump site and damage soils and aquifers, a nation's measured income does not decline. But if a government spends millions of dollars to clean up the mess, measured income goes up, because such expenditures are considered purchases of final goods and services.

If a firm undertakes the same cleanup itself, income does not rise, because the expenditures are counted as part of the costs of production. But if the site is left polluted and households incur medical expenses, income does rise: the national income accounts treat such costs as final consumption.

Robert Repetto, "Wasting Assets," 1991.

ful economists trying to concoct a new and more honest measure of productivity that will combine the insights of economics and ecology. The task is a daunting one.

Modes of Creating Wealth

Even if wealth in the physicist's sense cannot be created, wealth in a simpler human sense can. It is worth our while to review some of the better known means of improving the human condition.

First of all, potentially useful but diffusely distributed materials can be brought together, concentrated. For several thousand years human beings have been concentrating various metals from their ores (iron, copper, and so on), thus making possible the manufacture of tools and machines, which greatly increase our ability to wrest a living from nature. We never create atoms of copper or iron, but we certainly concentrate them and rearrange them into more useful configurations.

The capture of energy follows a somewhat different course. The iron in a machine is useful for a long time, though the atoms are ultimately disassociated from one another through friction and dispersed in the environment again (from which they can be reconcentrated through the expenditure of more effort and energy). But the energy (what physicists call "negentropy") resident in coal, oil, and gas can be used only once. Such useful energy is a capital accumulation from sunshine that was absorbed by the earth millions of years ago. Once used, the capital of negentropy is gone forever.

Another way of creating human wealth is by increasing the efficiency of human efforts. Two ways of doing this are obvious: either fewer human beings are used to carry out the job, or the time taken by one human being is reduced. As an example of reducing the number of human beings used in performing a task, consider the wheelbarrow. Up until the late Middle Ages the moving of materials was often accomplished with a two-man barrow—a platform or vessel with two shafts forward and two shafts aft.[16] One porter took the forward shafts, another the aft, and off they went.

Then some unsung genius realized that a wheel could be substituted for the forward porter, and *voila!* the work force required for the job was instantly cut in half. It is not often that a labor-saving invention cuts the input of labor by 50 percent. This advance came in what we, in our arrogance, are pleased to call the "Dark Ages."

The second way of increasing efficiency, through reduction of the time taken for the job, achieves its economic effect by virtue of a physiological truth: the calories of energy required by a human being can be divided into "maintenance calories" and "work calories." Just to stay alive, doing no useful work at all, requires about 1,500 calories per person per day. A moderately active clerk requires about 2,500 calories—1,500 maintenance calories plus 1,000 work calories per day. A lumberjack or miner may burn 5,000 calories per day (of which 3,500 are work calories).

Since maintenance calories are burned off at the rate of about 125 calories per hour, whether any work is being done or not, any improvement that saves human time saves energy (assuming the investment of work calories is the same). This is one of the principal virtues of modern transportation. (Think of the economizing of human time in flying across the Atlantic versus taking a slow boat.)

The benefits realized from an improvement do not necessarily go to those who are responsible for the innovation. The man who drills a new oil well gets only a fraction of the gain it brings to society. Others gain from trickle-down effects. Society tries to put primary innovators in a more favorable position by supporting a patent office to give inventors monopoly rights (for a limited time). We establish such legal rights partly out of a desire to be "fair" to inventors. An equally important reason is to encourage other ingenious men and women to make more inventions in the future.

Unlimited Breeding of Debt

Does usury create wealth? What is it that breeds when a bank account grows? Gold can't breed; neither can any other valued nonliving, material thing. Though material wealth cannot breed, *debt can*—and without limit, because its breeding is, inherently, a breeding on paper only. *Through usury we acquiesce in the breeding of debt.* When a depositor turns his gold over to a savings bank, two growth processes are set in train. The first growth process takes place in the mind of the depositor, who supposes that his cache of gold is growing in accordance with the compound interest formula (as visualized in Figure 8-2).

The locus of the second growth process is harder to specify because the process is diffusely distributed. At first glance it seems to be at the bank, perhaps in the mind of the banker who receives the deposit. But the banker is only an agent for the bank's board of directors, and these in turn act for the bank's borrowers who are required to pay back to the bank any money they may have borrowed, plus interest.

If many borrowers default on their payments, the necessity to pay the depositors devolves first, in part, on the directors, but then (more importantly, in the United States) on the FDIC (Federal Deposit Insurance Corporation). The funds of the FDIC come from thousands of member banks. If these funds are insufficient, the national treasury will be tapped, at which point the money comes from the taxpayers.

It is fair to say, then, that the locus of the growth process of debt is in the nation as a whole. The nation may eventually be called upon to make the figures on paper match the figures in the minds of the depositors. Without inputs from outside the system, a return of capital and interest in gold is not possible, as we have seen in the story of the People's Perpetual Bank of Jerusalem. There's nothing special about gold, of course: any material substance will fail as the "standard" of a usurious banking system. The obligations of a bank, of a banker, of the bank's board, of the borrowers, or of the FDIC to convert an ideational debt into material payments may be *legally* binding; but men do not write the laws of nature. Our species can, however, increase its drafts on the bounty of nature (within limits), and the efficiency with which we exploit this bounty (again, within limits). These increases constitute what we conventionally refer to as the "creation of wealth."

As far as the earth's economy is concerned there is a daily input of wealth from the outside in the form of radiant energy from the sun. Some of this energy is captured by the earth, so terrestrial wealth should steadily increse. The captured energy takes the form of plant material (corn, wheat, wood, and so on), or the form of water vapor elevated to the clouds from which rainwater discharges into mountain streams.

Sooner or later this energetic wealth is degraded by ingestion, digestion, and metabolism; by burning; or by being converted to electricity that illuminates light bulbs which heat up rooms. The ultimate form of this changeable wealth is heat and this, finally, is radiated out into space. If the heat were not so lost, the surface of the earth would eventually become unbearably hot. Over the long term the earth's "metabolism" can be epitomized as a zero-sum game: (input of solar energy) minus (radiation of terrestrial heat into space) = zero. (There can be a lag of several hundred million years in this equilibrating process, as, for example, when oil and coal deposits were laid down and remained as dormant stores of wealth until human beings brought this wealth to the surface and burned it.)

But let us return to the evanescent affairs of our civilization. The amount of debt can approach infinity; not so with the amount of any material goods that are specified as the coin of debt. After a long period of time a bank may be unable to extract from its borrowers (and the public) enough wealth to pay off its depositors. We are ordinarily saved from perceiving the fictional nature of usury by the complexity of the banking system. The complexity can befuddle even the managers of the system. Walter B. Wriston, chairman and chief executive officer of Citibank (New York's largest commercial bank), once authored a pamphlet in which he claimed that the modern world had outgrown the need for the great banks to back up their lending with any capital whatsoever, because (he maintained) a giant bank can always borrow whatever funds it needs by floating financial instruments in the market.[17] Thus is perpetual motion invented once more, this time by "hard-headed bankers."

The shaky foundation of the theory of usury was recognized early in this century by the nuclear physicist, Frederick Soddy (who, significantly, played a key role in the development of "breeders" in nuclear physics). The portentious implications of Soddy's work for economic theory have been almost entirely ignored by economists. Always, the priests of one religion (economics, in this case) are prone to ignore anything said by the priests of another (physics). Herman Daly is one of the few economists who have appreciated the revolutionary importance of Soddy's insights.[18]

The "bottom line" of an exact analysis of compound interest reads as follows: Though the inflow of solar energy increases the wealth of the earthly system, purely terrestrial processes do not increase the material wealth of the entire globe, whether under human control or not. On the contrary, material wealth is continually being degraded to less useful forms. Only debt can grow exponentially; and the convertibility of immaterial debt to material wealth should never be assumed.

Usury Running Wild

As we have seen, it took about a thousand years for the Arabic number system to be generally accepted by educated people. It took about five hundred years for graphing to reach a similar degree of acceptance. Must centuries also pass before the fictional nature of exponential growth is generally recognized?

Several considerations point to a pessimistic conclusion. First of all, there are some signs of the decay of education in our part of the world. Perhaps as a consequence of increasing the size of the clientele of our schools too fast the appropriateness of mathematics in general education has come under attack. The percentage of students learning algebra is falling. When we come to look at establishment members who might give voice to home truths about exponential growth, we note an unfortunate division. To the professional economists who understand the situation perfectly well it seems so boring a truism that they don't want to waste their time mentioning it. On the other hand investment counselors and the like stand to gain financially by not fully explaining the properties of exponential growth. Some of them even seem unaware that usury has no power over matter. As evidence thereof consider the following true story.[19]

In 1913 a wealthy man named Jonathan Holdeen set up a number of trusts, to run variously for five hundred to one thousand years. At maturity the benefits were to be distributed to family members and charities. At a modest 4 percent compound annual interest a bequest of $100 would amount to 33 billion dollars in five hundred years; continued for one thousand years, the accumulation in a single such account would be more than 10 quintillian dollars (1.08×10^{19}). And Holdeen set up 186 such accounts before dying in 1967!

When the trusts were challenged by a tax authority in 1975 most of the bequests held up in court, because (said the judge) there was no evidence that Holdeen himself benefited economically from his bequests. So far as the news report revealed, the court did not deal with the larger question, namely: What is the chance that such bequests can be paid off at maturity?

In evaluating a policy it helps to generalize a particular case to include many instances operating over an indefinite amount of time. Let us suppose that Holdeen's example was followed by others. About two million (2×10^6) Americans die each year. To be conservative, suppose that only 1 percent of these emulate Holdeen, each one leaving behind a single one-thousand year trust. That would be 2×10^4 trusts to mature a thousand years later. At 4 percent interest each trust should yield 1×10^{19} dollars, or 2×10^{23} for the whole bunch of trusts left by philanthropists in one year. How many Americans would be present to pay the beneficiaries of the trusts when payments became due? I don't think even the most immoderate pronatalist would suppose that the U.S. population would be more than 2×10^{10} a thousand years from now—which would be 20 times the present population of China.

Remember: wealth cannot breed—only debt can breed. The Americans on deck a thousand years from now would have to find the money to pay the obligations of the Perpetual Bank. The average American would then have to throw into the kitty 10^{13} dollars to pay off the trusts. That's 10 trillion dollars from each hapless citizen. And they could expect a similar bill the following year. And the next year.

Of course some of the same Americans would be beneficiaries under the trust deeds. Soddy's words give an apt description of such a situation: "[A]s a result of this confusion between wealth and debt we are invited to contemplate a millennium where people live on the interest of their mutual indebtedness."[20] In other words, money-at-interest, continuously operating without limit, produces a perpetual motion machine.

A judge in the Holdeen case who understood the imperatives of the default positions of science and scientific economics would have terminated the trusts pronto. A judge without this understanding would, I suppose, maintain that he is required to base his decisions on statute law only, leaving fundamental remedies to the legislature. But what if the ruling in a case depended on the assumption that the world is flat or that *pi* equals 3.0000 exactly? Sacred Hebrew documents make the second assumption.[21] What if a plaintiff, in the name of religious freedom, demanded that the court accept his commitment to the Hebrew value of *pi* in judging a commercial conflict? In such a case the courts would surely not hesitate to augment the roster of legislative laws with the laws of nature, acknowledging that nature is paramount over religion. The judge in *Holdeen* should have acknowledged that it is a law of nature that unlimited exponential growth is possible only for imaginary debt and not for material wealth.

Usury fails the policy test of being extensible over many people over long periods of time. We are never told about this in any of the promotional literature of financial institutions. Nor are children told this in public schools. (For that matter, how many university economics courses treat this matter candidly?)

Some state laws, it is true, strictly limit the length of time an inactive bank account can draw interest. We may laugh at the true story of Mr. Holdeen and at the myth of the People's Perpetual Gold Bank of Jerusalem, but promoters of savings banks don't hesitate to take advantage of the public's acquisitive impulses by *implying* that there are no limits to usury. Even today there is, in the District of Columbia, a chain of banks that has the word "perpetual" in its name. No doubt its more simple-minded depositers take the word at its face value.

The Necessity of Failure

Neither the Holy Land, nor any land less holy, has ever had the stability needed for the maturing of a usurious account over a period of two thousand years. Realistically, we admit that there is no reason to think that any of the world's present sovereignties will last two thousand years. Few will last even two hundred years. Going from the unreal world of theory to the real world of contingencies we see that the potentially ruinous consequences of usury are deflected by many sorts of failure.

Item: *bank robbery.* At first glance this might not seem an escape from the insidious threat of usury. If the robbers turn around and reinvest their loot in interest-bearing accounts, the act of robbery merely amounts to a redistribution of debt obligations. But the temperament needed to become a successful bank robber is unlikely to include much prudence. What with one thing and another, ill-gotten gains are likely to be squandered in ways that interrupt the interest cycle.

Item: *bank failures.* When a bank goes belly-up, its depositors lose some or all of their principal and interest; stockholders suffer losses, too. The community's aggregate burden of interest is lightened at the expense of some of its members. "Bad luck!" the rest of us say—and go about our business. (At least that's the way it used to be, before the FDIC.)

Item: *market crashes.* The paper value of stocks—the amount that may be demanded of somebody by the holders of stock certificates—falls dramatically in a stock market crash. The effect of this is to redistribute wealth—*paper* wealth. It has been calculated that the Wall Street crash of 19 October 1987 caused a loss of $1 trillion.[22]

Item: *repudiation of debts.* After 1492, the government of Spain, spoiled by unearned riches from the New World, settled into a mode of pursuing honor-through-war, moving ever closer to national bankruptcy. In the years 1557, 1575, 1596, 1607, 1627 and 1647—every fifteen years on the average—the government repudiated its debts.[23] Of course, it seldom did so candidly; instead it forced its creditors to exchange "old paper" for new, which was worth less and had built-in time delays on payments. "It couldn't happen here"? Don't be silly. Any government that wages war for honor's sake is suspect. ("Honor" is all too apt to mean, "We don't know what the hell we expect from this war—or even how to recognize victory if it dropped in our laps—but we're committed." Denial reigns; truth suffers.)

Item: *confiscatory taxes.* After World War II, England, in desperate economic shape, taxed capital gains at more than 100 percent. Such taxes removed not only the year's gain but also part of the capital that made the gain possible. (This is known as "killing the goose that lays the golden egg." Prudent political counselors advise against it.)

Item: *revolutions.* Bonds of the old imperial government of Russia were considered fine, conservative investments worldwide—until the Communist Revolution of 1917. The new government repudiated the debts of the old, of course. The delinquent imperial bonds (which were beautifully engraved) continued to be bought and sold in the capitalist world, though at disastrously reduced prices, for another twenty years. (Faith is wonderful.)

Item: *inflation.* This is far and away the most important of the systematic curbs on usury. It deserves a section of its own.

Inflation, the Ultimate Tamer of Usury

The general trend of economic history, albeit with many interruptions, is inflationary. Americans often complain of inflation, but they have never experienced more than the opening stages of the process. Our limited experience inclines us to make light of the danger of truly runaway inflation ("hyperinflation"). Perhaps it will help to have our noses rubbed in some accounts of truly destructive inflation. (It *can* happen here!)

Box 8-2 shows the course of inflation in the Roman empire over a period of some three centuries.[24] The economic measure is the number of drachmas (originally a silver coin) required to buy one artab—about a bushel—of wheat. During the first century and a half (from 30 A.D. to 180) money depreciated by some 80 percent in real value. Then for seventy years it was constant. In the next twenty years it depreciated 92 percent; and in the next thirty years, 85 percent more. Cumulatively, from 30 A.D. to the year 300, the drachma lost 99.76 percent of its value. In the year 301 the emperor Diocletian, in an attempt to arrest hyperinflation, instituted price controls, decreeing death or exile for violators.

Diocletian's laws didn't work, of course: stern measures imposed on a large population seldom do. Before another half-century had passed the drachma had

---

Box 8-2. Four Centuries of Inflation in Ancient Rome.

The price of an artab (approximately one bushel) of wheat in drachmas at various dates, anno Domini.

Date	Price
30	3
130	10
180	16
250	16
270	200
300	1,300
301 [Diocletian enacts his laws]	
314	10,000
334	84,000
344	2,000,000
410 [The Visigoths enter Rome]	

---

declined to 0.0015 percent of the value it had at the time of the death of Christ. Understandably, later administrators collected their taxes "in kind," that is, in wheat and other material goods, rather than in money. Not the least of the evils of inflation is the way it ruins a system of easy exchange (money). To put the matter another way: with hyperinflation a money economy degenerates into a barter economy. Barter economy may be fair, but it certainly squanders human time. (If my chickens produce more eggs than I can eat, how many trades must I engineer before I can acquire the bicycle I need?)

At some point a government becomes powerless to stop inflation, but it can always make it worse. Politicians often strengthen their position by actually promoting inflation. Controlled prices create a "black market." Morally, a government should try to stamp out this kind of market, but all too often rulers seek their personal advantage rather than the welfare of the nation at large. During World War II the Chungking government of China, riding inflation like a bucking bronco, was supported by infusions of U.S. money. At one time the $5 that bought one pack of cigarettes on the legal market would buy 162 packs on the black market. The Chungking government credited their American lender with Chinese money at the official rate, but spent the money at the black market rate. The suffering experienced by those who live through a period of runaway inflation can scarcely be imagined by the inexperienced.

The "normal," slow advance of inflation is dwarfed by rare and explosive outbreaks of hyperinflation. During the nineteenth century many government and private pension plans flourished in Europe. The funds in these systems were invested conservatively; perhaps none at more than 5 percent interest. Investors were told that their money was absolutely safe. Following the widespread destruction of capital goods in World War I, great readjustments of national currencies took place throughout Europe. At the worst, a German pensioner whose nest egg had accumulated 5 percent per annum compound interest lost in one day the capital it had taken him 3,033 days to accumulate. In four such days the loss would equal the accumulation of a working lifetime of thirty-three years. Less than a week destroyed all the pensioner's dreams of a gracious old age. It is no wonder that suicide became a substantial cause of death in what had once been flourishing economies.

"Bad Luck" and the Stability of Systems

That a conspiracy of silence surrounds the institution of compound interest is quite understandable. To encourage the loyalty of their workers, those in charge of any socioeconomic system feel they must claim that the system is absolutely stable. And, as we have learned, some bankers even have the nerve to incorporate the word "perpetual" in names of their institutions. (One can easily imagine what would happen to an institution that bore the honest name of "Perpetual-Till-the-Time-of-Troubles National Bank.") The brute, undeniable fact is that compound interest by itself creates an inherently unstable system in a world of finite physical resources— which is the only world available to us.

It is time to see how we have gotten where we are, and what we may expect in the future, as regards usury. The dominant attitude of the ancients is well expressed by Aristotle:

> There are two sorts of wealth-getting: one is a part of household management, the other is retail trade. The former is necessary and honorable, while that which consists in exchange is justly censored; for it is unnatural, and a mode by which men gain from one another. The most hated sort, and with the greatest reason, is usury, which makes a gain out of money itself, and not from the natural object of it. For money was intended to be used in exchange, but not to increase at interest. This term "interest," which means the birth of money from money, is applied to the breeding of money because the offspring resembles the parent. Of all modes of getting wealth this is the most unnatural.[25]

Sixteen centuries later we find Oresme saying much the same sort of thing: "It is monstrous and unnatural that an unfruitful thing should breed, that a thing specifically sterile, such as money, should bear fruit and multiply of itself."[26]

Oresme was one of the last of the supporters of the old view that usury is intrinsically abnormal and wicked. After Oresme, limited usury (renamed "a reasonable rate of interest") was supported by Christianity, and later by an overwhelming majority of economists.

It is easy to make a case that the progress of the European world into modern prosperity would have been greatly impeded by a ban on usury. Usury is justified by its fruits: debt, growing exponentially, marvelously motivates borrowers to find new ways of exploiting nature. The historical defence of usury can be reduced to the lines inscribed on a memorial to the architect Christopher Wren: *Si monumentum requiris, circumspice*—"If you seek [its] monument, look around you." Compare the wealth and the vast physical infrastructure of the Western world, where usury has been practiced for eight centuries, with the poverty of most of the countries where usury has not been systematically practiced. The man in the street regards usury as normal, decrying as abnormal the phenomena of inflation, bankruptcy, debt repudiation, and confiscatory taxation. But it is only through the persistence of the "bads" that the "good" called interest can continue to exist.

In this matter, as in others, the economist John Maynard Keynes stands out as an exception in his profession. In 1930 he expressed his opposition to usury not in a systematic development of an alternate proposal but in a familiar essay outlining the "Economic Possibilities for our Grandchildren." Some day we may, he said,

> return to some of the most sure and certain principles of religion and traditional virtue—that avarice is a vice, that the exaction of usury is a misdemeanour, and the love of money is detestable. . . . But beware! The time for all this is not yet. For at least another hundred years we must pretend to ourselves and to every one that fair is foul and foul is fair; for foul is useful and fair is not. Avarice and usury and precaution must be our gods for a little longer still.[27]

More than half of "another hundred years" have passed and usury still persists. Keynes's intellectual grandchildren are moving into power. Will the granchildren's grandchildren put an end to usury? Perhaps the best advice for those seeking prosperity for themselves and for the community at large may well be to follow the usurious path—for a perilous little while longer.[28]

The change, when it comes, may well be sudden and painful, because it will demand an inversion of traditional values. A postusurious society will insist that:

1. usury is abnormal (and it may be called "wicked");
2. inflation, bankruptcy, debt repudiation, and confiscatory taxes are the necessary corrective measures required for stability in a usurious society; and
3. for reasons of fairness, the practice of usury must be strictly regulated by the community, and banned in many instances.

For six centuries "informed opinion" has regarded the unlimited paying of interest on money as normal and generally desirable. People have assumed without question that material wealth can grow exponentially forever. Now we must admit that only debt can grow exponentially forever: that an exponential curve that soars off toward infinity can apply to nothing in the real world; and that such unpleasant events as inflation and debt repudiation are necessary correctives in a social system based on usury. The intellectual revolution demanded is a formidable challenge—for our children if not for us.

9

Exponential Growth of Populations

Historians took a long time to appreciate the importance of biological factors in human history. As the French naturalist Jean Henri Fabre (1823–1915) said: "History celebrates the battlefields whereon we meet our death, but scorns to speak of the plowed fields whereby we thrive. It knows the names of the King's bastards, but cannot tell us the origin of wheat." No doubt Fabre's criticism helped in turning the tide against the old-fashioned sort of history. History books now being written are more inclusive, more interesting. Some of them even mention population.

A century before Fabre was born, even the fact of population growth was denied by some otherwise well-informed scholars. In 1721 the Baron de Montesquieu asked, in all sincerity, "How does it happen that the world is so thinly peopled in comparison with what it once was?"[1] Until the nineteenth century the taking of censuses was a sporadic activity; most of the world, most of the time, lived uncensused. Primitive travel and slow communication made the counting of population over large areas difficult—and perhaps pointless. Without censuses or sampling, general impressions had to serve. When speaking of "the world" as "it once was," the baron, an educated European, no doubt had in mind the last days of the Roman Empire.

There is much uncertainty about the size of world population in the olden days, but the following estimates are probably not far off.[2] Over a period of about thirteen hundred years, ending in Montesquieu's time, the population of the world increased from some 190 million to about 610 million. This was more than a threefold increase, but an intelligent European could easily be unaware of both the direction and the extent of the change—for several reasons.

To begin with, most of the increase in population took place outside Europe. Despite reports like Marco Polo's, to European eyes Europe *was* the world. Viewing the sparsely inhabited ruins of Rome, eighteenth-century Europeans deduced a decrease in world population.

Awareness of long-term growth was made more difficult by erratic (but normal) fluctuations in populations. It was quite common for a region to lose a percent or two of its population during a single year because of disease. A 2 percent loss would be 20 times the average annual gain of 0.1 percent. During the Black Plague in the middle of the fourteenth century, Europe lost 25 percent of its population in just two years. Such a two-year loss was 125 times the average long-term gain.

Two centuries after the Black Plague, Europe was losing people by emigration to the New World. And of course, at all times wars took their toll of particular

regions, while migration within Europe itself redistributed considerable numbers
of people. Considering all the crosscurrents of history it would have taken unusual
ability to detect any long-term population growth. Fluctuations were obvious,
trends imperceptible: no wonder few historians were aware of the long-term growth
trend. As was pointed out in Chapter 3, the oldest paradigms of history are the
golden age and the endless cycle. Against this background Malthus's emphasis on
the reality and *ordinariness* of population increase struck many as astonishing. The
gist of his argument is reprinted in Box 9-1. Since the paradigm of progress was
developing rapidly in his day, the public soon equated growth with progress.

The new orientation speedily won support among the ruling class of England,
but as late as 1820 William Godwin was still denying that growth could be a normal

---

Box 9-1. Malthus: The Core Mathematical Argument.

In the United States of America, where the means of subsistence have been more than
ample, the manners of the people more pure, and consequently the checks to early marriages fewer than in any of the modern states of Europe, the population has been found
to double itself in twenty-five years.

This ratio of increase, though short of the utmost power of population, yet as the result
of actual experience, we will take as our rule, and say, that population, when unchecked,
goes on doubling itself every twenty-five years or increases in a geometrical ratio. . . .

Taking the population of the world at any number, a thousand millions, for instance,
the human species would increase in the ratio of—1, 2, 4, 8, 16, 128, 256, 512, &c. and
subsistence as—1, 2, 3, 4, 5, 6, 7, 8, 9, 10, &c. In two centuries and a quarter, the population would be to the means of subsistence as 512 to 10: in three centuries as 4096 to 13,
and in two thousand years the difference would be almost incalculable, though the produce in that time would have increased to an immense extent. . . .

The constant effort towards population, which is found to act even in the most vicious
societies, increases the number of people before the means of subsistence are increased.
The food therefore which before supported seven millions must now be dividied among
seven millions and a half or eight millions. . . . During this season of distress, the discour-
agement to marriage, and the difficulty of rearing a family are so great that population is
at a stand. In the mean time the cheapness of labour, the plenty of labourers, and the
necessity of an increased industry amongst them, encourage cultivators to employ more
labour upon their land, to turn up fresh soil, and to manure and improve more completely
what is already in tillage, till ultimately the means of subsistence become in the same proportion to the population as at the period from which we set out. The situation of the
labourer being then again tolerably comfortable, the restraints to population are in some
degree loosened, and the same retrograde and progressive movements with respect to happiness are repeated.

This sort of oscillation will not be remarked by superficial observors, and it may be
difficult even for the most penetrating mind to calculate its periods. . . .

Many reasons occur why this oscillation has been less obvious, and less decidedly con-
firmed by experience, than might naturally be expected.

One principal reason is that the histories of mankind that we possess are histories only
of the higher classes. We have but few accounts that can be depended upon of the manners
and customs of that part of mankind, where these retrograde and progressive movements
chiefly take place.

An Essay on the Principle of Population, (chap. 2), 1798.

characteristic of populations: "We have no authentic documents to prove any increase in the numbers of mankind."[3] If one italicizes the words *documents* and *prove,* Godwin's assertion has the sort of surface plausibility that sometimes wins cases in a court of law. But by 1820 most thoughtful people felt that Malthus had made a good case for the *naturalness* of the *drive* toward population growth. For a biologist, of course, it is difficult, if not impossible, to imagine a species of animal that lacks this drive.

Though Malthus did not use the word "exponential," it is clear from the passage in Box 9-1 that this pioneer economist had a clear conception of exponential growth and its important consequences for human populations.[4] Was he the first to be so impressed? Not quite: before him Benjamin Franklin had a glimpse of the phenomenon, but he referred to the matter briefly and then dropped it. The excerpt given in Box 9-2 reveals Franklin's position.

Note the difference in thrust of the statements by Franklin and Malthus. Malthus was trying to get people to worry about the consequences of exponential growth. In contrast, Franklin was saying "Not to worry": he wanted to relieve the English of anxiety that emigration to the colonies might depopulate their homeland. Reproduction would soon fill the places left vacant by out-migration. Franklin's essay was consistently upbeat about the exuberance of reproduction; it was the sort of message one might expect from a chamber of commerce—a quintessentially American institution not established in the U.S. until after Franklin's time.

So who should get the credit for understanding the exponential growth of human populations, Franklin or Malthus? The philosopher Alfred North Whitehead has written: "To come very near to a true theory, and to grasp its precise appli-

---

Box 9-2. Benjamin Franklin on Population.

There is in short, no Bound to the prolific Nature of Plants or Animals, but what is made by their crowding and interfering with each others Means of Subsistence. Was the Face of the Earth vacant of other Plants, it might be gradually sowed and overspread with one Kind only; as, for Instance, with Fennel; and were it empty of other Inhabitants, it might in a few Ages be replenish'd from one Nation only; as, for Instance, with Englishmen. Thus there are suppos'd to be now upwards of One Million English Souls in North-America, (tho' 'tis thought scarce 80,000 have been brought over Sea) and yet perhaps there is not one the fewer in Britain, but rather many more, on Account of the Employment the Colonies afford to Manufacturers at Home. This Million doubling, suppose but once in 25 Years, will in another Century be more than the People of England, and the greatest Number of Englishmen will be on this Side the Water. What an Accession of Power to the British Empire by Sea as well as Land! What Increase of Trade and Navigation! What Numbers of Ships and Seamen! . . . How careful should [England] be to secure Room enough, since on the Room depends so much the Increase of her People?

In fine, A Nation well regulated is like a Polypus; take away a Limb, its Place is soon supply'd; cut it in two, and each deficient Part shall speedily grow out of the Part remaining. Thus if you have Room and Subsistence enough, as you may by dividing, make ten Polypes out of one, you may of one make ten Nations, equally populous and powerful; or rather, increase a Nation ten fold in Numbers and Strength.

"Observations Concerning the Increase of Mankind," 1755.

cation, are two very different things, as the history of science teaches us. Everything of importance has been said before by somebody who did not discover it."[5] Franklin came close to stating a general population theory, but he did not quite make it. All things considered, there is no need to substitute "Franklinian" for "Malthusian" in the history of population thought,

Fertility, Like Usury, Needs to Be Curbed

To recapitulate the major point of the preceding chapter, *money is sterile.* This bald statement depends on two assumptions. First, by "money" we mean something that constitutes a demand on gold or some specified material substance found on or in the earth. (Real estate on one of Sirius's planets is out of the picture.) Second, by "sterile" we mean "not invariably fertile," that is, not indefinitely interest-bearing. The fertility of usury is bearable provided periods of compound interest are interspersed with corrective actions, such as the financial disasters discussed in Chapter 8.

The mathematics of biological reproduction is logically identical with the mathematics of usury. Money earns interest, animals have babies. In the living world different "accounts" (species) earn "interest" (babies) at different rates. The preferred form of the mathematical growth equation[6] during any period in which reproduction encounters no environmental resistance is this:

$$y = ke^{bt}$$

where y is the size of the population at time t, e is the base of natural logarithms, k is a scaling constant, and b stands for the "biotic potential" of the species. This information may be more than the reader hankers after, but it is given to arm him against the one-upmanship that mathematicians are inclined to practice in their dealings with the unanointed public. The equation for biological reproduction is the same as the one for money-at-interest: one merely has to redefine the symbols. In both cases, so long as b ("biotic potential," in biology) is greater than zero, by however small an amount, the potential of exhausting earthly resources must be met by countervailing forces. For usury, the corrective forces are the various financial disasters; for biology, the many modes of death.

Because usury can be continued indefinitely "on paper," the necessity of countervailing forces in economics escapes the attention of many people. The essential long-term instability of exponential growth (of debt) is not obvious. But where biology is concerned observors cannot long remain blind to the need for countervailing forces. Animal populations make withdrawals from the environment every day, every minute. The demand for "subsistence" (to use Malthus's term) never goes away.

The Rate of Growth—Does it Matter?

Even the most casual observer is impressed by the fecundity of living organisms. Unconsciously using our own species as a standard we are astounded when we learn that many female fish produce eggs by the hundred thousand, while a female oyster may release 50 million eggs at a time. Yet the world is not being taken over by either fish or oysters. There is little correlation between fecundity and ubiquity. Maybe fecundity doesn't matter?

What matters most is the fraction of fertilized eggs that survive to produce fecund adults. Demographers (in contradistinction to standard dictionaries) distinguish between "fecundity" and "fertility." *Fecundity* is defined as a measure of the *potential* reproductive power of a species; *fertility* is a measure of the *actual* increase from one generation to another. Since accomplishment is more important than promise, fertility is the more important of the two measures in accounting for the success of a species. Oysters are frightfully fecund, but their fertility is nothing to write home about.

Intent on convincing the public that human reproduction threatened humanity, Malthus took some pains to determine the maximum fertility of our species under the most favorable conditions. He settled on twenty-five years as the time required to double a population, obtaining that figure from Benjamin Franklin. Not only his critics, but Malthus himself spent an unpardonable amount of time trying to refine this fertility figure. The first edition of Malthus's *Essay* shows a fine grasp of essentials. Subsequent editions, three times as large, are overloaded with inconclusive data. Malthus seemed to think that the particular value for the human biotic potential (a term unknown to him) is something that needs to be determined with precision. He was wrong: it isn't.

Charles Darwin, a quarter of a century after Malthus's death, penetrated to the heart of the population problem when he showed that it matters very little how great the biotic potential is. He said: "There is no exception to the rule that every organic being naturally increases at *so high a rate*, that, if not destroyed, the earth would soon be covered by the progeny of a single pair."[7] Italics have been added to focus attention on the key point. The phrase "so high a rate" could easily mislead incautious readers to assume that *only* very high rates of fertility could produce this overwhelming result, but (without correcting his rhetoric) Darwin immediately set his readers straight with a telling example.

> The elephant is reckoned the slowest breeder of all known animals, and I have taken some pains to estimate its probable minimum rate of natural increase; it will be safest to assume that it begins breeding when thirty years old, and goes on breeding till ninety years old, bringing forth six young in the interval, and surviving till one hundred years old; if this be so, after a period of from 740 to 750 years there would be nearly nineteen million elephants alive descended from the first pair.

A little calculation shows that the doubling time for Darwin's elephants is thirty-five years, which corresponds to an interest rate of 2 percent per year. At that rate, would the earth "soon be covered by the progeny of a single pair" of elephants? "Soon" is undefined, so let us carry the calculations farther.

Assuming that the average elephant occupies an area of 12 square meters, the 148.847×10^6 square kilometers of land area could accommodate 12×10^{12} elephants. How long would it take the elephant population to reach that figure, starting with a single pair and increasing by 2 percent per year? Just 1,486 years—a mere three-quarters of the Christian era. Darwin's point is solidly established.

Habituated to interest rates on borrowed money ranging from 5 percent (on savings) to 19 percent (on credit card debits), many people find it hard to take a mere 2 percent rate seriously. But over time—and biological organisms have all the time in the world—any and every positive rate of interest must be taken seriously. In recognizing this fact Darwin showed his genius for seeing the significance of small causes operating over long periods of time.

To bring home the relative unimportance of the particular value of a species' fertility we can create a single curve that represents the growth rate of populations of *all* species (Figure 9-1). We do this by presenting a wide choice of scales on the horizontal dimension, ranging from minutes for common bacteria to years for elephants.

Note that this curve, like the curve for usurious increase, potentially heads off "toward infinity." As concerns the reproduction of biological species, *any rate even minutely greater than zero* is "so high a rate" of increase that, if some of the progeny were not destroyed, "the earth would soon be covered by the progeny of a single pair."

As for the human species, we now know that the doubling time of 25 years assumed by Franklin and Malthus underestimated the full horror of the human potential. Shortly after the end of World War II, in the name of national defense, the U.S. military decided it would have to use Bikini Island as a testing ground for

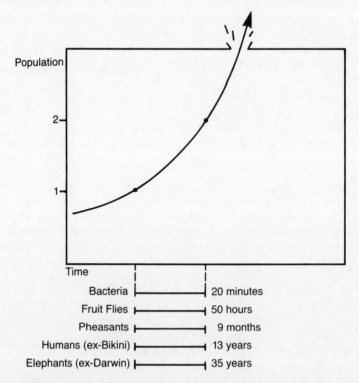

Figure 9-1. The potential population growth of any living species, headed for infinity in the absence of countervailing forces. By a suitable adjustment of the scale of the abscissa, "One curve fits all." The numerals on the vertical axis stand for hundreds, millions or whatever unit is convenient for a particular population.

nuclear explosions. Anticipating persistent radioactivity from the fallout of the explosions, our military evacuated the native population to other islands in the South Pacific. Our government then took on the responsibility of keeping the reluctant refugees alive and in good health in their new homes.[8]

With good health, and little to do but live and reproduce, this population grew from 161 in 1946 to more than 1,260 by 1985. The annual rate of increase was 5.4 percent. The doubling time, the shortest ever recorded for a human population, was thirteen years (which number is reflected in Figure 9-1). Today's Bikinians, living on charity, have lost their old skills. Had the experiment never been performed, the Bikinians would have remained self-supporting on Bikini, and their population might have been about 161 still. But the experiment *was* performed, and their numbers have swelled nearly eightfold. Unless the present policy is abandoned, in another 39 years the population will have swelled to more than 10,000; and in the next 39 years it should reach 80,000.

(Question for moralists: If the United States had massacred the Bikinians, the crime would have been called "genocide." America, by taking total responsibility for the refugees, has totally released Bikinians from personal responsibility. What name will the world give to the crime we *did* commit?)

In a finite world the destructive potential of usury is kept under control by such unwelcome events as inflation, bank failures, repudiation of debts, and the downfall of nations. *How, then, if humanity is to take control of its destiny, is the destructive potential of biological reproduction to be circumvented?* There, in a nutshell, is the "population problem."

When we try to deal rationally with this problem, our thinking is disrupted by primordial assumptions adopted long before men and women understood the nature and consequences of exponential growth. The biblical commandment, "Be fruitful and multiply," needs to be reexamined.[9]

Is Any Positive Rate of Growth "Small"?

Many influential writers deny that there is a human population problem. Others grudgingly admit that a problem may develop *someday,* but they judge this future to be too remote to worry about. Their denials may be punctuated by coughs caused by urban smog, curses at gridlocked automobile traffic, or anguished complaints about the inflating prices of real estate. That these discomforts have any connection with population growth seems not to occur to population optimists.

Psychological denial is a standard defense against unwelcome conclusions. In the present situation there are also understandable intellectual reasons for the denials. First, it is always difficult to detect a trend in the presence of great variation. During most of human history, the long-term trend toward global population increase was masked by much greater short-term fluctuations in local populations.

Consider a medieval village of 100 souls with an *average* annual increase of 0.1 percent over a period of 70 years. Figure 9-2 shows the population graph of our hypothetical village. The end point is 7 percent higher than the beginning point; but, in the light of the considerable yearly fluctuations, who would be so bold as to say that the population was growing? Today the population growth rate is many

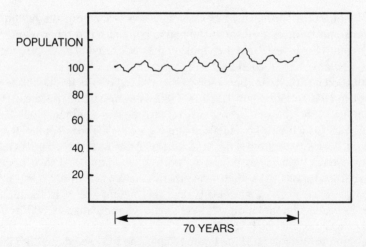

Figure 9-2. Hypothetical population history of a village in ancient, medieval, or Renaissance times, showing that year-to-year variations were more obvious than a lifetime increase of 7 percent.

times what it was in medieval days, and the yearly fluctuations less. An economics bias leads most people to dismiss a population growth rate of 1 percent as "miniscule."[10]

To a politician, all positive growth rates are good, since they supply him with more constituents. (Advertisers and merchants agree.) In 1987 a Canadian government agency issued a report that predicted the future population of Canada under various assumptions of fertility and immigration rates.[11] At no point did the prognosticators so much as mention the possibility that the aggregate population growth rate might ever be less than 1 percent: such a minimum rate was, for them, quite literally *unthinkable.*

For another example of unconscious and harmful bias, consider the implications of the following quotation from a literary periodical: "In recent years the alarmist view [of population growth] has been in retreat, in part because . . . instead of growing rapidly the global population growth rate fell back from 2 percent to 1.7 percent."[12] First, a factual correction is in order: population "alarmists" have *not* been saying that the growth rate itself would continue to grow rapidly, but rather that the present growth rate is (over time) insupportable. Even a much smaller growth rate would soon become insupportable.

Secondly, a decline in the growth rate from 2 percent to 1.7 percent is no reason to plan a celebration. For perspective, compare both rates with the average rate over the past million years of the human species' existence. Assuming that our species began with a single pair (Adam and Eve?) a million years ago, the average growth rate of world population has been just 0.015 percent per year (with a doubling time of 4,667 years). If we define this as normal, the recent fall in population growth rate has been from a rate 133 times normal to a rate 113 times normal. Admittedly, that's better than an increase in growth rate; but if there are good reasons for bringing population growth to an end, we are a long way from being out of danger.

Anyone who lectures to the general public on population frequently encounters comments like this: "I read in the paper that America's population has stopped growing. In fact we've already reached ZPG—zero population growth. So why worry?"

What such a questioner read in the paper was probably something like this: "America's growth *rate* has fallen; the rate is still declining. Our population is growing at a rate no greater than 0.7 percent per year; and the rate is expected to fall further." But a growth rate of 0.7 percent per year operating on a population of 250 million produces an increase of 1,750,000 per year. That's a long way from ZPG! If we ignore immigration, that's how fast the United States is growing as we approach the end of the twentieth century. (Immigration, inaccurately measured, may double the rate.)

The word *rate* apparently has trouble catching the eye of the average newspaper reader. Told that the "rate" of population growth is falling, his mind is all too likely to record "the population is now decreasing." Many journalists make the same mistake.

As for the world population, its growth *rate* has slowly declined from a bit over 2.0 percent per year in the early 1960s to 1.7 percent in the late 1980s. But a rate of increase of 1.7 percent per year operating on a base of 5 billion produces a yearly increase of 85 million—equal to the combined populations of the United Kingdom and Scandinavia.[13] For how long can population increase? That is one of the questions Malthus thought he had answered. But he had not, as we shall see in the next chapter.

Population Disappears from Economics

If ever someone constructs a carefully documented graph of the public attitude toward population after Malthus, it surely will look like a roller-coaster ride. Malthus, while not lacking opposition, was strongly supported during his lifetime by the power structure of Great Britain . (He died in 1834, three years before Victoria became queen.) He became a respected economist in his time, and was still highly praised by England's John Maynard Keynes a century later. But the position of population theory among the bulk of economists changed over that period. As the economist George Stigler noted: "In 1830, no general work in economics would omit a discussion of population, and in 1930, hardly any general work said anything about population."[14] The reasons for this puzzling change deserve to be investigated by historians of ideas.

No doubt many threads are involved in the tapestry of this history. One of the threads is the attitude of scholars toward rates that have small exponents. Scholars in economics and ecology differ sharply in the importance they assign to processes with small exponents. Economists tend to ignore such processes, no doubt because the rates economists professionally deal with can themselves change so fast. Ecologists, inspired by Darwin, take even the smallest of rates seriously. Working with nonhuman populations, ecologists tend to see rates as stable. Economists tend to see human rates as changeable; they know that speaking out sometimes changes them. (Economics is an information-mutable science.) Ecologists see the exponential growth curve (whether of money or organisms) as headed "out of this world." Economists merely see that the curve is headed up. And they seldom worry about the state of the world more than five years from now.

Ecology Enters History

Economists deserve no special blame, however, for their neglect of population principles: they have merely breathed in what Germans call the *Zeitgeist*—the spirit of the times (which, of course, they helped create!). Historians have breathed the same air. Well into the twentieth century some of the most fashionable histories diverged little from the style criticized by Fabre. The most ambitious history produced by a single individual in the present century was A. J. Toynbee's *A Study of History,* which was published in twelve massively documented volumes during the years 1934–1961. It aimed to be all-inclusive, but Aldous Huxley, the author of the novel *Brave New World,* pointed out the omissions and failings listed in Box 9-3.[15] Though Huxley's vocation was thoroughly in the literary milieu, he had numerous family associations with biology. His grandfather, T. H. Huxley, was "Darwin's bulldog"; his brother, Julian, did important work in animal behavior and was a successful science popularizer; another brother, Andrew, won the Nobel prize for his work in physiology; and a nephew became an expert on cacti. No doubt this scientifically rich family environment helped make Aldous aware of the human

---

Box 9-3. Environment & History: Huxley on Toynbee.

In the index at the end of the sixth volume of Dr. Toynbee's *A Study of History,* Popilius Laenas gets five mentions and Porphyry of Batamaea, two; but the word you would expect to find between these two names, Population, is conspicuous by its absence. In his second volume, Mr. Toynbee has written at length on "the stimulus of pressures"—but without ever mentioning the most important pressure of them all, the pressure of population on available resources. And here is a note in which the author describes his impressions of the Roman Campagna after twenty years of absence. "In 1911 the student who made a pilgrimage of the Via Appia Antica found himself walking through a wilderness.... When he repeated the pilgrimage in 1931, he found that, in the interval, Man had been busily reasserting his mastery over the whole stretch of country that lies between Rome and the Castelli Romani.... The tension of human energy on the Roman Campagna is now beginning to rise again for the first time since the end of the third century B.C." And there the matter is left, without any reference to the compelling reason for this "rise of tension." Between 1911 and 1931 the population of Italy had increased by the best part of eight million. Some of these eight millions went to live in the Roman Campagna....

One would like to know something about the Famines of earlier ages, but the nearest one gets to them in Mr. Toynbee's index is a blank space between Muhammad Falak-al-Din and Gaius Fannius.... Agriculture [is] not referred to in Mr. Toynbee's index, though Agrigentum gets two mentions and Agis IV, King of Sparta, no less than forty-seven.... One looks up Erosion ... but finds only Esarhaddon, Esotericism and Esperanto; one hunts for Forests, but has to be content, alas, with Formosus of Porto.

Tomorrow and Tomorrow and Tomorrow, 1956.

importance of biology: he, more than anyone else (except possibly Rachel Carson), is responsible for introducing the word "ecology" to the general public in the 1960s.

By contrast, A. J. Toynbee's distinguished relatives were all on the humanist side and unlikely to sensitize him to the importance of scientific facts. In fairness to the historian, however, it needs to be said that, in his last years, Toynbee acknowledged the importance of environmental and biological matters in the making of human history.

Has ecology produced the final restructuring of historical knowledge? Certainly not: each generation must rewrite history. Rewriting is done in terms of the latest increase in human understanding. We can do no better than use the ecological and evolutionary framework of our time. This is certainly better than that of the previous century, but the final word is never said.

10

What Malthus Missed

Though John Maynard Keynes had the highest opinion of his contributions to economics,[1] Malthus continues to be bad-mouthed by many of today's sociologists and economists. The passion displayed by some of his detractors is grossly disproportionate to the magnitude of his errors. A conscientious listing of the explicit statements made by Malthus would, I am sure, show that far more than 95 percent of them are correct. But for any writer who becomes notorious for voicing unwelcome "home truths," a correctness score of 95 percent is not enough. Envy, an all-too-human failing, is not unknown among critics.[2] Envy sharpens the critical faculties but dulls the sense of proportion.

Seeking a Counterbalance to Exponential Growth

The potentially unlimited growth of debt through the exponential growth of usury is counterbalanced, as we have seen, by such factors as bankruptcy, repudiation of debts, and inflation. Potentially exponential biological reproduction is also kept in check by counterbalancing forces. Every species "seeks" to convert the matter of its surroundings ("the environment") into more of its own kind, without limit. But since the amount and quality of convertible matter does have limits, so also must the growth of every population be limited. What in fact does limit the growth of populations?

Malthus was concerned only with the human species. Having found a mathematical expression for reproduction he then sought another mathematical expression for the limitation to human fertility. No one thinks he was successful in this second endeavor. We note that as a student at Cambridge he was graduated as Ninth Wrangler. The quaint term "wrangler" is awarded by the English to someone who takes honors in mathematics. Since Malthus placed ninth in his class we may assume that he was only modestly endowed with mathematical ability. We should not be surprised to learn that he made a serious mistake in applying mathematics to the problem of the factors limiting human populations. (Look again at Box 9-1 on page 88.)

In successive intervals of time, Malthus said, the human species has the potential of increasing as the numbers in the series 2, 4, 8, 16, etc. In this he was on firm ground. In the absence of environmental resistance, every species has this ability: the number expected at time t is 2^t, where the unit t is the doubling time for the species. Population growth is exponential (or, as Malthus said, "geometrical").

But where did Malthus get the idea that "subsistence" would increase only "arithmetically," as in the series 2, 3, 4, 5, etc.? Not from science, certainly. History is silent as to the origin of this postulate, but I have a suggestion to make. Is it perhaps significant that his ratios echo a passage in Francis Bacon? In a collection of succinct "Antitheses" published in 1623, under the heading "Nature," Bacon entered the following suggestive passage. *"Custom advances in an arithmetical ratio, nature in a geometrical. . . .* Custom against nature is a kind of tyranny, and is soon and upon slight occasion overthrown."[3] Did Malthus know of this passage? I know of no documentary evidence that he did. But Bacon's views on science and technology ("custom," in this quotation) were as much esteemed in Malthus's day as they are ignored in ours. It is possible that Malthus got his two ratios from Bacon: more we cannot say.

Be that as it may, the comparison of the two series, term by term, gave Malthus the result he wanted for his theory, namely a damping down of population growth with the passage of time. Apparently satisfied with the result, he stopped looking for an alternative theory. His complacency in the face of cogent and widespread criticism cannot be defended. Those who say that Malthusianism has been discredited are on solid ground if this aspect of his theoretical system is what they have in mind.

Malthus can be refuted by a comparison of the three ratios shown in Box 10-1. Line A is Malthus's arithmetic series used as a measure of increase in subsistence units—food, principally. Line B is the geometrical series for population growth, where the living units are labeled as "mouths" that eat the food. If the figures in these two lines are turned into a series of fractions, with the term in line A as the numerator and the corresponding term in line B as the denominator, the results (fractional term by fractional term) read: $1 - \frac{3}{4} - \frac{1}{2} - \frac{5}{16} - \frac{3}{16}$, and so on. Each fractional term shows the amount of *subsistence per individual* available at the moment of time given in the numbers above the double line in the box. The larger the population the less the subsistence per person. So said Malthus; but why in fact should this be so? Malthus did not answer this question; in fact he did not even ask the question. His opponents did.

Folk wisdom supported the critics. In Latin America it is said, "Every baby is born with a loaf of bread under his arm." Perhaps that places too much faith in Providence, which sometimes double-crosses babies. Europe boasts a more defensible aphorism: "Each new mouth brings with it a new pair of hands." This wisely proposes not providence but self-help as the pretext for optimism. Line C in Box 10-1 shows that the number of pairs of hands is exactly equal to the number of

---

Box 10-1. Malthus Refuted by Nature's Ratios.

Malthus reached his pessimistic conclusions by comparing series B with series A. His opponents justified their optimism by comparing series B with series C.

Elapsed Time:	2	3	4	5	6
A. Subsistence units (food)	2	3	4	5	6
B. Consuming units (mouths)	2	4	8	16	32
C. Labor units (pairs of hands)	2	4	8	16	32

mouths (Line B). The ratio of B to C is 1 throughout. Should it not be true, then, that the subsistence gained by human effort will forever be able to keep up with the demand created by human reproduction?—"How about that, Mr. Malthus?"

"Providence" Discourages Inquiry

Malthus may not have given enough attention to the mystery of the falling-off in the rate of population growth. An excuse for not trying hard was readily available in his day (as it is not in ours). This was the *panchreston*,[4] the "explain-all" called "Providence."

Etymologically, the word *providence* comes from the Latin *providere,* to provide. From "making provision for" it is easy to move to "exercising foresight." Early on, religious writers spoke of "God's providence," meaning his provision for man. The eighteenth century was the "Age of Enlightenment," when many thoughtful men abandoned "God" as an explanatory principle. But centuries of use of the word "God" made it socially risky to abandon entirely the thought behind the word. A compromise became popular among the elite of that century: they substituted the word "Providence" for "God" or "God's providence." Adopting this ploy amounted to playing both sides of the street: the hope was, no doubt, that both theists and atheists would accept the postulated "cause" of all that happens in the world.

Malthus, writing his essay at the end of the eighteenth century, turned out a sort of geological stratification of beliefs about the cause of the world as it is (see Box 10-2). Starting off with a supreme being (God) he shifts to the ambivalent concept

---

Box 10-2. Malthus on Providence.

The Supreme Being has ordained that the earth shall not produce good in great quantities till much preparatory labour and ingenuity has been exercised upon its surface. . . . The processes of ploughing and clearing the ground, of collecting and sowing seeds, are not surely for the assistance of God in his creation, but are made previously necessary to the enjoyment of the blessings of life, in order to rouse man into action, and form his mind to reason.

To furnish the most unremitted excitements of this kind, and to urge man to further the gracious designs of Providence by the full cultivation of the earth, it has been ordained that population should increase much faster than food. This general law . . . undoubtedly produces much partial evil, but a little reflection may, perhaps, satisfy us, that it produces a great overbalance of good. . . .

Leisure is, without doubt, highly valuable to man, but taking man as he is, the probability seems to be that in the greater number of instances it will produce evil rather than good. It has been not infrequently remarked that talents are more common among younger brothers than among elder brothers, but it can scarcely be imagined that younger brothers are, upon an average, born with a greater susceptibility of parts. The difference, if there really is any observable difference, can only arise from their different situations. Exertion and activity are in general absolutely necessary in one case and are only optional in the other.

That the difficulties of life contribute to generate talents, every day's experience must convince us.

An Essay on the Principle of Population, 1798.

of Providence. At the end of the passage he moves to a position that is even farther from a theistic commitment, to an explanatory principle that can only be called "the nature of things." Accepting without question the justness of primogeniture, Malthus points to the beneficial effects of short-changing younger brothers, who are thereby stimulated to greater effort. As a group it was supposed that their potentialities were developed more fully. Suffering was justified by its good "side effects" (as we might call them).

Having reached this convenient conclusion, Malthus (the sixth of seven children) was, like the first son under primogeniture, not strongly motivated to look harder for a better explanation of the forces that curbed exponential growth. Population growth in a limited world brought suffering to man, thus impelling him to exercise foresight in the planning of his life. Human suffering was part of God's plan to make human beings more energetic, more virtuous. For Malthus, the pains of overpopulation found their function in the nature of things. Like the Buddha, Malthus accepted the "sorrow" of life.

The Difficult Birth of "Diminishing Returns"

Whitehead's insight that a new idea is often first tripped over by someone who doesn't realize what he has "discovered" is well exemplified in Malthus's work. Though his concept of arithmetical ratios failed to explain satisfactorily the decline of population growth rates, Malthus did in fact stumble across the fundamental concept his theory needed—and never realized what he had found. To the second edition of his book, published five years after the first, he added the significant passage below ("corn" is British English for wheat, rye, or barley):

> [W]hen an additional *depopulation* takes place in a country which was before populous and industrious, and in the habit of exporting corn, if the remaining inhabitants be left at liberty to exert, and do exert, their industry in the same direction as before, it is a strange idea to entertain that they would then be unable to supply themselves with corn in the same plenty; particularly as *the diminished numbers would, of course, cultivate principally the more fertile parts of their territory, and not be obliged, as in their more populous state, to apply to ungrateful soils.*[5]

This assertion, like many facets of Malthusian theory, is based on a theory of human behavior. If, says Malthus, a farmer finds he no longer needs actively to work *all* his land, he will first stop farming those portions that require the most labor, thus living an easier life without sacrificing any of its good. A strict moralist, viewing such behavior in others might condemn it as laziness, but would the moralist behave any differently himself? If he would, he is a fool. The belief that the normal person seeks to minimize the time and effort he expends on essential work is an important *default position* of human psychology, as described in Chapter 5. This position in turn derives from the major default position of biology—that selection favors economizers.

The assumptions Malthus made about human behavior were, and are, ones that are subscribed to by most people. His prediction, without doubt a correct one, was that reducing population size somewhat would lead to greater agricultural productivity *per unit effort*. He just missed stating the law of diminishing returns. All he needed to do to make this discovery was to invert his example: to ask what would happen when the diminished population surged back to its initial, larger size. Obviously the marginal land ("ungrateful soils") that had been taken out of cultivation would have to be cultivated once more. This change would force agriculturalists as a group to work harder to produce the same amount of food per capita. When an increase in population requires a more-than-proportionate increase in effort to maintain the same per capita productivity, we say that *the point of diminishing returns* has been reached. Malthus never realized how an inversion of his example could furnish him with the growth-damping principle his population theory needed.

Worse: when, a decade later, several other economists explicitly stated the law of diminishing returns, Malthus just as explicitly denied that this was what he had been blundering toward when he proposed his arithmetic ratio. To the day of his death, almost two decades later, he never gave in. How many fruitless arguments might have been forestalled had Malthus had a more flexible mind!

History Apparently Makes a Mockery of "Diminishing Returns"

In a manner of speaking, history conspired to mock Malthus. Correcting for inflation, the real wages of British workers have been estimated for Malthus's day.[6] From 1800 (two years after the publication of the *Essay*) to 1824 (ten years before the author's death) the British population increased by 25 percent. During the same period the real wages *per worker* also increased by 25 percent: more people, living better—a most un-Malthusian development! In the next quarter of a century, while population increased by 56 percent, wages *per worker* increased another 40 percent. In what we call the "developed world" this trend continued during the succeeding century. It is not surprising, then, that many economic theoreticians came to feel that the law of diminishing returns either was not true or had been unduly emphasized.

Today's economists give much more emphasis to the opposite effect, called "economies of scale," or "returns to scale." In his *Wealth of Nations,* Adam Smith gave a general explanation for the observed ability of a large manufacturing firm to make things at a lower cost than a small firm: the "division of labor" whereby the job is subdivided into many small parts that can be more efficiently performed by workers specializing in mini-tasks. In the light of this practice, the "diseconomy of scale" implied by the law of diminishing returns needs to be accounted for.

"Diminishing Returns" in a Larger Context

What factors, acting jointly, determine the productivity of a piece of land? The principal ones are listed in Box 10-3. In Malthus's time the first factor listed was the principal determinant of the size of the crop: there was not much variation in the other factors in ordinary farming. Variation of different plots of soil with respect to inherent fertility can lead to diminishing returns. At each stage of agricultural expansion the most fertile hitherto unexploited plot is developed next. This means that the expansion of cultivated land under the pressure of population suffers from

---

Box 10-3. Agriculture: The More Obvious Production Factors.

Inherent fertility of the soil
Genetic quality of the seeds
Amount and quality of cultivation
Amount of fertilizer
Amount of pesticides
Amount and timing of water inputs

---

diseconomies of scale. Thus sayeth theory. In fact, from Malthus's time onward (ignoring fluctuations in the weather), the returns per acre actually increased, particularly in the twentieth century. How is a Malthusian to account for this embarrassing truth?

Peasant agriculturalists in the past did little to modify the factors listed in Box 10-3. The domestication of all the major grains took place before men learned to read and write, and so did much of the genetic improvement of the seeds, the improvement taking place slowly over the millennia. It wasn't until a century after Malthus that experimentalists learned how to bring about rapid improvements in seed quality.

Some significant improvements in the other factors of agricultural production occurred even in Malthus's time, accelerating later. Overall, the diminishing returns caused by the policy of using the best lands first have been overshadowed by the increasing returns resulting from improvements in other production factors. Yet with each factor there finally comes a level of application at which diminishing returns dominate the results.

Take, for example, the matter of fertilizer. The first additional unit of fertilizer may bring about a 10 percent improvement, say; as may a second, a third, and a fourth unit. Finally, some nth unit adds less than 10 percent; and the $n + 1$th still less. Ultimately, as many a backyard farmer learns, adding more fertilizer may actually be destructive: overfertilization "burns" the crop. How can a graph show both the good and the bad effects of increasing efforts (of a given kind) on productivity?

Figure 10-1 is a generalized graph of per capita productivity plotted against effort (pounds of fertilizer applied; gallons of water, hours of working the soil, or whatever). There is an early phase (initial to optimum, which we can abbreviate as I–O) during which economies of scale are realized. Then at the optimum the curve turns over, producing a plateau (O–B) that may be restricted in one case, extensive in another, until the effort reaches B, standing on the brink of disaster (D). Once the B–D phase has been entered, no sane person would knowingly call for more and more effort of the same kind .

The discipline of economics grew up when the industrial revolution was in the I–O phase; it is understandable that the idea of economies of scale became engrained in economic thinking; wishful thinking would have it so. Somewhat later, ecology was developed by students of the living world, for whom the opposite perception comes easily. Exponential reproduction moves each species rapidly through the I–O phase; what one might call the natural imperialism of the species soon brings it to the O point, the *carrying capacity of the environment*. The corrective role played by other species (predators, competitors, disease germs, and so on)

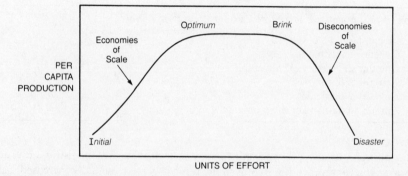

Figure 10-1. Reconciliation of economies of scale and diseconomies of scale. The generalized curve shows how per capita production is affected by units of effort. The O–B plateau may be either extensive or nonexistent. Optimists tend to see only the I–O segment, pessimists the B–D.

tends to keep the target species fluctuating around the O level. The imperialism of one species is kept from achieving too much demographically by the equally compulsive imperialism of others.

Trouble comes when man steps into the system of nature and tries to increase productivity *without limit.* Time after time greedy human beings move some production function onto the slippery slope of B–D. The consequences remind the greedy once more that there can be "too much of a good thing"—any good thing.[7] This means, of course, that *quantity matters* when we try to decide what is best or right.[8] A comprehensive ethical system must be numerate. Traditional systems of ethics, such as the Ten Commandments, are almost invariably innumerate.

Analysis that takes account of only one production factor at a time is finally not enough. All the factors can vary, and the optimum point for one is affected by the level of other factors. "Fertilizer" is a collective word for many substances, and the *balance* of nitrogen with phosphorus, for instance, matters. The working together, the *synergism,* of many factors is important. It is the task of scientific agriculturalists to try to work out the complex interaction of all the factors—a task that is not finished in a year or a decade.

The complexity of the real world does not justify assuming that economies of scale continue forever, at all levels of effort or population numbers. Emphasizing economies of scale while neglecting diseconomies is, of course, merely one more example of preferring optimism to pessimism, a dangerous attitude for a prophet to adopt.

Beyond Shiva

If, as European folk wisdom has it, each new mouth brings with it a pair of hands, how are we to view the fantastic changes brought about by the industrial-scientific revolution of the past two hundred years or so? Have we not now reached a stage at which each new mouth comes into the world with *more* than a single pair of hands? The woolgathering mind may recall statues of the Indian god Shiva, with his many (most commonly four) lively arms and busy hands.

If scientists were inclined to take up new gods (which they are not), Shiva would be a fine one for representing science and technology ("custom," in Bacon's language). Even before Malthus, technology began to increase the output of human hands (through such inventions as the wheelbarrow), but the change did not catch people's attention for a long time. Everyone is aware of it now. Especially in the developed world it has become obvious that material income per capita has increased greatly. The Shiva of Western technology is indeed a many-handed god.

As the beneficiaries of more than two centuries of rapid growth of science and technology, the masses cannot easily be persuaded that they should be worried about the future of population and the environment. Yet we would do well to remember that the Hindus' Shiva is a god of both creation and destruction. It is not without reason that we perceive a many-handed god as uncanny and frightening. Technology is a blessing to be sure, but every blessing has its price. The price of increased complexity is increased vulnerability. The growth of technology can be symbolized as an increase in the number of hands and arms of Shiva.

Now that *our* Shiva has a thousand arms, can we be entirely confident that all of them are, at all times, firmly under the control of a competent mind? What if the brain of the thousand-armed Shiva of technology goes berserk?

11

The Demostat

If the Old Testament preacher Koheleth could justly complain that "of the making of many books there is no end,"[1] then how much more reason do we have to complain now, some twenty-two centuries later! There are times when we fear that the snowballing "information overload" may be the downfall of civilization.

Fortunately there is a counterforce to information overload: *theory construction.* A good theory compacts a vast body of facts into a few words or equations. For example, before Gregor Mendel published his theory of heredity, some 8,000 pages of scholarly discussion had been produced on the subject. All these documents became useless upon the publication of Mendel's forty-page paper. Today, more than a century later, we can condense Mendel's findings into a single page.

The literature on human population growth is enormous. Blessedly, most of it can be safely ignored. A handful of principles enable us to incorporate the meaning of a great mass of data in a few images. The most important of these derive from "control theory," a development of the middle of the twentieth century. A careful reading of Malthus's *Essay* shows that control theory is implicit in his exposition.

Cybernetics

In 1948 the mathematician Norbert Weiner published *Cybernetics: or, Control and Communication in the Animal and the Machine.* This book briefly summarized and greatly extended a diffuse literature on the subject, introducing language that made it possible to talk more effectively about change and resistance to change. Wiener, the son of a classics scholar, derived the name of the science from a Greek word for "governor." Cybernetics deals with the logic of the mechanisms that govern the equilibrating functions of complex machines and animals. The thermostat is a convenient example.

In *A* of Figure 11-1 we see the graph of the temperature of a thermostated room: an irregular line fluctuating about the *set point,* the temperature reading at which someone has set the thermostat. As usual, time is oriented on the horizontal axis. Part *B* displays a *collapsed time diagram* of the same data: both possible excursions away from the set point are shown as alternate possibilities of the same moment in time. The "closed" nature of the resulting figure symbolizes the restriction of temperature within limits when a thermostat is in control. The material components of the control system—a bimetallic strip, electric wires, a furnace, and so on—have

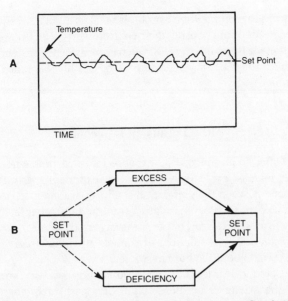

Figure 11-1. Records of the temperature of a thermostated room. Graph A is a "real time" record of the fluctuations about the set point of the temperature. Diagram B is a "collapsed time" representation of the same system, showing the logical elements of a negative feedback system. Dashed lines represent random or impressed changes, solid lines represent the inherent response changes.

been omitted from the diagram so as to focus our attention on the logical elements of cybernetic control.

Suppose the chosen set point is 68 degrees Fahrenheit. Dotted lines indicate changes that are impressed on the system by temperature changes in the room. What happens in response is determined by the construction of the thermostat. If the impressed change is an increase (note the rising, dotted arrow), the response of the system is to decrease the temperature by turning off the furnace (solid arrow). If a decrease is imposed on the room's temperature, the thermostat's response is to turn up the furnace. In each case the *response change is the negative of the impressed change:* hence the term *negative feedback.* Negative feedback is essential to produce stability in a self-adjusting system.

The logical nature of cybernetic control was first worked out for such man-made control systems as the governor of a steam engine. Then physiologists showed that the mammalian body is maintained in a nearly constant condition by myriads of cybernetic mechanisms. Body temperature is controlled by its own thermostat. The level of sugar in the blood is kept within very narrow limits by negative feedback. The concentration of many different salts in the blood is similarly stabilized. The plasma that surrounds the cells is derived from the blood; it plays the role of an "internal environment" for the cells. The normal functioning of "warm-blooded" animals depends on minimizing the fluctuations of this environment. The relative constancy of this internal environment permits warm-blooded animals to flourish over a wider range of external environments than is possible for "cold-blooded" creatures like reptiles and amphibians. This ability gives warm-blooded animals greater freedom in choosing their environments. The French physiologist Claude Bernard made this point in 1878, when he said: "The constancy of the internal environment is the necessary condition of the free life." Paradoxically, *control increases freedom.*

The Malthusian Demostat

For a few years after an animal species expands into a favorable new territory the population may increase explosively—that is, by exponential growth. The explosion comes to an end when the population stabilizes around a set point called the *carrying capacity* of the territory. Climatic variations (and other factors) cause this capacity to vary from year to year, but over a long period of time the carrying capacity is essentially stable. For populations of animals other than man this description is patently true. What about the human species?

For the past three centuries the human population has been growing rapidly. People assume that whatever has been true for the past three generations will be true forever. The phrase "from time immemorial" usually means "for three generations." Three hundred years is about twelve human generations—an infinity of time to many people.

Contemporary Americans find it difficult to imagine a world with zero population growth. Some find the thought not only difficult, but even immoral to entertain. An enormous body of rhetoric supports this position: "Grow or die" and "You can't stop progress" are examples in point. Nevertheless, during most of human existence, the average rate of population growth has been very, very close to zero. If "normal" means *most common,* then over the long time span of human existence zero population growth must be judged normal.

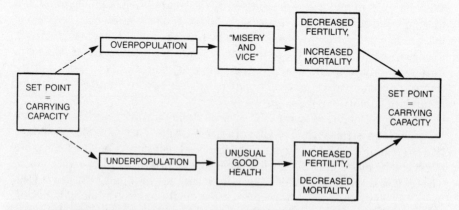

Figure 11-2. The Malthusian demostat, the heart of Malthus's theory. In this "collapsed time" diagram the dashed arrows stand for random changes imposed by the environment; solid arrows stand for necessary changes inherent in the cybernetic system and made in response to imposed changes.

Malthus was both lucky and unlucky in living at the interface of two eras. Enough of the old era persisted so that it was natural for him to think in terms of static conditions; but a new era was developing rapidly, an era that (unluckily for his reputation) undermined his static theory, instigating (luckily for his memory) a controversy that attracted an enduring audience. Had he published his essay two hundred years earlier, the name Malthus might be unknown today.

Unaware of social and technological changes that were picking up speed in his time, Malthus described a cybernetic control system that would have elicited no excitement whatever during most of the millennia of human history. What Malthus proposed, we now realize, was an analog of the thermostat that controls the temperature of our rooms. This mechanism is called the *Malthusian demostat.* Of this mechanism Malthus gave only a verbal description in which the details are more implicit than explicit. The demostat balances the inherent tendency of every population to increase against factors that tend to reduce its numbers.

The human demostat is shown in the collapsed-time diagram of Figure 11-2, the elements of which should be compared with Malthus's rhetoric (given in Box 11-1). As before, impressed change (dotted arrows) leads to the negative feedback of response change (solid arrows). Whenever the population falls significantly below the set point, the increased prosperity (leading to better nutrition among women) causes a rise in fertility, which soon brings the population back up to the carrying capacity of the environment.[2] On the other hand, when the population moves beyond the carrying capacity, "misery and vice" diminish fertility and survival, thus driving the population down. "Misery and vice" are Malthus's terms for such negative feedbacks as premature death caused by famine, epidemics, infant neglect, criminal violence and the mortality of war. Such is the way the Malthusian demostat works, given a stable set point. (The consequences of a moving set point are the subject of the next chapter.)

The Malthusian demostat is *the* central concept of population theory. The demostat necessarily follows from the two primitive assumptions of (1) exponential growth, (2) operating in a world of real limits. Did no one have an inkling of the demostat before Malthus?

Tertullian's "Blessing"

"What's new is not true, and what's true is not new" is a time-honored way of wittily damning views one refuses to consider. Damning views dams discussion. Some critics have disposed of Malthus's theory with the first excuse, others with the second. We can best reopen the dialogue by admitting the truth of the second objection, namely that Malthus was not entirely original. (But who is?)

That misery can act as a negative feedback to population growth was recognized by Tertullian, a lawyer who shaped much of the theology of the Roman Catholic church. Writing in the third century A.D., he said: "The strongest witness is the vast population of the earth to which we are a burden and she scarcely can provide for our needs; as our demands grow greater, our complaints against nature's inadequacy are heard by all. The scourges of pestilence, famine, wars, and earthquakes

Box 11-1. Intimations of the Demostat in Malthus.

We will suppose the means of subsistence in any country just equal to the easy support of its inhabitants. The constant effort towards population, which is found to act even in the most vicious societies, increases the number of people before the means of subsistence are increased. The food therefore which before supported seven millions must now be divided among seven millions and a half or eight millions. The poor consequently must live much worse, and many of them be reduced to severe distress. The number of labourers also being above the proportion of the work in the market, the price of labour must tend toward a decrease, while the price of provisions would at the same time tend to rise. The labourer therefore must work harder to earn the same as he did before. During this season of distress, the discouragements to marriage, and the difficulty of rearing a family are so great that population is at a stand. In the mean time the cheapness of labour, the plenty of labourers, and the necessity of an increased industry amongst them, encourage culti- vators to employ more labour upon their land, to turn up fresh soil, and to manure and improve more completely what is already in tillage, till ultimately the means of subsis- tence become in the same proportion to the population as at the period from which we set out. The situation of the labourer being then again tolerably comfortable, the restraints to population are in some degree loosened, and the same retrograde and progressive movements with respect to happiness are repeated. [Chapter 2]

. . . it would appear, that the population of France and England has accommodated itself very nearly to the average produce of each country. The discouragements to mar- riage, the consequent vicious habits, war, luxury, the silent though certain depopulation of large towns, and the close habitations, and insufficient food of many of the poor, pre- vent population from increasing beyond the means of subsistence; and, if I may use an expression which certainly at first appears strange, supercede the necessity of great and ravaging epidemics to repress what is redundant. Were a wasting plague to sweep off two millions in England and six millions in France, there can be no doubt whatever, that after the inhabitants had recovered from the dreadful shock, the proportion of births to burials would be much above what it is in either country at present. [Chapter 7]

Famine seems to be the last, the most dreadful resource of nature. The power of pop- ulation is so superior to the power in the earth to produce subsistence for man, that pre- mature death must in some shape or other visit the human race. The vices of mankind are active and able ministers of depopulation. They are the precursors in the great army of destruction; and often finish the dreadful work themselves. But should they fail in this war of extermination, sickly seasons, epidemics, pestilence, and plague, advance in terrific array, and sweep off their thousands and ten thousands. Should success be still incom- plete, gigantic inevitable famine stalks in the rear, and with one mighty blow, levels the population with the food of the world. [Chapter 7]

An Essay on the Principle of Population, 1798.

have come to be regarded as a blessing to overcrowded nations, since they serve to prune away the luxuriant growth of the human race."[3]

In our time not many people are willing to call such negative feedbacks a "bless- ing," cybernetic or otherwise: but Tertullian's phrase, "have come to be regarded," implies that in his time many people appreciated the benefits of timely death and elimination. Why then do we not more often hear of Tertullian's early statement of the demostatic point of view? Several issues are involved.

In the first place, in the work quoted, Tertullian was not primarily concerned with population: he was chasing another hare. The passage occurs in the treatise *De Anima*—"On the Soul,"—a queer place, one might suppose, to look for demographic theories. In this treatise Tertullian was intent on disproving the ancient theory of the "transmigration of souls." In one variant of this theory the world at its beginning was presumed to have been supplied with all the human souls it would ever need. Each time a person died his or her soul was stashed away in a celestial warehouse where it would remain until called for by a new birth. But, said Tertullian, this theory cannot be true: the original supply of souls would be insufficient for the much larger number of people now swarming over the earth. The greatness of population in his day was, Tertullian said, "the strongest witness" against the theory of transmigration.

The transmigration theory was Tertullian's interest at the moment and he did not follow up on the demographic implications of his position. Here we see one more instance of the truth of Whitehead's aphorism: "Everything of importance has been said before by somebody who did not discover it." What Tertullian *said* in the third century had to be *discovered* at the end of the eighteenth century.

Even before Malthus made his appearance another citizen of the Enlightenment showed that he understood the balance produced by the opposing forces of fecundity and mortality. This was the Comte de Buffon.[4] It is hardly to be wondered at that his remarks were little noticed by later demographers, for they were buried at the end of the forty-four volumes of his *Natural History*, the last of which was published after his death in 1788. Buffon implied demostatic control for human populations as well as for animal populations, but his treatise was used principally as a reference work by zoologists who had little interest in human populations.

If one had to put forward a single sentence that summarizes the heart of Malthusian theory, I think it would be this: *Exponential growth is kept under control by misery.* To speak, as Tertullian did, of the need to prune away the luxuriant growth of the human race, is to adopt the viewpoint of farmers. First farmers try to get something to grow. Then, finding they have encouraged life too much, they are faced with the necessity of destroying some of it. A farmer who was so unwise as never to thin, cull or prune away superfluous life would produce not greater, but smaller crops than neighbors who had no such compunction. Rural people know this to be true for their crops; consequently they have less difficulty than city folks in understanding that the same principle also applies at some stage to the growing crop of human beings. But anyone who utters such truth in the twentieth century is sure to be called heartless.

It is true first, that the inextinguishable drive toward exponential growth creates a need for some counteracting force; and second, that Tertullian's "pestilence, famine, wars, and earthquakes" *can* serve as the forces that quench exponential growth. But it is also true that the ingenuity of men and women is equal to the task of finding more gentle controllers of population than the ones Tertullian knew. Birth control pills are gentler than starvation. Only when gentler substitutes are in place throughout the world can we truly say that the post-Malthusian revolution has arrived.

Tertullian, though no doubt city bred, lived at a time when the experiential gap between city life and country life was not as great as it is today. Rural habits of thought still guided the thinking of city dwellers in the third century. Today, the very grossness of our multimillion-person metropolitan aggregations makes infection of urbanites by rural habits of thought unlikely. Many city dwellers are descended solely from urbanites three, four, or more generations back. They have essentially lost their rural roots and with them they have lost the farmer's way of thinking. This defect is ludicrously apparent when, in response to some emergency, an urbanite takes up gardening. Then, when nature in her usual fashion produces too much life in the row of vegetables or the cluster of trees, the urbanite-turned-gardener has great difficulty mustering the moral courage to uproot superfluous seedlings, to knock down three-quarters of a too-exuberant "set" of tiny fruit, or to prune crowded branches off a tree. Similarly, after wolves have been removed as the controllers of deer populations, soft-hearted city dwellers often lack the courage to diminish the suffering of overcrowded deer herds by harvesting the excess animals. The sentimentality that urbanites are pleased to call "respect for life" corrupts those who have never farmed, fished, or hunted. True respect for life must include respect for the functions and necessity of death.

Though little literature on human population problems was produced until the nineteenth century, it is reasonable to assume that many of our ancestors (insofar as they thought about such matters at all) were Malthusians-before-Malthus. In a sense, Malthus had to rediscover what common folk had always known. This he did in a day when new and powerful contrary currents of thought had set the stage for controversy where there had been little before. His critics were right when they said of his theory, "what's true is not new." For some time, truths that bookish, urban people found unpleasant had been ignored or suppressed in polite literature.

Malthus made the world acutely aware that there is a puzzle to be solved. The puzzle is this: the coexistence of the potentially limitless exponential growth with the reality of essential stability in population size. *An "obvious" fact that is ubiquitous is hard to see.* As Einstein once asked: "What does a fish in the depths of the sea know of water?" Long-term demostatic stability was an unremarked reality for most of human history. It is only in modern times that continual population growth has been mistakenly perceived as a permanent truth.

One might expect that the crowding that comes with an increase in urbanization would make city dwellers readily admit the reality of overpopulation. Not so. Permanent urbanites are more comfortable attributing the ills of city existence to politics, injustice, and other whipping boys of moralistic thinkers. Overpopulation is, for many people, simply *unthinkable.*[5] And we must not forget that many people profit personally from the consequences of overpopulation, which causes real estate prices to rise, thus enriching speculators in land and buildings. Such beneficiaries of overpopulation are apt to deny the existence of the condition that makes them rich.

Individualism, Population, and Posterity

Tertullian is strong medicine. Were he alive today, I think he could defend himself well. He did not say that a painful death was a blessing to the *individual* who suffered it; the blessing of many such deaths accrues only to those who survive, particularly to later generations. The blessing is a group blessing. In terms of the standard cybernetic diagram (Fig. 11-1B), the blessing is to be found in the solid arrows of the response change, which corrects for the harm caused by the dotted arrows of impressed change.

The common conflict between individual-oriented and community-oriented value systems needs to be underlined. Tertullian's "blessing" is conferred on an overcrowded nation, that is, on the community. Concerned with its welfare *over a period of time,* Tertullian could easily see the blessing of reducing the numbers in an already overcrowded community. The immediate effect of such a reduction is greater misery for some individuals, but in the long run the total number of individuals made miserable is less when the needed corrective feedbacks are brought into play *at an early date.*

Community-oriented ethical thinking was no doubt commoner in the third century than it is today. Today the greatest honor is accorded to speakers who focus on individual interests to the exclusion of community interests. Demagogues derive their power by appealing to the selfish interests of many individuals. Individuals vote: this is the reality. The abstraction called "the community" cannot vote. But, in time, the abstraction called "community" becomes the reality of posterity, which must suffer for the lack of imagination and courage of its ancestors.

Malthus, an ordained minister, came on the scene more than a century after John Locke had persuaded intellectuals to couch moral questions in terms of the interests of the individual rather than in terms of community interest. Malthus's theory implicitly gives priority to community interests—and "the community" includes limitless posterity. Lockeans, focusing on the individual and having difficulty in seeing the community, accused the author of the *Essay on Population* of being a misanthrope. As was pointed out in Chapter 4, however, Malthus opposed population growth not because it generated more people but because it multiplied misery.[6]

The imputation of hard-heartedness continues to be leveled against Malthus and his followers by people who reckon morality only in an individualistic, community-blind mode. (Community-blind includes posterity-blind.) Stung by criticism Malthus said: "I must be prepared to hear unmoved all those accusations of 'hardness of heart' which appear to me to be the result of ignorance or malice."[7] Thus was the critics' charge of misanthropy met with his countercharge of malice. The argument needs to be moved to a higher level than the *argumentum ad hominem.*

Is "Killing the Messenger" Ever a Solution?

An ancient story has it that a messenger bringing news of a military defeat to a Persian king was executed by the displeased monarch. In the mind of that king the battle evidently marked the end of a segment of time: killing the messenger created a happy ending. But if the end of the battle is perceived as the beginning of a segment of time that reaches far into the future, killing the messenger is foolish. Planning for the future demands the best possible assessment of where we are at present, regardless of who is to blame for the misfortune. Illusions are a treacherous foundation on which to lay plans. (But it's pleasanter to blame others than to reform oneself.)

Commercial interests, which penetrate to the farthest corners of our society, tremble at predictions of the ultimate exhaustion of our stores of fossil energy (oil, coal, gas); at confirmation of the greenhouse effect; at speculations about the agricultural consequences of this effect; at news of massive deforestation and runaway soil erosion; and at the condemnation of unlimited "development" implied in the blunt truth that "asphalt is the land's last crop."[8]

Inspirational pundits like to say that our civilization will be saved only when we ascend to a higher moral level. They may well be right, but phrases like "a higher moral level" are too vague to be of much help. What we need most is a brief calendar of specific practices that must be given up if we are to survive. Ecologists suggest that the first item on the list should be this: *Stop killing the messengers.*

12

Generating the Future

An enduring problem of social life is what to do about the future. Can we predict it? Can we control it? How much sacrifice are we willing to make in the present for the promise of a better future? The questions are harrowing, and agreement comes hard.

The year 1921 was a time of famine in some parts of the newly formed Soviet Union. An American journalist, visiting a refugee camp on the Volga, reported that almost half of the people had died of starvation. Noticing some sacks of grain stacked on an adjacent field, he asked the patriarch of the refugee community why the people did not simply overpower the lone soldier guarding the grain and help themselves. The patriarch impatiently explained that the seed was being saved for next season's planting. "We do not steal from the future," he said.[1]

It would be too much to claim that only the human animal is capable of imagining what is yet to come, but it is difficult to believe that any other animal can have so keen an appreciation of the demands of the future. Alfred Korbzybski (1879–1950) called man "the time-binding animal." Binding the future to the present makes sense only if understandable mechanisms connect the two.

This understanding was notably missing in the writings of the anarchist-journalist William Godwin. Unlike Malthus, he could make no sense of the fluctuations of human numbers. "Population," he said, "if we consider it historically, appears to be a fitful principle, operating intermittently and by starts. This is the great mystery of the subject. . . . One of the first ideas that will occur to a reflecting mind is, that the cause of these irregularities cannot be of itself of regular and uniform operation. It cannot be [as Malthus says] 'the numbers of mankind at all times pressing hard against the limits of the means of subsistence.'"[2]

Rather than trying to see how appearances might be reconciled with natural laws, Godwin simply said there were no natural laws. His proposal to replace law with "fitfulness" led one of his critics to comment: "Perhaps Godwin was simply carrying his dislike of law one step farther. Having applied it to politics (1793) and to style (1797), he now applied it to nature (1820). He deliberately placed a whole army of facts out of the range of science."[3]

But science does not advance by preemptive surrender. Certainly when it comes to the study of population the surrender is not necessary. In the light of cybernetic principles there is nothing fitful or irrational about population growth: net growth is the outcome of a "struggle" between opposing forces. Vary the relative strength of the forces and the outcome varies.

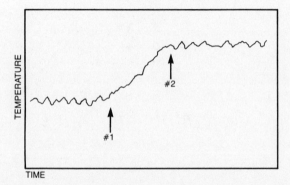

Figure 12-1. Temperature of a room under thermostatic control. At arrow #1 someone starts slowly moving the set point upward, until a new stable set point is established (arrow #2). Even during a slow secular shift negative feedback mechanisms have some effect.

Both *growth* and *no-growth* can be fitted into a single theoretical framework. Before taking up the biological example it will help to examine analogous phenomena in the temperature of a room controlled by an ordinary nonliving thermostat. Figure 12-1 shows the temperature of a hypothetical thermostated room over a period of time. At first the fluctuations clearly center about a set point. Then, at arrow number 1, the temperature line moves upward; this movement stops at arrow number 2 and the room temperature equilibrates about a new set point.

Should such a record be called "fitful"? Does it defy logical explanation? Hardly: beginning at point 1 some unseen hand evidently started slowly changing the set-screw of the thermostat, moving the temperature upward. If the change took place slowly enough, even during the upward course the temperature would be fluctuating about a set point, only it would be a *moving* set point. When the unseen hand ceased its interference, a new equilibrium was established. Cybernetics operates at all times; a directional shift takes place when something outside the basic control system moves the set point. Directional change is sometimes referred to as *secular change,* to distinguish it from random, nonprogressive fluctuations.

So it is with population. For a long time, sometimes for centuries, the demographic set point may do no more than fluctuate. Then nature (weather, perhaps) or human ingenuity (a significant new invention) introduces a secular change in the set point. Population growth soon follows, the number equilibrating eventually around a new set point (the carrying capacity of the changed environment). Even during an upward secular shift the demostat is working through the negative feedbacks of "misery and vice," though not quite so strongly. "Law"—that is, an understandable set of mechanisms—not "fitfulness," is in charge at all times.

The Three Great Demographic Revolutions

Now let us look at the whole of human history. The word "history" may properly be used in either of two senses: in a restricted sense, refering to that part of the human story that is authenticated by written records; or, in a broader sense, the story that includes the entire account of humanity's evolution over time. Adopting the latter definition, the word "human" is also subject to varying definitions. It can refer not only to *Homo sapiens,* the present species, but also to some of our *humanoid* ancestors, such as *H. erectus.* The several species of humanoids will not here be distinguished. For simplicity, we will assume that the humanoid line began with a single couple, "Adam and Eve," at about 1,000,000 B.P. ("before present").

If it took a million years for a population of just two individuals to increase to a population of some five billion, the average growth rate was only a bit more than two hundredths of one percent per year. To get a feeling for this enormously slow rate of growth, imagine a population of 5,000 individuals growing at that rate: in one year's time it would increase to 5,001. No one would call this a population explosion. Moreover, the long-term trend would be completely obscured by the year-to-year fluctuations caused by disease and human conflict.

It is certain that the human population has not grown in a steady manner; but, to make trends more apparent, from this point on our graphs will ignore fluctuations. Most of the time the long-term trend has produced a growth rate of less than 0.02 percent per year, with a few remarkable spurts corresponding to the long-recognized "revolutions" of history. Each revolution occurred because human beings learned to extract sustenance from the environment more efficiently: the tool-making revolution, the agricultural revolution and the scientific-industrial revolution.

Because of the long time and the large numbers involved, graphing the population history of humankind presents problems. Figure 12-2 shows two ways of dealing with the great range of numbers. On the vertical axis we graph the logarithms of population numbers. "Logs" have the effect of compressing large numbers: the larger the number the greater the compression. On the horizontal axis the long extension of time is managed by inserting gaps in the record during those periods when the population was scarcely growing.[4] Without these gaps the graph would

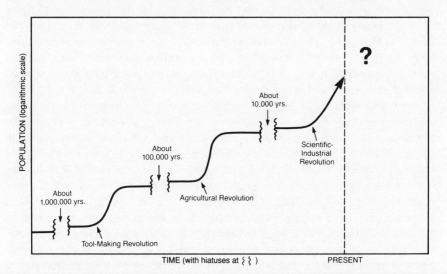

Figure 12-2. Human population history, compressed. Short-term fluctuations are ignored. Question: does the past tell us what lies beyond the veil of the present (dashed line)?

have to be about three hundred feet from left to right—the length of a football field and rather too much to fit on this page. The graph of population growth stops at a dashed vertical line. But time has no stop; population will continue; the future is a question mark.

Revolution Through Coevolution

When planning began for the reconstruction of the House of Commons after World War II, Winston Churchill insisted that it be rebuilt exactly as it was before the bombing. He attributed its excellence as a debating chamber to the intimacy of its space. "We shape our buildings," he said, "and they shape us."[5] Thus did he recognize the reciprocal effects of human beings and their artifacts—things that artisans make to achieve human ends. Seldom anticipated is the fact that an artifact, in the end, changes its makers.

It is not difficult to deduce the effect on human beings of the tools that were invented during the tool-making revolution—axes, bludgeons, cutting flints, bows, arrows and spears. Since skill was required to use them well, these artifacts must have selected for genetic types who could best develop these skills. Though making an invention may be possible only for rare geniuses, once the artifact exists, it exerts selective pressure on the whole genetic community. Individuals who are too stupid or too clumsy to use them well will be progressively eliminated from the population. A major invention is one that generates a new future for the human race.

The bundle of artifacts we call "agriculture" selected for an acute sense of the future and its demands. The first great insight must have been the realization that inconspicuous seeds could grow into conspicuous plants, given time and tending. The conceptual connection must have been made many thousands of years ago (and there was no writing to memorialize the advance).

As soon as it was recognized that different kinds of seeds grew into different kinds of plants, the way was opened to human selection within each species of plants. Natural selection (which takes place at all times) was augmented by human selection. Plant species judged to taste good were favored over "weeds." As the human population grew in numbers the global proportion of crop plants to weed plants shifted in favor of the former.

Some forms of human selection were unconscious. The clusters of seeds of wild grains shatter early, dispersing the seeds widely. This makes collection of seeds for human use inefficient. Very rarely, a nonshattering mutation occurs in a plant favored by human beings. Since the seeds of a nonshattering mutant are more easily collected by human beings, such mutants will be favored by human agriculturalists. A nonshattering gene that has a negative value for a plant subject only to nature's selection, has a positive value for a domesticated species, that is, a species subject to human protection and propagation (Box 12-1). Plants and human beings then make a co-evolving system. After millenia of selection, many varieties of domesticated plants and animals are unfit to live in the wild. Examples: slow, clumsy, great-uddered milch cows; and navel oranges, which produce no seed and have to be "vegetatively" reproduced by slips and grafts. Co-evolution moves the set-point for

Box 12-1. The Meaning of "Survival of the Fittest."

The effects of "shattering" of seed-heads on the survival of seeds in different selective environments. "Fittest" is always defined relative to a particular environment.

Selective Environment	"Fittest" Genotype
With no human beings	Shattering
With people who are very neat eaters	Shattering
With people who are sloppy eaters	Outcome depends on the degree of sloppiness
With people who purposely save seed for planting	Non-shattering
With people who save the "best" seed for planting	Non-shattering; plus whatever other characteristics are called "best"

human population numbers upward. The end result of co-evolution is mutual dependence. We would have trouble surviving without any of our domesticated partners; and some of them could not survive at all, in their present "improved" forms, without the care of human beings.

"Future Orientation": Its Selective Consequences

The story of the Russian patriarch that began this chapter points to an enduring problem of the human species: how does one weigh future (possible) good against present (certain) bad? In various ways this problem surfaces again and again in agriculture.

Going back to the earliest days there must have been many occasions on which there was a strong temptation to serve the present rather than the future. The young of domesticated animals put on weight at different rates. The largest and fattest of a litter is more tempting to eat than its scrawny litter-mates. It is possible (but not always certain) that the difference in size is partly ascribable to heredity. If so, concern for the future dictates that the farmer should eat the scrawny animals, saving the biggest for breeding stock. This advice is based on probability, and so is easily ignored by those whose greed is greater than their trust in logic.

An illuminating survey of civilization could be built around the development of future-oriented decisions. A modern industrial civilization cannot be understood without a searching analysis of the institutions that demand the kind of people who are capable of giving preference to the future. Close observers of criminals have noted a striking inability of career criminals to give adequate weight to future (possible) punishments as they succumb to the temptation of present gain.[6] Students of poverty often call attention to the fact that their subjects, as a group, seem to be deficient in the ability to defer the gratification of their desires to a distant (and always somewhat uncertain) future.[7] Bluntly put, at least some of the reasons why people are poor are internal to the persons themselves.

Modern life apparently demands a stronger future orientation than many people possess. Conflicts of interest between present-oriented people and future-oriented people can become intense, even violent. A nation in which only a tiny minority of the people are sufficiently future-oriented may not be able to survive in competition with nations in which a larger proportion have this orientation.

Every step on the road to future orientation must have been a difficult one. Deferring gratification is always risky, for how does one know that a predicted future will ever arrive? When present pain is certain, what is there to support faith in some future gratification?

The revolution we are now living through—the scientific-industrial revolution—incorporates to some extent the two preceding revolutions. Not only are we inventing such novelties as lasers and silicon chips, we are also reinventing agriculture. After a relative stasis that lasted for centuries, agricultural productivity multiplied more than twofold in a few decades as hybrid corn and other genetic innovations were brought to fruition in the twentieth century. The recently developed "genetic engineering" may do even more.

And What Does Our Future Hold?

We can never, for sure, see beyond the moving curtain that separates the present from the future, but our evolution-selected, future-oriented decision abilities drive us to try to peer behind the veil of time-unborn. The big question mark in Figure 12-2 covers too much; we can replace it with three question marks, as has been done in Figure 12-3. This change is less an addition to knowledge than a way to so emphasize our ignorance that we cannot ignore it.

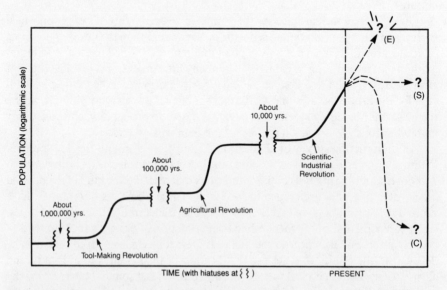

Figure 12-3. Human population history extended into the future. Which will it be? E = Ever greater growth; S = Stationery state; C = Collapse following overshoot of the carrying capacity.

The thrust of invention during the past two centuries, together with the resultant growth of population, naturally created an expectation that both would continue—*forever* (as some people think). What better indication of the future can we have than the recent past? People who habitually bet on a continuation of trends are, on the whole, winners. But we should not expect too much of this type of conservative policy. As René Dubos was fond of saying, "Trend is not destiny." In the last of the Mesozoic era, reptilian investment counselors (if there were such) would have been unanimous in predicting a brilliant future for the dinosaurs. But where now are the dinosaurs of yesteryear?

Figure 12-3 categorizes the possible futures into three types:

E = Ever greater invention-supported population growth, as the trend of the past three centuries is continued without limit. The upper horizontal boundary of the graph is broken to indicate the presupposition of this theory. (The other two theories assume no such breakthrough.)

S = Stationary state achieved as the population adjusts to the reality of limiting factors. This flattening out is a repetition of the conclusion of the other technological revolutions, but—by the hypothesis of ultimate physical limits— ours is probably the *last* revolution that will increase the size of the terrestrial population of human beings.

C = Collapse of a global population that has vastly overshot the sustainable carrying capacity of its environment. A mere dislike of this possibility is no reason for refusing to consider it, for if it *is* a possibility, we should know this so we can take timely action to minimize its unwanted consequences.

The Riddle of Decline

Malthus's "pessimistic" view was born into a world that was already converting to technological optimism. The literature supporting the E-category of ever greater population growth is immense: all advertising is committed to this view, as is most economic literature. Politicians mention no other. The perpetual growth of wealth, population, and everything good is the faith of demagogues in the twentieth century.

Among professional economists there was one in the nineteenth century who took exception to the "growthmanship" view: John Stuart Mill.[8] In 1848 he penned a much quoted defense of the "stationary state" (see Box 12-2). He thought that his view would prevail in the future, as is indicated by his referring to those who believed otherwise as "political economists of the old school."

But Mill did not prevail. It was more than a century before his eulogy of noneconomic values was taken up again, not by economists this time, but by environmentalists, ecologists, and nature lovers. John Muir, Paul Sears, and Aldo Leopold were most influential in advancing the broader view of human goals. Gradually, economists joined in the chorus. With hindsight we can see why Mill was whistling in the dark. The accelerating pace of technological change made his view seem quaint.

Box 12-2. John Stuart Mill on the Stationary State.

It must always have been seen, more or less distinctly, by political economists, that the increase of wealth is not boundless: that at the end of what they term the progressive state lies the stationary state. . . .

[The] impossibility of ultimately avoiding the stationary state—this irresistible necessity that the stream of human industry should finally spread itself out into an apparently stagnant sea—must have been, to the political economists of the last two generations, an unpleasing and discouraging prospect; for the tone and tendency of their speculations goes completely to identify all that is economically desirable with the progressive state, and with that alone. . . .

I cannot . . . regard the stationary state of capital and wealth with the unaffected aversion so generally manifested towards it by political economists of the old school. I am inclined to believe that it would be, on the whole, a very considerable improvement on our present condition. . . .

There is room in the world, no doubt, and even in old countries, for a great increase of population, supposing the arts of life to go on improving, and capital to increase. But even if innocuous, I confess I see very little reason for desiring it. The density of population necessary to enable mankind to obtain, in the greatest degree, all the advantages both of co-operation and of social intercourse, has, in all the most populous countries, been attained. A population may be too crowded, though all be amply supplied with food and raiment. It is not good for man to be kept perforce at all times in the presence of his species. A world from which solitude is extirpated is a very poor ideal. Solitude, in the sense of being often alone, is essential to any depth of meditation or of character; and solitude in the presence of natural beauty and grandeur, is the cradle of thoughts and aspirations which are not only good for the individual, but which society could ill do without. Nor is there much satisfaction in contemplating the world with nothing left to the spontaneous activity of nature; with every rood of land brought into cultivation, which is capable of growing food for human beings; every flowery waste or natural pasture ploughed up, all quadrupeds or birds which are not domesticated for man's use exterminated as his rivals for food, every hedgerow or superfluous tree rooted out, and scarcely a place left where a wild shrub or flower could grow without being eradicated as a weed in the name of improved agriculture. If the earth must lose that great portion of its pleasantness which it owes to things that the unlimited increase of wealth and population would extirpate from it, for the mere purpose of enabling it to support a larger, but not a better or a happier population, I sincerely hope, for the sake of posterity, that they will be content to be stationary, long before necessity compels them to it.

Principles of Political Economy, 1848.

Inventions and discoveries have produced the upward thrust of each revolution, but until recently the principal driving force of invention has been the one identified by Aesop twenty-five hundred years ago: "Necessity is the mother of invention." In the nineteenth century a new ball game developed. Not waiting for the prod of necessity, certain clever and ambitious people began putting elements of the world together in new ways and then looking around for places to insert their novel creations. Paradoxically, *invention became a breeder of necessities.* Thomas Edison was the prototype of the agent involved in creating a trans-Aesopian world. A few industrial concerns like Du Pont, Eastman, Bell Telephone, and 3-M paid people to invent first and worry about applications later. Nylon. Scotch Tape. Velcro. Zippers. Transistors. Of course, dedicated inventors discovered many interesting things for which an important use was never found, for example, Silly Putty. Truly, as Whitehead said: "The greatest discovery of the nineteenth century was the invention of the method of invention." Invention became a driving force in the third revolution, far beyond what it had been in the preceding cultural revolutions. The end is not yet in sight.

Will growth go on forever? Will there be infinite progress? Careful writers are chary of using words of the "infinity" family, but the priests of progress, from Condorcet down to the present, have not hesitated to claim that progress would continue "indefinitely." What a beautifully ambiguous word! It suggests the infinite without specifically claiming it. Operationally it translates into: "I don't want to think about limits."

Growthmanship has determined the thrust of commercial propaganda. In the minds of many people limitless growth has gained the status of a "right." But the growthman's "limitlessness," like Godwin's "fitfulness," evades the discipline of numeracy, which is committed to finding numbers and working with them. Growthmanship and fitfulness do not welcome rationality.

If we are rational, we must admit at least the *possibility* of a downfall of our civilization. Civilizations have collapsed in the past—for instance the Mayan civilization of Central America. In just 100 years—from 850 to 950 A.D.—the population of the south and central Maya lowlands declined by about 85 percent (from a high of 3 million people to about 450,000).[9] That meant a decrease in population of about 1.9 percent per year. The underlying cause was dependence on an unsustainable agriculture. It is a tragic truth that the rise and fall of civilizations is not a symmetrical affair. As Will Durant put the matter (with only a slight exaggeration), "From barbarism to civilization requires a century; from civilization to barbarism needs but a day."[10]

As we reluctantly abandon the illusion of perpetual growth we realize that one of the greatest needs of our time is for a greatly improved educational system (where "education" is understood to include not only schools but also comic books, popular song lyrics, television, and the press). The bifurcated path of the Buddha needs to become part of the innermost guide of many more people: we need to learn the causes of human sorrow and the ways to free ourselves of sorrow (insofar as this is possible). Choosing between present and future gain, between "the bottom line" and a principled program, necessarily causes some sorrow. We must face the sorrow, and decide what to do about it.

In keeping with the common preference for optimism over pessimism, the millions of words devoted to recounting success stories—in business, in politics, in personal lives—vastly outweigh the literature alloted to the description of failures. Perhaps this is as it should be, but the total omission of pessimistic accounts endangers the future. Until recently the curricula of business administration programs have almost entirely lacked accounts of how businesses fail.[11] What M.B.A. students crave most are success stories. But they must be reminded that news of military victories were what the legendary Persian monarch wanted too.

At some of the stronger business schools the faculty now tell their students that they may learn more from failures than from successes. *(Don't kill the messenger!)* Reform is in the air: as one professor put it, dealing with business declines has become something of a "growth industry."

Growth? Stagnation? Collapse? What does the immediate future hold for our civilization? *It's no use looking at trends.* We must look at fundamentals, at the substantive base of human actions. We must measure quantities of potential supplies against quantities of obdurate demands to see what the future holds. Malthus tried to do just that, but the tools he used were too crude. His answer was not convincing.

We should be able to do better.

13

Limits: A Constrained View

In the real world—beyond pedagogy, beyond hypocrisy—language has two purposes: to facilitate thought, and to prevent it.[1] Seldom does a writer skilled in the arts of persuasion call attention to the second purpose because to do so would be to arouse suspicions of his own verbalizations. Rhetoric—ambiguous, deceptive, delusive rhetoric—stands ever ready to help writers of all persuasions to "throw dust in the jurymen's eyes." Population pundits use this tactic when they entitle an article or book "Standing Room Only." In getting the reader's attention those three words substitute trivia for fundamentals. Before another work with that title is published let's see why "Standing Room Only" is so silly.

How much of the earth's land area would now be occupied if the present five billion inhabitants were crowded together on a "standing room only" basis? Taking the space occupied by the average human being, standing up, as three square feet (a rectangle 3 × 1 feet), a square mile could accommodate just a little more than 9 million standees. Five billion people (the population of the earth in 1987) could be accommodated on a mere 556 square miles, just 46 percent of the area of Rhode Island, our smallest state. A perfect square, 24 miles on a side, could accommodate the world's entire population, standing up. Alaska, with an SRO capacity of 5 trillion, could accommodate a thousand times the present world population.

Let's look at some more absurd statistics.[2] If all the land area of the earth were covered by SRO patrons, what would be the total population? And how long would it take the present population to reach that figure, if the recent rate of world population increase (1.7 percent per year) could be maintained? The earth's land area $(1.48 \times 10^{14}$ square meters) divided by the area occupied by one person (0.28 square meters) $= 5.29 \times 10^{14}$, or 529 trillion human beings. It would take 5 billion people, increasing at 1.7 percent per year, just 686 years to swell to that number. That time lapse is only 34 percent as great as the total Christian era to date. (And of course the most absurd aspect of this exercise is the assumption that the present monstrous global growth rate of 1.7 percent per year could be long maintained.)

Ghost Acres

The fact that so little area would be required for all the world's people on an SRO basis is sometimes offered as a proof that the world is not at present overpopulated. But the Bible is right: man does not live by bread alone. Neither do human beings

121

live on standing room only. Much additional space is required for the growing of crops, the operation of mines, and the garnering of potable water, as well as for the accommodation of houses, factories, stores, and roads. We should not forget what John Stuart Mill (Box 12-2) said about the importance of "flowery waters," natural pastures, and bird-filled hedgerows for the nurturing of the human spirit. We need space. How much space do human beings use?

The answer depends on the scale of living presupposed. Let's take the United States. Consider the people whose address is Manhattan, New York City. The area involved is 14,310 acres. The 1980 population of residents (surprisingly, somewhat smaller than the 1970 population) amounted to 1.4 million. So there were 105 residents per acre. Reciprocally, each resident "occupied" about one one-hundredth of an acre. That's 435 square feet—a square of about 7 yards by 7 yards. And each resident had to share "his" space with commuting office workers and visitors from out of town. (But of course multi-storied buildings greatly diminish the perceived crowding—at the expense of increased traffic milling around the roots of the tall buildings.)

Do 1.4 million people *live on* Manhattan? Language is tricky: much depends on how you interpret the words "live on." If you mean, "are supported by," the answer is a flat *no*. Some 1.4 million people live *in* the borough of Manhattan, but they are not solely supported by the island's produce. They live *on* wheat produced in Kansas, eat cattle started in Wyoming and fattened in Missouri, and drink water gathered by a protected and almost uninhabited watershed of upper New York State. They use electricity generated in Canada, coffee from Colombia, cocoa from Ghana, and minerals produced by mines scattered all over the world. The list goes on and on.

Without too much error we can assume that the imports and exports of the United States are in balance as concerns the area required to produce food and other basic goods. Using standard tables,[3] we find that the average American draws upon the resources of the land to the following extent:

Cropland	1.9 acres
Pastureland	2.4 acres
Woodland	2.6 acres
Other land	2.2 acres

Cropland can produce human food directly: wheat, corn, and so on, (as well as cotton and other non-foods). Pastureland produces food indirectly: cows eat grass, and we eat the cows. "Woodland" includes not only recognizable forests but also smaller woody plants (bushes). That woodlands produce lumber and fuel is widely known; what is not widely appreciated is the importance of forestland as a ground cover that protects the watersheds that furnish city people with drinking water and saves lowland people from disastrous floods. "Other land" in the table includes the area used for factories, houses, roads, and other types of construction as well as wilderness and miscellaneous recreation areas. The total of the four categories adds up to almost exactly 9 acres per American.

As far as the Bureau of the Census is concerned, the residents of Manhattan live *in* Manhattan. As concerns the larger reality, however, Manhattanites also live *on* the produce of the entire country (and that statement neglects the rich resources of foreign countries that Manhattanites also live on to some extent). Every resident of Manhattan, whether he knows it or not, and no matter how crowded he may feel, lives on more than nine acres of land. Since most of the acreage the average citizen "occupies" is out of sight and out of mind, the agricultural geographer Georg Borgstrom suggested in 1961 that we call it "ghost acreage." The essential life of an educated urban dweller, from birth to death, is lived out on ghost acreage. Urbanites, lamentably unconscious of this support base most of the time, live a life of illusion. This does not make for ecologically realistic thinking; illiterate farmers of the poorest countries are often closer to ecological realities than are the most sophisticated city dwellers. Unfortunately urbanites, in most countries and in most times, control both the media and the political system.

Because the inhabitants of industrialized and urbanized countries are poorly prepared to "see" ghost acres, a cocktail-hour discussion of overpopulation is all too often interrupted by someone snapping: "What are you talking about? This country isn't overcrowded! I flew from coast to coast last week and I was appalled at the amount of empty space I could see from the airplane."

For a quick rejoinder one should ask, "If that space is so empty and so available, why aren't you living there?" Of course the typical urbanite wouldn't be caught dead in Wyoming or Utah: he regards the wide open spaces as fit only for quail, coyotes, and *other people.* Since he is deficient in meaningful experiences with the sources of his being, the urbanite must have reality brought home to him through the intellectual gimmick of "ghost acreage." Without some appreciation of the breadth of their dependency on the outside world, city dwellers are apt to adopt political plans that erode the foundations on which their survival depends. Urbanization may, in the end, prove to be a fatal disease.

Can a world controlled by prisoners of illusion educate their urban children to understand the ecological roots of their well-being? The problem is something like that of lifting oneself by one's bootstraps. At what density does "overpopulation" begin? Are we overpopulated now? Technology may, in the future reduce the per capita ghost acreage somewhat. On the other hand, when the energy now available in the concentrated forms of oil and coal has to be supplied by the more diffuse source of solar energy, the ghost acres per citizen will have to increase considerably. And if we "conquer poverty" (which some reformers think is possible) the per capita provision of ghost acres will have to rise even more. The correct answer to the question "When does overpopulation begin?" may well be "Centuries ago!"

The Scale Effect

One of the most important elements of Galileo's *Dialogues Concerning Two New Sciences,* published in 1638, is his argument for what we now call the *scale effect.* A portion of the dialogue between two of the fictional characters is presented in Box 13-1.[4] After establishing the mathematics governing the strength of such structures as beams in engineering, Galileo develops the implications for living organisms.

Imagine a man swelling proportionally in all his dimensions (as a photograph might be enlarged optically). Enter, the scale effect: the weight increases as the third power of the man's height, while the ability of his long bones to sustain his weight

Box 13-1. Galileo Explains the Scale Effect.

Salviati: It would be impossible to build up the bony structures of men, horses, or other animals so as to hold together and perform their normal functions if these animals were to be increased enormously in height; for this increase in height can be accomplished only by employing a material which is harder and stronger than usual, or by enlarging the size of the bones, thus changing their shape until the form and appearance of the animals suggests a monstrosity. . . .

I have sketched a bone whose natural length has been increased three times and whose thickness has been multiplied until, for a correspondingly large animal, it would perform the same function which the small bone performs for its small animal. . . . you can see how out of proportion the enlarged bone appears. Clearly then if one wishes to maintain in a great giant the same proportion of limb as that found in an ordinary man he must either find a harder and stronger material for making the bones, or he must admit a diminution of strength in comparison with men of medium stature; for if his height be increased inordinately he will fall and be crushed under his own weight. Whereas, if the size of a body be diminished, the strength of that body is not diminished in the same proportion; indeed the smaller the body the greater its relative strength. Thus a small dog could probably carry on his back two or three dogs of his own size; but I believe that a horse could not carry even one of his own size.

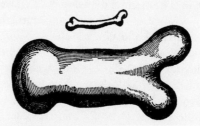

Simplicio: This may be so; but I am led to doubt it on account of the enormous size reached by certain fish, such as the whale which, I understand, is ten times as large as an elephant; yet they all support themselves.

Salviati: Your question, Simplicio, suggests another principle, one which had hitherto escaped my attention. . . . keeping the proportions of the bony structure constant, the skeleton will hold together in the same manner or even more easily, provided one diminishes, in the proper proportion, the weight of the bony material, of the flesh, and of anything else which the skeleton has to carry. . . . that fish are able to remain motionless under water is a conclusive reason for thinking that the material of their bodies has the same specific gravity as that of water; accordingly, if in their make-up there are certain parts which are heavier than water there must be others which are lighter, for otherwise they would not produce equilibrium.

Dialogues Concerning Two New Sciences, 1638.

increases only as the second power. What can be done easily to an image by optical means could not in fact be done to a real man by simple growth. The bones would become unequal to the task of supporting his weight. Something else has to change.

Galileo illustrated the problem with a drawing of one of the bones of the human body (here included in Box 13-1). (The sketch he used, presumably of a humerus, is not very good: one wishes Galileo had cribbed from the excellent work of his fellow-Paduan, Vesalius, who worked a century earlier. However the drawing will do.) Galileo's figure shows the monstrous deformation that would have to be imposed on the long bone of the human arm if a person were to grow to an enormous height. The other bones would, of course, have to become equally gross. Galileo could have made his point more memorable had he employed a competent artist to draw the entire human giant, with muscles to match its bones. One wonders what effect this visual novelty might have had if Jonathan Swift, nearly a century later, had looked at the resulting figure before writing *Gulliver's Travels.* If some travelers in our world should ever stumble across Lilliputians and Brobdingnagians, we can be sure that they won't look at all like the merely optical transformations depicted in Swift's book. The six-inch high little people will be more like insects, and the big people will be, to use Galileo's word, monstrosities. Proportions must change with size.

Several aspects of Galileo's procedure will bear emphasis. Notice that he lets one of his fictional characters (Simplicio) criticize the theory by citing a counterexample, namely the whale, which is much larger than an elephant but does not have disproportionately large bones. It is of the essence of science to try to disprove a new theory: if the originator does not try to do this himself, he can be sure someone else will (Simplicio, in this instance). Note how Salviati (Galileo) rises to the challenge, pointing out that the *effective* weight of an animal immersed in water is very little, and so it has no need of monstrous bones. Thus we see that a good scientific theory is one that is deepened, not weakened, by counterexamples.

Note also how Galileo strengthens the plausibility of his theory with a "thought experiment" (a term that was not coined until three centuries later). Imagine, he says, that we test the strength of the long bones by stacking one animal on top of another—making perhaps a tower of four, all told. An animal as insignificant as a small dog could probably survive a load of three dogs; but it is most improbable that one horse could support the weight of three horses. Such an experiment has not, thank goodness, ever been performed; the thought experiment is good enough to make the point.

When a change in size is contemplated, this question constantly arises: will the change make any significant difference in function? Will the change make things better or worse? Perhaps a bit of both: much depends on the "initial size" and the magnitude of the change. "Other things being equal," increasing the size of basketball players from five feet to six feet would improve the performance of a team; but five men all nine feet in height would not win the pennant.

Scale effects are found everywhere. By the nineteenth century looking for scale effects had become routine in science and engineering. This guiding question made slower progress in economics and business, which have unfortunately been all too often guided by the single bias, "bigger is better." Many people have difficulty in admitting the disadvantages of large size.

The Law of Diminishing Returns

As was pointed out in Chapter 10, Malthus just missed discovering the law of diminishing returns. The initial application made was to agriculture, where it is the consequence of the natural impulse to "farm easy acres first." (One might call this a "laziness policy," but that would not be to condemn it; this sort of laziness is rational.)

Diminishing returns come into agriculture in another way. If you increase the labor applied to a field by 10 percent, you may well increase production by 10 percent; 20 percent more labor may yield a 20 percent larger harvest. But at some high level, the addition of another 10 percent input (of labor, fertilizer, or whatever) yields less than a 10 percent increase in output, because a point of diminishing returns has been reached. (Look again at Figure 10-1.) Whenever there is an optimum point in a production curve, diminishing returns come in beyond that point.

The application of this idea to fields other than agriculture was not so straightforward or noncontroversial. Take manufacturing. Since heavy equipment is very expensive, economists first took note of "economies of scale" when the share of capital cost per unit produced went down because the equipment was used more hours per day. At first sight one might think there would be no point at which the returns per unit cost would start diminishing, but this expectation is refuted by many experiences in industry.

Gigantism creates problems. As economies of scale are achieved by using more massive machinery and a larger population of workers, the relations of workers to management, and workers to each other, changes. Ultimately a point is reached at which diseconomies start to creep in. Quite understandably, workers on rigidly controlled assembly lines sometimes suffer from boredom as well as alienation from management and society at large. Because the psychology of the situation is appreciated by so few, the onset of diseconomies of scale is seldom foreseen. Workers may demand higher wages. If won, these ultimately turn out to be an inappropriate solution to the real problem. Disaffection grows. As the workers win ever higher wages, management may try to keep costs down by introducing automation. This response generates new worker-management disputes.

The technical factors that create economies of scale are easy to define intellectually. The psychological factors that make for diseconomies of scale are more difficult to foresee and define. They are none the less real. As a population grows in size, counterproductive forces take over. But compulsive optimists miss seeing the change soon enough.

Energy as the Limit

An inquiring mind that becomes aware of the limitless potential of unhindered exponential population growth naturally looks for a countervailing factor. Malthus solved the problem by deciding that "subsistence" increased at a slower rate than population. The principal component of subsistence was food. Unfortunately for Malthus, even in his lifetime increases in food production outran population growth. After his death the inequality of the rates became even greater. The behavior of subsistence does not fit the needs of his theory; and neither, as we have seen, does simple space. What else should we consider?

Energy is the next thing that springs to mind. At this moment in time it may seem foolish to propose that the energy supply could limit population growth because almost everyone knows about nuclear energy. "The atom" has been heralded as a "near-infinite" source of energy. And so it is, in a sense; but there are serious questions about the safety of "peaceful atomic energy." These questions will be treated at length in Chapter 15. For the the present, *let us presume ourselves back in the nineteenth century*—back before 1905, before radioactivity, before Einstein.

Antagonistic Worldviews

It would be an enormous error to assume that our picture of the world is built only on logic. No matter how hard-headed one tries to be, one's thinking is shaped by the biases of all-encompassing worldviews derived from assumptions of which one is barely (if at all) conscious. (One's opponent often sees these assumptions more clearly. Since the relation is mutual, it is obvious that we need each another as critics, if nothing else.)

There are times when one wonders if the human species wasn't divided at its inception into two types or subspecies. Though giving names to the postulated groups leads to arguments, the risk must be run. In Box 13-2, I present—with some hesitation—two "baskets of attitudes." The terms in each basket are certainly not simple synonyms; they are not even all the same parts of speech. The postulations underlying these collections of terms have been variously designated as theories, hypotheses, *Weltanschauungen,* Worldviews, images, visions, and paradigms. (No doubt tomorrow some new collective term will be proposed.) Christening a basket of attitudes is like trying to pin a label on a mound of Jello; but distinguishing between the two contrasting assemblages helps us understand many persistent human conflicts.

Though the categories are not sharply separable, the members of one basket are, on the whole, more closely related to each other than they are to members of the contrasting basket. There is no reason to think that anybody would identify himself wholly with one group; in truth, each of us is an impure composite (though in the heat of argument we may insist that our opponents are pure—that is, purely wrong!)

Box 13-2. Two Baskets of Attitudes.

The characteristics suggested by the terms listed in each column tend to be associated in the psychological makeup of an individual. It is doubtful if a more precise statement can be supported.

Basket 1	Basket 2
pleasure	duty
freedom	fate
comedy	tragedy
optimism	pessimism
liberal	conservative
progress	stability
unconstrained	constrained
free-form	structured

I was led to assemble this box by Thomas Sowell's insightful introduction of two terms—the next-to-last pair in the list.[5] With a wealth of examples Sowell has shown how nonproductive many disputes are unless we recognize that the antagonists are being guided by two different "visions of reality," as he calls them—one (relatively) *unconstrained,* the other (relatively) *constrained.* People of the unconstrained persuasion tend to say, "Do your own thing!" Those of the constrained sect are apt to murmur: "Duty . . . duty!" Members of the first group—Charles Dickens's Mr. Micawber comes to mind—worry very little because they are sure that "something will turn up." Members of the second group worry about untoward effects of present actions in determining the future.

Since no pair of contrasting labels is wholly satisfactory, it is always tempting to invent new ones. Never a person to resist linguistic temptation I have coined my own terms. Sowell's term *constrained* implies that the conservative stance necessarily entails a loss of freedom. I think this assumption fails to take account of a real gain in meaning and power that can come from accepting guidance by a highly *structured* image. To Hegel is attributed the remark that "Freedom is the recognition of necessity." This is the kind of freedom sought in a *structured view* of nature. The opposing view can be called *free-form.* I will use these contrasting terms hereafter.

Creative individuals in most fields of human endeavor can be divided into those who submit happily to the discipline of structured thinking and those who do not. In poetry, for example, Wordsworth sang the praises of submitting to the rigid discipline of the sonnet—fourteen lines with an invariable rhyme scheme. "Nuns fret not at their convent's narrow room," Wordsworth said, from which he derived this moral:

> In truth the prison, unto which we doom
> Ourselves, no prison is: and hence for me,
> In sundry moods, 'twas pastime to be bound
> Within the Sonnet's scanty plot of ground;
> Pleased if some Souls (for such there needs must be)
> Who have felt the weight of too much liberty,
> Should find brief solace there, as I have found.

It would be rash to claim that one of the two predispositions in the structuring of ideas is wholly right, the other wholly wrong. Yet as a "consumer" of poetry rather than a producer, I confess I favor Wordsworth's structured view. In my younger days I found it easy to memorize sonnets. I doubt if I ever remembered so much as ten consecutive words of "free verse." Some minds—mine at any rate— feel most free when the constraints are real *and make sense.* (Furthermore, I doubt if any worshiper of free forms has read all the way to this point in this book. Voluntary self-segregation averts many an argument!)

Structured Views in Science and Technology

A case can be made for the proposition that the books that have had the most influence on the development of human thought have been ones that included a generous provision of ambiguities. In such works antagonists find support for opposing positions: praise can then come from many sides. Condorcet's posthumous book (discussed in Chapter 3) is such a work.

Even the language of the book (French) furnished Condorcet with ambiguities not readily available in English. The title was *Esquisse d'un tableau des progrès de l'esprit humain,* which is rendered in English as "Sketch for an historical picture of the progress of the . . ."—of the what? *Esprit* may be rendered as either "spirit" or "mind," words which seem rather different to English-speaking people. It is unfortunate that we who speak English must do without the fertile ambiguity of the Gallic *esprit.*

"The work I have undertaken," wrote Condorcet, "will be to show, through reasoning and through facts, that nature has assigned no limit to the perfecting of the human faculties, that the perfectibility of man is truly indefinite." But how is one to show that improvements in "esprit" or "human faculties" have taken place? The simplest way is by pointing to the *material products* of a spirit or mind at work. And so, Condorcet displayed the many inventions of human beings and the technological revolutions through which history has passed. As a result of this and other writings of the nineteenth century, the idea of progress shifted away somewhat from its original base—the mind or spirit of man (which is difficult to capture in words or pictures)—to the products of the mind: inventions and technological marvels (which are easy to photograph and describe).

The shift has had some unfortunate consequences. For one thing, "You can't stop progress!" is often taken to mean that, having invented LSD and other "mind-blowers"—as well as leaf-blowers, dune buggies, and supersonic transport planes—human beings are now obligated to use every one of them no matter what the consequences may be. Personally, I like to think that a true follower of Condorcet would say, "Let us look critically at each of these inventions to see if it improves the situation *de l'esprit humain.* If not, then to hell with so-called progress!"[6]

Capital-P Progress has come to be something of a religion for hundreds of millions of people. (Whatever else a religion may be, most long-surviving religions call for a commitment that discourages the asking of questions.) Some scientists, as well as most engineers, worship at the religious shrine of Progress. Engineers have a saying, "The difficult we do immediately, the impossible may take a little longer." Some of them behave as if the tablets that Moses brought down from Mount Sinai included this commandment: "Thou shalt use every invention that thy inventors inflict upon thee." Such is the *technological Imperative.* Free-form thinking, coupled with the technological imperative, leads to a new kind of slavery.

Technology grows out of science, and "pure science" is concerned with discovering the "laws" of nature. "Law" in this context is only a metaphor, but it has the merit of implying a restriction of freedom. Science covers a broad spectrum, running from technology at one end to pure science at the other, where investigators seek to put into precise words and equations the reality-that-must-be-obeyed: the limits, the boundaries of the possible. The variety of temperaments characterizing scientists and technologists spans an equally wide spectrum.

The idea of progress, in its purest technological form, gained greatly in popularity during the nineteenth century, and for good reason: never before had there been such an epidemic of inventions. At that point the emotional impact of the asserted "laws" of nature was weakened as free-form thinking came to displace structured thinking in determining the expectations of the public. Science fiction multiplied and flourished.

Energy: What Is Conserved and What Is Not

Paradoxically, the progress of free-form thinking was matched by equal progress in structured thinking, but of this the general public knew little. Many factors account for this difference in awareness. For one thing, it is easier to "sell" the products of free-form thinking; the constrained products of structured thinking, since they imply restrictions on human actions, require salesmanship of no mean order. A few examples should make this clear.

The "conservation of matter" was an early and important product of structured thinking in the nineteenth century. Like all important ideas this one had ancient roots (in the thought of Anaxagoras and Epicurus, in the fifth and third centuries B.C., respectively), but the principle was not made fully explicit until after the work of Lavoisier (and Madame Lavoisier, be it noted) on the threshold of the nineteenth century. Lavoisier lost his head to the guillotine on 8 May 1794, so it was left to others to incorporate the conservation of matter into scientific literature. As honest and accurate accounting is essential to business, so also are conservation principles essential to chemical investigations. Unfortunately most people find the structured idea of conservation about as exciting as a description of business accounting. The free-form idea of progress is much "sexier," and so receives much more attention in the popular press.

Also in the nineteenth century, the conservation of energy was made explicit. Again, the operational merit of the principle is that it makes exact accounting possible—which means that it makes dishonest or incompetent reports easier to detect. This law is often called the "first law of thermodynamics."

It was soon followed by enunciation of the "second law of thermodynamics," or more briefly, the "second law," which is often stated in terms of the peculiar concept of *entropy.* "In a closed system, entropy always tends to increase." And what is entropy? We are told that entropy is a *measure of disorder.* At this point John Q. Public may feel that the explanation is more confusing than the puzzle. A homely example may help.

Consider a room with an electric refrigerator in it. The refrigerator is connected to the world outside the room through electric wires, which put it in communication with a generator somewhere, perhaps a hundred miles away. Initially the interior of the refrigerator is colder than the room. We pull the plug, thus disconnecting the refrigerator from the world outside the room. We now have a more limited "system" consisting of {room + refrigerator}. The *difference* in temperature inside and outside the refrigerator constitutes a sort of *order* in this restricted system.

To the extent that order exists, the entropy (disorder) of the system is less than the maximum possible. We can even speak of the system's *negentropy,* or negative entropy (positive order). The language is certainly curious, but since physicists are such influential people, we must learn to put up with their language.

Just after we've unplugged the refrigerator, the interior of the box is cold; but since the insulation of the refrigerator from the room is not perfect, heat seeps from the room into the refrigerator. The temperature of the unplugged refrigerator rises as the temperature of the room falls (slightly). In the system as defined, negentropy is lost, entropy is gained. Ultimately, room and refrigerator are at the same temperature, and entropy is then at its maximum.

Of course we could plug the refrigerator back into the electric outlet and lower its temperature. But that would be taking something from outside the defined system of {refrigerator + room}. We would be piping in negentropy. The defined system would no longer be closed, which means that the second law would be inapplicable.

The two laws can be put in simple terms:

First law: Energy can be neither created nor destroyed.
Second law: Useful energy (negentropy) is constantly being lost.

Energy: The Global View

"All flesh is grass," reads Isaiah 40:6; this basic insight came independently to people in many different cultures. Grass grows and feeds the cows, and we eat the cows; in a manner of speaking we human beings are only so much processed grass. And what makes the grass grow? Sunlight. So the sun is the material author of our existence. Religions that revolve around sun worship make a sort of sense: we eat sunshine. Sunshine clothes us as well. It also houses us, and moves us from place to place.

By the middle of the nineteenth century the sages of our culture had exposed the many ways in which the sun is important to human existence. The negentropy of sunlight enables plants to synthesize high-energy organic compounds. These compounds are removed from the plant world by plant-eating animals. But this is not the end of the line. The herbivores in turn may be eaten by carnivores; the organic compounds in herbivore flesh are then recycled into carnivore flesh. Alternatively, herbivore flesh is reprocessed by saprophytes (decay organisms, like bacteria and molds). We human beings are omnivores: we eat "grass" of some sorts (wheat), as well as animals (both herbivores and carnivores), and even some saprophytes (mushrooms). But no matter what food we eat, we are really eating sunshine. Energetically, human beings are only so much sunlight, many times reprocessed.

Until the nineteenth century high-energy carbon compounds could be synthesized only inside living bodies. (Low energy carbon dioxide can be made in many ways, but it is not a food.) High-energy carbon compounds were called *organic* because it was thought that only *organisms* could synthesize them (inside their bodies). Early in the nineteenth century some imaginative chemists began to look forward to synthesizing organic compounds "in the test tube," that is, outside living bodies. In 1845 Adolph Kolbe carried out the first such synthesis "from the elements." After that, there was no stopping the chemists. Long before the twentieth

century arrived, hundreds of organic compounds had been synthesized by technological man; but we still call such carbon-containing compounds "organic," an
adjective that used to constrain thought severely but no longer does.

All the essential amino acids and carbohydrates, as well as most of the vitamins
required for life, have already been synthesized in the laboratory. Plants are no
longer essential. As a matter of economics, however, there is no early prospect of
dispensing with plants because they can synthesize many organic compounds far
more cheaply than chemists can; and serious gourmets won't settle for a purely
chemical cuisine. But, *in principle,* all food problems are convertible into energy
problems. The problem of getting enough food (which Malthus assumed was
humanity's major problem) is basically a problem of getting enough energy.

Before the discovery of nuclear energy, sunshine was the only important source
of energy for human beings. (The few exceptions like tidal and geothermal power
were—and still are—*relatively* unimportant.) Coal, oil, and gas, which have
become important sources of energy during recent times, are really "fossil sunlight," since they were derived from the corpses and waste products of plants and
animals that grew because the sun was shining hundreds of millions of years ago.

One of the scientists who clarified energy cycles in the nineteenth century was
William Thompson, Lord Kelvin. Kelvin was a brilliant child. At age twenty-two
he was appointed professor of natural philosophy (which we now call "physics") at
the University of Glasgow. He was politically and socially influential in establishing
physics as the most prestigious of the "hard" sciences. But his failures are as interesting as his successes, because they show how impossible it is to make a scientific
advance when certain essential information is lacking. Without meaning to belittle
this great man, let us look at his most spectacular mistakes.

First, his calculation of *the age of the earth.* The major beds of sedimentary rock
are, on the average, fifteen hundred feet thick. The measured rates of deposition of
sediments observed today (for example, at the mouths of rivers) imply that it took
many millions of years for sedimentary beds of such thickness to be laid down. Victorian geologists were confident that the age of the earth had to be measured in the
hundreds of millions of years.

Kelvin, pursuing a different line of thought, concluded that the earth was much
younger. The side of the earth that faces the sun absorbs radiant energy—during
the "day." At "night," when the same portion of the earth faces away from the sun,
it reradiates the heat out into space. Fact: on an annual basis, *the amount of heat
lost from the earth is greater than the amount gained from the sun.* The excess, said
Kelvin, must be derived from an initial endowment of heat at the time the earth
was formed as a hot, possibly molten mass. Straightforward mathematical calculations showed that the earth could be as hot as it still is only if it was no more than
about a million years old. Geologists like Charles Lyell, and evolutionists like
Charles Darwin, demanded hundreds of millions of years for the plants, animals,
and rocks to change as much as they evidently have changed. (Present-day scientists
demand billions of years.) Kelvin would allow, at most, a few million years. The
physicist's prestige was such that his views were accepted as correct in his day. But
Kelvin was wrong. He didn't dream of the apparently perpetual production of new
heat by radioactive disintegrations taking place in the bowels of the earth. And with-

out this information his sophisticated and exact mathematical calculations could only lead him to wrong answers.

Consider Kelvin's theory of *the history and future of the sun.* Once the dependence of earthly life on the sun is recognized, the question naturally arises, How long has this been going on? And what does the future hold, for the sun and for human life?

The principal local source of energy on earth is the burning of high-energy compounds, as in the oxidation of coal or petroleum. The sun, though it is 334,000 times as massive as the earth, would not last long if its output of radiant energy came only from the oxidation of a fixed supply of fuel. Looking for another source Kelvin settled on the plunging of meteors and meteorites into the solar atmosphere; he postulated that meteoritic friction produced enough heat to account for solar radiation.[7] It was not Kelvin's happiest conjecture. But, ignorant of nuclear disintegrations, he could hardly do better.

There is a moral in these two failures of Kelvin. The theory of education at the elementary level relies heavily on the concept of "reading readiness." When a very young child makes no progress in learning to read, competent educators no longer write him off as "stupid." Individual children (like all young animals) mature at different rates. Some children are developmentally ready to learn to read at three years, others may be scarcely ready at six. (As a "preschooler" Albert Einstein was a backward child.) If you try to stuff reading into a child before he is developmentally ready for it, you will "break your pick," and (what is worse) you may break his spirit.

In the development of the sciences there is a strong analogy to human development. A scientific puzzle must reach a stage of "solution readiness" before much good can come from an all-out effort to solve it. The puzzles of the age of the earth and the history and future of the sun were not "solution ready" during the years 1860–1890, when Kelvin was most active. This was long before the days of huge government grants for research; but we can confidently say that had there been such grants, handing out millions of pounds sterling to physicists in Kelvin's day for attacks on these problems would not have hastened their solutions. Solution readiness had to await unforeseen discoveries in apparently irrelevant fields of investigation. (And it is never easy to get funding for research that seems to be irrelevant to the perceived problems of the day.)

In the nineteenth century the origin of the sun's energy was a mystery, but its importance for life on earth was well understood. Taking solar energy as a *given* we are now in a position to throw new light on the history and development of civilization, seen as problems in the management of energy.

14

From Jevons's Coal to Hubbert's Pimple

In a commercial society like ours it is understandable that money-makers should be the ones who pay the greatest attention to the implications of economics. Historians have been a breed apart, with most of them (until recently) paying little heed to the ways in which economics affects history. Yet surprisingly, a basis for the eventual integration of economics, ecology, and history was laid in the nineteenth century.

The Victorian who tackled history from the economic side was William Stanley Jevons (1835–1882). The distinction made in the previous chapter between living *in* a area and living *on* it was a paraphrase of what Jevons wrote about the material basis of English prosperity: "The plains of North America and Russia are our cornfields; Chicago and Odessa our granaries; Canada and the Baltic are our timber forests; Australia contains our sheep farms, and in South America are our herds of oxen; . . . the Chinese grow tea for us, and our coffee, sugar, and spice plantations are in all the Indies. Spain and France are our vineyards, and the Mediterranean our fruit-garden."[1] A century before the term "ghost acres" was coined, Jevons had clearly in mind the idea behind the term.

Half a century before Jevons was born—in fact in the year the Bastille was stormed by French revolutionaries (1789)—an English mineral surveyor by the name of John Williams had asked, in *The Limited Quantity of Coal of Britain,* what would happen to the blessings of the industrial revolution when England no longer possessed the wherewithal to power the machinery that produced her wealth? Optimism is so deeply engrained a characteristic of busy people that this warning, like most first warnings, was little noted. It remained for Jevons to rouse the British public in 1865 with the publication of his book, *The Coal Question.*

Jevons's life coincided in time with the period when the nature and significance of energy (in its prenuclear formulation) was becoming manifest to physical scientists. Since energy was needed to turn the wheels of industry, and coal was the most readily available source of energy, Jevons reasoned that the continued political dominance of Great Britain was dependent on the bounty of her coal. This naturally led to the double question, How long would English coal and the British Empire last?

Twin Mysteries: Buried Resources and the Unborn Future

To determine how long a supply will last, surely one needs to know the magnitude of the supply. Desirable, said Jevons, but not absolutely necessary. A contemporary of his, Sir William Armstrong, had remarked that "The tendency of progress is to quicken progress, because every acquisition in science is so much vantage ground for fresh attainment. We may expect, therefore, to increase our speed as we struggle forward."[2] Translated into modern language, what Armstrong said was that technological progress creates a system of change that has positive feedback: improvements multiply exponentially.

At this point a modern ecologist is apt to call our attention to an often overlooked cost of progress. The nonrenewable resources on which progress depends must diminish at the same rate that progress advances. We are delighted to think of progress advancing exponentially; but a concomitant exponential attenuation of supplies should make us uneasy.

Using English data, Jevons showed that "we do each of us in general increase our consumption of coal. In round numbers, the population has about doubled since the beginning of the century, but the consumption of coal has increased eightfold, and more. *The consumption per head of the population has therefore increased fourfold.*"[3] In other words, consumption (in a progressive economy) increases as an exponential function *of an exponential function* (population growth). In Jevons's time—and ours—consumption has been *doubly* exponential in its mode of increase. "We cannot," said Jevons, "but be struck by the fact that *the consumption of the last ten years is half as great as that of the previous seventy-two years!*"[4] Jevons wrote:

> [T]he exact amount of our stock of coal is not the matter of chief moment. The reader who thoroughly apprehends the natural law of growth, or multiplication in social affairs, will see that the absolute quantity of coal rather defines the height of wealth to which we shall rise, than the period during which we shall enjoy either the growth or the climax of prosperity. For, as the multiplication of our numbers and works proceeds at a constant rate, the numerical additions ... constantly grow. ... It is on this account that I attach less importance than might be thought right to an exact estimate of the coal existing in Great Britain.[5]

In spite of this assertion Jevons went to a great deal of trouble to try to zero in on a defensible figure for Britain's total coal resources. He did not strongly defend his estimate, for the reason just given: the doubly exponential rate at which they were being exhausted tended to trivialize the importance of any particular estimate of the supply.

The significance of these qualifications largely escaped his critics. In the twentieth century the same argument has had to be erected again by the authors of *The Limits to Growth.*[6] Once more critics responded by focusing on the limited reliability of the estimates of supply when they should have concentrated on the significance of the doubly exponential demand curve.[7] On this shaky ground today's critics refer to the "discredited work of the authors of *The Limits to Growth.*" (What a marvelous economy of critical effort the adjective "discredited" provides!)

When the Victorian man in the street asked, "When will our coal mines be exhausted?" Jevons responded:

> The expression "exhaustion of our mines," states the subject in the briefest form, but is sure to convey erroneous notions to those who do not reflect upon the long series of changes in our industrial condition which must result from the gradual deepening of our coal mines and the increased price of fuel. Many persons perhaps entertain a vague notion that some day our coal seams will be found emptied to the bottom, and swept clean like a coal-cellar. Our fires and furnaces, they think, will then be suddenly extinguished, and cold and darkness will be left to reign over a depopulated country. It is almost needless to say, however, that our mines are literally inexhaustible. We cannot get to the bottom of them; and though we may some day have to pay dear for fuel, it will never be positively wanting.[8]

Had our economist been thoroughly au courant with the developing physics of his day, he would have made the expensiveness—in money—of the fuel play second fiddle to the energy cost of it. With coal-as-a-fuel, as with petroleum-as-a-fuel (see Chapter 7), the mining of the energy resource should be stopped when the energy used in extracting it from ever deeper strata becomes greater than the energy obtainable from burning the fuel. The rise in energy cost will be *only roughly* paralleled by a rise in money cost. This is fortunate: the increase in price gives a signal to one and all that they should try to reform the infrastructure of society so as to use less of the resource. The end of our honeymoon with fossil energy need not be suddenly and devastatingly painful.

One other point about Jevons's statement needs footnoting. The statement that "our mines are literally inexhaustible" would be less criticizable if *practically* were substituted for "literally." Jevons's choice of adverb is defensible, of course, if the audience is made up exclusively of economists, who can argue that "economically ruinous to exploit" is the same thing as "literally inexhaustible," since an unexploited resource will never give out. But economic convention is a poor defense for imprecise rhetoric.

Though Jevons was not eager to give any estimate of the date when England's coal supplies would become practically useless, he was, like all authors of forward-looking books, under strong pressure from the public to commit himself to a "bottom line" estimate. After setting forth many qualifications he yielded to the pressure.

> I draw the conclusion that I think any one would draw, that *we cannot long maintain our present rate of increase of consumption; that we can never advance to the higher amounts of consumption supposed. But this only means that the check to our progress must become perceptible within a century from the present time;* that the cost of fuel must rise, perhaps within a lifetime, to a rate injurious to our commercial and manufacturing supremacy; and the conclusion is inevitable, that our present happy progressive condition is a thing of limited duration.[9]

Like so many speculative time schedules, this one was sabotaged by history. The mistakes Jevons made were ones that lie in wait for anyone who tries to estimate the practical life span of a mineral resource. Mineral wealth is underground—sometimes far underground—so one can never be sure that the technological limits of detecting it have been reached. Moreover, time brings unforeseen improvements in getting resources out of the ground. Technology is also involved in making use of the mineral resource, and this technology is sure to improve. The net result of all these improvements is an extension in the life of the resources. The supply may be exhausted at a rate that is somewhat less than doubly exponential. (On the other hand, the optimism bred by the apparent increase in resources may result in an increase in the rate of population growth, thus undoing, in part at least, the beneficial effects of improvements in technology.)

Yet another factor diminished the prescience of Jevons's pessimistic view: the development of petroleum as a major source of energy. The pioneer "Drake well" in Pennsylvania came on line in 1859, six years before the publication of *The Coal Question;* but it would be historically unreasonable to indict Jevons for failing to foresee the eventual importance of the new source of energy so early in its development.

In the light of the best estimates we can make, the total amount of energy available in the earth's liquid petroleum is only about 6 percent of that present in coal.[10] (The energy in oil shale is said to be 8 times as much as the energy in coal,[11] but the environmental costs of exploiting oil shale border on the forbidden.) The practical importance of petroleum derives from other factors than its total energy content. All things considered, oil is more easily extractable from the ground than coal is. Over all, its exploitation probably produces less pollution; being a liquid, it is more easily engineered into industrial systems; and the accidents associated with the pumping of oil snuff out fewer lives than coal mining does.

The Twenty-Year Horizon

Since Jevons's day petroleum has replaced coal as the principal spur to industrial civilization. Modern transportation would be seriously handicapped if it had to depend only on coal, lignite, and peat. (These other resources can, of course, be converted into liquid fuel, but with considerable loss of useful energy in the conversion.) Almost a century after Jevons's cry of "wolf!" was refuted by history, it was natural that scepticism should be focused on the next wolf-outcry, which was stimulated by worries about the early exhaustion of oil supplies.

A graph of the course of extraction of oil from the ground looks very much like the graph of the exponential growth of debt given previously in Figure 8-2. A "cornucopist" who finds it natural to suppose that the debt curve is a curve of the increase of wealth may well find it easy to assume that the curve of energy "production" will soar upward forever. If challenged he will justify his position by saying that his optimism is based on the idea and reality of "substitutability." He uses history as a justification for this assumption.

A long time ago we used wood for energy; then we found out we could use coal; now we use oil; when the oil runs out, we can go back to coal; and by the time that runs out we will no doubt have found some other energy source. The greatest "other" of course is nuclear energy, the discussion of which is postponed to the next chapter. For the present we will look into the limitations of petroleum as a future source of energy for industrial civilization.

The alarm about petroleum was sounded early in this century. Looking over

the oil industry's data some pessimistic prophets predicted an early end to petroleum supplies, usually in about twenty years. Then twenty years passed, and oil was
found to be as plentiful (relative to demand) as before. At this point (naturally)
some new prophet proclaimed that the exhaustion of oil lay only *another* twenty
years ahead. The pessimists' horizon seemed to be a constant twenty-years-to-
doomsday. Such a moving target is hardly the sort of thing to inspire public confidence in the nervous peepings of our Chicken Littles!

Why were pessimistic prophets repeatedly wrong? The most important reason
was this: the forecasters confused petroleum *resources* with petroleum *reserves.* As
was stated in Chapter 7, "resources" refers to the total amount of oil estimated—
or "guesstimated"—to be in the ground. Obviously not much precision can be
claimed for this figure. "Reserves," on the other hand, refers to the total amount of
petroleum that has already been discovered and is waiting to be pumped up. This
figure can be fairly closely estimated by standard methods—provided the owners
of the reserves (the oil companies) are willing to share their "proprietary" information with others (which they usually are not).

Reserves seldom amount to more than a twenty-year supply at the predicted
rate of use. There are good financial reasons for this limitation. It takes money to
drill wells, and borrowed money costs money. It doesn't make economic sense to
borrow money to discover oil that won't be pumped up and sold until many decades in the future. A twenty-year reserve is quite enough. All too often our Chicken
Littles look only at reserves, while cornucopists pin their hopes on resources.
Though less precisely known than reserves, the resources are certainly much larger
and they are not wholly fictitious.

Hubbert, the Persistent Prophet

Petroleum prophecy took a new turn in 1948, the 150th anniversary of Malthus's
essay. M. King Hubbert (1903–1989), a petroleum geologist employed at that time
by Shell Oil, introduced a sophisticated new method of analysis.[12] His method was
based on *effort per barrel*—the drilling effort expended per barrel of oil discovered
and brought to the surface. The money price of oil will, "other things being equal,"
increase with scarcity; but as long as people are willing to pay the price, oil companies have no reason to stop drilling. Ultimately, however, the energy price of
obtaining oil will exceed the energy derivable from the product; beyond that point
there is no rational defense for "producing" more fuel oil. Hubbert noted that the
barrels of oil produced per unit effort required for the discovery of the reserves had
been decreasing regularly for a long time. Projecting the curve into the future he
predicted the "end of oil" for the United States and for the world. These terminal
dates were much closer to hand than the ones assumed in the front office of the
major oil companies. Understandably, Hubbert was promptly labeled as the latest
reincarnation of Chicken Little.

Hubbert persisted, extending and refining his methods during the next two decades. He predicted that in the early 1970s the price of petroleum would take a sharp
turn upward. When the oil shock of 1973 came—the first oil shock we now call it—
Hubbert was vindicated. We cannot ignore the fact that international politics

played a role in producing the oil shock of 1973: price fixing by OPEC, the cartel of the major oil-exporting nations, touched it off. But the cartel could not have made its high prices stick in the absence of the relative shortage predicted by Hubbert.

The decade preceding the 1973 oil crisis was marked by sharp debates between the supporters of Hubbert (the "pessimists") and his opponents, the "cornucopists"—who occupied positions of power in industry and government. While Hubbert estimated that the lifetime production of petroleum in the United States would be from 150 to 200 billion barrels, A. D. Zapp, of the U.S. Geological Survey, estimated 590 billion. The opponents were working with the same data.

A significant difference in their methods involved the estimate of oil found per foot of drilling *in the future.* Zapp assumed that the future would be like the past. This approach no doubt seemed conservative to many people, but it was not: Zapp was assuming that the extended future would be like the immediate past, which is a mere moment in time. A true conservative would use not the *moment* but the *trend* in constructing a telescope for looking into the future.

Hubbert was a conservative of the second sort. Extrapolating the trend of increasing effort that was apparent in the history of drilling, Hubbert concluded that *the future will be worse than the past.* Cornucopists of course called this attitude "pessimism." Perhaps it is: but history has vindicated Hubbert. The yield per effort has gotten steadily worse. To expect otherwise would be to assert that petroleum geologists are incompetent. Faced with many possible drilling sites, a company geologist will advise his firm to drill the most hopeful ones first. If he is competent, the potential of the yet undrilled sites will diminish steadily with the passage of time. Productivity per foot drilled goes down, cost goes up. (If Zapp were right—if petroleum geologists were incompetent—then oil companies might as well save money by firing their geologists and choosing their drill sites by flipping coins.)

For a decade the influential director of the USGS "bought" Zapp's estimate and opposed Hubbert. When the first oil shock came, two national committees (one within the USGS) were appointed to evaluate the situation. Both committees endorsed Hubbert. Finding his professional authority undermined, the director of the USGS resigned. Hubbert, for so long a "prophet without honor in his own country," was fully vindicated.

Yet the biblical description of a "prophet without honor" is not entirely appropriate in this case. Pessimistic prophets and whistle-blowers are often given a hard time by their bosses. It is, therefore, a pleasure to report that the executives of Hubbert's own company, the Shell Oil company, though not pleased with what he was saying, supported him during his "years in the wilderness."[13] In 1963 M. King Hubbert joined the faculty of Stanford University, from which he retired in 1968. After his victory in 1973 the "retired" prophet was in great demand as a speaker on the significance of physical resources for the survival of civilization.

History Through an Inverted Telescope

The pivotal role of energy in determining the quality of human life is now widely recognized. In what follows I will, unless otherwise stated, use the phrase "quality of life" to refer to the *physical* quality of life—to the possibility of enjoying such amenities as a pleasant ambient temperature, good food, freedom from pollution of many sorts (including noise pollution), ease of moving from one place to another, and so on. This emphasis does not deny the importance of nonphysical aspects of living—the charms of art, music, nature, animal pets, and human friendship, for example. But the connection of nonmaterial treasures with simple physical wealth is not easily clarified.

The ease with which useful energy can be captured has a great deal to do with the physical quality of life. Cheap energy means abundant supplies of energy-requiring goods; when energy becomes expensive, people start complaining of shortages. In the last three centuries an increasing fraction of our daily energy supply has come from petroleum, gas, and coal. What can we say about human history in the light of the supplies of fossil energy?

Graphing the rate of use of each fossil energy source yields a bell-shaped curve. Figure 14-1 gives Hubbert's projection of the world's use of petroleum over time. Until the year 1900 the level of world production was too low to show on the scale of this figure. Then it rose exponentially almost until the present. After 1973 the path departed more and more from an exponential curve due to increasingly tighter supplies. At some point (here estimated to be about 1995, but the date is not precise) the curve of petroleum use will bend over and start heading downward. As indicated in the figure, 80 percent of the oil will be used up in a mere fifty-six years, scarcely more than a moment in the history of mankind. All but a small percentage of the extractable oil will be taken from the ground in less than two centuries.

A similar graph for coal extraction would look much the same, but it would begin earlier and peak later than the oil curve. Comparable curves must hold for natural gas, tar sands, oil shales, and peat, but the numerical data are less reliable. Lumping all the energy data together produces the graph shown in Figure 14-2. This curve has come to be known as "Hubbert's pimple."

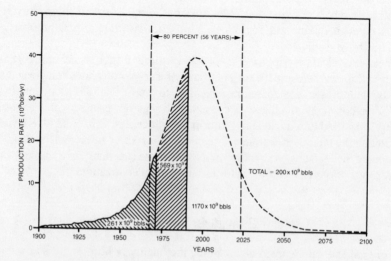

Figure 14-1. Complete lifetime curve for world petroleum "production." (After Hubbert, 1974.)

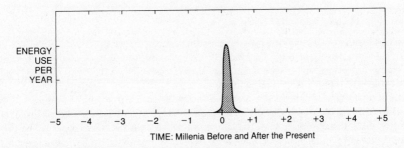

Figure 14-2. "Hubbert's pimple" on the face of history, showing past and future course of fossil energy use by human beings.

The part of the curve that lies in the future is conjectural, of course, but there can be little doubt of its essential correctness. To feel the full impact of reality, one should, in imagination, extend the curve far beyond the bounds of the printed page. The leftward extension would go beyond the four thousand years shown (which take it only back to 2000 B.C.). *Homo sapiens*—our species—has been in existence for about one hundred thousand years. The progenitor species go back at least a million years. Were we to extend the curve backward a million years it would reach to the left of this printed page for about forty feet.

For all but a few hundred years of that time the curve of fossil fuel usage is nearly flat on the horizontal axis, not visibly above the level of usage = 0. The curve started rising only yesterday, as it were—specifically, about six hundred years ago, when we started using coal in significant quantities. From all the signs, the human species is only a few score years away from the peak of the curve. After that the curve will fall rapidly until it once more lies prostrate on the zero line. The prosperous period of our fossil-energy-fueled-civilization can be no more than a pimple on the lifeline of human existence.

Chapter 8 made the point that the ability to extract meaning from graphs is an essential part of "numeracy." Hubbert's pimple is a test of that ability. As one traces this curve from the evanescent present into the unavoidably near future the numerate viewer experiences something of a cold chill traveling down his spine. If words will help, the restrained summary Hubbert wrote in 1981 should be of aid (Box 14-1).[14] Those who understand Hubbert's pimple find its implications as incompatible with easy optimism as Gibbons' *Decline and Fall of the Roman Empire*.

To date, from the beginning of time until we become entangled in the veil of the future, the curve of human population growth is essentially identical with the curve of fossil energy usage. The near identity of the two curves must be more than coincidence. Human life and civilization require steady inputs of energy. The number of human lives, and the scale of energy use per capita to which we have become accustomed, produce so high a rate of energy demand that the thought of exhausting fossil energy resources is scary. To see what lies ahead of us—*and not very far ahead of us, at that*—we need to look at a magnification of the yet-to-be-developed part of the curve where the turning takes place (Figure 14-3).

Too many of our people unfortunately expect the curve of available energy (the dashed line) to continue to increase exponentially forever. As energy inputs start to

Box 14-1. History through Hubbert's Eyes.

Human history can be divided into three distinct successive phases. The first, comprising all history prior to about 1800, was characterized by a small human population, a low level of energy consumption per capita, and very slow rates of change. The second, based upon the exploitation of the fossil fuels and the industrial metals, has been a period of continuous and spectacular exponential growth. However, because of the finite resources of the Earth's fossil fuels and metallic ores, the second phase can only be transitory. Most of the ores of the industrial metals will have been mined within the next century. The third phase, therefore, must again become one of slow rates of growth, but initially at least with a large population and a high rate of energy consumption. Perhaps the foremost problem facing mankind at present is that of how to make the transition from the present exponential-growth phase to the near steady state of the future by as noncatastrophic a progression as possible.

"Energy from Fossil Fuels," 1949.

fall short of our exponential expectations there will be a period that is characterized by widespread fear and denial of the facts. This will be followed by what we can only designate by the pitifully inadequate word "shock." Beyond that lies the pain of "social chaos"—also inadequate words.

All this is within the veil of the future, so it cannot be dignified by the name

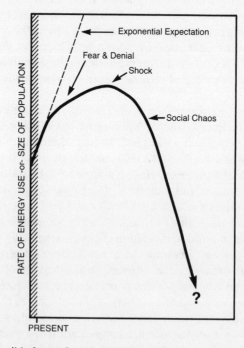

Figure 14-3. A plausible future for the coupled variables of energy use and population size, unless the human species mends its ways.

"fact." The exhaustion of fossil fuel resources is certain enough to be called a fact. The human reactions of fear, denial, shock, and pain are also facts; but, being information-mutable facts, they are facts of a different order. Such facts are subject to some control (modification) by human decisions, by human effort and by human will. (But what sort of fact is *human will*?)

Can we develop a new and significant supply of energy? Is nuclear energy such a one? Theoretically, the *per capita supply* of energy can be increased by reducing the number of people making demands on the environment. Or a "shortage" can be done away with by lowering per capita energy demands. Both possibilities are denigrated as "utopian" by most people, but the mythical man-from-Mars (who is, by hypothesis, a perfectly intelligent and all-knowing being) might well, after examining the human situation on earth, ask: "What's the trouble? There's no reason on earth you earthlings cannot accept, in plenty of time, the necessity of *stopping* exponential growth. When you understand what has to be done, *stop*."

No reason on earth why exponential expectations cannot be eliminated? Quite so: no reason *on earth*. The trouble is not exactly "on earth": the problem is *in our heads*. Not in one human head, but in a collectivity of many human heads. Solving problems that are "in our heads" is much more difficult than solving problems "on earth." We need to take a closer look at some of the curious processes that take place in the minds of human beings as they become aware of problems created by human successes in gaining a partial mastery of nature.

Judging Prophets: The Double Standard

There is a family resemblance between the predictions of pessimists and the story of the boy who cried wolf. It may be argued that doom sayers, unlike the fabled boy, do not intend to deceive. Perhaps this is generally true; but Keynes, who gave a sympathetic reading to Jevons, called attention to the fact that Jevons was a prodigious hoarder of brown packing paper, of which he bequeathed so large a supply to his heirs that they still had not exhausted the supply fifty years later. Keynes went on to postulate that Jevons's conclusions in the coal question "were influenced, I suspect, by a psychological trait, unusually strong in him, which many other people share, a certain hoarding instinct, a readiness to be alarmed and excited by the idea of the exhaustion of resources."[15]

In the days when scholars thought that logic alone was enough for the discovery of truth, a postulation like Keynes's merited condemnation as an *argumentum ad hominem*—an argument against the man who advances a view, rather than an argument addressed to the facts. But Freud has taught us to mitigate our logical purity: justified or not, critics' opinions of a man's doctrines are shaded by their evaluation of his personality. Different critics, different evaluations, different judgments.

Pessimists are not given an easy time in this world. Prophets are subject to a double standard: optimists are permitted many mistakes; pessimists, none. One well-publicized mistake—and it may not even be a large one—and a doom sayer's words are heavily discounted from then on. People hunger for pleasant truths. This is understandable: but should this hunger be encouraged? If there must be a failure in prophecy, which is the more dangerous: the optimistic prophecy that is refuted by events, or the pessimistic prophecy that blessedly proves false? What is the true path of prudence? (That, however, may be a poor appeal to make: when was the last time you heard the word *prudence* used in public? In today's world many people are embarrassed to claim this virtue: Why?)

Abandoning psychologism, can the frightening implications of Hubbert's pimple be escaped? This is the question that is now before the house.

II

LOOKING FOR THE BLUEBIRD

15

Nuclear Power: A Nonsolution

Constrained, structured thinking has been the predominant habit of successful operators in both business and science for at least two millennia—at least since Epicurus of Samos. Only occasionally have surprising discoveries upset the equilibria of scientists, and then only for a little while. Surprises are soon reconciled with old pictures of reality: structure and constraint reign once more. But in the disequilibrium of the interim, believers in a free lunch have a field day.

By the latter half of the nineteenth century the laws of conservation of matter and energy seemed to have tied everything up into one neat package. Then in 1896 Becquerel discovered radioactivity and the old constrained view of energy was in trouble. During a decade of intense experimentation the properties and significance of radioactivity and radioactive decay were investigated, culminating in 1905 in the publication of Einstein's celebrated equation, $E = mc^2$. Conservation was redefined in terms of a new synthetic entity, *mass-energy*. Constraint ruled once more.

Limitless Energy?

Despite Einstein's rescue of conservation, there was still some turmoil because, from a practical point of view, the fact that a tiny mass could be converted into a great quantity of energy made the conservation of mass-energy seem rather academic. In 1916 the English physicist Ernest Rutherford pointed out that the energy resident in a single pound of radioactive material was equivalent to that obtainable from the combustion of 100 million pounds of coal. Since his country was then at war, it is not surprising that the physicist should have expressed a hope that radioactive energy would not be available to human beings until they had learned to live in peace with one another.[1]

Scientists of considerable stature sometimes denied the possibility of an atomic bomb. In 1930 Robert A. Millikan, a Nobel laureate in 1923 and at the time president of the California Institute of Technology, called the prospect of an atomic bomb a hobgoblin and a myth. "It is highly improbable that there is any appreciable amount of available energy for man to tap." That the grounds for Millikan's conclusion were not wholly scientific was apparent when he confessed his faith that humanity can "sleep in peace with the consciousness that the Creator has put some foolproof elements into His handiwork, and that man is powerless to do any titanic physical damage."[2] Nine years later Hahn and Strassmann found that apparently

Millikan's benevolent Creator had, in a moment of absentmindedness, neglected to insert the needed foolproof elements into his handiwork. Six years after that came Hiroshima.

From the earliest days of atomic research it was realized that the enormous sources of energy released by exploding atomic bombs could (theoretically) be directed into peaceful channels. All during World War II, for reasons of national security, a tight censorship was imposed on public discussions of atomic energy, even of possible peaceful applications. But before the censors took over, and almost a year before the United States entered the war, a research scientist turned popularizer, writing in *Popular Mechanics,* predicted the development of a nuclear reactor the size of a typewriter, which could be installed individually in millions of homes, thus doing away with unsightly power lines. The cost of energy would then be less than a tenth of a penny per kilowatt-hour. In this new utopia "energy has become so cheap that it isn't worth making a charge for it. . . . This means that freight as well as passenger transportation are public utilities; like the heat and light and water in your house, you don't have to pay for them at all."[3] (One is impelled to ask, who paid the monthly utility bills in the writer's home? Perhaps his wife— and the scientist-turned-writer never even knew it. Or perhaps he lived in a city apartment where all the bills were silently included in a single monthly rent payment—another example of how urban bias can blind intelligent people to the reality of resource limitations.)

In 1949, with the war over, the atomic utopia was revived in the pages of *Popular Mechanics:* "Unlimited power will mean the production of ample food, clothing, housing, and other necessities as well as myriad luxuries, for everyone. Poverty and famine, slums and malnutrition will disappear from the face of the earth."[4] Implicit in this statement is a hypothesis that turns up time after time in Utopias generated by technologists. This hypothesis can be reasonably reduced to the following syllogism:

> All social evils—poverty, famine, crime, social disorder, and the like—are caused
> by resource shortages;
> Atomic energy will put an end to all resource shortages;
> Therefore atomic energy will put an end to all social evils.

Put so baldly, the syllogism would attract criticism. But it is never so clearly stated, and technological optimists continue to "solve" the world's social problems with dreams of physical abundance.

The technological optimism of scientists was eagerly supported by politicians. Harold E. Stassen, a perennial candidate for the presidency, proclaimed in the *Ladies' Home Journal* that in the near future nuclear energy would create a world "in which there is no disease . . . where hunger is unknown . . . where food never rots and crops never spoil . . . where 'dirt' is an old-fashioned word, and routine household tasks are just a matter of pushing a few buttons . . . a world where no one stokes a furnace or curses the smog, where the air is everywhere as fresh as on a mountain top and the breeze from a factory as sweet as from a rose."[5]

Now, nearly half a century later, what do we find? In our homes we certainly have come closer to a push-button world, but pollution problems outside the home are still very much with us (and many of them are worse).

Technologists sometimes outdid the politicians in dreaming. During the 1950s there was insufficient appreciation of two problems: (1) the problem of living with the dangerous byproducts of nuclear reactions, and (2) the problems created by the sheer bulkiness of a reactor *plus* its associated hardware. The theoretically small size of a reactor *considered by itself* led enthusiasts to foresee the day when nuclear reactors would power trains, commercial ships, rockets for peaceful uses, aircraft, and even automobiles. Enthusiasts seldom thought about the consequences of collisions.

Seeking peaceful uses of atomic power in his "Atoms for Peace" speech of 8 December 1953, President Eisenhower gave his blessing to "Project Plowshare." (The name came from the Bible, from Sarah: "They shall beat their swords into plowshares, and their spears into pruning hooks . . .") As part of this idealistic program, Glenn Seaborg, Nobel laureate in physics, proposed that nuclear explosions be used to dig a harbor at Point Barrow, Alaska, excavate a channel across the Aleutian Islands, and deepen the Bering Strait. Edward Teller, the reputable but irascible opponent of Robert Oppenheimer and reputed "father" of the hydrogen bomb, proposed that a new sea-level Panama canal be excavated by nuclear explosions. He also suggested we should use explosives to close the Straits of Gibraltar—which were geologically closed in the prehistoric past—so that the Mediterranean Sea, fed by inflowing rivers, could "rise and freshen to the point that it could be used to irrigate the Sahara."[6] He neglected to mention that the higher level of the inland sea would destroy Venice, the "Pearl of the Adriatic."

Who Benefits? Who Pays?

Looking backward at the mid-century proposals of nuclear enthusiasts, it is clear that their principal deficiency was a lack of ecological insight. (The Rachel Carson revolution came along ten years later.) In terms introduced at the end of Chapter 2 we can say that the propaganda for the "peaceful atom" was splendid in its literacy, excellent in its numeracy, and abysmal in its ecolacy. The ecolate questions that needed asking fall into two categories.

And then what? "Time has no stop," and it certainly won't stop at the first favorable effect of an intervention in the environmental order of things. Raising the level of the Mediterranean doesn't merely furnish water for the Sahara. Digging a new Panama canal by blasting and irradiating billions of tons of dirt doesn't merely produce a more efficient waterway. As ecologists repeatedly say: We can never do merely one thing.

Cui malo? Cui bono? Long before Christ was born, sceptical Romans asked, "To whom the bads? To whom the goods?" Or: Who benefits? Who pays? Developers, promoters, and salesmen of all sorts are quick to tell us the benefits of an intervention, but they have a thousand and one ways of diverting our attention from the question, Who pays? When posterity is the group left paying the bill, it is easy to deflect attention in this way, because the bill payers are not yet present to ask their question.

It is also easy for do-gooders of the industrialized world to forget about bill payers who live in the nonindustrialized world. Fat-cat industrialists love to build billion-dollar dams in poor countries, taking little thought of the thousands of peasants that a dam uproots from homelands their people have lived in for many generations. The unconscious "no limits" assumption of the fat cats allows them to assume casually that there is plenty of equally satisfactory land elsewhere to which the displaced can flee. "Developers" separated by thousands of miles from the havoc they cause do not notice when development-displaced refugees start farming steep hillsides, thus causing massive soil erosion; or turn wetlands into farmlands, thus diminishing the breeding areas for aquatic and marshland species.

An Unforgiving Technology

In searching for those who pay in one sense or another for the blessings of nuclear power, we focus first on those who are closest to the system itself, to the experimenters who discover and build it and to those who operate the completed system. From the earliest days of the atom bomb research it was apparent that physicists had a dragon by the tail. One sufficiently chilling account given by Otto Frisch makes clear the peril in which investigators worked at Los Alamos (Box 15-1).[7] In spite of their appreciation of the dangers, physicists suffered a number of fatal accidents, and no doubt some cancers developed later because of excessive exposure to radiation.

After the investigations are finished and a design for a nuclear reactor is accepted, the dangers are still not over. The very magnitude of the engineering strains designing ability to the utmost. Philip R. Morse has described the formidable problems of a typical reactor:

> The huge amounts of heat evolved are to be carried away by air-flow, nearly half a
> million cubic feet per minute, an amount requiring careful aerodynamic design to

---

Box 15-1. Otto Frisch: Beyond the Critical Mass—An Unforgiving Technology.

On one occasion I was making . . . an assembly (nicknamed Lady Godiva because there was no neutron-reflecting material round it), and just as we were getting close to critical size the student who was assisting me pulled out the neutron counter which he said seemed unreliable. I leaned over, calling out to him to put it back, and from the corner of my eye I saw that the neon lamps on the scaler had stopped flickering and seemed to glow continually. Hastily I removed a few pieces of uranium-235, and the lamps returned to their flickering. Obviously, the assembly had briefly become critical because my body—as I leaned over—reflected neutrons back into it. By measuring the radioactivity of some of the uranium-235 bricks afterwards, we could calculate that the reaction had been growing by a factor of 100 every second! As it happened I had received only about one standard daily dose in those two seconds; but it would have been a lethal dose if I had hesitated for two seconds longer.

There were others less lucky. . . . one of the students who helped with the critical assemblies dropped a heavy block of reflector material at the wrong moment, and although he instantly swept it aside he received enough radiation so that two weeks later he died.

"Somebody Turned on the Sun with a Switch," 1974.

Box 15-2. Radioactivity in a World of Illiterate Badgers and Restless Tumbleweeds.

Richland, Washington. A badger broke through the security lines here at the world's first plutonium factory in 1959. He ignored all the warnings and dug a hole in one of the waste pits. After he left, rabbits began to stop by for an occasional lick of salt, but it was no ordinary salt they had found. Before long, they scattered 200 curies of radioactive droppings over 2,500 acres of the Hanford Reserve. . . .

Hanford also has trouble with ground squirrels, burrowing owls, pocket mice, insects, and plants like rabbitbrush and tumbleweed. With roots that can grow 20 feet, tumbleweeds reach down into waste dumps and take up strontium-90, break off, and blow around the dry land.

Eliot Marshall, "Hanford's Radioactive Tumbleweed," 1987.

---

avoid large pressure drops, and requiring super-blowers to drive. All this, of course, must be accomplished without any leaks in the whole system, from intake to the top of the 300-foot stack. The control rods, which regulate the intensity of the nuclear reaction, must be able to move five feet in a tenth of a second, and must be controllable within fractions of a millimeter. An inkling of the problems involved may be obtained from the simple statement that once the pile is in full operation no one can ever go inside the shield thereafter, to repair or lubricate or adjust any of the reloading or control equipment inside. If an important part of it becomes inoperable, we shut the reactor down and build another one.[8]

Human beings have, of course, had to deal with dangerous new technologies before, and have satisfactorily solved the problems they presented. When first built, steam boilers exploded often, killing many people; but they were eventually tamed. Naturally, we hope the history of nuclear plants will have an equally benign ending. But there is one problem with the new technology that is different *in kind* from the problems posed by other technologies: this is the problem of waste.

When the useless remains of a steam plant are "thrown away," the result may be esthetically unsightly, but at least people aren't harmed in any simple sense by the mess. Not so with the waste products of nuclear reactors and the trash that must be taken care of when a generating plant is ultimately "decommissioned" after only a few decades of operation. Since the essential mechanism is by this time highly radioactive it must be disassembled by remotely controlled robots, a tricky operation at best. The costs of this are still unknown, but they must be great. And if disassembly proves impossible, about the only measure left is to encase the "dead" but dangerous reactor in concrete, the effectiveness of which over thousands of years is unknown.

The ease of detecting tiny quantities of radioactive substances has made us keenly aware of how many forces operate to encroach upon the supposed security of the "aways" we throw things into. Not only are the geological agents of groundwater, ground movements, and earthquakes to be considered; less obvious but equally persistent biological agents do their bit to undermine security. Radioactive atoms can be transported surprising distances by plants and animals with no malevolent intent whatsoever. Box 15-2 describes some of the troubles biological agents have caused when people tried to sequester dangerous radioactive material in a sparsely settled area.[9] Radionuclides escaping into a desert can enter underground aquifers that furnish water to foodplants that feed human beings in distant cities. That such hazards exist is likely never to occur to people with a strongly urban bias. Bad as it is, the disposal problem will become even worse as the supply of "empty space" decreases—as it must with continued population growth in a world of limited size.

Energy Too Cheap to Meter?

From the very beginning the extravagant dreams of Project Plowshare were heavily discounted by most scientists. The workaday plans for generating electricity by nuclear means were taken more seriously. A leader in this development was the financier Lewis L. Strauss, chairman of the Atomic Energy Commission. In a speech in 1954 he said: "It is not too much to expect that our children will enjoy in their homes electrical energy too cheap to meter, will know of great periodic regional famines in the world only as matters of history, will travel effortlessly over the seas and under them and through the air with a minimum of danger and at great speeds, and will experience a life span far longer than ours. . . . This is the forecast for an age of peace."[10] Because of Strauss's powerful position as chairman of the AEC, his statement received wide publicity—and no doubt was widely believed. People want to believe in safe air travel, in greater longevity, in peace and in food enough for all—even when the connection of the atom to these benefits is less than crystal clear.

The slogan "too cheap to meter" was too good to forget. This phrase reverberated through the press. Yet at the outset it was obvious to anyone with the slightest knowledge of the economics of electric utilities that this goal could never be reached, for a simple reason. Half the cost of household electricity is accounted for by the expenses of distribution: the capitalized costs of power lines, transformers, and so forth; the electrical losses in distribution; the costs of household meters; and the costs of reading meters and sending bills to householders. If the actual cost of generating electricity fell to a flat *zero,* a 50 percent reduction in the cost of delivered energy would be the most that one could hope for. Half-price is *not* "too cheap to meter."

Of course a few costs could be eliminated by doing away with meters, meter reading, and billing. But if that were done, if householders never again received a bill for the electricity they used, a new cost would develop: the inevitable wasting of wealth that is held in common. Aristotle understood this as long ago as the fourth century B.C.: "That which is common to the greatest number has the least care bestowed upon it."[11] Chairman Strauss's claim that nuclear energy would be "too cheap to meter," means that the cost *perceived* by the users would be zero, and Aristotle's prediction would be realized: users would waste electricity. To control costs, society would ultimately have to intervene and install meters after all. By this reductio ad absurdum, "too cheap to meter" is unmasked. Notice that it is not technology that produces the collapse of a dream, but human nature.

As domestic electricity from nuclear reactors became a reality, the public learned of costs that were not obvious in 1954. First, there are the costs of accidents which, in the real world, can never be entirely avoided. Then there is the possibility of sabotage. So far this has not been great, but the amount of sabotage is a function of the magnitude of political disorder, and this can increase despite our best intentions. Then there is the cost of waste disposal. Because of the long half-life of radioactive elements, the criteria for really safe disposal are severe. So far, after more than three decades of power generation, accompanied by a considerable accumulation of nuclear wastes in "temporary" depots, our managers have not been able to agree on a safe method of disposal. We would like to just "throw away" the wastes, but (as ecologists are ever ready to remind us), *there is no away to throw to.*[12]

What About Fusion?

Even before the first fission bomb was successfully constructed and exploded it was realized that an alternative energy-producing nuclear change was possible: the fusion of light-weight hydrogen atoms instead of the fission of such heavy-weight atoms as uranium and plutonium. Whereas the latter reaction produces radioactive by-products, the former is a radioactively "clean" reaction. Fusion is technically more difficult to achieve than fission, so this possibility was put on the back burner until after the war.

As the dangers of fission became more widely recognized during the 1950s, research into the fusion possibility was intensified. The military version (the "Super" or "hydrogen bomb") was soon achieved, but a peaceful, controllable fusion reaction eluded the efforts of competent scientists. In spite of this, optimism ran high in the nuclear community.

At first, success was prophesied within five years. Unfortunately, the five year horizon not only retreated year by year, it lengthened. When last heard from the peaceable fusion horizon was somewhere around the year 2020 A.D. By that time, "if present trends continue," the human population that "needs" more energy will be more than 3 billion larger than it is now. The expressed "need" will increase by more than this 70 percent, for two reasons: (1) earthly resources will have been depleted even further, and (2) the "revolution of rising expectations" will have infected even more of the earth's peoples, causing more widespread dissatisfaction with poverty.

The casual reader of the daily papers is unaware of how distant the prospect of successful fusion power is. This is principally because of the extreme competence of the public relations office at the Livermore Laboratory, a federally supported facility in northern California. For many years the publicity agent at this lab, guided by the presence and spirit of Edward Teller, announced a significant new "breakthrough" in fusion research every three months.[13] If paper "breakthroughs" could be converted into peaceful power, the United States would be awash in electricity by now.

Since we do not yet have fusion power, we do not know what problems a working system will present, but at the moment, despite all the clever publicity, we doubt that it can be a truly clean system. The heart of it would be "clean," but the fusion reaction has to be ignited by a "dirty" fission reaction. Moreover, the essential mechanism will probably have to be surrounded by a football-field sized installation that would be made steadily more radioactive by the intense radiation coming from the heart. Like all other nuclear power systems it would finally have to be decommissioned. Then what? Should it be buried in concrete? How safe would that be, considering the slow erosive powers of ground water? Or should it be taken apart? By whom? Before the "hot" parts could be transported elsewhere the giant plant would have to be cut up, by remotely controlled robots, into transportable pieces. Then comes the question: transported by what means? What if the vehicles (railroad cars or trucks) have accidents? And where is the "away" for this dangerous trash to be thrown to?

How Safe Are Nuclear Reactors?

The most defensible answers to this headlined question are: *We still don't know. We will probably never know.*

If those statements do not shock you, you must not be living in the modern world. Those for whom science technology is a religion will judge those sentiments either lèse-majesté or blasphemy. But they can be justified.

Let's look first at the history of the growth of the nuclear power industry. From the very beginning it was realized that we were dealing with a technology more dangerous than any other. That being so, what would be the truly conservative way to proceed? Surely it would be to make a quantitative estimate of the dangers before building the reactors. Was such a policy followed? No: some sixty reactors were built and licensed *before* a detailed quantitative estimate was made of the hazards. ("Fly now, pay later," as one airline used to advertise.)

Finally the Nuclear Regulatory Commission (the NRC) authorized a study that Congress underwrote to the tune of $2 million. It was carried out under the direction of Norman Rasmussen of the Massachusetts Institute of Technology and was variously known as the "Rasmussen report" and "WASH-1400." As is common among flights into the unknown, the analysis cost more than had been budgeted: somewhere between $4 and $5 million. The conclusions were released in 1975 in a 2,400-page document, available to the curious for $200. As one might suppose, this book did not make the best-seller list. But the NRC very foresightedly released a twelve-page "Executive Summary,"[14] and this *was* widely noticed. Significantly, the summary was released *fourteen months before* the complete study.[15]

Here we stop to note a deceptive strategy that is often employed in politically sensitive matters: couple an unreadable magnum opus with an eminently readable short summary. Newspaper reporters work under tight deadlines. Given twenty-four hundred densely printed pages of data and equations, plus twelve pages of ordinary prose on Monday noon, with a story deadline of ten o'clock that evening, what does the reporter read first? Need we ask? In fact, how probable is it that he will ever get around to looking carefully at the twenty-four hundred pages? And when, as in this case, the report trails the summary by more than a year, the final report is published into a vacuum of public attention.

Bureaucrats are not unaware of the way human nature works. It is not uncommon for the executive summary to be optimistic when the full report is anything but. How is John Q. Public to know where the truth lies? Since he has his daily bread to earn he can hardly carry out an investigation of his own.

It should be noted that the reception of the full Rasmussen report by the scientific community was unfavorable from the beginning. The American Physical Society appointed a special committee to evaluate it. The committee said that the prime method of attack, the "fault tree analysis," was erroneous, obsolete, and merely educated guessing. In another report several physicists pointed out that, in a nuclear reactor, the number of possible sequences of events that could lead to accidents is extremely large, perhaps of the order of billions. In general, it is impossible to demonstrate that a fault tree is complete.[16]

The possibility of sabotage was brushed aside by the Rasmussen report. Admittedly, this is a difficult factor to quantify; but the risk remains none the less. Criticisms were serious enough by 1979 to cause the NRC to withdraw its support of the Rasmussen report. Several million dollars had gone down the drain.

No new study was planned, nor is it likely that one ever will be. The problem of nuclear safety is intractable. An estimation of risks has to be made on the basis of experience or theory. For experience to be of value there must be many repetitions of similar accidents. Insurers can rationally estimate the risk of having an automobile accident because they have years of experience (thousands of accidents) to work with. Risk assessors have no such long run of nuclear accidents. And when it comes to theory, we are even worse off: there is no agreement on the best theories to use.

What one tries to do in a theoretical analysis is estimate the probability of each small malfunction and then (by the rules of probability) combine the separate estimates into one over-all figure. Unfortunately some of the rules are ambiguous. Moreover, when the work is finished, how do you know that you have taken account of *every* possible interaction of the parts? It is always possible that the interaction of safety elements may actually cause an accident: we have no way of surely ruling out this possibility. Then if (like the committee), you don't even consider the effect of the aging of metals, of human failure, and of sabotage by human beings— of what value is your final answer? Not much.

The American Three Mile Island near-disaster in 1979 was caused by human failures that were not anticipated in the Rasmussen report. The Russian Chernobyl disaster in 1986 was also caused by gross human failures.

How hopeless the estimation of nuclear risk really is, is indicated with blinding clarity by the behavior of business and government toward the proposal that insurance be created to cover the possible losses from nuclear accidents. When the federal government first broached the possibility of taming the atom to generate electricity, business interests immediately let it be known that they would not join in the effort unless they were freed of legal liability for any accidents. So the government said it would underwrite the necessary liability insurance, *but only to the extent of some $560 million per accident* (the Price-Anderson Act). Yet from the beginning it was apparent that an accident causing billions of dollars in damages was a real possibility. Recently in Russia, in the Chernobyl accident, possibility became reality. It is obvious that under the Price-Anderson Act, if we continue with the generation of electricity by nuclear means, some of our citizens (or their heirs) will some day have to accept a recompense of a few cents on the dollar.

Time after time during the past forty years government spokesmen have assured us that the probability of a serious nuclear accident is trifling. But in insurance, betting, and business, the best test of sincerity is this: *Put your money where your mouth is.* The Price-Anderson Act clearly says that the government's large mouth is almost empty.

A New Priesthood?

One of the persistent defenders of nuclear power has been Alvin Weinberg, long-time director of the Oak Ridge National Laboratory in Tennessee, and active in the development of both the atomic bomb and peaceful power. In 1972 he wrote a much-quoted defense of nuclear power that, while frankly acknowledging the hazards, gave an optimistic "spin" to the prognosis (Box 15-3).[17] Two years later he returned to the problem, saying:

> The price that we must pay for this great boon is a vigilance that in many ways transcends what we have ever had to maintain: vigilance and care in operating these devices, and creation, and continuation into eternity, of a cadre or priesthood who understand the nuclear systems, and who are prepared to guard the wastes. To those of us whose business it is to supply power here and now, such speculations about 100,000 year-priesthoods must strike an eerie and unreal sound.[18]

No nation has ever been stable for 1,000 years, much less for 100,000; our nation is a mere stripling less than 300 years old. It is difficult to imagine a stable priesthood in an unstable nation. The thought of a nuclear priesthood that persists over 100,000 years is indeed "eerie and unreal." We have seen many governments

---

Box 15-3. Alvin Weinberg: A Technologist Calls for Religious Dedication.

We nuclear people have made a Faustian bargain with society. On the one hand, we offer an inexhaustible source of energy. . . . But the price that we demand of society for this magical source is both a vigilance and a longevity of our social institutions that we are quite unaccustomed to. . . .

We make two demands. The first, which I think is the easier to manage, is that we exercise in nuclear technology the very best techniques and that we use people of high expertise and purpose. Quality assurance is the phrase that permeates much of the nuclear community these days. It connotes using the highest standards of engineering design and execution; of maintaining proper discipline in the operation of nuclear plants in the face of the natural tendency to relax as a plant becomes older and more familiar; and perhaps of managing and operating our nuclear power plants with people of higher qualification than were necessary for managing and operating nonnuclear power plants; in short, of creating a continuing tradition of meticulous attention to detail.

The second demand is less clear, and I hope it may prove to be unnecessary. We have relatively little problem dealing with wastes if we can assume always that there will be intelligent people around to cope with eventualities we have not thought of. . . .

Is mankind prepared to exert the eternal vigilance needed to ensure proper and safe operation of its nuclear energy system? This admittedly is a significant commitment that we ask of society. What we offer in return, an all but infinite source of relatively cheap and clean energy, seems to me to be well worth the price.

"Social Institutions and Nuclear Energy, 1972.

collapse in our time. We have no reason to think that ours is immune to dissolution. If a government dissolves into chaos, what happens to the priesthood that is charged with guarding and monitoring its accumulated nuclear wastes? What then happens to the grandchildren born into a world without order?

Monitoring Made Explicit

A great merit of Weinberg's analysis is that it makes very clear that system reliability is *not* a problem that can be solved by technology: the heart of the problem lies in human nature.

Consider what it must be like to be employed in a nuclear plant. Imagine yourself sitting, day after day, watching the excursion of scores of dials and the flashing of signal lights. Because the system is well designed, built-in automatic responses take care of most of the situations that arise. Days go by, and you don't have to do a thing. Weeks go by; months, perhaps even years pass without incident: you might as well be a knot on a log for all the good you're doing. Then . . .

At some unforeseen moment something significant happens. Hastily you try to remember what it is that you are supposed to do. You take down your manual of procedures and, with clumsy and clammy fingers, you try to find the right page. Maybe you find it. If you don't, in a panic you shout: "Hey, Joe, what do I do now?"

Time passes. . . .

And remember, on the scale of nuclear events a second is a near-eternity. If you, who never finished high school and have only the benefit of a special "quickie" course of instruction in the operation of some of the most sophisticated scientific equipment of our time, fail to come up with the best response to a "deviation," are you to blame? Blameworthy or not, the survival in good health of tens of thousands of people may depend on your doing the right thing the first time. That's a fearsome load to lay on a high-school dropout!

Obviously (some may say) we should hire Ph.D. physicists to man our nuclear plants. Sounds nice; but try to do it! Try to find people who are bright enough and ambitious enough to fight their way through to a Ph.D. in physics who will be content to spend the rest of their lives sitting on their fannies in front of a control panel *doing nothing* month after month. Would any wages society offered be enough to entice such people to take on such a job? Almost certainly not. Or, if the persuasion offered or the coercion exerted would be enough to staff such positions today, how likely is it that persuasion and coercion would be effective generation after generation into the indefinite future?

In engineering publications the interrelationships of the various elements of a complex system are indicated by lines (or arrows) linking nonhuman elements. The fact that human beings are involved is not shown on such "flow charts." The reader is assumed to know that. But deliberate omission breeds unconscious forgetting. In the interests of safety *the human elements should be included in every linkage of a systems diagram.* The major categories of system linkages should be shown in somewhat the following fashion.

Facility assembled *by human beings.* Assemblies checked *by human beings.* The human checkers are themselves checked *by human beings.* When the system is operating, the dials are read *by human beings.* The dial readers' reports are checked *by human beings.* The records of the checkers are vouched for *by human beings.* Emergencies are met by steps taken *by human beings.* The personnel are vetted for reliability *by human beings.* Evidence of the aging of equipment must be noted and reported *by human beings.* The reports of malfunctions due to aging must be taken seriously *by human beings* outside the control rooms.

The human element that is here only barely indicated actually involves thousands of human beings. And who are these human beings? Weinberg said they should be "people of high expertise and purpose," and their vigilance should be "eternal." So what people does one find inside our nuclear power plants? Conscientious Quakers? Men and women with Ph.D. degrees in physics? Albert Einstein? Enrico Fermi? Or . . . Alvin Weinberg?

Hardly! The degradation of the moral atmosphere in nuclear control rooms is suggested by the large number of reported cases of operators' buying, selling, and using drugs; drinking alcohol; and even sleeping on the job. Their behavior in emergencies has often been what one would expect—certainly not that of a dedicated priesthood. As for their technical training, few have any training in physics, few have any sort of university degree, and many have not even graduated from high school.

Adam Smith could have predicted all this. In effect, he did, as the quotation in Box 15-4 makes obvious.[19] One of the weaknesses of "bottom line" thinking in business is that the bottom line comes at the end of the next fiscal quarter (or, at its latest, at the end of the fiscal year). In the short run it is economic to design work to be as routine as possible so that it demands no intelligence, no initiative. In the long run, short-term efficiency can be disastrous.

In this analysis we see one more instance of the importance of asking the ecologist's question, *And then what?* Repeated acts generate policies, and policies have consequences. Adam Smith saw the first consequence of rewarding purely routine work: selection, within each individual, of behavior that would in the long run be counterproductive. To Smith's insight we can now make an addition: selection among individuals, at the hiring level, for temperamental types that will accept boring employment. In despair, pessimists are tempted to conclude that *we have infinite faith in the unreliability of man.* But this is too global a statement. More prosaically it should be said that (1) people differ, and (2) selection ultimately wreaks its consequences—wanted or not, foreseen or not.

Now and then a voice is raised to point out a *conceivable* solution to the nuclear problem: engineer into the system a few infrequent, unpredictable accidents to keep

---

Box 15-4. Adam Smith on Deadly Boring Work.

The man whose whole life is spent in performing a few simple operations, of which the effects too are, perhaps, always the same, or very nearly the same, has no occasion to exert his understanding, or to exercise his invention in finding out expedients for removing difficulties which never occur. He naturally loses, therefore, the habit of such exertion, and generally becomes as stupid and ignorant as it is possible for a human being to become.

The Wealth of Nations, 1776.

the monitors on their toes. The mortality need not be great, but a little mortality would get more attention than none. Even though the long-term loss of life might be less with such an operational system than without it, there is no chance that responsible engineers would, given our moral values and our legal liability laws, ever consent to create such a system. The reaction of the engineer Samuel Florman may be taken as typical:

> No right-thinking person will wish for casualties in order to make a point. (I recall the revulsion with which I read an article by an anti-nuclear advocate entitled "What This Country Needs Is a Meltdown.") But there is no denying that in the absence of outrage many things are ignored that ought not to be ignored, and nothing produces outrage as readily as large numbers of simultaneous, accidental civilian deaths.[20]

One last unwelcome thought: what if incompetence were enriched with malevolence? What if the ethnocentrism, social friction, violence, and terrorism experienced by our society during the past few decades should escalate further? How long could a Weinbergian priesthood remain nonpartisan in a society that frequently mandates the "politically correct" education that encourages separatism, ethnic sovereignty, and obligatory "diversity"?[21] How long could thick sanctuary walls insulate a nuclear priesthood from the surging troubles of the outside world?

The Reductio ad Paradoxum of Nuclear Energy

What do technological optimists seek as a solution to "the population problem"? Surely it is this: that despite unfettered reproduction we should have prosperity and good health for all. Since unlimited reproduction is possible only if resources are without limit, two proposals have been made. First, that we tap the unlimited resources of space; second that we find unlimited resources here on earth. In Chapter 2 we saw that the resources of space could be tapped only if the passengers on board the Spaceship Mayflower would submit to absolutely rigid control of their reproduction for the centuries it would take to reach a distant colonizable planet. But it was the rigid control of reproduction that the spaceship passengers sought to evade by emigration. So this "solution" to the population problem was invalidated by a reductio ad paradoxum.

Now we see that the case for a nuclear solution to the population problem here on earth runs up against a similar reductio. Hoping to support unlimited reproduction with an "all but infinite source" of terrestrial energy, we find that that can be done only if human society can muster a dedicated nuclear priesthood that will remain uncorrupted for thousands of years. But if the human species is so amenable to discipline as to submit to this sort of control, why not solve the population/ resources problem more simply by taking two measures: (1) by making fewer demands on terrestrial resources; and (2) by submitting human reproduction to human control? Both measures would involve an increase in the control of individuals by society, but both together would be less oppressive than the "nuclear priesthood" required to make a dependence on nuclear power work.

16

Trying to Escape Malthus

Before Malthus appeared on the scene, William Godwin recognized that the expanding population might ultimately produce an unfavorable ratio of population to resources which could create a problem. Five years later Malthus viewed this problem as an inevitable result of human nature reacting to a world of limits. Godwin, however (in the passage previously quoted at the end of Box 3-1) had proposed to solve the population by changing human nature. He suggested that some day our species might "cease to propagate." Since this was written in England two hundred years ago, in the absence of contradictory evidence we can only assume that Godwin was postulating an end to human sexual activity. He no doubt thought the sacrifice would be worthwhile because, in his utopia, there would be "no war, no crimes, no administration of justice, as it is called, and no government. Besides this, there will be neither disease, anguish, melancholy, nor resentment."[1]

Most of Godwin's suppositions are too ridiculous to linger over, but one of them deserves an extended analysis because it touches on a general principle that will be called upon repeatedly as we continue to look for ways to avoid overpopulation. There is not the ghost of a chance that the human species will ever "cease to propagate." The reason is found in the great discovery made by Charles Darwin sixty years later: *selection.*

Natural Selection, a Basic Default Position of Biology

Suppose, following Godwin, that the natural fertility of our species evolves almost all the way to zero. Then what? Initially, fertile individuals might be but a tiny minority of the whole; but, over time, selection would ensure the dominance of the fertile fraction. If there were even the slightest genetic basis for fecundity in human beings (as indeed there is in other animals) then fertile human beings would in time replace the infertile. To postulate a *selection for universal sterility* (as Godwin's scheme would require) is to perpetrate an oxymoron.[2] Nature does not work with oxymorons.

We who are alive now are the descendents of an unbroken line of fertile ancestors. This line extends back millions of years to the first humanoids—indeed, billions of years to the beginning of sexual life of any kind. Powerful though she is, Nature cannot create a self-sustaining, totally infertile, sexual species. (Nonsexual, vegetative reproduction is common among plants, of course, but not many people are interested in promoting that.)

160

The history of population disputes is a long litany of attempts to evade problems rather than solve them. This book began with a demonstration that population problems cannot be solved by fleeing to the stars. Escaping biology here on earth is equally impossible.

The Doctrine of Human Exemptionism

Godwin's astonishing postulation of a zero-fertility society had its roots in the anthropocentric bias of most religious views of man's place in nature. ("Man" is entirely correct in this sentence—not "man and woman"—because most surviving religions are male biased.) As the God of Genesis said: "Let us make man in our image, after our likeness, and let him have dominion over the fish of the sea, the birds of the air, the domestic animals, the wild beasts, and all the land reptiles."[3]

Since only man was made in God's image, did this not mean that man must be essentially and inescapably different from all other animals? In Judeo-Christian ideology the unity of living things plays second fiddle to the differences between men and animals. (It is only since Darwin that Christians have been able to speak of "men and *other* animals.") It was insisted that man was exempt from the laws that governed the others. This, the *exemptionist doctrine,* survived the decay of conventional religion in the eighteenth century as it was incorporated into the romanticism of the nineteenth. The German poet and playwright Friedrich Schiller (1759–1805), in a letter written to a fellow wordsmith six weeks before his death, said: "After all, both of us are idealists, and should be ashamed to have it said that the material world formed us, instead of being formed by us."[4] Would Schiller be proud of his species if he were told of all the instances we now know of man's making a mess of the material world? How joyful would Schiller be—Schiller, the author of the "Hymn to Joy" of Beethoven's Ninth Symphony—were he told how man has turned half of India into a desert? No other single species of animal could have done it; is this the glory of exemptionist status?

In a few crucial respects, man *is* superior to the "beasts" (to use a word much favored in the nineteenth century). For instance: no beast writes or reads books. Literacy creates a great gulf between men and beasts. With respect to the subject that is the burden of this book (the causes of human population growth), Condorcet pointed out that man clearly transcends animal limitations, for "he alone, among all the animals, has found a way to separate, in the act which should perpetuate the species, the gratification inherent in that act and the procreation which, in other species, is the involuntary cause of it."[5] That's a pretty delicate way of mentioning contraception, but it didn't fool Malthus who, strange as it may seem now, disapproved of artificial birth control.

Buried in the bias created by the human exemptionist doctrine, sociologists William Catton and Riley Dunlap discern the following four important elements:

1. People are fundamentally different from all other creatures on earth, over which they have dominion.
2. People are masters of their destiny; they can choose their goals and learn to do whatever is necessary to achieve them.

3. The world is vast, and thus provides unlimited opportunities for humans.
4. The history of humanity is one of progress; for every problem there is a solution, and thus progress need never cease.[6]

Challenges to this anthropocentric and optimistic set of beliefs are now being made because it is patently unecological. Most of the abilities of men, however one measures them, are shared with other animals; only a few, like literacy, are confined to the human species. Unfortunately, as Dunlap pointed out, exemptionism still "appears to be the majority position in the social sciences, particularly within economics."[7]

Materialism Equals Pessimism?

The essence of Malthus's contribution to population theory is not his geometric and arithmetic series, but the demostat that is implicit in his writings, the essence of which is diagrammed in Figure 16-1, a simplification of the earlier Figure 11-2. Temporary changes in population size due to environmental fluctuations are shown by dashed arrows. The resulting mismatch of population and resources ("misery" or "felicity") produces a response change that reduces or increases the population, as shown by the solid arrows. Because of its functional significance, negative feedback can be called "corrective feedback."

Most of the time, in most animal populations, the demostat adequately accounts for the facts. Even in human populations demostatic control has been tightly maintained during most of human history. It is only the rapid upward shift in the set point during the past few centuries that has encouraged doubts of the generality of the demostatic model. The rapid progress of the scientific-industrial revolution caused the shifting of the set point.

Those who hold that the resources of the world are ultimately limited conclude that the upward movement of the set point must finally come to an end. At this

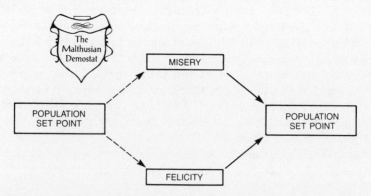

Figure 16-1. The Malthusian demostat in its simplest form. Dashed lines show changes impressed on the population by fluctuations in resource availability. These impressed changes are countered by natural response changes (solid lines), which restore the population to its set point size.

Box 16-1. Boulding on Malthus's "Utterly Dismal Theorem."

A good example of [an explanatory model] is the Malthusian theory. This is the famous dismal theorem of economics that if the only check on the growth of population is starvation and misery, then no matter how favorable the environment or how advanced the technology the population will grow until it is miserable and starves. The theorem, indeed, has a worse corollary which has been described as the utterly dismal theorem. This is the proposition that if the only check on the growth of population is starvation and misery, then any technological improvement will have the ultimate effect of increasing the sum of human misery, as it permits a larger population to live in precisely the same state of misery and starvation as before the change.

There are enough known examples of the operations of Malthusian systems in history to make the model highly relevant even in the present day. . . . The experience of Ireland is an extremely interesting case in point. In the late seventeenth century, the population of Ireland was about two million people living in misery. Then came the seventeenth-century equivalent of [foreign aid], the introduction of the potato, a technological revolution of first importance enabling the Irish to raise much more food per acre than they had ever done before. The result of this benevolent technological improvement was an increase in population from two million to eight million by 1845. The result of the technological improvement, therefore, was to quadruple the amount of human misery on the unfortunate island. The failure of the potato crop in 1845 led to disastrous consequences. Two million Irish died of starvation; another two million emigrated; and the remaining four million learned a sharp lesson which has still not been forgotten. The population of Ireland has been roughly stationary since that date, in spite of the fact that Ireland is a predominantly Roman Catholic country. The stability has been achieved by an extraordinary increase in the age at marriage.

The Image, 1956.

---

point the Malthusian demostat clearly takes over as the two regions of disequilibrium, "misery" and "felicity," govern feedback. This diagram is implicit in Malthus (who drew no diagrams), but it remained for the economist Kenneth Boulding[8] to make it fully explicit. It does not disturb people to learn that a decrease in population leads (other things being equal) to an increase in the reproductive rate; this seems a rational response to an increase in felicity. But the other response of the demostat—a decrease in the reproductive rate following an increase in misery— has offended the admirable humanitarian spirit that has grown up during the past two centuries. "Isn't it enough," some say, "that the poor are *poor?* Must we also say they must be deprived of the joys of parenthood?"

A Malthusian may feel just as much empathy with the poor, but he warns us of the probable consequences of any increase in the food supply, as may be caused by improved technology or generous foreign aid. In his day, Malthus condemned domestic "poor relief" because production was thus encouraged, while misery was continued at a higher level of population. It was this legitimate deduction from Malthusian theory that led Boulding to speak of the "utterly dismal theorem" (Box 16-1). Tender-hearted humanitarians use the deduction as an excuse for denying the truth of Malthusian theory. Boulding accepted the truth.

The Malthusian demostat is a major default position for all of biology. The advice implied by Figure 16-1 makes evolutionary sense: invest in success (an increase in the resources/population ratio), but disinvest in failure (a decrease in the resources/population ratio). Nonhuman animals behave according to this pattern: natural selection favors such species-rationality. If human beings insist on interfering with the natural mortality of the young in a community that has overshot the carrying capacity, they must balance this policy with another, namely making aid to the poor contingent upon the adoption of fertility-reducing measures (such as sterilization or an enforceable contract to have fewer children). Many humanitarians are shocked at such suggestions: "Unthinkable!" they exclaim. If it is indeed unthinkable, civilization has arrived at a disastrous cul-de-sac.

Are Human Beings Rational?

Human affairs are certainly more complicated than the affairs of other animals. The apparent lack of consistency in human behavior creates a formidable gauntlet to be run by every theory proposed. Even before the demostat was implicitly advanced by Malthus, several observers noticed contrary behavior that would later be cited to challenge the Malthusian explanatory scheme. Long before Malthus, Adam Smith called attention to the great fecundity of some poor Scots mothers[9] (Box 16-2). But notice that he pursued the matter further, pointing out that a very *fecund* mother might be notably *infertile*—that is might leave few descendents to become parents in the next generation. The quoted passage clearly describes a Malthusian demostat in the days before the welfare state. With the coming of the welfare state compassion created new problems for the would-be exceptionalist species *Homo sapiens.* (How long would a genetic line of nonhuman animals last if compassion caused it to invest in failure?)

No doubt about it, human behavior does create problems. Boswell's Dr. John-

---

Box 16-2. Adam Smith on Human Fertility.

Poverty, though it no doubt discourages, does not always prevent marriage. It seems even to be favourable to generation. A half-starved Highland woman frequently bears more than twenty children, while a pampered fine lady is often incapable of bearing any, and is generally exhausted by two or three. Barrenness, so frequent among women of fashion, is very rare among those of inferior station. Luxury in the fair sex, while it inflames perhaps the passion for enjoyment, seems always to weaken, and frequently to destroy altogether, the powers of generation.

But poverty, though it does not prevent the generation, is extremely unfavourable to the rearing of children. The tender plant is produced, but in so cold a soil, and so severe a climate, soon withers and dies. It is not uncommon, I have been frequently told, in the Highlands of Scotland, for a mother who has borne twenty children not to have two alive. . . .

Every species of animals naturally multiplies in proportion to the means of their subsistence, and no species can ever multiply beyond it. But in civilized society it is only among the inferior ranks of people that the scantiness of subsistence can set limits to the further multiplication of the human species; and it can do so in no other way than by destroying a great part of the childen which their fruitful marriages produce.

The Wealth of Nations, 1776.

son, who left few human actions unjudged, touched on the motivations that lead human beings to procreate. In the conversation of 26 October 1769 (when Malthus was only three years old) Johnson said: "It is not from reason and prudence that people marry, but from inclination. A man is poor; he thinks, 'I cannot be worse, and so I'll e'en take Peggy.'"

This remark calls attention to the fact that the Malthusian demostat assumes that human beings are rational. When it is very hard to eke out an existence, would a rational person make his (or her) situation worse by assuming an obligation to keep additional persons (babies) alive? Certainly not, yet Dr. Johnson says that people sometimes behave that way. Anyone of wide experience can cite corroborative instances. Either people sometimes act irrationally (which casts doubt on the explanatory power of the demostat), or there are other human motivations that the abstract scheme of Figure 16-1 does not encompass.

By contrast, many instances are known in the nonhuman world in which caretaking animals accurately match their family commitments to the probable quality of future environments.[10] Birds, for instance, commonly lay fewer eggs in inclement weather than they do when food is more abundant. Perhaps those who so passionately defend the doctrine of human exemptionism would settle for the conclusion that the human species, unlike lesser species, is uniquely susceptible to attacks of irrational behavior?

Can Charity Make an Antidemostat Work?

The Malthusian demostat predicts that prosperity will increase the growth rate of the population, while hard times will diminish it. Even in Malthus's time critics called attention to a correlation that appeared to contradict the Malthusian prediction: prosperous countries often have a lower fertility rate than poor countries. The data have led to alternative theories.

The first important anti-Malthusian theory was advanced in 1832 (two years before Malthus's death) by Thomas Rowe Edmonds (1803–1889)[11] (see Box 16-3). The anti-Malthusian scheme he proposed is quite simple: the poorer a people are the greater will be their fertility because (he said) the only amusement they have is sexual intercourse. Among the wealthy, sex must compete with other amusements. As wealth increases fertility falls.

To appreciate fully the lunacy of Edmonds's proposal we must call on the resources of graphing. An intellectual descendant of Oresme (Chapter 8) would convert Edmonds's prose into the diagram of Figure 16-2. In both directions, this antidemostat suffers from *positive* feedback (runaway feedback): misery-caused fertility produces even greater fertility, while the relative sterility caused by prosperity lowers the fertility. A tender-hearted philanthropist who admitted this would deprive himself of the emotional comfort of shipping food to the starving. The antidemostat implied by Edmonds and his spiritual descendants offers, in the end, two equally unacceptable results: universal starvation through overpopulation, or universal sterility through excess prosperity. Of course the end-points of the anti-Malthusian theory are seldom mentioned: at each moment all that is requested is just a little more "charity." In the 1970s, the rallying cry of the international anti-Mal-

---

Box 16-3. Edmonds: An Implicit Anti-Demostat Makes its Appearance.

Population does not actually increase in strict conformity with the received opinions upon that subject. It is quite possible for the ratio of increase to be small in countries possessing a lavish abundance of food. . . . Amongst the great body of the people at the present moment, sexual intercourse is the only gratification; and thus, by a most unfortunate concurrence of adverse circumstances, population goes on augmenting at a period when it ought to be restrained. To better the condition of the labouring classes, that is, to place more food and comforts before them, however paradoxical it may appear, is the wisest mode to check redundancy. On this principle many singular anomalies in Ireland can be explained. The increase of poverty in that country, which has certainly taken place within the last generation, has increased the number of births, and probably also the adult population. Were that country to emerge from her present condition, and were the object to restrain a further supply of labourers, the wisest course would be to give the people a greater command over the necessaries of life. When they are better fed they will have other enjoyments at command than sexual intercourse, and their numbers, therefore, will not increase in the same proportion as at present.

An Enquiry into the Principles of Population, 1832.

---

thusians became "Take care of the people and population will take care of itself." Before we join in this crusade we should note that failure has been the result of all attempts to control overpopulation among herds of game animals by bringing in food. Professional game managers have constantly to struggle against tenderhearted "animal lovers" whose demands for more food derive from the antidemostat unknowingly postulated by Edmonds.

If human populations were indeed governed by an antidemostat, we would be confronted with a clear instance of human exemptionism. No ancient animal species could have survived to the present had its population been governed by an antidemostat. If an antidemostat determines the future of the human species, then our species cannot survive much longer. In that case we shall soon be the conscious witness of our own extinction. (Now there's a distinction that *cannot* be claimed by any other species. There's exemptionist doctrine with a vengeance!)

Obviously Edmonds never thought in terms of graphs. Edmonds (not surprisingly) failed to follow the procedure that should guide anyone who aspires to be the author of a robust theory:

> *Rule 1.* Take a simple idea.
> *Rule 2.* Take it seriously.

Taking an idea seriously means developing its logical consequences, *and never denying them.* No other species of animal could survive for more than a geological moment of time if it were governed by an antidemostat; and no mechanism has been proposed that would ensure the persistence and survival of human populations governed by an antidemostat. Nonetheless (as we shall presently see) from 1832 to the present, one antidemostatic agent after another has been proposed for the control of human populations. Why have such irrational theories always managed to gain a respectable following?

As far as Edmonds is concerned, it is probable that one of the most attractive features of his argument was his assertion that among the unwashed masses, "sexual intercourse is the only gratification." Though it was five years before Victoria would ascend the British throne, 1832 was already well into the Victorian era, culturally speaking, for sex was already a taboo topic. But poverty was an embarrassing one, so it was all right if one imputed great sexual activity to the uneducated, uncultured masses. The privileged classes could see themselves as above that sort of thing and claim *reproductive restraint,* even if it implied some infertility. Edmonds's argument pandered to the class pride of those rich enough to buy his book.

An equally powerful attraction of his argument lay in its proposal of a form of action that was much esteemed in his century (and ours). Charity is praised by all major religions, but both the praise and practice of charity increased markedly in the nineteenth century (partly, no doubt, because increasing prosperity made the practice of charity less costly in real, personal terms). Unlike Malthus who, with

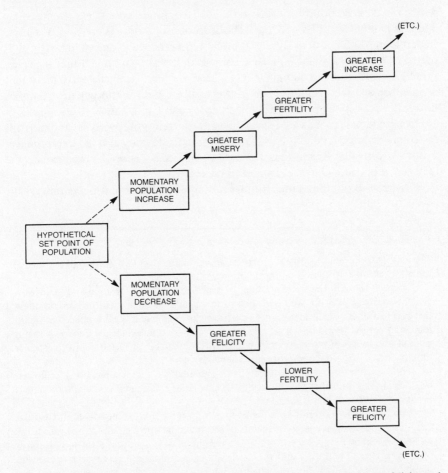

Figure 16-2. A hypothetical antidemostat created by an inverse relation between felicity and fertility. The hypothetical set point is doubly unstable: positive feedback tends to extinguish the population through either zero felicity or zero fertility, which (by hypothesis) results from unlimited felicity.

Christ, assumed that the poor must always be with us (Matthew 26:11), Edmonds accepted the ideas of progress and human exemptionism, saying that to counteract the superfluity of the poor we need only "place more food and comforts before them."

Charitable people waxed enthusiastic over Edmonds's proposal. Away with the pessimism of Malthus's utterly dismal theorem! Down with the demon demostat that supports it! Up with the optimism of the antidemostat! Malthusians just sit on their hands and watch the poor suffer, while really nice people feed them and furnish them with new diversions. Such are the sentiments that guided charity in the nineteenth and twentieth centuries.

Does Physiology Provide an Antidemostat?

A decade after Edmonds another variant of the antidemostat was proposed by Thomas Doubleday (1790–1870).[12] The heart of his position is given in Box 16-4. In developing his argument Doubleday followed a procedure long endorsed by biologists: he looked at what plants and animals did, and then argued that the same principles must apply to human beings. This procedure has the negative merit that it does not assume exemptionism; however if the author chooses his examples unwisely he can easily be led astray. Doubleday chose unwisely.

If caged female rabbits are fed very generously they grow overly fat and may fail to become pregnant. Female pigs (sows) that are too fat may also fail to reproduce. From these rustic observations Doubleday deduced a general law: fecundity is inversely proportional to the richness of the diet.

His error, to put the matter simply, was in using domesticated creatures as his

---

Box 16-4. Doubleday: Gluttony as Feedback in the Anti-Demostat.

There is in all societies a constant increase going on amongst that portion of it which is the worst supplied with food; in short, amongst the poorest.

Amongst those in the state of affluence, and well supplied with food and luxuries, a constant decrease goes on. Amongst those who form the mean or medium between these two opposite states, that is to say, amongst those who are tolerably well supplied with good food, and not overworked, nor yet idle, population is stationary. Hence it follows, that it is upon the *numerical proportion* which these three states bear to each other in any society that increase or decrease upon the whole depends. . . .

It is a fact, admitted by all gardeners as well as botanists, that if a tree, plant, or flower, be placed in mould, either naturally or artificially made too rich for it, a plethoric state is produced, and fruitfulness ceases. . . .

[Similarly] There cannot be a doubt that, with animal creation—including in that term birds and quadrupeds (of the habits of fish we know little or nothing)—fecundity is totally checked by the plethoric state. . . . This is more or less the case even with the most prolific animals. The rabbit and the swine are extraordinary in this respect; yet every schoolboy knows that the doe, or female rabbit, and every farmer and breeder knows that the sow will *not* conceive if fed to a certain height of fatness; and that the number of the progeny is generally in the *ratio* of the *leanness* of the animal.

The True Law of Population, 1842.

model rather than wild ones. In the wild, for instance, there is a nearly zero chance that a female rabbit will take in enough nourishment to sterilize herself. Advancing the argument two decades to the time when Darwinian reasoning took over, one must point out that, in the wild, an obese animal would soon fall prey to a swifter predator and so its fertility would no longer be an object of selection. The relative sterility of obese domestic animals does not reveal *The True Law of Population* (Doubleday's book title).

Under natural conditions, when fecundity is affected at all by diet, it is directly (not inversely) proportional to the adequacy of the diet. In terms of evolution this correlation makes sense (as the converse relationship does not). When an animal is grossly malnourished it would be dangerous for it to channel the few available calories into the production of babies, because the early death of the parent might condemn the offspring to die. Only animals that are adequately nourished can afford the luxury of reproduction, which (for females) is an energetically expensive business. The fact that grossly overfed animals are sterile has no more evolutionary significance than the fact that human beings in an atmosphere of 100 percent oxygen die in a few hours. Food is good, oxygen is good: but under artificial conditions it is easy to impose "too much of a good thing" on man or beast.

Putting analogical arguments aside we note that there is a gratifying consistency in the data on the fertility of human beings as a function of the level of nutrition. Studies by Rose Frisch have shown that well-nourished women are statistically more fecund than poorly nourished ones.[13] And Ancel Keys's studies of civilian populations during the World War II revealed that severely malnourished adults in occupied Europe virtually ceased to reproduce.[14] This was not because they made greater use of artificial contraceptives (which were often hard to come by). What one might call the natural contraceptive of physiological change accounted for the infertility. Starving women failed to ovulate (as indicated by their failure to menstruate); starving men failed to produce the plethora of sperm cells that are required for male fertility. And with the most severe malnutrition, sexual desire itself disappeared in both sexes. From a selectionist point of view the findings all make sense (as Doubleday's hypothesis does not). Nature, unlike theoreticians, is seldom stupid.

The antidemostatic interpretation of nutrition is effectively dead in the scientific community; but in the literate world this theory, like Lazarus, comes to life again every now and then. In 1952 a Brazilian author, Josué de Castro, devoted a whole book to such a theory, identifying proteins as the antidemostatic factor. In *The Geography of Hunger* he wrote that "The groups with highest fertility are those who have the lowest percentage of complete proteins, animal proteins, in their regular diets."[15] (See Box 16-5 for the two closing paragraphs of his book.) His argument was less based on physiology than it was on a somewhat mystical appeal to good-hearted people to share their food with the starving. The human impulse to share food with the needy is felt by Malthusians too, but they are more aware than most people that sharing food today with extremely needy people will, unless balancing measures are adopted, actually *increase* suffering tomorrow.

Two faults can be charged against de Castro. The first concerns the way he handles statistics. Kingsley Davis, a demographer and sociologist, flatly said that "De Castro's mishandling of statistics throughout the book can hardly be attributed to

---

Box 16-5. De Castro Praises the Humaneness of Anti-Malthusian Controls.

The road to world survival, therefore, does not lie in the neo-Malthusian prescriptions to eliminate surplus people, nor in birth control, but in the effort to make everybody on the face of the earth productive. Hunger and misery are not caused by the presence of too many people in the world, but rather by having few to produce and many to feed. The neo-Malthusian doctrine of a dehumanized economy, which preaches that the weak and the sick should be left to die, which would help the starving to die more quickly, and which even goes to the extreme of suggesting that medical and sanitary resources should not be made available to the more miserable populations—such policies merely reflect the mean and egotistical sentiments of people living well, terrified by the disquieting presence of those who are living badly.

The world, fortunately, will not let itself be carried away by such defeatist and disintegrative conceptions. In spite of their scientific aura, these ideas cannot show us a road to survival. They can only point the way to death, to revolution and to war—the road to perdition.

The Geography of Hunger, 1952.

---

ignorance. . . . It seems due, instead, to passionate cheating because the mishandling always favors his argument."[16] The second and more general criticism is this: correlation is ambiguous. When a high protein diet is correlated with relative infertility does this mean that protein ingestion *causes* sterility? Or that people who voluntarily refrain from having too many children thereby enjoy a higher disposable income, some of which they spend on luxury foods? Or, more generally, that childless people have more money to spend on both good food and forms of recreation that distract them from the beastly activity condemned by Edmonds? When it comes to deducing *cause* from *correlation,* "You pays your money and you takes your choice."

Professionals who discussed de Castro's book almost uniformly gave it a low score. In so doing some reviewers pointed to an important reason for its appeal to the general reader. As Henry Pratt Fairchild said: "One must applaud the liberal spirit in which the author approaches his subject, his sincere feeling for humanity, his obvious distress over human suffering wherever found."[17] And in Paris, demographer Alfred Sauvy concluded his unfavorable review by granting that the book "has the shining merit of proposing a humane solution."[18] In other words, if you want to attract a popular following when talking about overpopulation (its ills and their cure), wear your heart on your sleeve and assert that we must find—somehow, somewhere—a cost-free and painless solution.

The Child Survival Hypothesis

Three years after the English publication of de Castro's book, the biologist Marston Bates[19] criticized him for discussing the effect of nutrition on fertility at the physiological level, saying: "I think that in man the cultural factors overwhelm any likely physiological effects." This thought was later expanded by Lester Brown, the founder of World Watch, a Washington think-tank devoted to population and environment matters. In a passage to which italics have here been added, he wrote:

> An assured food supply plays an important role in reducing birth rates. When malnutrition is widespread, even common childhood diseases are often fatal. The relationship between nutrition and human fertility is summed up in the observation that *good nutrition is the best contraceptive.* It is no coincidence that virtually all well-fed societies have low fertility, and poorly fed societies have high fertility. The effect of nutrition on fertility is in large measure indirect, through its effect on the infant mortality rate and on over-all life expectancy. Where malnutrition is widespread, it is virtually impossible to achieve low infant mortality rates.[20]

The theory here sketched by Brown is known as the "child survival hypothesis." This explanation of human fertility moves the focus from simple physiology to psychological and cultural forces—a permissible form of human exemptionist doctrine (which may or may not be true). Though seldom explicit, the framework of the theory is the following set of assumptions:

Rationality rules in the determination of family size.

When infant mortality is high, parents will have many children, to ensure that they have someone to take care of them in their old age.

When infant mortality is low, parents will stop their breeding at a smaller family size because they understand that few is plenty.

These facts justify a simple policy recommendation: To reduce the birthrate of a people, FIRST save their babies.

By contrast, the theory of the Malthusian demostat predicts that saving babies first will result in a faster rate of growth of population. This is what happened in Europe after Malthus's death, a period that saw the rise of both scientific bacteriology and private philanthropy. These factors, working together, increased the survival rate of babies; and the population grew faster.

Yet even in the earliest days of medical microbiology, in 1847 to be exact, an anonymous translator of Sismondi's *Political Economy* wrote in the preface: "Sanitary improvements, and *whatever tends to lengthen life,* are the most effectual means of restraining a too great increase of population."[21] The hypothesis ingrained in the italicized words was built into the original strategy of the Planned Parenthood movement—the birth control movement—in the twentieth century. One of the leaders expressed the strategy this way: "Parents will be most ready to learn family planning from the health workers who have gained their confidence by contributing to the survival of their children."[22] Explicitly put: save babies first, then use the prestige thus earned to sell birth control programs to the prolific poor. The strategy is plausible, and it has the merit of gaining financial support for Planned Parenthood organizations. But will a lower infant mortality really persuade parents to reduce the size of their families?

The question is hard to answer. One looks for supporting data from countries in which the child survival rate has increased to see what has happened to the birth rate—one looks for *empirical* evidence. But the trouble with empirical evidence is this: in each country *many* things are happening simultaneously, so how is one to know for sure *what causes what?* And what time frame shall we take for our analysis—a year, a decade, or two generations?

Empirical evidence can be found on both sides of the child survival argument. As demographer A. J. Coale pointed out: "The modern decline in mortality in Germany began at the same time as the decline in fertility . . . but when province-by-province records are examined, it is found that in about half the provinces the decline in fertility preceded the decline in infant mortality; so it is an open question which trend is the cause and which the effect."[23]

There is enough empirical evidence against the child survival hypothesis[24] to make an individual philanthropist think twice before investing his own money in projects based on this hypothesis. Of course, the administrators of a philanthropic organization, and the legislators of a republic, cheerfully invest the donations or taxes *of other people* in such projects, since the generosity of decision makers costs them but little (their share of the increased taxes, which come out of a commons). What do retrospective audits of the effects of such philanthropy show? Here is a sample.

A careful statistical study of Bangladesh showed no support for the child survival hypothesis. Improvements in the survival of infants resulted in a 4 percent decrease in fertility, which was overpowered by a 7 percent increase in the infant population due to greater survival.[25] Turkey: rural land redistribution—a favorite reform recommended to the governments of poor countries by socialistically inclined citizens of rich countries—caused former sharecroppers to double the number of their children, the average number rising to 6.4 per family.[26] "The Kenyan government's "assessment of its population policy in 1984 was that, while the maternal child health component had considerably improved the health of mothers and children, the family planning program had had little success. Despite the 'substantial effort' that had been put into the family planning programme, the government's economic survey for 1984 stated that attendance at family planning clinics had declined in recent years."[27] In Guatemala:

> Perceived child survival chances seem to have little influence on whether or not a woman desires additional children. . . . Reductions in child mortality may have the short-term effect of accelerating population growth, until enough experience with decreased mortality is accumulated to effect a change in fertility desires. . . . [The results suggest] that mortality declines must occur over two generations (her mother's and her own) to make a significant impact on a woman's desire for additional children.[28]

Finally we have the testimony of a high official of the Ford Foundation, which has invested many millions of dollars in bringing medicine and contraception to poor countries:

> In the short term . . . reduction of infant mortality does not assure reduction in fertility. Detailed studies of specific populations demonstrate that for every ten infant deaths prevented, from one to five fewer births result. In the short run, therefore, lowering infant mortality may lead to larger families and increased population growth, but in the long run, as more children survive, parents will want fewer children in order to provide them with better nurture and education.[29]

A careful reading of the rhetoric of the last statement makes it crystal clear that the asserted adverse short-term effect is based on experience, while only faith supports the asserted favorable long-term effect. Some philanthropists hold that the hoped-for long-term effect is adequate excuse for financing *today* the child-saving measures that will result in lower fertility at some unspecified *tomorrow*. This policy would not pose a serious danger if it were adopted only in nations that were grossly *under*populated. In such nations the population is (by definition) far from the carrying capacity of the land. A well-intentioned intervener would hope that long before the carrying capacity was reached the people would have lowered their fertility to the point at which a sustainable economy became a reality.

But, with few if any exceptions, poor countries are ones in which the population has already grown far beyond the humane carrying capacity of the land. Within two generations, birth control might indeed bring the fertility rate down to the zero population growth level. But in two generations the population of a country like Kenya, with an increase of about 4 percent per year, can soar fourfold—from, in Kenya's case, 25 million in 1990 to 100 million in the year 2025. To visualize what this might mean to Kenya in the future, it will help to compare Kenya's circumstances with America's.

In both area and population there was, at the end of the 1980s, almost exact equality between the nation of Kenya and the combined American states of Minnesota, Iowa, Illinois, and Indiana. The gross national product (GNP) per capita for Americans in general at that time was 15 times that of Kenyans. (GNP, though only a crude measure of well-being, is of some use.)

A major source of national income to Kenya is tourism. The principal reason tourists come to East Africa is to see the wild animals. With less soil and forest, and four times as many farmers demanding land in Kenya, how much would be left of the wildlife in 2025? Kenya is already suffering from deforestation and soil erosion. How much soil and forest would be left by the time, two generations later, when the postulated beneficial population effects of saving babies took effect?

Unfortunately deforestation and soil erosion are, in terms of ordinary human history, essentially irreversible evils. So also is the loss of wildlife. Saving human lives in the hope of selling population control is more certain than Russian roulette to lead to disaster. This reality poses a serious problem for conventional ethics and traditional religion.

Is Humanity a Cancer on the Face of the Earth?

From Edmonds to de Castro some very persuasive writers devoted their considerable talents to providing "soft" answers to population problems. The fact that their postulated antidemostatic mechanisms made no rational sense did not prevent the general public from taking the "optimists" to its bosom.

Rationalists who asserted their confidence in demostatic mechanisms have been castigated as "pessimists" and "misanthropes." It has taken courage to be an outspoken rationalist in this area. Such courage was shown by the physician Alan Gregg (1890–1957), a vice-president of the Rockefeller Foundation, an agency that spent many millions of dollars in saving lives in distant and overpopulated countries. As he neared retirement age Gregg asked some hard questions of his organization's philanthropic policies (Box 16-6).[30]

Box 16-6. Alan Gregg: Humanity as a Cancer of the Earth.

I propose to offer only one idea regarding the population problem. . . . It is . . . the view of one who has had a medical training—a single idea around which subordinate reflections of a rather general sort present themselves. . . .

New growths of any kind . . . involve an increase in the number of some one kind of cell and, hence, a corresponding increase in the size of the organ or tissue involved. . . . In all but one instance, organs and tissues in their growth seem to "know" when to stop. The exception, of course, is . . . cancer. . . .

I suggest, as a way of looking at the population problem, that there are some interesting analogies between the growth of the human population of the world and the increase of cells observable in neoplasms. To say that the world has cancer, and that the cancer cell is man, has neither experimental proof nor the validation of predictive accuracy; but I see no reason that instantly forbids such a speculation. . . .

What are some of the characteristics of new growths? One of the simplest is that they commonly exert pressure on adjacent structures and, hence, displace them. New growths within closed cavities, like the skull, exert pressures that kill, because any considerable displacement is impossible. Pressure develops, usually destroying first the function and later the substance of the normal cells thus pressed upon. For a comparison with a closed cavity, think of an island sheltering a unique form of animal life that is hunted to extinction by man. The limited space of the island resembles the cranial cavity whose normal contents cannot escape the murderous invader. Border warfare, mass migrations, and those wars that are described as being the result of population pressures resemble the pressures exerted by new growths. We actually borrow not only the word *pressure* but also the word *invasion* to describe the way in which new growths by direct extension preempt the space occupied by other cells or types of life. The destruction of forests, the annihilation or near extinction of various animals, and the soil erosion consequent to overgrazing illustrate the cancerlike effect that man—in mounting numbers and heedless arrogance—has had on other forms of life on what we call "our" planet.

Metastasis is the word used to describe another phenomenon of malignant growth in which detached neoplastic cells carried by the lymphatics or the blood vessels lodge at a distance from the primary focus or point of origin and proceed to multiply without direct contact with the tissue or organ from which they came. It is actually difficult to avoid using the word *colony* in describing this thing physicians call metastasis. Conversely, to what degree can colonization of the Western Hemisphere be thought of as metastasis of the white race?

Cancerous growths demand food; but, so far as I know, they have never been cured by getting it. Furthermore, although their blood supply is commonly so disordered that persistent bleeding from any body orifice suggests that a new growth is its cause, the organism as a whole often experiences a loss of weight and strength and suggests either poisoning or the existence of an inordinate nutritional demand by neoplastic cells—perhaps both. The analogies can be found in "our plundered planet"—in man's effect on other forms of life. These hardly need elaboration—certainly the ecologists would be prepared to supply examples in plenty of man's inroads upon other forms of life. Our rivers run silt— although we could better think of them as running the telltale blood of cancer.

At the center of a new growth, and apparently partly as a result of its inadequate circulation, necrosis often sets in—the death and liquidation of the cells that have, as it were, dispensed with order and self-control in their passion to reproduce out of all proportion to their usual number in the organism. How nearly the slums of our great cities resemble the necrosis of tumors raises the whimsical query: Which is the more offensive to decency and beauty, slums or the fetid detritus of a growing tumor?

A Medical Aspect of the Population Problem, 1955.

Gregg was a revered and powerful figure in the medical world, and his remarks were widely noted—and widely condemned. Gregg observed: "Cancerous growths demand food; but they have never been cured by getting it." This was later called "Gregg's Law."[31] The frankness of this "law" affronted the foreign aid establishment, which had the feeding of overpopulated countries as one of its major missions. After a brief period of notoriety, Gregg's Law disappeared from public consciousness. His paper is seldom included in anthologies on either population or the environment, though Dr. Gregg himself recognized that his argument had an important bearing on the environmental movement then in the process of being born.

One might have expected Alan Gregg's insight to play an important role in the genesis of Rachel Carson's *Silent Spring,* which appeared seven years later, but the index of Carson's book does not include Gregg. Carson was a voracious reader; she surely must have noticed Gregg's address at the time. Did she repress knowledge of it because she herself was suffering from a terminal cancer when she wrote her influential book? Or did she not refer to Gregg because she felt that the mere mention of so "controversial" a message might harm her cause?

The foreign aid establishment continued to distribute annually hundreds of millions of dollars overseas in the faith that antidemostatic mechanisms would ultimately prevail. Only after the political reversals of Marxism in Europe, culminating in the crises of the autumn of 1989, did the wealthy nations start to disassemble their most extreme and least productive "humanitarian aid" apparatus in sub-Saharan Africa, where diminution of the death rates had been accompanied by a disastrous increase in infant survival rates.[32]

Returning to the Rockefeller Foundation, we have to ask: did it, in the light of the statement made by its own vice-president, mend its ways and cease to promote population growth in already overpopulated countries? It did not. The saving of infant lives may originally have been intended as the means whereby poor people would be induced to accept contraception, but the means had become the end.

A Trip to Disneyland

Two different "baskets of attitudes" seem to divide the human species. (Look again at Box 13-2.) Thomas Sowell deals with them by distinguishing between "unconstrained" and "constrained visions of reality." With a slight difference in emphasis one can speak of "free-form" and "structured" organizations of knowledge. Both schemata are intellectual descendants of a distinction made almost a century ago by the psychologist William James: "tender-minded" versus "tough-minded."[33]

James called attention to the fact that the two contrasting types of human beings often "have a low opinion of each other. . . . The tough think of the tender as sentimentalists and soft-heads. The tender feel the tough to be unrefined, callous, or brutal. . . . Each type believes the other to be inferior to itself; but disdain in the one case is mingled with amusement, in the other it has a dash of fear." James identified himself as a member of the first group.

The distinction is useful in understanding the difference in people's reactions to poverty in distant parts of the world. Thinking about the needs of these poor people (the Third World) most of us can agree that two goals are desirable above all others: to make the people more comfortable, and to bring their population growth to a halt. When it comes to assigning priority to these goals we part company. Tough-minded Malthusians want to give priority to population control, arguing that increased well-being will follow from that achievement. Tender-minded anti-Malthusians argue that we should first make the poor richer and more comfortable, secure in the faith that increased well-being will eventually result in diminished fertility. The child survival hypothesis is clearly a tender-minded, anti-Malthusian conjecture.

The Malthusian position is supported by a powerful generalization that extends far beyond demography. Experimental psychology rests firmly on an expectation backed up by thousands of years of success in the training of animals, whether for work or performance in circuses: *performance first, then reward.* By contrast, anti-Malthusian theories cling to the opposite hope, namely "reward first, then performance." Which assumption is the better guide in our relations with needy societies? To throw light on the problem I offer two parables.

> It is spring. Mr. and Mrs. Tough have two immediate goals: to get the house cleaned, and to take the children to Disneyland. Seeking to fulfill these goals Mrs. Tough says: "Now look, children, this house desperately needs a good spring cleaning. But our spirits need a spring cleaning too! Wouldn't it be nice to pack up and go to Disneyland? If you children will really pitch in and help with the house-cleaning for three days then off we'll all go to Disneyland for a good time! How about it?"
>
> Meanwhile the Tender family next door approaches the problem differently. Mrs. Tender presents her children with this proposition: "Wouldn't it be fun to go to Disneyland tomorrow? Two days: then when we get back we'll all pitch in and give the house a good spring cleaning? How about it?"

Which house do you think will get a better spring cleaning at the hands of the children? Is there any doubt?

A tough-minded person, whether Malthusian or psychologist, would say there is no doubt. A tender-minded anti-Malthusian might still hold out, saying that he personally has known of a family where the tender-minded strategy worked. And no doubt it does work, now and then. But which strategy is the better gamble? The success of a policy is connected with some very subtle interactions of family members, with the nature of promises (explicit or implied), and with the manipulation of conscience, guilt, and other hard-to-define entities. So the decision, as concerns family operations, is not open and shut. But the odds of success favor the tough-minded one. *Performance first; then reward:* this is surely a major default position of rational policy sciences.

Scale effect greatly increases the odds. At the scale of nations, how can millions of needy people make promises that other millions can rely on? Perhaps you think gratitude can motivate cooperation between nations? Experience throws grave doubt on the reality of national gratitude. Intermediary events may interfere. For instance: bags of grain that have been sent to starving nations have often been found relabeled as the gifts of a local politician or military leader.

How does a poor population respond to a gift of food? The response is generally Malthusian: fertility goes up. The antipsychological, anti-Malthusian policy of *reward first, then performance,* though it may work in a group as small as the family, simply does not "scale up" to the level of nations. Pious pronouncements about "the family of man" are powerless to negate the scale effect.

In discussions of foreign aid there is seldom a mention of tender- and tough-mindedness. William James commented long ago on the silence about the psychological substrate of controversies. Mentioning these temperaments borders on the argumentum ad hominem and so is unacceptable in argument. Consequently anyone who argues in public for a certain position is careful to advance only impersonal reasons. Said James: "There arises thus a certain insincerity in our philosophical discussions: the potentest of all our premises is never mentioned."[34]

Insincerity infiltrates discussions of foreign aid, as many people subconsciously recognize that birth control should precede death control, though the ruling mores interfere with candor. To date, no political figure in the United States has dared even to suggest the truth. But continuing to give death control priority over birth control insures that populations will continue to increase. The further growth of a population in an already overstrained environment insures the further destruction of that environment through loss of soil, loss of forests, loss of wild species, and loss of productivity. In brief, giving death control priority over birth control ultimately increases the death rate. Tender-mindedness, uninformed by carrying capacity thinking, may prevail in the short run, but in the long run such tender-mindedness will produce the tragedy of a population crash.

17

The Benign Demographic Transition

The child survival hypothesis is immensely popular with politicians, religious leaders, and executives of organizations engaged in foreign philanthropy, because it justifies the anti-Malthusian and tender-minded belief that reducing infant mortality will automatically bring about a reduction in fertility. The belief easily converts into policy, because saving babies is something we know how to do. Nonetheless, the term *child survival hypothesis* is not widely known outside professional circles. By contrast, the theory of the "demographic transition" has been extensively popularized over several decades. Its meaning can, however, stand a bit of clarification.

Demographic Transition Theory: the Benign Form

The theory was born French: in 1934 Adolphe Landry wrote of the *révolution démographique.*[1] A decade later this was translated into the familiar English form. By 1969 a widely used population textbook expressed the common, if not the predominant, opinion of demographers when it identified the theory as "one of the best documented generalizations in the social sciences."[2] *Documented* it certainly is: the literature is appallingly large.

But documented does not mean *proved.* Ironically (in the words of demographer Michael Teitelbaum), "its explanatory power has come into increasing scientific doubt at the very time that it is achieving its greatest acceptance by nonscientists. In scientific circles, only modest claims are now made for transition theory."[3] That was said in 1975. Ten years later Teitelbaum and Winter put the matter more forcefully: "It is doubtful whether this theory was ever truly a theory at all (that is, a set of hypotheses with predictive force)."[4]

Before we look into its predictive abilities we need to find out exactly what the theory asserts. This is not easy because the theory is almost never carefully and rigorously described. We need once more to call upon the art of graphing.

Transition theory assumes a finite world. For most of the world, most of the time, both birth rate and death rate have been in the neighborhood of 40 per thousand population per year.[5] When the two rates are equal, zPG (zero population growth) prevails. Despite perennial fluctuations in population size at different locations, the *average* growth rate of the entire human population for the past million years has been very close to ZPG, namely 0.02 percent per year. At this growth rate the population doubles every 3,500 years—hardly a population explosion!

About three centuries ago the situation started to change significantly as the escalating rate of scientific advances, principally in the areas of medicine and agriculture, made it possible for many more people to live on our finite globe. The death rate plunged, particularly in Europe, while the birth rate remained about the same, or even rose a bit here and there.

But, given the restrictions of a nongrowing globe, a population cannot increase forever. Escape from ZPG can be only temporary. Ultimately birth and death rates must again become equal. Obviously, "given our druthers," we would like to keep the death rate low, hoping that the birth rate will drop to equal it. Figure 17–1 is an idealized picture of this outcome. The inequality between death rate and birth rate creates a "demographic gap." On a finite globe, the gap must soon be closed.

(In passing, note that before a new equality of the two rates is achieved, the death rate must rise somewhat. This rise does not bespeak a failure of science and technology: it is just a statistical fluke. At the present time the death rate in the United States is about 10 per thousand per year. *If the population were in equilibrium* with respect to the proportions of the various year classes, a death rate of 10 per mil would imply an *average* length of life of 100 years. There is no present prospect of such longevity. Recent "baby booms" have created an excess of people in the low-mortality, high-breeding years—15 to 45 years of age—and hence an abnormally low death rate. Even with no further technological advances, so long as the inherent length of life of human beings remains the same (about 75 years), the death rate must eventually rise to about 13 per thousand per year as the larger proportion of older people die of the diseases of old age. Then, as ZPG is re-established, the paradoxically rising death rate will meet the falling birth rate.)

A technicality like this needs to be widely understood because, if and when the demographic gap is closed in this way, we can be sure that journalists will view the rising death rate with alarm, supposing that it indicates a worsening of human

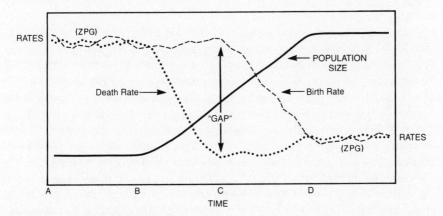

Figure 17-1. Demographic transition theory in its idealized *benign* form. Death rates in dots; birth rates in dashes. "GAP" is the demographic gap which produces population growth, as illustrated by the solid line.

Box 17-1. Fluctuations in Natural Increase in Europe.

Natural increase is defined as the birth rate minus the death rate, the result being given as the percentage increase (or decrease) per year. The figures below are taken from the World Population Data Sheets of the Population Reference Bureau of Washington, D.C., and really apply to the year completed before the year given at the head of the column.

		Year	
Region	1972	1976	1988
Europe	0.7	0.6	0.3
Denmark	0.5	0.4	−0.1
West Germany	0.2	0.1	−0.1
East Germany	−0.2	−0.2	0.0
Hungary	0.3	0.6	−0.2
Malta	−0.7	0.0	0.7
Portugal	0.8	−0.4	0.3

health. A death rate of 13 per thousand is 30 percent higher than a death rate of 10 per thousand—but so what? In the history of the demographic transition it will be just a statistical aberration.

So much for the idealized theory: has it been realized any place? It is not certain that it has. Europe is commonly cited as a region in which the transition has been completed, but this is not so. The table in Box 17-1 shows that the rate of natural increase is falling, but as of 1988 it was still 0.3 percent per year, which is 15 times as high as the all-time average for the world population, and corresponds to a doubling time of 233 years. Moreover, if we look at the various rates for the particular countries listed in the box, we find that a rate may fall below zero and then rise again later. East Germany, for instance, fell to a minus rate in 1972, then rose to ZPG by 1988; With Malta the change was even greater. Empirical data alone are not enough to establish the validity of a population theory because "trend is not destiny" and "no inning is the last inning."

The Possibility of a Malign Demographic Transition

To be honest we must admit that a new ZPG might be attained in another way, namely by the death rate *rising* to the level of a still-high birth rate. The slight rise in death rate shown in Figure 17-1 is replaced by a decided rise in Figure 17-2; a statistical fluke is replaced by a real increase in mortality. Obviously this is "a consummation devoutly *not* to be wished," but it is a possible way to close the demographic gap. The result could well be called a "malign demographic transition."

Not infrequently sceptics ask, will population ever be controlled? The answer is *yes, certainly: by nature, if human beings fail.* Following the creation of a demographic gap by scientific progress, a *malign* demographic transition can take place automatically, without further human intervention. There is no reason to think that a *benign* transition will occur in the absence of conscious human intervention.

Can humanity agree on the interventions to be made? Therein lies an important aspect of "the population problem."

Waterproof Theories Are No Good

Scientific theories must have predictive force. This is not possible when predictions are ambiguous. It is both amusing and worrisome when demographers unconsciously document the ambiguity of the demographic transition theory, as in the following example:

> Both in historical Europe and in the recent past in developing countries, fertility has frequently undergone a period of increase prior to the advent of sustained decline. Such increases seem to be intimately linked with subsequent falls. . . . The conclusion that both historical and contemporary populations underwent pre-decline rises makes it easier for us to accommodate the experiences of both types of populations within a single formulation of transition theory that allows for an initial phase of fertility rise. Indeed, in light of the findings of historical demography, perhaps we should even regard it as reassuring that most fertility time series for contemporary developing countries also show such a rise.[6]

Cutting away the superfluous verbiage we see that the authors justify "predecline rises" by these implied assertions:

1. If the fall in death rate occurs immediately and is followed by a fall in birth rate, the demographic transition theory is validated;
2. If the fall in death rate is followed by a rise in birth rate, the demographic transition theory is validated.

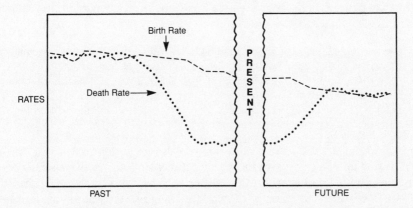

Figure 17-2. A possible *malign* form of the demographic transition. This actually threatens Third World countries if they do not reduce their birth rates significantly in the near future. In the malign form the demographic gap is closed by a rising of the death rate to meet the birth rate.

Still more briefly: *Heads I win, tails you lose.* Such is the essence of a *waterproof theory,* which is simply not admissible to the realm we call science. Given the tolerant attitude expressed in the above quotation, the demographic transition theory must be judged (and condemned) as a waterproof theory.

Historicism Is Not Science

More cautious, but no more scientific, are the essays and books that present the benign transition theory as a historical inevitability. The argument, usually only implied, can be reduced to these propositions: (1) Europe has already gone through the transition; (2) what has happened in Europe is the model for all other nations to follow; and (3) you can't stop "progress."

It cannot be confidently said that the transition has yet been completed in Europe, and history cannot guarantee predictions of the future. Retrospective eyesight can so easily pass as 20/20 vision! To assume that prospective eyesight is equally keen is to be guilty of what philosopher Karl Popper has called *historicism.*[7]

Marx, more than any other person, was responsible for selling historical determinism to the world. At his grave in 1883 his great friend Friedrich Engels proudly said that "Just as Darwin discovered the law of development of organic nature, so Marx discovered the law of development of human history."[8] But Darwin never claimed to find a deterministic law of evolutionary development: he uncovered the forces of mutation and selection that *contingently* determine what happens. How one species evolves is dependent on how many associated species evolve. No one can successfully predict the exact path of biological evolution.

Human political history is also ruled by contingency. Marx did not discover any all-embracing and deterministic law of historical development, for there is no such law. Nevertheless, a passionate belief in historicism has motivated Marxist activists. The "true believer" *knows* which way history is now going—his way, of course—and unwavering belief has been a source of great political strength for the "Marxist hero," as John Silber has explained:

> He renounces all claim to, indeed all belief in, individual effort or worth; unselving himself, he finds his place within the historical dialectic. History for him is made, not by individuals, but by dialectic forces operating through social classes. He submerges himself, not merely *accepting* his destiny as an obscure member of society, but also *seeking* this as his fulfillment. The Marxist theorist Plekhanov describes him well: "He not only serves as an instrument of necessity and cannot help doing so, but he passionately desires this, and cannot help desiring to do so."[9]

Looking to the future we cannot escape the conviction that all future history is contingent upon unforeseeable events. Who, in 1987, seventy years after the Russian Revolution, predicted *any* of the world-shaking events of the autumn of 1989? Yet, *retrospectively* it was easy to make historical sense of these surprising events. Future history is still a problem. (Is "future history" an oxymoron?) The Nobelist Dennis Gabor, inventor of holography, has aptly pointed out, "The future cannot be predicted, but futures can be invented."[10] The question is, What future do we wish to invent? It is in the realization of invented futures that the glory of the human species is to be sought. Submission to historicism is an abrogation of the gift of humanity.

Take-Off Theory—Another Mistaken Determinism

A rhetorical variant of the benign demographic transition theory that gained a large following in the second half of the twentieth century was the "take-off theory" of W. W. Rostow.[11] It depends on an aeronautical image.

The changing of a poor country ("developing country") into a rich one ("developed country") was compared to the take-off of an airplane. When various industries and traditions are introduced into a primitive economy, the early stages bring much expense and little profit, just as the early stages of the acceleration of an airplane over the ground use up a lot of fuel before the plane can become airborne. A developing country may be too poor to finance the early stages of modernization, for which it needs the financial help of wealthier nations.

Then, at some critical stage of development, income exceeds expenses, and the formerly primitive country "takes off." At that point external philanthropy can be discontinued because the country can take care of itself. Rostow's theory promised an end to international philanthropy: this made it attractive to *donor* countries. It also gave good reasons for *massive* foreign aid, for whoever heard of an airplane taking off at a low speed? This aspect of the theory made it attractive to *recipient* countries.

For a bit more than a decade the take-off theory was the fair-haired boy of the foreign aid establishment; then references to it suddenly ceased. Ecologists usually (but economists seldom) found the no-earthly-limits assumed by the theory unacceptable. This assumption is apparent in the concluding sentences of Rostow's paper: "[T]ake-off requires that a society find a way to apply effectively to its own peculiar resources . . . the tricks of manufacture; and continued growth requires that it so organise itself as to continue to apply them in an unending flow, of changing composition. Only thus, as we have been correctly taught, can that old demon, diminishing returns, be held at bay."

The world available to human society is *inescapably finite* (Chapter 8); and returns ultimately become diminishing returns (Chapter 13). Therefore Rostow's vision of a country taking off into perpetually accelerating prosperity is so much pie-in-the-sky. When he says "we have been correctly taught" that this pie-in-the-sky is possible, "we" *does not include ecologists*. Scale effects, of which diminishing returns are but one example, are pivotal principles of the science of ecology. It is to be hoped that within another generation the principle of diminishing returns will be accepted once more as a legitimate member of the family of economic truths. (How many of the economic disasters growing out of political-economic measures taken in the appalling 1980s stemmed from the widespread miseducation of economists? Historians will someday recognize this question as worthy of research.)

Rostow's simile furnishes a plausible excuse for being generous. But when the take-off image is developed more thoroughly, it just as plausibly gives the rationale for *not* supporting foreign aid. Suppose the foreign aid is not quite generous enough—what then? What happens to an airplane that moves faster and faster on the ground but never quite achieves take-off speed? We all know the answer: it crashes, and the greater the less-than-take-off speed the worse the crash. Rostow did not mention this aspect of the image; but the failures of the past four decades of foreign aid now add a bitter aftertaste to the words *take-off.*

Africa south of the Sahara furnishes many shocking examples of progress in reverse. Etienne van de Walle has concluded that "central Africa is one vast contradiction of [transition] theory: mortality has fallen, and fertility has risen, for two generations, with no end in sight."[12] Ester Boserup predicts that "Population increase will be rapid in Africa for many decades."[13] The hopes of "transitionists" are contradicted by trends in Kenya, where "the fertility rate remained high, and possibly even rose, between the early 1960s and the late 1970s, at the same time that contraceptive prevalence rose from virtually zero to about 7 percent of the married women of reproductive age. In other parts of Africa, fertility is likely to rise in the future."[14]

It is distressing to have to report that African fertility is approaching a high never before reached in the history of large groups—50 per thousand per year. There are various reasons for this peak, among them the improved health of mothers. Tragically, this is occuring in areas of immense environmental destruction due to over-population.

Another factor is this: at the instigation of foreign missionaries polygamy is being replaced by monogamy. In polygamous earlier times an African woman often had some respite from child-bearing when she went to her mother's home with her newborn child, where she might stay a year or more. During this time her husband satisfied his sexual needs with another wife. Under polygamy the average married *man* has more children, but the average married *woman* has fewer children. In addition, many men in a polygamous society never marry; their heterosexual contacts may be limited to prostitutes, a notoriously sterile group. It follows from all these considerations that the change from polygamy to monogamy causes population to increase faster (in the absence of compensating cultural changes). It is doubtful if European missionaries foresaw the populational consequences of conversion to Christianity (or that they would have cared if they had foreseen it).

We've looked for the bluebird of painless population control, but anti-Malthusian theories about child survival effects and the demographic transition have been found wanting. It is time to look for other ways of controlling population, within the ecological boundaries of Malthusian theory, from which there is no rational escape.

III

BITING THE BULLET

18

Making Room for Human Will

Anything to be *done* about human populations necessarily depends on the will to do it. But what does the word *will* mean? Much has been written about it, but most of the rhetoric is nonsense. Rather than add one more explicit (and probably faulty) definition to the roster I will treat "will" *ostensively,* that is by pointing to passages that throw some light on its meaning (Box 18-1).

The contributions of academics are commonly belittled by "practical" people, who trust more in the guidance of intuition. In a classic statement John Maynard Keynes argued that such guidance often came through unconscious memory.[1] Because of the heavy demands on their time, politicians seldom read any work of substance after the age of thirty. Their responses are, Keynes said, distilled "from some academic scribbler a few years back." Looking at the situation with a different orientation in time, we argue that it is worthwhile for the inventor or scholar to try to get his views accepted by those who are young and powerless *now* because some of them may have political power two decades from now, when their days of leisurely reading are long past.

In the unending development of human civilization what men think will happen can influence what does happen. The connection between the original ideas and their conversion into action is not rigid, determinative, or well understood: but there is a connection, and this appeals to the ambitions of social inventors. Consequently, as Dennis Gabor says, "The future cannot be predicted, but futures can be invented." As concerns the size of future populations, humanity's problem is to invent the answer. What size do we *want* human populations to be? On what assumptions do our answers rest? Precisely *how* can human consent be engineered?

What Is Scarcity?

There is no *pure* population problem: the problem is one of population and resources. The well-being of a population depends on the ratio of the size of the population to the magnitude of available resources. What the future holds for population considered by itself is simple enough, as Malthus knew: the perpetual threat posed by population's ability to increase exponentially. But resources? Malthus stubbed his toe on this one, and people are still arguing. The arguments center around the concept of scarcity and the relevance of statistics to predicting the future.

Box 18-1. The Power of the Human Will: Ostensive Definitions.

The ideas of economists and political philosophers, both when they are right and when they are wrong, are more powerful than is commonly understood. Indeed the world is ruled by little else. Practical men, who believe themselves to be quite exempt from any intellectual influences, are usually the slaves of some defunct economist. Madmen in authority, who hear voices in the air, are distilling their frenzy from some academic scribbler a few years back. I am sure that the power of vested interests is vastly exaggerated compared with the gradual encroachment of ideas. Not, indeed, immediately, but after a certain interval; for in the field of economic and political philosophy there are not many who are influenced by new theories after they are twenty-five or thirty years of age, so that the ideas which civil servants and politicians and even agitators apply to current events are not likely to be the newest. But soon or late, it is ideas and not vested interests which are dangerous for good or evil.

John Maynard Keynes, *General Theory of Employment, Interest, and Money,* 1936.

The future cannot be predicted, but futures can be invented. It was man's ability to invent which has made human society what it is. The mental processes of invention are still mysterious. They are rational, but not logical, that is to say not deductive. The first step of the technological or social inventor is to visualize, by an act of imagination, a thing or a state of things which does not yet exist, and which to him appears in some way desirable. He can then start rationally arguing backwards from the invention, and forward from the means at his disposal, until a way is found from one to the other. There is no invention if the goal is not attainable by known means, but this cannot be known beforehand. The goal of the technological inventor is attainable if it is physically feasible, but for the realisation he will be dependent, just like the social inventor, on human consent. The difference is that while in the past many technological inventors failed tragically by not being able to obtain consent, this is today not only easy but often far too easy. For the social inventor on the other hand, the engineering of human consent is the most essential and the most difficult step, and I do not think that this has become more easy in democracies where the masses must be persuaded, instead of perhaps one enlightened monarch.

Dennis Gabor, *Inventing the Future,* 1963.

The most sophisticated statistics have been developed in the service of the natural sciences, but natural scientists have some reservations about the use of statistics to solve problems in the behavioral (or social) sciences. Strongly recommended is a light-hearted book by a public-spirited statistician, *How to Lie with Statistics.*[2] One must be constantly alert to arguments that confuse reserves and resources. *Resources* are the total quantity of useful materials available on earth, most of it underground and difficult to measure, while *reserves* are the well-measured quantities that frequently change with more exploration and advances in technology. (Recall the confusion of petroleum reserves and petroleum resources described in Chapter 6.)

In drawing up plans for the future, natural scientists focus on the earth's resources. Since the earth is of finite size, the quantity of resources must also be finite. Every time we draw on useful materials we must reduce the supply. How could it be otherwise? Science and common sense agree in this conservative conclusion.

Ecologists, the quintessential conservatives of the scientific community, would base economic policy on the inescapable finiteness of terrestrial *resources.* Many economists, focusing on variations in the estimates of terrestrial *reserves,* reject conservative thinking. A team of economists headed by Harold J. Barnett dismissed the common sense views of ecologists as no more than "widespread belief."[3] Barnett's and Chandler Morse's analysis of 1963 rests solely on empirical findings,[4] with no acknowledgment of what we now call the default positions of science (Chapter 5). Empirical findings are so numerous and so ambiguous that almost any conclusion can be supported by a plausible argument. But empirical studies have great prestige in our science-sensitized society, particularly because they can be so selected and arranged as to seem to support faith in perpetual growth, the religion of the most powerful actors in a commercial society.

There is some sleight of hand in the report of Barnett and Morse. Adding italics to one of their key statements makes the point easier to see: "Our empirical test has *not* supported the hypothesis . . . that *economic scarcity* of natural resources, *as measured by the trend of real cost* of extractive output, will increase over time in a growing economy." Natural scientists are interested in true scarcity, while economists talk of "economic scarcity," which is measured by *cost* and is a different thing altogether. Many factors in addition to true scarcity can affect the cost of a resource. Most notable during the past century has been the cost of petroleum, which has played a key role in the extraction and transportation of resource derivatives. This cost has trended downward because of admirable technological advances in the discovery and utilization of petroleum. Commodity markets deal with the cost of petroleum; no market deals with the values of wilderness and unspoiled nature which have been sacrificed to satisfy the gluttony of a petroleum-based civilization. So the downward trend in the market price of commodities is to be taken with a grain of salt. It should also be pointed out that the faster oil prices move downward, the more rapidly true resources of other sorts are exhausted.

In 1984 Barnett and his associates documented what has come to be the conventional economic conclusion: "in the United States, during the period 1870–1970, the theory of increasing economic scarcity of minerals is not supported by the facts. This is important evidence. The period is a long one; the USA is the largest minerals producer and consumer; and the studies were carefully done."[5]

A significant admission was made four pages later in the same study: "While several of the minerals have increased substantially in price since 1970, the periods of increase are as yet too short or too inconsistent to be termed 'trends.'" Does this mean that no apparent reversal will be accepted as fact until the period of rising prices is as long as the earlier period of falling prices? Must we wait until 2070 A.D. to say that the betting is 50–50? Are economists echoing the maxim of MAD Magazine's Alfred E. Newman, "What! Me worry?"

To some people the year 2070 may seem impossibly far off; but it is only a little farther in the future than the year 1930 is in the past, and no well-educated person finds it difficult to imagine the days when the stock market crashed and Lindbergh flew across the Atlantic. It cannot be too often pointed out that "It takes imagination to recognize the truth." Does that mean that imagining the finitude of resources is too difficult a mental task for some professional economists?

"Progress"—The 200-Year Binge

The discipline of economics is founded on a "conviction of the mind"—Whittaker's term—that finds its expression in the dictum that "There's no such thing as a free lunch." Unfortunately economic policies sometimes become detached from their foundation.

The reasons for the separation are understandable. The growth of the academic discipline of economics has been historically concurrent with the growth of modern science and technology. Time after time asserted limitations of human wealth and income have had to be revised upward because of new ways of exploiting the wealth of nature. Discovery has been confused with creation. The upward revisions in limits have been an important historical factor only in the last couple of centuries. But, for most people, a mere three generations is an eternity.

Box 18-2. A Bouquet of Growth Posies.

The means which the earth affords for the subsistence of man, are subject to no assignable limits.

William Godwin, literary anarchist, 1820.

Prosperity has no fixed limits. It is not a finite substance to be diminished by division. On the contrary, the more of it that other nations enjoy, the more each nation will have for itself.

Henry Morgenthau, U.S. Secretary of the Treasury, 1933.

I cannot conceive a successful economy without growth.

Walter Heller, U.S. President's Council of Economic Advisers, 1962.

The existing propensities of the population and policies of the government constitute claims upon GNP itself that can only be satisfied by rapid economic growth.

U.S. President's Council of Economic Advisers, 1971.

Never has growth been more important. You can never feed the poor or ease the lives of the wage-earning families, ameliorate the problems of race or solve the problem of pollution without real growth.

John B. Connally, U.S. Secretary of the Treasury, 1972.

The concept of sustainable development does imply limits—not absolute limits but limitations imposed by the present state of technology and social organization on environmental resources and by the ability of the biosphere to absorb the effects of human activities. But technology and social organization can be both managed and improved to make way for a new era of economic growth. The Commission believes that widespread poverty is no longer inevitable. Poverty is not only an evil in itself, but sustainable development requires meeting the basic needs of all and extending to all the opportunity to fulfill their aspirations for a better life.

U.N. World Commission on Environment and Development, 1971.

In a finite world, high growth rates must self-destruct. If the base from which growth is taking place is tiny, this law may not operate for a time. But when the base balloons, the party ends: A high growth rate eventually forges its own anchor.

Warren E. Buffet, one of America's most successful investors, 1990.

Any trend that has lasted a century is presumed to hold during the indefinite future. Economic predictions beyond five years are untrustworthy; but clinging to the presumption of perpetual growth is irresponsible. Contemporary economics is not *conservative*—not as scientists use the adjective; but it shows signs of improving.

Box 18-2 displays an assortment of growth-related statements, most of which are anticonservative. It is noteworthy that anticonservative views that are rejected by scientists are supported by both political liberals and political conservatives. Their reasons may be somewhat different: political liberals want the economy to grow forever so the poor can become rich, while political conservatives want growth to continue so that they themselves can become richer.

Is perpetual growth possible? Suspicions that it may not be have begun to percolate through the ranks of the prophets. How growth-intoxicated dreamers get around this awkward possibility is often interesting from a semantic point of view. The clarity of a statement is usually inversely related to its length. The longest statement in the box was written under the chairmanship of Gro Harlem Brundtland, sometime prime minister of Norway.[6] Does "development" necessarily involve growth? The commission muddied the waters by introducing a new entity, "sustainable development." The fact that this rather academic substitution has been eagerly embraced by commercial interests makes one suspect that "sustainable development" is being used as a covert substitute for "sustainable growth," and this, as economist Herman Daly has pointed out, "should be rejected as a bad oxymoron." He makes his point more telling by calling our attention to the fact that two years after the commission's report Brundtland insisted that global economic growth must increase by a factor of 5 to 10 to make so-called "sustainable development" possible.[7] The amount of global pollution generated if the world turnover of nature's bounty were to become 5 to 10 times greater than it is now should give pause to even the most "optimistic" of anticonservatives. Few economists have bothered to say a word against Brundtland's "optimistic" remedy for the world's ills. Natural scientists, however, delight in quoting the words of Kenneth Boulding, onetime president of the American Economic Association: "Only madmen and economists believe in perpetual exponential growth."[8]

Justifying Default Positions

Close observation of scientific investigations shows that progress is possible only if legitimacy is conferred on a small roster of "default positions" (Chapter 5). In practice, *default status places the burden of proof on any assertion to the contrary.* The conservation of matter and energy is a case in point. Without a decision on the placement of the burden of proof, the efforts of scientists would be frittered away investigating every ill-supported claim (for example, perpetual motion machines or ways to annul earthly resource limits).

A discipline that rejects default statements is at the mercy of empirical data. In the most rigorous sense, empiricism is endlessly inconclusive: the impulse called *will* is made all but impossible. The so-called social sciences, as they have developed during the past century, have gloried in their sensitivity to volatile data and their rejection of "common sense" (default positions). This is the meaning of their categorization as sciences that are "data rich and theory poor."

Discriminating intolerance is a necessary part of science. Since intolerance is always dangerous, how can scientists ever justify it? The ecological-economic world is immensely complex. Depending on how fine the analysis is, it reveals dozens or thousands of "ecosystems," with no two alike. Of sovereign nations there are nearly two hundred. Of economic systems there may, basically, be no more than three different ones, but these have many variants. Multiply these numbers together and you have a shockingly large population of situations in which to look for cause-and-effect relationships.

In the past three centuries the people of Europe have, in real terms, become richer; and their birth rates have fallen. Did they become richer *because* they had fewer children? Or did their fertility fall because they became richer? The *history* question—the question about the past—does not interest some people; but the *policy* question—the question of what to do in the future—should be of concern to everyone. In the light of European experience should we, when we try to help poor and densely populated nations elsewhere, try to make them rich first, or less fertile first?

Post hoc ergo propter hoc—"after this, therefore because of this"—is the name of a long recognized fallacy in logic. Statistical analysis offers techniques for circumventing the fallacy, but unfortunately the number of variables involved usually vastly exceeds the number of equations to be worked with, which means that analysis can yield no certain answers. But that doesn't prevent slipshod statisticians from "snowing" us with meaningless statistics. To get ahead with the world's work we have to regain some of our traditional faith in common sense. The noncreation of energy is common sense, even if we cannot rigorously prove it. (How does one prove a negative?)

Eddington said that the second law of thermodynamics occupies a "supreme position" in the hierarchy of scientific statements. Note the special reference to the image of *position*. This image is found (in implicit form) in a very famous religious statement. On 18 April 1521, on the eve of the Diet of Worms, Martin Luther, under attack for his heretical opinions, said: "Here I stand! I cannot do otherwise. God help me!"

The image of *standing* is a positional image that implies an element of choice. It is much more compatible with the scientific temperament than is *law,* which sounds too rigid. Returning to science we can say that a perpetual motion machine may indeed be possible, but the burden of proof falls strongly on whoever claims to have found one. Two plus two may equal five, but don't be surprised to find scientists intolerant of such a claim. The scientific mind is not irrevocably closed: it is merely intolerant of wasting time on the proposals of those who are too lazy to submit themselves to the necessary discipline of science.

Perpetual Growth: Possible and Impossible

In spite of the "no free lunch" axiom of economics, economists themselves have often been guilty of *presuming*—and occasionally *stating* nonconservation. It was at a meeting held in preparation for the 1974 World Population Conference that Paul Ehrlich reported the following: "As each new perpetual-motion-machine was propounded, one of the biologists or physicists would simply point out that it violated the second law. Finally, in frustration, one of the economists blurted out, 'Who knows what the second law of thermodynamics will be like in a hundred years?'"[9]

When economist Walter Heller said (Box 18-2) that he could not conceive a successful economy without growth, he meant economic growth—growth in the rate of use of materials and energy. Without too much trouble, it would be possible to assemble dozens of similar statements made by other reputable economists. Herman Daly's book, *Steady-State Economics,* is a rara avis in the literature of economics.[10] When the science of economics undergoes the evolutionary change that it must, it will no longer be necessary to add the modifier "steady state" to the name "economics," because that will be the predominant kind.

Perpetual economic growth would necessarily entail perpetual increase in the use of energy by human beings. That this is not possible was shown a generation ago by the physicist J. H. Fremlin.[11] Despite the fact that energy from the sun is continually raining in on the earth, the surface does not become unbearably hot because radiation into space (predominantly during the night) keeps the temperature in a fluctuating balance. Were human beings to learn how to produce significantly more energy from new sources such as nuclear energy, the balance point would shift upward. The operation of our machines would also produce heat. At some point the perpetual growth of the economy *and of the human population* would have to stop because the release of heat by human metabolism would push the balance point beyond the level at which life is possible. Fremlin estimated that this limit would be reached when the human population reached a density of about 120 per square meter of the earth's surface (which would be covered everywhere by high skyscrapers). The total number of people would be between 10^{16} and 10^{18}. (In words, the larger number is a *billion billion.*) The upper estimate is 100 times as great as the lower, which shows how crude the estimate is; but the reasoning is correct and the order of magnitude of the numbers must be in the right ball park.

The economists' dream of perpetual growth must be abandoned. Without documenting the argument I think almost all scientists would bet that the limiting human population will be *far less* than 10^{18}. In fact, once we have come to the end of our fossil fuels the sustainable population will probably be far less than the present 5 billion human beings. Our species is living on borrowed time. Unfortunately academic economists are almost completely unprepared to deal with a steady-state world, though it may be "right around the corner."

Underwood and King (1989) point out that the invisible hand of classical economics cannot "manage the interaction between economic growth and the integrity of the biosphere over an infinite future."[12] In the past, academic economics has been very careful to monitor all exchanges between human beings and human institutions ("no free lunches!"), while being resolutely blind to inflows of wealth from the nonhuman environment, as well as to outflows of costly wastes into the world around us. With such a philosophy of accounting it was easy for economists to ignore the laws of thermodynamics. For its own good, say Underwood and King, academic economics must now be restructured: "The fact that there are no known exceptions to the laws of thermodynamics should be incorporated into the axiomatic foundation of economics."[13] Evasive terms like "side effects" have long made free lunches seem plausible.

Most economists find the thought of a conservative science frightening. Fortunately there is a rapidly growing band of academics who are bringing classical economics and classical ecology together; they have found their first professional home in the International Society for Ecological Economics, which has, since 1989, published its own journal. Italians have organized a European Association for Bioeconomic Studies, while the Swedes have generated an "Eco-Eco Group."

In the past "no growth" has been despised as if it were a rejection of life itself. A society that does not grow economically has been vilified as stationary, torpid, and petrified. *Grow or Die!* is the title of one book. The implication is that this is the wisdom of biology. Not so. As far as over-all growth in weight and height is concerned, the normal course of human development is to grow until about 18 years of age, then to live on in a nongrowing state for another sixty years or so. Most of the years of human life are spent in a nongrowing condition. (The man or woman who grew perpetually would soon be in trouble.) As a policy "grow or die!" is at once greedy and suicidal.

Such is the situation as concerns weight alone. Actually, new cells are being laid down all of our lives—but old cells are being destroyed at the same rate. The body is in a steady state most of its life. Constant changes take place hand-in-hand with essentially constant size. "Dynamic balance" is the name for this arrangement. Steady state is the norm for human life; it is surely a worthy model for economic life as well.

Matter and *energy* are conserved, and therefore the perpetual growth of either is impossible. But scientists recognize a third entity called *information,* and this is not conserved; it can grow forever (so far as we know). Music, the visual arts, literature, science, philosophy—these can grow without limit, and there is no reason they cannot grow vigorously in a steady-state economy. (They may or may not grow in fact: the necessary conditions for their growth are poorly understood.) As the burgeoning scarcities of material resources compel the adoption of steady-state economics, it is to be hoped that the superstition of perpetual material growth will be abandoned, thereby making possible a conversion of the present economic system into one that makes better ecological and human sense.

Of Will and Necessity

From Epicurus onward thinkers who have left a permanent imprint on human knowledge have followed the structured, constrained path. Francis Bacon said that "Nature to be commanded must be obeyed." In the light of this restriction Hegel redefined freedom: "Freedom is the recognition of necessity." In our own time the psychologist B. F. Skinner has pointed out that the obverse of Bacon's coinage is "Once obeyed, nature can be commanded." Pessimism, deeply understood, can be rhetorically converted to a sort of optimism.

From time immemorial many men and women have carried over into adulthood the unstructured, or perversely structured, thinking of the fairy tales they heard in childhood. The free-form mode was given new life by the success of Jules Verne in foretelling the wonders of technology to come. The social results have been particularly damaging to the development of academic economics. "There's no such thing as a free lunch" has been too often assumed to apply only to the narrow present: given time enough those marvelous magicians, the scientists, would surely furnish us with a new free lunch! Unfortunately, for a couple of centuries, science and nature did seem to furnish one free lunch after another, thus apparently justifying the refusal of economists to take limits seriously.

Many of our generation have been conditioned into a schizoid view of the future. As concerns *material* change they admit no limits: they think perfectly safe fusion power, anti-gravity machines, and travel faster than the speed of light may well be ours tomorrow. (Remember, they say, how people once scoffed at Jules Verne's submarine?) But when it comes to *political* change the common man retreats into unmitigated conservatism: the present social and political institutions are, in their essence, presumed to be unchangeable. It's as though, after several thousand years of significant changes in political arrangements we had arrived at the final, perfect state.

The schizoid attitude toward change is understandable. The acceptance of material innovations requires, in general, no *obvious* change in social and political arrangements. (In fact, over a period of time, material inventions do often bring about substantial sociopolitical changes. For a telling example, think of the spreading social effects of that great material innovation of our time, the contraceptive pill. But social changes can be fiendishly hard to predict.)

The vast majority of the populace is poorly schooled in science but well educated in the practicalities of social and political life. Their experiences tell them that social change to a new stable or quasi-stable state is difficult to bring about. They are well advised to be conservative about social institutions—*most of the time.* The two incongruent kinds of education received by Everyman result in his being naively hopeful of perpetual motion machines and free lunches, while being extremely resistant to accepting desperately needed social and political changes.

The increasing growth of pollution of all sorts and the increasing signs of social and political strain show that our age is no longer part of "most of the time." Like it or not, we must muster the courage to invent, test, and adopt new social arrangements.

Elite spokesmen do not always know what is going on. In speaking of the problem of population control, Sir James Steuart spoke of the need for some "restraint upon marriage." The taboos of his class apparently prevented him from taking a more general view of the problem. The domain of marriage has been so eroded that we would now reword Sir James' statement to acknowledge that we have not yet agreed on "how to lay a restraint upon child-bearing without shocking the spirit of the times."

Since "most of the time" is gone, we must invent and evaluate many conceivable restraints upon child-bearing (within marriage, or outside of it), seeking to determine the social and political price of each innovation. We should not seek a costless change, for there is none. To the best of our abilities we must investigate the comparative costs of proposals already made—and look for better ones.

No definitive answer to "the population problem" will be presented here. None is possible at present. The preceding chapters have given an account of the present state of the relevant sciences. The chapters that follow give a survey of social and political problems that have been unintentionally raised by scientific advances. Conceiving a workable system of population control is the work of the future, in which many minds must participate. Making the required political and social changes will involve the human will in a way in which it was not involved when merely technological changes were the focus of attention.

19

Major Default Positions of Human Biology

In Chapter 5 it was shown that physics, generally accepted as the very model of a rigorous discipline, cannot escape common-sense assertions that are supported by nothing more than "a conviction of the mind," to use the words of E. T. Whittaker. On this apparently fragile foundation have been erected powerful sciences and fruitful technologies.

The biological sciences also rest on the common sense of a few default positions. Human behavior being as variable as it is, human biology must deal with a great mass of data. The classical error of *Post hoc ergo propter hoc*—"after this, therefore because of this"—lies ever in wait for those who are too trusting of empirical studies. Thus it came about (as we saw in Chapter 16) that the benign demographic transition theory managed to survive for nearly half a century, though it was implausible in principle and unprovable in practice.

Tools of investigation can serve pathological goals. Psychiatrists have long recognized the abnormality called "logorrhea"—verbal diarrhea, or diarrhea of the larynx. Statistical analysis can develop into a similar disease. The opaqueness of statistical arguments makes it easy for analysts to "get away with murder." In befuddling the public, logorrhea has been joined by "arithmorrhea," number diarrhea. Statistics, though often wonderfully useful, can also serve as a substitute for thought.

The default positions of biology, like those of the physical sciences, place a heavy burden of proof on any assertion that violates common sense. Of course, the default status must be assigned with discriminating care, or serious errors will be made. For a cautionary instance consider these remarks by an early nineteenth-century critic of Malthus: "Everywhere [man's] length of life, the chances of his existence are nearly the same. . . . The ratio of our increase, the proportion of our mortality, appear to be amongst the most unalterable laws of our nature; they depend on no accidents; they are not influenced, they cannot be, by any human institution."[1] Even the most casual observations of health, length of life, and fertility in various regions of the world should have shown the author that he had chosen his default position unwisely.

It is understood of course that all the default positions of the physical sciences are accepted in biology; to these a few others must be added in order to deal with population problems. This chapter is devoted to a listing of the major biological default positions that are of significance in population studies.

Our Earth Is the Total World for Most of the Human Species

To date, a dozen human beings have managed, for a brief period of time, to get as far from the earth as the moon, about 240,000 miles distant. In the lifetime of people now living, a few men and women *may* go further abroad for longer periods of time. But for the totality of the human species no such escape is possible (as was demonstrated in Chapter 2). Most of the thousands of millions of men and women are stuck on earth; they must reconcile themselves to making the best of it. Dreamers who promise otherwise do a disservice to their fellow human beings. With the rarest of exceptions, space novels, space movies, and space dramas on television constitute an "escape literature" in the worst sense. Such "hope operas" no doubt help NASA at budget hearings in Congress, but they divert citizens from taking a hand in caring for the world from which they cannot escape.

Rewards Determine Behavior

"Rewards determine behavior" sounds like such a truism, an axiom so painfully obvious, that it should not need to be said. Unfortunately policies are often built around the faith that wanted behavior can be evoked without positive rewards, or even with negative rewards. The belief that behavior is determined by rewards is essential if we are to make sense of the more puzzling aspects of human behavior. Consider the enigma of juvenile delinquency. At first glance it may look as though a juvenile criminal is behaving in an utterly irrational way, since he is aware of the laws that specify punishment for what he is doing. But close investigation shows that there are also positive rewards for criminal activity, such as membership in close-knit gangs and the admiration of one's peers. Evidently these positive "reinforcements" of criminal activity sometimes outweigh the negative reinforcements of apprehension and conviction, which are only probable, not certain. If a society aspires to change criminal behavior—not merely to punish it when the offender is caught—it must identify the total reward system that impinges on the juvenile. An understanding of juvenile delinquency has been made difficult by the subtlety of the rewards impinging on the young. (It does not follow that a successful study will put an end to delinquent behavior; penal punishments may still be needed as part of the reward system.)

The "profit motive" of economics appeals to the motivation of individuals. "You get what you pay for" is a valuable reminder to reformers. In evolution theory, "you get what you select for" and "survival of the fittest" point to natural selection, which also is driven by environmental rewards. Darwinian selection is just a special instance of results being determined by rewards. Natural selection is so obvious (now that Darwin has pointed it out) that we cannot imagine a world in which it does not operate.

Population policy must allow for the fact that the rewards of parenthood are subtle and imperfectly understood. As we uncover the literature on human populations, we will frequently run across theories that are built upon an unconscious rejection of the selection principle.

"We Can Never Do Merely One Thing"

Wishing to kill insects, we may put an end to the singing of birds. Wishing to "get there" faster, we insult our lungs with smog. Wishing to know what is happening everywhere in the world at once, we create an information overload against which the mind rebels, responding by a new and dangerous apathy.[2]

I thought I was being splendidly original when, in 1963, I first made the assertion that *we can never do merely one thing*. Others thought so too, as became clear when *Fortune* magazine published an editorial in which they said that "Hardin's Law" (as they called it) was "something like a very clean glass door—you're not sure at first glance whether anything is there. But those seven seemingly casual words express a profound truth about human affairs."[3]

I am not about to beat my own drum. The most important point to make about the so-called "Hardin's Law" is that it is *not* original, despite what I may have thought in 1963. The miscarriage of plans, partial or complete, has been noted in the oldest of human literature; no doubt even before writing was invented, some human beings (parents, for instance) were aware of this reality. But reformers often repress this wisdom. In tackling the pervasive puzzle of why people do so many stupid things it would be well to ask first, why do we forget so much so fast? And second: why do basic truths have to be rediscovered generation after generation?

I suggest that we call the aphorism under consideration the *first law of human ecology,* because it is the ecological interaction of things that constantly surprises us and negates our laboriously worked out plans for reform. Some of the statements of this law that have been made over the centuries are gathered together in Box 19-1. Their differences deserve comment.

The statements of Anaxagoras, Thompson,[4] Muir[5] and Commoner,[6] are very *global* in their reach. "Global" is a favorite praise word of our time, but it sometimes implies too much. The Australian philosopher John Passmore summarizes the criticism well.[7] If everything is literally hitched to everything else in the universe, and we say nothing about the closeness of the hitching, we unnecessarily burden ourselves with a boundless obligation to round up all the influences.

Both the strengths and the weaknesses of the environmental movement are apparent in Francis Thompson's poetic words. From his final assertion that merely stirring a flower affects distant stars one might assume that Thompson had been meditating on Newton's law of gravitation, which tells us that every particle attracts every other particle in the universe. If we were to load Thompson's flower into a rocket and shoot it away into the stars beyond Saturn, the subsequent movements of Alpha Centauri, 25 million million miles away, would surely be altered: but no measurements that we can make would convince a court of law that Alpha Centauri had shivered because of our action. The inverse square law for gravitational attraction tells us that the asserted effect is practically unmeasurable and surely unimportant.

Numbers matter, but Francis Thompson took no notice of them. His upbringing was typical of literary figures. As a schoolboy he "excelled in English, Latin, and Greek. Of twenty-one competitive exams held in essay writing during his seminary days, he won first place in sixteen; he was usually first in English and often first or

Box 19-1. Interrelatedness and the Rhetoric of Conservatism.

Nothing exists apart; everything has a share in everything.

Anaxagoras 5th century, B.C.

There is nothing which is truly indifferent. All things in the universe are connected together. It is true that many of these links in human affairs are too subtle to be traced by our grosser optics. But we should observe as many of them as we are able.

William Godwin, 1798.

> All things by immortal power
>   Near or far
>   Hiddenly
> To each other linked are,
> That thou canst not stir a flower
> Without troubling of a star.

Francis Thompson, 1897.

When you try to pick out any thing by itself, you find it hitched to everything else in the universe.

John Muir, 1911.

The first law of ecology: Everything is connected to everything else.

Barry Commoner, 1971.

There is certainly a risk that we shall be utterly discouraged by the implications of Barry Commoner's "first ecological law" . . . for this makes it appear that to act at all is the height of imprudence. But fortunately I do not, before I swat a mosquito, have to calculate the consequences of my act on the sun's output of cosmic rays or the eutrophication of Lake Erie. It is just not true that everything I do has effects on *everything* else. What we do need always to remember, however—and this is sufficiently alarming—is that the unintended consequences of our actions are often surprisingly remote in time and place from those actions. (Skin cancer forty years after exposure to the sun; the excess fertiliser from my garden feeding algae in a remote stream.) Commoner's "law" somewhat resembles the old Heraclitean dictum "expect the unexpected." Valuable as a warning, it is useless as a guide to action.

John Passmore, 1974.

second in Latin. He also fell to last place in mathematics."[8] Society does not expect poets to be numerately oriented, but the shortcoming shown in Thompson's verse has become a serious defect in the popularizations of ecology. Popularizers are so tempted to take a "global" view of everything that their writings may be of little use in reaching practical decisions. We can't wait for all the facts to come in before we act; we can't understand everything. Overly global presentations of the world's problems have understandably caused a backlash among citizens who are charged with making practical decisions.

Since the "first law" is repeatedly encountered in new contexts, it is repeatedly renamed. Economists refer to it as the "law of unintended consequences." The social scientist Robert Merton has referred to it as the "unanticipated consequences of purposive social action."[9] Political scientist Robert Leone describes it in somewhat different terms: "Every act of government, no matter what its broader merits or demerits for society at large, creates winners and losers within the competitive sector of the economy. . . . This outcome is so predictable that it constitutes virtually an Iron Law of Public Policy."[10]

The frequent rediscovery of this default principle is understandable in terms of normal human development. It is natural that the young should first become aware of simple cause-and-effect relationships, only gradually realizing that they must substitute multiple "causal factors" for unitary "causes" in their explanations of the world.

Awareness of multiple consequences is fostered by a burgeoning interest in conserving the existing environment. At first the word "environment" may refer only to the world external to human beings. When it becomes apparent that the first law of ecology applies also to the world of human affairs, growth in conservatism takes place. The tendency of the first law to encourage inaction needs to be offset by the reflexive truth that *not to act is to act*. Or, as one psychoanalyst put it: "'Nothing' never happens."

"There's No Away to Throw to"

This may be called the second law of human ecology. Its relationship to the conservative position of Epicurus is apparent. It took the development of environmentalism to end some erroneous assumptions that had long been accepted by the movers and shakers of the commercial world, for example:

"The solution to pollution is dilution."

"Out of sight, out of mind."

"Muck is money!"—the defense in the nineteenth century to Blake's horror of the "dark Satanic mills" of newly industrialized England.

As Dan McKinley has pointed out, these dangerous illusions can be derived from the single assumption that "Private property includes the smokestack, but not what comes out of it."[11]

Environmentalists are now heavily engaged in bringing the general public around to the acceptance of the truth of the second law. The conviction that there is no "away" must be bred in the bone, from elementary school on, if we are to make rapid enough progress to save humanity from polluting itself into extinction (or at least into great misery). Acknowledging the reality of the "greenhouse effect" and modifying human behavior to reduce its consequences will require changes in education and human economy throughout the world. We may fail; if so, we will surely be the first species to have foreseen its own demise.

When "Guilty!" Is the Default Position of Choice

A major change in American law took place in the last half of the twentieth century. Focusing on criminal acts, ancient Anglo-Saxon law had decreed that the default position of the law should be "innocent until proven guilty." For the criminal law this is undoubtedly the best assumption. But when it comes to laws that govern the everyday activities of citizens living in an ever more crowded world, the assumption is perilous. Chemists have synthesized more than a million compounds, and a wealth of experience indicates that the effects on human beings of most of the compounds is bad. Society would soon be bankrupted if it had to prove, in courts of law, the harmful effects of every one of these compounds, while determining the threshold concentration of each at which harm is first observed. The most rational policy is to put the burden of proof on the entrepreneur who is hoping to make a profit from introducing one more compound into the human environment. The cost of proving harmlessness then becomes one of the costs of a profit-oriented business—as it should be.

It was not until 1962 that the burden of proof was put on manufacturers and distributors. That this should have occurred first in the area of human health is understandable. Human beings are, quite properly, so jealous of their health that, where health is involved, they can easily open their minds to the possibility of a revolutionary change in the law. *Guilty until proven innocent* was the new default position established by the Kefauver-Harris amendments to the food and drug laws.

In 1970 the National Environmental Policy Act (NEPA) extended this principle to environment-altering proposals. Manufacturers, real estate "developers," mining and lumber companies, and others with financial interests fight against this new default position, but the ever greater impingements of growing populations on the environment result in extending the application of the act, year by year.[12]

The Impact Law

The role of overpopulation and population growth in causing environmental deterioration is summarized in the equation: $I = P \times A \times T$.[13] The impact (I) of any group or nation on the environment can be viewed as the product of its population size (P) multiplied by per-capita affluence (A) as measured by consumption, in turn multiplied by a measure of the damage done by the technologies (T) employed in supplying each unit of that consumption. The $I = PAT$ equation shows immediately that, all else being equal, doubling a population's size will double its impact on the environment. And if, through great effort, individual impact ($A \times T$) is halved while the population doubles, the total impact will remain the same.[14]

The $I = PAT$ equation may be called the *third law of human ecology*. Though it is no more than common sense, it is often denied, usually implicitly, by people who should know better. Sometimes the denial is even explicit, as it was in a recent statement made by a professor of philosophy: "Pollution results not from our numbers . . . but from our lifestyles and our rate of consumption."[15] This was said nine years after the $I = PAT$ equation was given wide publicity.

Population buffs are often criticized for dwelling too much on the population factor (P) of the $I = PAT$ equation. Sometimes the criticism is justified. But focusing only on the A and T factors of the equation—affluence and technology—implies that population is of no importance. Yet common sense tells us that any impact of people on the environment must be proportional to the number of people. "Population is a multiplier," it is often said.

$I = PAT$ expresses an essential default position of ecology. In 1984, ecologists were astounded at the official position taken by the United States at the U.N. conference on population and the environment in Mexico City: our spokesmen said that "population growth is neutral." This was also the position taken by the Vatican. All other delegations supported the default position, I = PAT.

To deny the relevance of population size is to support a kind of fatalism: denial implies that absolutely nothing can be done about the human control of human population. At the same time, many of the people who focus only on the A and T factors assert that we in the developed world are under no obligation to reduce the physical quality of our lives by foregoing congenial technology and consuming fewer resources. It is at least implied, and sometimes asserted, that rich nations are guilty of keeping overpopulated nations miserable.

What should be the role of guilt in developing environmental policy? Many of the great world-religions use guilt as a tool to persuade individuals to consider the community. Psychoanalysis, an alternative way of working toward the same end, emphasizes understanding rather than guilt. Environmental activists are divided into the same two camps. Environmental guilt-mongers are generally more colorful and more noticed by the public. They also make more enemies. In the long run, how wise is it to call on guilt to motivate the rich to share with the world's poor?

Concern for the poor and powerless is admirable, but is it wholly selfless? Sociologist James Coleman has pointed out that a new virtue has become fashionable among opinion makers, namely the virtue of *conspicuous benevolence:*

> What are the kinds of results that most strongly elicit disapproval by one's colleagues in universities? The answer is not always and everywhere the same, but I believe that for many academics in many settings, the following can be said: There are certain policies, certain public activities, that have the property that they stem from benevolent intentions expressed toward those less fortunate or in some way oppressed. The intended consequences follow transparently from the policy. These are policies designed to aid the poor, or to aid blacks or Hispanics or women, and any result that would hinder one of these policies is subject to disapproval and attack. These are policies intended to display egalitarian intentions. For many academics they replace the patterns of conspicuous consumption that Thorstein Veblen attributed to the rich. They might be called policies of conspicuous benevolence. They display, conspicuously, the benevolent intentions of their supporters.[16]

Admittedly, the world would be better with a greater supply of benevolence; but when it comes to intentions, we should be guided by proverbial wisdom: "The road to hell is paved with good intentions."

20

Carrying Capacity

An often quoted passage of Arthur Conan Doyle's story "Silver Blaze" makes the point that the absence of data can be a datum. When the mystery of the purloined racehorse seems insoluble, Police Inspector Gregory asks Sherlock Holmes:

> "Is there any point to which you would wish to draw my attention?"
> "To the curious incident of the dog in the night-time."
> "The dog did nothing in the night-time."
> "That was the curious incident," remarked Sherlock Holmes.

The dog that does not bark attracts no attention to itself. It takes insight to recognize that a nonhappening can be an alarm. Herman Daly[1] showed a Holmeslike insight when he called attention to the bark that was absent from a would-be authoritative study made by a group of economists reporting to the prestigious National Research Council in 1986 on population growth and economic development.[2] In 108 pages of text there is not a single mention of *carrying capacity,* a concept that should be central to all discussions of population and environment. It is as though gravity were left out of a treatise on the dynamics of the solar system; or assets and liabilities were left out of a textbook on business accounting. If civilization survives another century, and if there are still economists, a history of what will then be called "modern economics" may well begin with a belittling account of the "premodern" economics of the twentieth century in which carrying capacity plays no role. Nothing shows so well the impermeability of the barriers between academic disciplines as the silence of economists about a concept that dominates discussions of game management, a discipline concerned with population and environment problems as they affect animals other than *Homo sapiens.* Economists, dealing only with human populations, probably unconsciously embrace the human exemptionist doctrine (Chapter 15), though their commitment is seldom no more than implicit in their statements (Box 20-1).[3]

Two serious criticisms can be leveled against most of the authors quoted in the box. First, it is obvious that they desperately yearn for a world without limits. This is particularly evident in the last quotation, by Gro Harlem Brundtland, who chaired the United Nations commission that issued this statement. One can praise the heart of the commission without agreeing with the head. Brundtland says we *must* supply a population that is twice as large as today's, therefore we *must* have continued economic growth, the implication being that we dare not inquire into the resource base on which such growth would have to be based. The earth has a mass of 5.983×10^{27} grams, only a tiny fraction of which can be turned into human

Box 20-1. Denials, Implicit or Explicit, of Carrying Capacity.

1. Cruelly, you [Western demographers] intend to adjust the population to the economy, while we Communists want to adjust the economy to the population.

Yugoslav delegate to U.N. Population Commission, 1947.

2. I would consider it barbaric for the Commission to contemplate a limitation of marriages or of legitimate births, and this for any country whatsoever, at any period whatsoever. With an adequate social organization it is possible to face any increase in population.

Ukrainian delegate to the U.N. Population Commission, 1947.

3. The problem is undue population growth: the enemy is not a number, however large, but a rate.

Bernard Berelson, 1965.

4. In relation to the special human carrying capacity of the earth, it is obvious that it is infinitely greater than present levels.

Osorio do Alameda, 1973.

5. There is no burden on the rest of the community if the parents bear the costs of rearing and educating the children. If they do not bear these costs, then there is a burden until the children become self-supporting. But this burden is unaffected by the size of the total population. Moreover it would be present even if a family had only one child.

Peter T. Bauer, 1976.

6. A politician from Upper Volta, who last year attended a preparatory meeting for the Desertification Conference, was told of the results of a case study that showed that intensive development was turning an area of the Sudan into a desert. "We cannot accept such conclusions," the politician said, "and if the UN Conference reaches such conclusions we cannot accept them either." His country, he said, intended to increase its population from 6.5 million to 30 million, all of whom, he insisted, would have the same standard of living as the inhabitants of California.

Edward Goldsmith, 1977.

7. Because of increases in knowledge, the earth's "carrying capacity" has been increasing throughout the decades and centuries and millennia to such an extent that the term "carrying capacity" has by now no useful meaning.

Julian Simon & Herman Kahn, 1984.

8. Economists and environmentalists do not understand each others' languages, as was evidenced in an informal meeting held [at the World Bank in 1984]. The economists at the meeting rejected the idea that resources could be finite. Said one: "The notion that there are limits that can't be taken care of by capital has to be rejected." Said another: "I think the burden of proof is on your side to show that there are limits and where the limits are." They were suspicious of well-worn ecological terms such as "carrying capacity" and "sustainability." Said one: "We need definitions in economic, not biological terms."

Constance Holden, 1987.

9. The World Commission on Environment and Development concluded in its 1987 report, *Our Common Future,* that sustained economic growth, which is a precondition for the elimination of mass poverty, is possible only within a more equitable international economic regime. The commission called for a new era of economic growth. . . . And without growth, how can we provide for twice the present population some time in the next century, when we cannot provide for everybody today? . . . The commission found no absolute limits to growth. Limits are indeed imposed by the impact of present technologies and social organization on the biosphere, but we have the ingenuity to change. And change we must.

Gro Harlem Brundtland, 1989.

beings and their appurtenances. It is pleasant to have one's dream ship propelled by the sail of conspicuous benevolence, but the ship of state needs an anchor in reality. Brundtland, denying the existence of absolute limits, embraces the concept of "sustainable development." In response, Donald Mann, the president of Negative Population Growth, Inc., maintained that "The concept of sustainable development is little more than a gigantic exercise in self-deception," because those who advocate sustainable development really mean "sustainable economic growth." This, in a world of limits, is "a thundering oxymoron if ever there was one."[4]

The second serious criticism is this: implicitly these statements presume some sort of perpetual motion machine ruling economics. Item 8 in the box includes the anti-Epicurean assertion that there are no "limits that can't be taken care of by capital." Herman Daly has responded cogently to this remarkable assertion: "Production functions that allow virtually unlimited substitution of capital for resources are clearly unrealistic. Otherwise we could make the same house with half the lumber [resources] but two or three times as many saws [capital]!"[5]

Human existence is caught in the nexus of the general production function introduced in Chapter 7:

$$\text{Source} \longrightarrow \text{Production} \longrightarrow \text{Sink}$$

The material source of all economic "production" is of two sorts: matter and energy. Aside from the atmosphere the matter that is practically available to our species is probably no more than the outer five-mile sheath of the globe. This, by our cleverness, we rework into forms useful to us, a re-formation that we, in our arrogance, call "production."

The artifacts we produce are not stable; they eventually degenerate into useless forms that are "thrown away" into the terrestrial "sink." Energy is required for the re-formation processes, and this we get almost entirely from solar radiation. Until the last few moments of historic time, solar radiation has been almost the only source of re-formation energy; when we exhaust the supplies of fossil fuel ("fossil sunlight," really), we will once again be dependent on the daily inflow of solar energy (unless, as was pointed out in Chapter 17, we pull off the miracle of creating the *absolutely reliable* human beings required for the safe production of nuclear power). Whatever its source, energy is incorporated in the materials produced. This energy eventually deteriorates into useless heat energy ("entropy").

Since the degeneration of the produced materials is not instantaneous, while the inflow of solar energy is continuous, there is some accumulation of produced materials, and this we call "capital." The accumulation of capital allows for some increase in the population. Population cannot increase forever, however, because of the second law; eventually a steady state must exist. In that state, most of the gift of solar energy will be expended on reworking materials that accumulate in the "sink," which will then become our only "source." At that point all economic "production" will be only a recycling of matter previously drawn from the "source" and deteriorated into "waste." The maximum human population possible will be determined by the carrying capacity of the earth subject to this production function. Before we tackle the complicated question of what the human carrying capacity of the earth might be, it will be well to study the much simpler question of the meaning of carrying capacity for nonhuman species.

Carrying Capacity in Animal Husbandry

For the simplest case, we imagine a pasture of fixed dimensions in a mild climate; in this are pastured a constant number of cows that have no other source of food the year around. The carrying capacity of the pasture is the maximum number of animals that can be sustained by this food source *year after year, without diminution of the quality of the pasture.*

Since photosynthesis is less in winter than in summer, a stable carrying capacity *must be tied to the least favorable conditions* (winter), not to the most favorable. This follows from "Liebig's law of the minimum," named after Justus von Liebig (1803–1873), a chemist who contributed important insights to biology. Some grass will "go to waste" in the summer. Moreover, we must allow for the variability of the climate by tying carrying capacity to the least favorable years (perhaps allowing for the one year in a hundred when things are really bad). This sort of provision for the unexpected is what engineers call a "safety factor." The greater the safety factor, the greater the "waste" of unused resources in ordinary years. The greedier the manager, the less the "waste"—and the less also is the safety of the total system.

We must not forget the power of exponential growth that drives every population. A proper number of cows will soon increase to a highly improper number, unless the animal husbandman does something about it. Increase must be prevented by getting rid of the excess. Management may be made more flexible by allowing a larger number of animals in the summer, provided one eliminates the excess before winter sets in.

Why be so careful not to exceed the carrying capacity? Because of the consequences of exceeding it, consequences first for the pasture and secondly for the animals themselves. Selective grazing by animals results in a progressive replacement of "sweet grass" by "weeds" (in the cattle's estimation). If the cattle are too numerous the trampling of the soil contributes to the selection effect and also makes the soil more easily eroded (thus further adversely affecting the growth of sweet grass). In time, the ability of the ground to hold water between rains is diminished. All of these factors combine to reduce the carrying capacity of the territory, stepwise, year by year, until scarcely any animals at all can be supported on what was initially a rich resource.

A sorry aspect of this process is that there is no fully matching restoration process; or, if restoration does occur it takes much, much longer than destruction. The two inches of soil lost in a few years may take a thousand years to be regenerated. Many, perhaps most, of the deserts of the world have been produced by biological populations that exceeded the carrying capacity.

The Eleventh Commandment: Ecology's Contribution to Ethics

Exceeding the carrying capacity in one year diminishes the carrying capacity in subsequent years. The ultimate result of such transgression is the ruin of the environment. It is for this reason that ecologists speak of the "Eleventh Commandment":[6]

Thou shalt not transgress the carrying capacity.

Box 20-2. Plato on the Transgression of the Carrying Capacity in Attica.

[In earlier days Attica] yielded far more abundant produce. In comparison of what then was, there are remaining only the bones of the wasted body; all the richer and softer parts of the soil having fallen away, and the mere skeleton of the land being left. But in the primitive state of the country, its mountains were high hills covered with soil, and the plains were full of rich earth, and there was abundance of wood in the mountains. Of this last traces still remain, for although some of the mountains now only afford sustenance to bees, not so very long ago there were still to be seen roofs of timber cut from trees growing there, which were of a size sufficient to cover the largest houses; and there were many other high trees, cultivated by man and bearing abundance of food for cattle. Moreover, the land reaped the benefit of the annual rainfall, not as now losing the water which flows off the bare earth into the sea, but, having an abundant supply in all places, and receiving it into herself and treasuring it up in the close clay soil, it let off into the hollows the streams which it absorbed from the heights, providing everywhere abundant fountains and rivers, of which there may still be observed sacred memorials in places where fountains once existed; and this proves the truth of what I am saying.

The wisdom of this should be obvious, but to many it is not, in our predominantly urban times. As the economist E. F. Schumacher pointed out, "The people who now control our destiny almost universally have a city orientation."[7] How urbanity has corrupted perception becomes clear when we note what the twentieth-century novelist Henry Miller said about Greece, as compared with what Plato said twenty-three centuries earlier. Miller claimed that present-day Greece (1941) "is what you expect the earth to look like given a fair chance. It is the subliminal threshold of innocence. It stands, as it stood from birth, naked and fully revealed."[8] Plato (427–347 B.C.), in his *Critias,* gave a strikingly different interpretion of the Greek landscape (Box 20-2).[9] Plato knew that the Greece he lived in was not as it had been "from birth," that its present nakedness was something imposed on it by the ill-advised actions of men. Whatever the carrying capacity of ancient Greece might once have been, human beings and their domestic animals transgressed it well before Plato's time. The transgression has continued to the present day. (Does this mean that mankind is incapable of learning?)

The devastation of Greece had two principal causes: deforestation for the sake of fuel and lumber, and overgrazing and overbrowsing by a multitude of uncontrolled goats (who thrive on seedling trees). Semiarid lands are especially vulnerable to such destruction. What happened to Greece and most of the lands bordering the Mediterranean is now happening in parts of the United States. In 1981 a committee of the Council on Environmental Quality concluded that "about 225 million acres of land in the United States are undergoing severe desertification—an area roughly the size of the 13 original states."[10]

The Carrying Capacity for Wild Populations

Populations of domesticated animals must be kept from increasing beyond the carrying capacity of their territories by killing the yearly increase. (If the increase is harvested and sold alive to someone else, that amounts to the same thing, because sooner or later the "dividend" will be "liquidated," that is, killed.) But what about populations of *wild* animals, which are not subject to human oversight? Since *all* species tend to increase exponentially, what keeps wild animals from "eating themselves out of house and home"?

We find a general answer in the account of an unplanned experiment on a remote Alaskan island.[11] In 1944, for reasons that are now obscure, some men released twenty-four female reindeer and five males on St. Matthew's Island in the Bering Sea. There had been no mammals on this island until then. Without predators to contend with, and with plenty of reindeer moss to eat, the herd increased rapidly. In nineteen years time the population swelled to some six thousand animals, a yearly increase of 33 percent. In the heavy winter snows of 1963 virtually the entire population died. In 1966 only forty-two animals were found there, only one of which was a male, and he was suspected of being sterile. Presumably the population has since died out.

Calling the severe 1963 winter the *cause* of the disaster would be a mistake; the weather was only the coup de grace. A professional game manager has estimated that the carrying capacity of the island was five reindeer per square kilometer. In 1963 the population had reached a density of eighteen per square kilometer, or 3.6 times the sustainable number. This horde ate the moss down near the starvation level, and the animals themselves went into the winter badly underweight.

How could the disaster have been prevented? By a high death rate imposed years earlier. The agents might have been human hunters, but this island is so difficult to get to much of the year that such visits would be hard to arrange. An alternate remedy would have been to add wolves to the island's fauna: these could certainly have put an end to the transgression of the carrying capacity by the reindeer.

Wolves would have produced a different nemesis for the ungulates. Without adequate hiding place on their barren island the deer would have been unable to escape their enemies, ever. As the predators increased in number the prey would have decreased faster and faster. Finally the wolves would have "eaten themselves out of house and home," and then died themselves. That a stable predator-prey system needs something in the way of sanctuaries for the prey was recognized as far back as 1786 by a thoughtful and observant English clergyman, Joseph Townsend.[12] This was almost a century before Ernst Haeckel named the science of ecology, and Charles Darwin started it on the high road—and nearly two centuries before Rachel Carson brought the news to the general public.

Many well-meaning people resist admitting and acting on the insight that predators serve a useful function for prey populations—useful even by narrow human standards. For centuries such stories as "Little Red Riding Hood" have conditioned children to think of prey as innocent and predators as wicked. Why this emphasis? The cynical explanation is that subconsciously men have seen wolves and lions as the competitors of the human species, the supreme predator-over-all. Man has trained his children to hate his competitors. (Other explanations of the folktales are possible.) Whatever the truth may be, the fact is that wolves have had an undeservedly "bad press."

How effective early childhood conditioning can be is apparent in the story of the life of Aldo Leopold (1887–1948), one of the patron saints of the ecology move-

ment.[13] He started his professional life as an enthusiastic enemy of wolves, mountain lions, and other "varmints" that were decimating flocks of sheep in the South-
west of the United States. Many of his writings during the period from 1915 to 1920
bear testimony to his enthusiasm for killing wolves. In 1920 he said that "the last
one must be caught"—and killed. In 1925 he modified his position only to say that
we must avoid the danger of exterminating *all* predators, adding "but there is no
danger of this yet." For the next ten years his position was ambivalent and waver-
ing.

Then in 1936 he took a trip to the Sierra Madre in the state of Chihuahua, Mexico, a land in the same climatic zone as New Mexico, where Leopold had spent so
many years. He was thunderstruck by the beauty of the landscape, in which many
animal species were abundant but none were overabundant. "All my life," he said,
"I had seen only sick land, whereas here was a biota still in perfect aboriginal health.
The term 'unspoiled wilderness' took on a new meaning." Such was Leopold's road
to Damascus; his conversion, like Saint Paul's, produced an emotional and intellectual turn of 180 degrees. From being the enemy of predators, he became their
friend and champion. From one who had sought to maximize the number of deer
lives, he became the proponent of the temperate killing of prey animals—by predators preferably, but by human hunters if necessary; in any case, *a killing of prey
animals for the good of their own kind.*

How many years' experience did Aldo Leopold have to live through before he
underwent his damascene enlightenment? *Twenty-one:* from 1915 to 1936, during
all of which time he was obsessed by the problems of game management. When we
despair of the backwardness of ordinary citizens in understanding population principles we should remind ourselves of the Leopold story. If it took a dedicated professional twenty-one years to see the light, we should not be surprised at the slower
progress of nonprofessionals. (They have other things on their minds.)

From 1936 to the end of his life twelve years later, Aldo Leopold carried the
ecological gospel to the people, and was much abused for it. The reception of
nature's word was made much more difficult by the appearance of the Walt Disney
film *Bambi* in 1942. The film's message is childishly simple: the lives of sweet, cud-
dly deer should be cherished, always, and protected against those wicked old hunters and wolves. No qualifications; not the slightest recognition of the reality of carrying capacity. No wonder that an energetic attempt to reduce the tragic
overpopulation of deer in Wisconsin, made in the following year, should meet with
passionate public opposition. The opposition continues to this day.[14]

Leopold was a member of a commission that called for an "antlerless season"—
an open season on shooting *all* deer, instead of just the bucks (males). Why is legal
hunting usually restricted to the killing of bucks? No doubt because of the traditional sentimental attitude toward the female of the species: "women and children
first," we say in rescue situations.

Ecological insight gives a new twist to this old directive. When it comes to overpopulation in a polygynous species like deer you had better concentrate your fire
on the females, for they are demographically the more dangerous sex: they bear the
babies. If hunters shoot 90 percent of the males, the remaining 10 percent of the
bucks can "service" all the females. On the other hand, if hunters should shoot 90
percent of the females, population growth will be reduced by 90 percent for that

season. As for killing little Bambis, in an overpopulated species they won't be missed when next year comes. There will be time enough to cherish the young after the population is reduced to a point *below* the carrying capacity of the land. *Thou shalt not transgress the carrying capacity.* So speaks rationality; sentimentality is shocked.

Leopold was the guiding spirit of the Wisconsin commission that tried to justify the 1943 all-out deer-killing season. When questioned about the size of the deer population Leopold admitted that the figure given was not the product of a careful census; it was merely an estimate. This admission provoked an angry open letter to the governor and legislators.

> The infamous and bloody 1943 deer slaughter was sponsored by one of the commission members, Mr. Aldo Leopold, who admitted in writing that the figures he uses were PURE GUESSWORK. . . .
>
> Imagine our fine deer herd shot to pieces by a man who rates himself as a Professor and uses a GUESS instead of facts? Mere fawns just out of their spots were sacrificed by our conservation commission. Does, with young already conceived, young, immature bucks, in fact, everything that ran was indiscriminately slaughtered, not by sportsmen, but by a bunch of hungry meat hunters, spurred on by the commission's poison propaganda.[15]

This sort of criticism is common among people who have never been introduced to the logic of the "default position." A census of shy deer in a bushy environment is difficult to take, but we do not need an exact number; nor do we need to have a figure for the amount of photosynthesis carried on by the edible plants; nor the number of pounds of deer food produced per season. When the deer population has surged beyond the carrying capacity of the territory we need only to do this: *Read the environment.* When there are too many animals, tender new seedlings of trees and bushes are rare, and the browse line on the bark of trees is as high as deer can reach. *Look at the animals:* when they are skinny and have more intestinal parasites than usual you know they are suffering from malnutrition.

Once it is recognized that the carrying capacity has been transgressed, the battle continues along other lines. As Leopold said, "Herd reduction is like paying the national debt; nobody wants to do it *now.*"[16] The rhetorical tactics conjured up to escape the logical demands of carrying capacity theory are sometimes wonderful to contemplate. A full generation after deer suffered the "Massacre of Forty-Three," on 4 March 1979 to be exact, the National Geographic Society aired an hour's television show on the problems posed by excess elephants in the highlands of Kenya. "Last Stand in Eden" told how protected elephants were pillaging the native farms, leading to demands that they be killed or removed. That killing was unthinkable was made clear by showing some film clips of the gory slaughter of more than a hundred elephants in Ruwanda several years earlier. So attempts were made to drive the elephants out of the highlands, using the noise of low-flying helicopters. For awhile it worked. But the elephants, perceiving the lesser attraction of the lands they were driven to, and (apparently) becoming inured to the hideous helicopter noise, ended up by returning to the land where the eating was good. On the tape frequent statements made by local game managers expressed their horror of elephant killing and called for "understanding" and "patience" while they tried to persuade the elephants to change their tastes and their ways. Not once was the term "carrying capacity" used, nor was the concept introduced in any other way. "Understanding" and "patience" indeed! All this cowardly nonsense was committed to tape thirty years after the death of Aldo Leopold! One suspects that some of the African game managers had wiser things to say but that diffident Society editors in Washington expunged them from the final tape.

The "sanctity of life" is more than a shibboleth of Western man: it stands for a strong commitment to try to preserve human life no matter what the consequences. In recent years the commitment has, among a significant fraction of the population, spread from the human species to the lives of lesser "animals." (The quotation marks are needed because the animals so protected are only large animals, most often mammals and birds. Microsopic protozoa and roundworms do not qualify as "animals" worthy of protection.) Time after time the rational advice of biologists is rejected, though the end result is a great increase in the suffering inflicted on cherished but too numerous animals. Mere life, even mere animal life, is held sacred by "animal lovers."

One last instance. Angel Island in San Franciso Bay is populated by a herd of about 150 deer, a number far beyond its carrying capacity, even with the artificial feeding supplied by the government and visitors. The animals are in miserable shape. Proposals to shoot the excess aroused a storm of protest among "animal lovers." So in 1981 a university game manager proposed that a few coyotes be introduced to the island. These, by their predation on the fawns, would eventually reduce the deer population. Even this natural population control was viewed with horror by an official of the local Society for the Prevention of Cruelty to Animals, who said: "We do not want to see a slaughter of Angel Island deer, whether by man himself, or through a man-made solution such as introducing predators."[17] (Since when has predation been an invention of the human species?) In the objections made by the SPCA there was no indication of an understanding of limits and exponential growth. When the heart so overrules the head, even in animal affairs, it is obvious that resistance to the logic of carrying capacity will be even greater when human populations are involved.

Cultural Carrying Capacity

The concept of carrying capacity is implicit in Malthus's theory. What he failed to realize (as did most others of his time) was that he was living in a time when the "set point" of population was rapidly moving upward, as a result of technological and industrial advances (see Chapter 10). Anti-Malthusians generalized the trend of a couple of centuries and presumed that population would never again press against limits. Economics being the handmaiden of business and industry, it was natural for economists to lose patience with the idea of carrying capacity (as well as with diminishing returns, absolute scarcities, and other concepts infected with the idea of limits).

When the concept of carrying capacity is defined in terms of energy, another difficulty has to be faced: the problem of values. An adult human being requires about 2,300 calories of energy a day to remain alive and be moderately active.[18]

Recent estimates put the energy consumption of the average American at 230,000 calories per day—100 times as much as the minimum. What are all those extra calories used for? Manufacturing and driving automobiles and airplanes; building and maintaining the infrastructure needed for transportation; producing and washing clothes; constructing buildings; heating, lighting and cooling them; manufacturing and enjoying radios, television, and movies; manufacturing, using, and throwing away paper, plastic, and metal objects, as well as maintaining our entire technological civilization.

It should be clear that the question, "What is the carrying capacity of the earth, for human beings?" is not sufficiently specific to lead to a satisfactory answer. On the American scale of living the carrying capacity of the earth is only about one one-hundredth as great as it would be if people would be content with the barest minimum of goods—no clothes, no autos or airplanes, no radio, no TV or movies, no space heating and cooling, no libraries, no schools, no mechanical recreation, and so on.

Moreover, some goods—the amenities—impose costs that cannot easily be stated in terms of energy: the solitude of lonely beaches, access to wilderness and areas rich in flowers, birds, and butterflies, together with time to enjoy these amenities as well as music and the visual arts. The ability to furnish these goods is also part of the human carrying capacity of the environment: more important to some people, less so to others. "What is the carrying capacity?" and "What is the optimum human population?" are complicated and subtle questions.

Because it is not immediately apparent that carrying capacity has a different meaning for human beings than it has for deer, for instance, some rather ridiculous answers have been given to the question, "How many people can the globe support?" One physicist, for instance, guesstimated that the answer might be as great as 50 billion people.[19] It is more than doubtful that this man—or any other—would be content to live with no more than his proportionate share of the environment if the total population swelled to that number.

The logic of the carrying capacity is the same when we shift to the human condition, but the definition needs to be changed to take account of all the cultural amenities that people hope to enjoy. As the Bible says, "it is not on bread alone that man lives, but it is on everything produced by command of the Lord that man lives."[20] Though he did not develop the idea of carrying capacity, Malthus himself had an intuitive understanding of it. A German translator of his works wrote that Malthus's maxim was that "there should be no more people in a country than could enjoy daily a glass of wine and a piece of beef with their dinner."[21] Prohibitionists and vegetarians might disagree with the particular "goods" used as examples, but the point is a general one: at a sustainable size of population, *the quality of life and the quantity of it are inversely related.* Choices must be made.

The relativity of life's quality and quantity has been seized upon by some critics as sufficient reason for rejecting the concept of carrying capacity. Some call it subjective: perhaps it is, but who says that it is forbidden for men and women to deal with subjective matters? Some critics imply that unless carrying capacity can be assigned a precise, unique value it is meaningless. Still others imply that if our determination of this capacity does not yield a constant figure over time, then we are justified in supposing that carrying capacity is infinite. As William Catton says,

"Politicians and industrialists grasp such straws all too eagerly."[22] Perpetual growth is a religious tenet.

Modern men and women, ecologically sensitized, are inclined to include wilderness among their amenities.[23] To make sure that our calculations of the possible *and acceptable* size of the human population take account of the many goods and amenities that may mean nothing to deer, coyotes, and rabbits, we need to enlarge the measuring standard to what we can call the *cultural carrying capacity* of the environment.[24] Thus does the problem of the optimum human population become inextricably interwoven with problems of values.

The reason economists have shied away from carrying capacity should by now be no great mystery. Adam Smith began his professional career by tackling questions of value in his 1759 opus, *The Theory of Moral Sentiments.* Some of the answers he sought could be found in an analysis of the apparently value-free questions of efficiency, waste, and so on. He concentrated on these when he wrote his *Wealth of Nations* (1776). To an increasing extent the economists who followed Smith began their work where he ended his, in the investigation of apparently value-free questions. For a long time economists have been uncomfortable with questions of values. The convenient and comfortable way became the canonical. By 1984 it was possible for two spokesmen for economics (neither of whom, incidentally, was trained as an economist) to assert without contradiction by the economic community at large that the term "carrying capacity" had "no useful meaning" (statement 7 in Box 20-1). The large questions that had led Adam Smith to give human structure to economic questions were no longer tackled by many leading economists, or even admitted to be meaningful questions. The baby had been thrown out with the bathwater.

Practitioners of a discipline can, of course, limit their inquiries in any way they choose, but economists who rule out all questions of value trivialize their subject. Human ecologists studying population growth and its consequences cannot indulge in this luxury. Inevitably questions of value bring up questions of distribution, to which we now turn.

21

The Global Pillage: Consequences
of Unmanaged Commons

Great is the power of words when manipulated by a master who has his finger on the public pulse. In the 1960s the Canadian Marshall McLuhan evidently tapped a major stream of consciousness when he proclaimed the coming of "the global village," a world in which nearly instantaneous communication would weld together the aspirations of mankind. A sharing world. A land of heart's desire. Unfortunately his image took no account of the effects of scale or the consequences of the rules of distribution. When these variables are plugged into the equation, the dream of a bucolic global village dissolves into a nightmare of global pillage. Humanity has now completed some political experiments that reveal the nightmare.

The Soviet State: The Finale of a Delusion

How will our time be remembered a hundred years from now? It is at least plausible that the twentieth century will be commemorated as the era in which Marx's ideas were at last given a fair trial and found wanting. From the spring of 1917, when Lenin returned to Russia to stir things up, to the cataclysms of the autumn of 1989 was seventy-two years—the biblical lifetime of a man. Three generations. Quite enough time to allow Marxism in its various forms to reveal its inherent deficiencies. Yet, when the end came, almost everyone was surprised at the speed with which nearly 300 million people revealed their disillusionment and set about trying to put the pieces together into a better political pattern.

We wonder of course why Marx's ideas were so resistant to the intellectual cold showers that beat against them for three score years and ten. The literary critic Lionel Trilling put his finger on a force that caused "intellectuals" to cling to the Left during the period between the two world wars. As Trilling expressed the mind-set of these influential people: "One need not be actually *for* Communism; one was morally compromised, turned toward evil and away from good if one was *against* it."[1] To use James Coleman's term, adopting the Marxist position was the most fashionable way to practice "conspicuous benevolence." Supporters of free enterprise were almost uniformly painted as promoters of unmitigated selfishness.

Only one thread of Marxist thought need be followed here, a thread that is intimately involved in the theory of population. It is the idea to which Marx gave such unforgettable form in 1875, when he said that the ideal of the good society was one in which the distribution of wealth and duties would be in accordance with this double rule: "From each according to his abilities, to each according to his needs!" (The exclamation point in this double imperative is Marx's.)[2]

No doubt one of the reasons for the prompt popularity of this pronouncement is found in its echo of several passages in the Bible. In the second chapter of Acts of the Apostles, we are told of a community of Christians who "had all things in common," and among whom goods were distributed according "as every man had need." Similar texts occur in other religions. Marx was drawing on an ancient store of religious sentiment when he expressed this formula for the good life. Considering Marx's poor opinion of organized religion ("the opium of the people") there is some irony in his indebtedness. This basic similarity of ideals in Christianity and Marxism helps explain the phenomenon that fascinated the self-taught philosopher Eric Hoffer, namely the ease with which a "true believer" can shift from Marxism to Christianity, and vice versa.[3] In the twentieth century the hierarchy of the Roman Catholic Church has had difficulty making peace with its idealistic offshoot, "liberation theology," which has more than a tinge of Marxism in it.

Irony is joined to tragedy when we realize that a definitive disproof of the Marxist imperative had been given four decades before 1875 by an obscure Oxford professor of mathematics and economics, William Forster Lloyd (1794–1852).

The Rural Roots of Distribution Theory

The heart of the argument propounded in Lloyd's publication of 1833 is given in Box 21-1.[4] In traditional animal husbandry the animals themselves were generally made private property long before the pastures on which they grazed were privatized. So long as there is a great sufficiency of pastureland, commonized real estate is efficient: no fences need be maintained and there is little call for human supervision. Such pasturelands qualify as "unmanaged commons."

But as the number of people and cattle increase, the amount of pastureland becomes a limiting factor to animal production (be it milk to drink or beef to eat). It is then observed (as Lloyd pointed out) that the cattle on common land are "puny and stunted" as compared with the cattle on a privately owned pasture. The reason is simple. It pays a private landowner *not* to put too many cattle on his land because he will himself have to assume all the loss that comes from overpasturing. By contrast, if the pasture is owned by a multitude of herdsmen, and if each is free to add as many animals to the pasture as he wishes, the costs imposed by overpasturing will be shared by all the owners (since the pasture is common property), whereas the benefits of having more cattle will come to each cattle owner (since the cattle are private property).

So long as the population of cattle on the pasture is well below the carrying capacity, these considerations are of little importance because the costs imposed on the land by the cattle are negligible and are speedily corrected by photosynthesis. But once the number of cattle exceeds the carrying capacity, the costs of overpasturing are appreciable. Furthermore, with continued overpasturing, the costs grow greater each year as weeds replace sweet grass and the soil is eroded away. That

---

Box 21-1. William Forster Lloyd on the Unmanaged Commons.

Suppose two persons to have a common purse, to which each may freely resort. The ordinary source of motives for economy is a foresight of the diminution in the means of future enjoyment depending on each act of present expenditure. If a man takes a guinea out of his own purse, the remainder, which he can spend afterwards, is diminished by a guinea. But not so, if he takes it from a fund, to which he and another have an equal right of access. The loss falling upon both, he spends a guinea with as little consideration as he would use in spending half a guinea, were the fund divided. Each determines his expenditure as if the whole of the joint stock were his own. Consequently, in a multitude of partners, where the dimunition effected by each separate act of expenditure is insensible, the motive for economy entirely vanishes. . . .

[This analysis shows] how the future is struck out of the reckoning, when the constitution of society is such as to diffuse the effects of individual acts throughout the community at large instead of appropriating them to the individuals, by whom they are respectively committed. . . .

Why are the cattle on a common so puny and stunted? Why is the common itself so bare-worn, and cropped so differently from the adjoining inclosures? No inequality, in respect of natural or acquired fertility, will account for the phenomenon. The difference depends on the difference of the way in which an increase of stock in the two cases affects the circumstances of the author of the increase. If a person puts more cattle into his own field, the amount of the subsistence which they consume is all deducted from that which was at the command, of his original stock; and if, before, there was no more than a sufficiency of pasture, he reaps no benefit from the additional cattle, what is gained in one way being lost in another. But if he puts more cattle on a common, the food which they consume forms a deduction which is shared between all the cattle, as well that of others as his own, in proportion to their number, and only a small part of it is taken from his own cattle.

Two Lectures on the Checks to Population, 1833.

---

being so, one might suppose that rational herdsmen who were aware of all the facts would change their policies and reduce the size of their herds. *Not so,* said Lloyd: the system of {commonized pasture + privatized herds} *actually rewards each "rational" herdsman for doing the wrong thing.* In modern times this insight has been spelled out in greater detail:

As a rational being, each herdsman seeks to maximize his gain. Explicitly or implicitly, more or less consciously, he asks, "What is the utility *to me* of adding one more animal to my herd?" This utility has one negative and one positive component.

1. The positive component is a function of the increment of one animal. Since the herdsman receives all the proceeds from the sale of the additional animal, the positive utility is nearly $+1$.

2. The negative component is a function of the additional overgrazing created by one more animal. Since, however, the effects of overgrazing are shared by all the herdsmen, the negative utility for any particular decision-making herdsman is only a fraction of -1.

Adding together the component partial utilities, the rational herdsman concludes that the only sensible course for him to pursue is to add another animal to his herd. And another. . . . But this is the conclusion reached by each and every rational herdsman sharing a commons. Therein is the tragedy. Each man is locked into a system that compels him to increase his herd without limit—in a world that is limited. Ruin is the destination toward which all men rush, each pursuing his own best interest in a society that believes in the freedom of the commons. Freedom in a commons brings ruin to all.[5]

Lloyd had expressed the same point somewhat differently. In his day people often spoke of the "faculties" of the mind, one of which was the "faculty of reasoning." Lloyd said, "[T]he obligation to prudence being placed [whenever a common is involved] upon the society collectively, instead of being distributed to the individual members, the effect is, that, though the reasoning faculty is in full force, and each man can clearly foresee the consequences of his actions, yet the conduct is the same as if that faculty had no existence."[6]

One more aspect of the situation deserves notice. In our day any malfunctioning in the distribution system is very likely to be blamed on people. For instance, the destruction of an overpastured common is likely to be blamed on the greed of individual herdsmen. *Blaming misses the point.* Each human being, like every other animal, is genetically programmed to seek his own good. "Prudence is," as Lloyd said, "a selfish virtue"—and, since prudence makes for survival, natural selection justifies the word *virtue.* (The genes of postulated ancestors who *selflessly* insisted on acting imprudently would soon be competitively eliminated from the hereditary stream.) The only blame that can reasonably be assigned to the herdsmen of an overpopulated common is blame for clinging to the system of the commons once the carrying capacity has been transgressed. The tragedy is brought on not by individual sin ("greed"), but by the system itself; or by clinging to a system that won't work once the carrying capacity has been reached. The tragedy of the commons is a consequence of scarcity. The Marxist distributive rule, "From each according to his abilities, to each according to his needs," where each person is free to judge his own needs, necessarily leads to tragedy in a world of scarcities.

The Three Basic Distribution Systems

So how should a supply of goods be distributed among petitioners? We can avoid that tricky little word "should" by asking more precisely: What will be the consequences of various methods of distribution? Consequences are determined by the lines of responsibility. A great deal of nonsense has been written and said about "responsibility." We can escape much of this nonsense if we adopt philosopher Charles Frankel's definition: "A decision is responsible when the man or group that makes it has to answer for it to those who are directly or indirectly affected by it."[7] Three basic systems of distribution need to be examined for their responsibility content.

Commonism

The system of the unmanaged commons has just been described and found wanting. Personal responsibility is so dilluted by the rule of "to each according to his needs" that disaster is certain once scarcity has taken charge.

Privatism

When both the land and the animals are owned by the same person, full Frankelian responsibility prevails. The owner suffers fully for his errors of judgment. Equally, he benefits from good decisions. No sermonizing is called for.

Suppose, however, that the land is owned by one person and the herd by another; and suppose the cattle owner is free to move elsewhere when the pasturage deteriorates? The dangers of such "tenant farming" have long been known. Arthur Young (1741–1820), an English writer on agriculture, pointedly described them: "Give a man the secure possession of a bleak rock and he will turn it into a garden; give him a nine year's lease of a garden and he will convert it into a desert." Ownership that can be separated from occupancy and operation is an open invitation to the occupant to strive for short-term profits at the expense of long-term conservation.

In several thousand years of mutation, private property has differentiated into many modes; think of stocks and bonds; of options; of "commodity futures"—and so on. The analysis of these in the light of Frankelian responsibility has been largely neglected. We cannot indulge in that sort of inquiry here, beyond pointing out that legally qualifying as "private property" does not guarantee full Frankelian responsibility.

Socialism

A managed commons is a form of socialism. A group of owners appoint a manager for their common property, and then leave him to enforce the rules (and perhaps even to make them). If he manages well, he will be rewarded; if poorly, he will be punished or fired. The manager is subject to *contrived* responsibility. This raises the practical question of *Quis custodiet ipsos custodes?*—Who will watch the watcher himself? No single answer fits all cases.

Commonism—privatism—socialism: which is the best system of distribution? There is no general answer. Large modern nations are a mixture of the three systems, and the mixture changes from time to time. Looking only at America we note that a small business is often simply private property; a large business is "incorporated" so that many stockholders "own" a fraction of the equity, while the managers manage with (sometimes) virtually no financial stake in the corporation. Our sidewalks are pure socialism: each person uses them as much as he needs to, independently of the taxes he has paid. Most automobile roads are socialized, but major roads may be privatized and tolls collected from the users.

The restriction of rights requires community agreement. The body politic must agree to coerce its individual members into giving up some of their freedom—for their own good in the long run. If this restriction comes about democratically it can be described as *mutual coercion, mutually agreed upon.* And of course, since unanimity is difficult to come by in large groups, the members of the community must accept the will of the majority. (How large the required majority must be is open to negotiation.) "Coercion" is something of a dirty word to many people today; it is important to recognize that every democratically achieved "social contract" involves mutual coercion.

Obstacles to Prudence in the Population Commons

The most radical of Lloyd's contributions was his application of the theory of the commons to population problems (Box 21-2).[8] Practical men and women have always been aware of how small a role prudence plays in the decision to have a baby—if "decision" is the right word! Boswell tells us that his idol, Dr. Johnson, on 26 October 1769, opined that "It is not from reason and prudence that men marry, but from inclination. A man is poor; he thinks, 'I cannot be worse, and so I'll e'en take Peggy.'" This was said, of course, in the days when birth control methods were primitive, and marrying was almost synonymous with begetting children.

Suppose the begetting is imprudent? Suppose the parents cannot support the child, perhaps because a crop failure has pushed the price of food beyond their reach? It is hard for people today to imagine the equanimity with which society, only two centuries ago, accepted the death of poor children in hard times. Three years after Dr. Johnson in England commented on the imprudence of Peggy's friend, the biologist Carl Linnaeus described the effects of a famine in Sweden:

> I fear that I shall not have any under-gardeners this summer to do daily work, for they say they cannot work without food, and for many days they have not tasted a crust of bread. One or two widows here are said not to have had any bread for themselves or their children for 8 days, and are ashamed to beg. Today a wife was sent to the castle [dungeon] for having cut her child's throat, having had no food to give it, that it might not pine away in hunger and tears.[9]

Box 21-2. William Forster Lloyd: Prudence Nullified by a Population Commons.

Marriage is a present good. The difficulties attending the maintenance of a family are future. But in a community of goods, where the children are maintained at public tables, or where each family takes according to its necessities out of the common stock, these difficulties are removed from the individual. They spread themselves, and overflow the whole surface of society, and press equally on every part. All may determine their conduct by the consideration of the present only. All are at liberty to follow the bent of their inclinations in an early marriage. But . . . it is impossible to provide an adequate supply of food for all who can be born. Hence, supposing the form of the society to remain, the shares of subsistence are continually diminishing, until all are reduced to extreme distress, and until, ultimately, the further increase of population is repressed by the undisguised check of misery and want. . . .

[T]he simple fact of a country being overpopulous, by which I mean its population pressing too closely against the means of subsistence, is not, of itself, sufficient evidence that the fault lies in the people themselves, or a proof of the absence of a prudential disposition. The fault may rest, not with them as individuals, but with the constitution of the society, of which they form part.

Two Lectures on the Checks to Population, 1833.

It is clear where Linnaeus's sympathies lay, but it is equally clear that he was not moved to action. Nor was anyone else. Such inactivity seems cruel to us now because people who are rich enough to read books like this can scarcely imagine living in a world in which there is a genuine shortage of food. But in Linnaeus's day it would have done no good for the rich to donate money to a community chest because the food for a large population of needy people was simply not available for purchase. In a world of genuine scarcity a rich minority can offer the too numerous indigent little but sympathy.

Unlike many "primitive" societies, the modern Western world does not approve of infanticide as a corrective for reproductive imprudence (or simple bad luck). But need often breeds solutions beyond the imagination of the law. The historical researches of William Langer have shown that Europe, in the eighteenth and nineteenth centuries, invented a legal way to correct for reproductive imprudence: hospitals and homes for foundlings. Officially, the purpose of a foundling home was to save the lives of babies whose mothers felt they could not support them. In practice, such a home had quite the opposite effect. In those pre-Pasteurian days babies that were crowded together were swept away by periodic epidemics of disease. The historian has described the consequences:

> In all of France fully 127,507 children were abandoned in the year 1833. Anywhere from 20 to 30 percent of all children born were left to their fate. The figures for Paris suggest that in the years 1817–1820 the "foundlings" comprised fully 36 percent of all births. In some of the Italian hospitals the mortality (under one year of age) ran to 80 or 90 percent. In Paris the *Maison de la Couche* reported that of 4,779 babies admitted in 1818, 2,370 died in the first three months and another 956 within the first year. . . . Many contemporaries denounced it as legalized infanticide, and one at least suggested that the foundling hospitals post a sign reading "Children killed at Government expense."[10]

The sarcasm indicates that the climate of opinion was changing in Lloyd's time. In part this was because the public could afford to liberalize their views. The amount of food per capita was trending upward, so it was becoming possible (given suitable changes in distribution) to save more lives among the imprudently begotten. Then too, the birth control movement, which may be said to have begun in earnest in 1822 in England, offered another way of escaping the temptation to infanticide. In 1821, the economist James Mill wrote guardedly of "prudence; by which, either marriages are sparingly contracted, or care is taken that children, beyond a certain number, shall not be the fruit." Unfortunately, many of those who practiced personal prudence also exerted themselves mightily to prevent the general public from learning about birth control Did these moralists regard contraception as a greater sin than infanticide? One wonders.

It is not generally known that prudence was, in earlier times, often mandated by the state itself. One aspect of the Elizabethan Poor Law of 1601 was summarized thus in 1651: "[T]hey who could not maintain a wife, might not marry; for a License they could not have . . . usually none were permitted marriage till the man were thirty five at least, and the woman thirty."[11]

That people would accept this "restraint upon marriage" (to use Sir James Steuart's phrase) seems almost incredible to us now because of the growth of radical individualism since the time of Elizabeth I. To what extent was the Elizabethan law on marriages enforced? It is not certain; but it seems to have been a "blue law" long before Steuart and Malthus appeared on the scene. To achieve population control Malthus recommended an internalization of prudence through "moral restraint," by which he meant delaying marriage, and practicing considerable continence within marriage.

But Francis Place, a courageous fighter for the rights of laborers, saw little hope in "moral restraint." In financial and political matters he himself showed considerable prudence, rising by his own efforts from poverty to affluence and political power. Reproductive prudence he had not. Imprudence seems to be of the essence of youth, and we both commend and condemn it. And it is the young who produce most of the children. Prudence develops slowly in a person's life.

Place had either fourteen or fifteen children—significantly, the accounts vary— of whom five died in childhood. There is a letter of Place's to a friend in which he comments bitterly about "moral restraint, which has served so well in the instances of you and I—and Mill, and Wakefield—mustering among us no less I believe than 36 children—rare fellows we to teach moral restraint."[12] Rather than attack the spontaneity of youth, Place elected, at considerable personal sacrifice, to urge a separation of sexual intercourse from reproduction. He was the first great promoter of artificial birth control.

Demographic Consequences of Imprudence

Western societies no longer have decrees that mandate reproductive prudence: such decrees are incompatible with the prevailing conception of freedom. The right to reproduce is given a paramount position in the roster of individual rights. The growth of individual freedom posed no overwhelming danger of overpopulation as long as the family was wholly responsible for the survival of its young: death from deprivation eliminated imprudently conceived infants, together with whatever genes for imprudence they might carry. Few people felt that there was any community obligation to save brats whelped by the feckless.

Sixty years intervened between the time of Linnaeus's letter and 1832, when Lloyd gave the lecture on which his publication in the following year was based— just two generations. We now have histories of childhood in Europe that show that public concern for the well-being of children increased greatly during that time. To a small extent this concern translated into community action—enough, at any rate, to enable Lloyd to recognize the incipient commonization of the costs of child rearing. The "welfare state" was born in the nineteenth century. Lloyd foresaw that an unlimited extension of the commonized arrangement could ultimately diminish everyone's "shares of subsistence" until "all are reduced to extreme distress," the population finally being controlled only by "the undisguised check of misery and want." But Lloyd did not blame the people who produced these consequences for lacking "a prudential disposition." In his view the principal fault lay not with individuals "but with the constitution of the society, of which they form part."

Why Was Lloyd's Work Lost?

To appreciate the revolutionary character of Lloyd's paper, we need to place it in its historical setting. Lloyd's argument that, in a climate of freedom, good intentions could produce bad results was advanced in a world in which quite the opposite view was gaining ground. The idea that there is a providence that will take care of us is very old: in the fourth century B.C., Chuang Tzu claimed that "good order results spontaneously when things are let alone."[13] To this comforting thought a new twist was added in the eighteenth century: the assertion that even men's *bad* intentions, under conditions of freedom, could sometimes work for the good of the community at large. Such was the message of Adam Smith's *Wealth of Nations,* published in 1776 (italics have been added to the following famous passage):

> [E]very individual necessarily labours to render the annual revenue of the society as great as he can. He generally, indeed, neither intends to promote the public interest, nor knows how much he is promoting it. By preferring the support of domestic to that of foreign industry, he intends only his own security; and by directing that industry in such a manner as its produce may be of the greatest value, he intends only his own gain, and he is in this, as in many other cases, led by *an invisible hand* to promote an end which was no part of his intention. Nor is it always the worse for the society that it was no part of it. By pursuing his own interest he frequently promotes that of the society more effectually than when he really intends to promote it. I have never known much good done by those who effected to trade for the public good. It is an affectation, indeed, not very common among merchants, and very few words need be employed in dissuading them from it.[14]

The "invisible hand," first introduced by the Scottish economist in 1759, raised the potency of providence to new heights. In two centuries of struggling against the stranglehold of "mercantilism," economists had produced much evidence to show the harm that could be produced by the state control of commerce. Laissez-faire spelled freedom, and freedom promised prosperity.

Lloyd's denial of the providential result of freedom to breed in a system tied to the commons must have made his message unwelcome to a society in which Adam Smith had become a patron saint. More prosaic personal reasons may also have played a role in obliterating Lloyd from the literature of scholarship. Lloyd was a member of a sickly family. In five years he gave only a very few lectures at Oxford before retiring, with private means, to Prestwood, Great Missenden, where he lived "in apparent obscurity" until his death from a stroke at age fifty-eight.[15] In the learned world, as in others, repetition and self-advertizement contribute mightily to the amassing of a reputation. Lloyd said his piece only once, and with great brevity. His message that "to each according to his needs" was a recipe for suicide was welcomed neither by Christians nor (later) by Marxists. Marx might have been spared his worst errors had he known of Lloyd's work, but there is no evidence that he ever heard of Lloyd.

A setback to the possible recognition of Lloyd came with the publication in 1953 of a massive survey of population literature by a United Nations committee. Out of the 330,000 words of *The Determinants and Consequences of Population Trends* only forty-three are devoted to Lloyd's work; they occur toward the end of a long footnote. The anonymous U.N. authors say that "since the gain from restricting family size is largely diffused to others, the individual *under capitalism* has little incentive to restrict family size."[16] Italics have been added to call attention to the fact that the committee got their facts wrong by 180 degrees. Under pure capitalism (as illustrated in Linnaeus's letter) parents *do* have an incentive to restrict (if they can) their families to a size that will spare them mental suffering. It is when the nurture of the children is imposed on the commons of the welfare state that the tragedy of uncontrollable population growth is brought into play.

How a Global Village Begets Global Pillage

The error committed by the UN authors of the population survey was no accident. It was a natural consequence of what Lionel Trilling identified as the unconscious leftward bias of the intellectuals of that day. As was pointed out at the beginning of this chapter, "conspicuous benevolence"—in words, if not in deeds—was the fashion. It was supported less by rigorous argument than by heart-warming rhetoric that had ancient roots in religion. We need to ask: What theoretical framework is *implied* by the following oft-repeated fragments of rhetoric?

> "Am I not my brother's keeper?"
> "The brotherhood of man"
> "The family of man"
> "The global village"

The thrust of all four expressions is surely toward the unity of all human beings, away from discrimination and toward a promiscuous sharing of wealth. But, as we have just learned, sharing wealth globally according to the formula "to each according to his needs" amounts to embracing a commons of distribution. But a commons-driven distribution system eventually ends in total ruin. A "just" sharing of the world's wealth among all the inhabitants, without coercive control of individual reproduction, would result in a continual, exponential growth of the human population. Unfortunately the resources on which human beings depend cannot grow. A desperate, globally sharing population pillages the riches of the environment.

All appeals to "conspicuous benevolence" depend for their effectiveness on certain assumptions about human altruism. Altruism is not a simple idea. Before we can go much farther in our analysis of population problems, we must try to determine what altruism means, and what are the practical boundaries to its practice.

22

Discriminating Altruisms

Sooner or later discussions of population problems raise the issue of altruism. Why should I refrain from exploiting the environment because posterity may some day wish that I had? Or because today's poor want a larger share of the world's wealth? Is altruism natural? Is it *safe*?

Altruism, like "will," may be one of those topics on which universal agreement is impossible. In both cases opposing arguments seem quite convincing—until you listen to the other side! In general, having names for things makes for clarity in discussion; but one wonders if that is so in this instance. For thousands of years people worried about the best balance between self-considering actions and actions that focus on the interests of others, but the disputes may have become more acute since neat names were coined. The earliest use of the word "egoism" recorded in the *Oxford English Dictionary* is 1722, with "altruism" appearing in 1853. Often the creation of a noun ("substantive") seems to presume the presence of a substance, a physical *thing*. Students of mental functions used to waste a great deal of time looking for the "faculties" of the mind; ultimately psychologists abandoned that substantive. Should "egoism" and "altruism" also be jettisoned?

Perhaps not yet: but many arguments can be curtailed if we note two different *referents* of the word altruism. Sometimes the reference is to the *motives* inside the mind of the altruist; at other times we are interested in the *consequences* of the action. Philosophical and religious writers are more concerned with the former; students of politics and bioethics with the latter. Religions are interested in promoting virtuous thought, but all assertions about motives suffer from the "egocentric predicament," the inability of each of us to really know what is going on inside any other mind.[1] (Assertions made by the *other* do not help because how can I *know* he is telling the truth?) Determinations of consequences do not have this shortcoming since consequences lie outside the brain of the actor. Bioethicists adopt a consequential approach to altruism. This is the path followed here.

Does Altruism Exist?

For centuries philosophers have played with the idea that maybe the motive called altruism does not exist. The argument is as follows: if the altruist derives personal pleasure from performing his actions, then do we not have to say that it is his own pleasure that he seeks rather than the good of the other party? The position is log-

225

ically defensible, but it often evokes strong reactions. Consider this story from the family of Sigmund Freud.

> [T]he children were not only not to have any anxiety about money, but even to know as little as possible about it—nothing in fact beyond their own little allowances . . . . it might have been easier for them had they been taught something of the part money necessarily plays in life . . . . His eldest daughter . . . once saw her aunt paying money to a servant and asked her what it was for. On being told it was wages she vehemently asserted that her mother did nothing of the sort; their servants, and above all her Nannie, worked purely for love. When she was contradicted and told the truth she broke into tears and wept the whole night through.[2]

The girl's reaction was extreme, but it reveals a deep desire to believe in the motive of altruism. It is a sweet story. One much less sweet was reported not long ago from Omaha, Nebraska: "An enraged man who had been turned down as a blood donor went on a rampage in a donor center, fatally stabbing the director and a woman and wounding several others."[3] There is an apparent conflict between the two stories. The Freud daughter yearned after altruism in others, while the Nebraska man yearned to be allowed to practice altruism himself. But the conflict is only apparent: the process of psychological *identification* converts the stories into two sides of the same coin. It is not surprising that many people resent being told that altruism is merely a disguised form of egoism. In various wordings this idea appears in many of the statements made about altruism over the past 2,000 years (Box 22-1).[4]

Altruism and Natural Selection

Some light can be thrown on the human problem by first observing other animals. We must at the outset deny the truth of an assertion made not long ago in a religious journal: "It is one of the unique features of the human being that he is willing to forego survival for the sake of a person he loves or some cause he strongly believes in."[5] It is astonishing that such a claim of human uniqueness could be made as late as the last half of the twentieth century. The claim is, of course, but one more example of the doctrine of human exemptionism (Chapter 16). It has been known for centuries that worker bees protect their hive by stinging, even though this action has a high probability of killing the bee that stings. Surely not many religious authors are ignorant of this fact?

It is altruism *within* a species *(Homo sapiens)* that we are most concerned with, but the first great analytical step was made by looking at altruism *between* species. Before Darwin, a large and sentimental literature had grown up citing instances in which Providence had designed one species to help another. Principally, of course, the stories showed how other species served human beings: bees, for instance, were supposed to make honey *for the sake of* man. Darwin's theory substituted "natural selection" for "providence," and then asserted that animal adaptations could not be explained as instances of altruism between species. (The honey that bees make primarily serves the bees' purposes: human use is incidental and is not the originating cause.)

Box 22-1. Altruism: Historic Defences, Doubts, and Qualifications.

1. If I am not for myself, who will be for me? And if I am for myself alone, what am I? And if not now, when?

Hillel, circa 50 B.C.

2. It is solely through good laws that one can form virtuous men. Thus the whole art of the legislator consists of forcing men, by the sentiment of self-love, to be always just to one another.

Helvetius, 1758.

3. Self-preservation, and the propagation of the species, are the great ends which nature seems to have proposed in the formation of all animals.

Adam Smith, 1759.

4. By making the passion of self-love beyond comparison stronger than the passion of benevolence, He [God] has at once impelled us to that line of conduct which is essential to the preservation of the human race.

Thomas Robert Malthus, 1806.

5. At one time the benevolent affections embrace merely the family, soon the circle expanding includes first a class, then a nation, then a coalition of nations, then all humanity, and finally, its influence is felt in the dealings of man with an animal world.

W. E. H. Lecky, 1869.

6. The more uncertain I have felt about myself, the more there has grown up in me a feeling of kinship with all things.

Carl Jung, (1875–1961)

7. When faced with hypothetical situations suggesting the imminence of death, e.g., "If you could do only one more thing before dying, what would you choose to do?." the characteristic choices of the mentally ill patients tend to give priority to activities of a social and religious type, e.g., "give my belongings to charity," "stop war if possible," "know more of God," etc. This is in contrast to the responses from the normal groups which emphasize personal pleasures and gratifications, e.g., "travel all over the world," "live in a new home," etc.

Herman Feifel, 1959.

8. [In the novel *The Brothers Karamazov* "an elderly and undoubtedly clever man" spoke] . . . in jest, but in mournful jest. "I love humanity," he said, "but I can't help being surprised at myself: the more I love humanity in general, the less I love men in particular, I mean, separately, as separate individuals."

Fyodor Dostoyevsky, 1880.

9. A sensible human once said, "If people knew how much ill-feeling Unselfishness occasions, it would not be so often recommended from the pulpit"; and again, "She's the sort of woman who lives for others—you can always tell the others by their hunted expression."

C. S. Lewis, 1942.

10. I have heard that people may become dependent on us for food. To me that is good news—because before people can do anything they have got to eat. And if you are looking for a way to get people to lean on you and be dependent on you, in terms of their cooperation with you, it seems to me that food dependence would be terrific.

Senator Hubert Humphrey, 1957.

11. *Cui servire est regnare:* "To serve is to rule."

The motto of Groton School.

Darwin's treatment of altruism is part of a more important argument dealing with natural selection, his great contribution to scientific thought. To appreciate fully the words quoted below one must realize how undogmatic was Darwin's habitual style of reporting. He hesitated twenty years between the time when he conceived his theory and the time when he first presented it to the public. He leaned over backwards trying to present fairly all the counterarguments. In *The Origin of Species* Chapter 6, "Difficulties of the Theory," occupies 6 percent of the first edition in 1859, and 8 percent of the sixth (last) edition of 1872. "However," and "on the other hand" characterized his approach to any subject. But when Darwin came to assess the reality of natural selection and its bearing on altruism he did not equivocate.

> Natural selection *cannot possibly* produce any modification in a species exclusively for the good of another species, though throughout nature one species incessantly takes advantage of and profits by the structures of others. But natural selection can and does often produce structures for the direct injury of other animals, as we see in the fang of the adder, and in the ovipositor of the ichneumon, by which its eggs are deposited in the living bodies of other insects. *If it could be proved that any part of the structure of any one species had been formed for the exclusive good of another species, it would annihilate my theory,* for such could not have been produced through natural selection.[6]

From other discussions in the *Origin* (and elsewhere), it is clear that when Darwin writes "structures" he usually means both structures and behaviors. Pure altruism between species would, by definition, be behavior that benefited *only* the species that *received* the altruistic services. If such altruism between species exists, natural selection is a mirage. Darwin staked his all on this admission, and time has shown that he wagered wisely. Never does one species do something *exclusively* for the good of another.

Pure consequential altruism between species does not exist.

The nonexistence of pure altruism between species is one of the major default positions of biology. Default positions, as E. T. Whittaker said (recall Box 5-1), spring from "a conviction of the mind" that all attempts to explain things otherwise are bound to fail. Only features that are of advantage to a species will be selected for. More exactly: though it might exist for a moment in the history of a species, pure altruism cannot *persist* over many generations.

Darwin justified his certitude by an argument that is only implicit in his work. In making it explicit we assume that species B has an adaptation that produces no benefit for its own members, but does benefit species C. The production of any adaptation exacts a cost of some sort. The mutation process is unstoppable. Whenever a mutant of B appears that lacks the hypothetical adaptation, that mutant will have a competitive advantage over the "normal" members of species B, because it will not be wasting its efforts on improving life for species C. To say that the mutant has a competitive advantage is to say that it will (on the average) produce more surviving offspring than will the "normal," altruistic versions of species B. Gradually, over the generations, the mutant type will replace the hypothetical altruistic type. Ultimately species B would thus be purged of its species altruism.

The argument that rules out consequential altruism between species serves equally well to rule it out within a species. The mechanism that cleanses a species of its altruism is the same in both cases. Suppose every member of a species prefers to benefit some other member of its own species rather than itself. Again: every beneficial act imposes a cost of some sort on the actor. If now a mutant should appear that acts egoistically rather than altruistically this mutant will have a selective advantage over the "normal" types since uncompensated costs are not imposed on it. Natural selection favors the egoistic mutant over the purely altruistic type, and in time the egoistic mutant will become the predominant form. Q.E.D.

The Selfish Gene

It is an irony of history that less than a decade after the term "altruism" was coined (by August Comte, who also coined the name "sociology"), the nonexistence of altruism *in the strict sense* was proved by Darwin's theory of natural selection. Yet respectable writers still use the term "altruism." How come?

In choosing our language there's such a thing as being too pure. For instance: probably all languages have the two contrasting terms "hot" and "cold," yet we have known for more than a century that there's redundancy in these terms. In nature there is only heat, of which objects may possess varying amounts. Should we, then, rewrite literature to take account of this insight of physics? Keats, remember, wrote:

> St. Agnes' Eve—Ah bitter chill it was!
> The owl, for all his feathers, was a-cold—

when, had he possessed the knowledge of physics that developed soon after his death—the knowledge that heat is a measure of molecular motion, of which only positive amounts are possible—had Keats understood all this he might have written:

> St. Agnes' Eve—Ah insufficiently hot it was!
> The owl, for all his feathers, was losing heat too fast.

We would be ridiculed if we tried to revise the entire *corpus* of English literature to fit the most recent views of science. Even scientists, though they know that only heat exists, do not hesitate to speak of both heat and cold.

As for altruism, though there is not, in the consequentialist sense, any such thing as *pure* altruism, we can continue to use Comte's term provided we don't forget what Darwin taught us. "Pure altruism," like frictionless pulleys and weightless levers in physics, is a fictional construct that makes the analysis of real situations easier.

Biology boasts many startling examples of impure altruism. Consider the following. There is a species of cricket in which the mother permits her numerous brood of offspring to eat her up, thus getting a good start in life.[7] This extreme form of "mother love" undoubtedly increases the probability that each tiny cricket will survive (and reproduce) while reducing to a flat zero the mother's probability of surviving longer and breeding again. If this behavior does not deserve the adjective "altruistic," what does?

In passing, we should note a linguistic error that crept in with Darwinism. In the story of the crickets it is certainly true that natural selection does not exist for the good of the cannibalized mother. For whose good, then, does selection operate? For a long time biology textbooks said that selection operated "for the good of the species." But this cannot be true. Among crickets one never finds a female that will let just any baby crickets eat her up: she makes this sacrifice only for her own children. Conceivably, the sacrificial cricket mother may be moved by altruistic feelings, but her genes are acting "selfishly" as they "seek" to further their own reproduction into future generations.

Quotation marks have been used in the previous sentence to call attention to the fact that a profound knowledge of biology sometimes stretches the limits of language. We have to shift the focus from individuals *to their genes.* In crickets, the genes for maternal cannibalism are present in both the mother and her progeny. If, by eating their mother, cricket youngsters greatly increase their own rate of survival, the loss of the relevant genes in the cannibalized mother will be less than the gain in the number of the same kind of genes in the surviving young. There is a sense in which we can label the genes, rather than the individuals, as the egoists in this melodrama.

At an implicit level Darwin understood this, and reasoned correctly about many instances of natural selection in social insects. But he did not quite succeed in bringing about the needed change in language. "Natural selection," he said, "will never produce in a being any structure more injurious than beneficial to that being, for natural selection acts solely by and for the good of each." For the word "being" we would now substitute "the genes of a being." But the concept of genes was not made clear until the twentieth century. It remained for Richard Dawkins, in 1976, to clarify the connection of language to biology in his book, *The Selfish Gene.*[8] There may be some awkwardness in the new language, but it mirrors as best our language can the underlying reality. The behavior of selfish genes can produce results that, in everyday speech, we are pleased to label "altruistic." Parental behavior is an undeniable example.

This behavior of crickets is not unique: it is found in many species of spiders as well. Furthermore, even in our own species, which does not practice maternal cannibalism, there is more than a smidgen of parental sacrifice. All parenthood entails costs, small or large, imposed on one parent at least, and often on both. Whatever our conclusion about motivational altruism, consequential altruism truly exists.

In Praise of Discrimination

Individually altruistic but genetically selfish actions have been classified as "kin altruism." Natural selection favors this kind of behavior only because the genetically supported helping impulse is accompanied by genetically supported discrimination. In our day the word "discrimination" is almost always a term of condemnation. This is unfortunate because *discrimination is a necessary part of every persisting altruistic behavior.* Why? Because without discrimination the good effects of "altruism" would be *commonized* over the entire population. (In the preceding chapter we saw the weakness of the system of the commons.) The benefits of altruistic actions would then be so diluted that they would be less than the benefits to be gained by more egoistic alternatives, which (by definition) are not so commonized and are not diluted. Without discrimination, altruism in a large population has a negative selective value. Some well known examples will make the point clear.

A bird does not take care of eggs until it has laid its own. Then it does not care for just any old eggs, but only for those in its own nest; and the nest has to be in the right place. If a human experimenter moves the nest a few feet, the bird, even though it observes the action, will not sit on its own eggs once the total gestalt fails to match the one that was earlier impressed on its brain. (Not without cause do we use "birdbrain" as a pejorative!) Caring *and* discrimination are both genetically programmed. (In fairness to birds we should point out that the avian brain is mostly dedicated to the difficult art of flying. Natural selection has hardly had enough time to adjust it to the curious problems created by busybody scientists.)

The cuckoo takes advantage of the limited discriminatory ability of other birds, laying its egg in the nest of some other species. Its egg is enough like the host's so that the host is unaware of the piratical invasion. When the eggs hatch, the young cuckoo promptly ejects the host young, thus securing all the foster-parental care for itself. (By that time its *biological* mother is engaged in laying eggs in other nests.) There's no point in faulting a host mother for discriminating so poorly; she is doing the best she can with her meager mental equipment. Nature stories like this (and they are many) strengthen the conviction that altruism must be discriminating.

Individualism and Reciprocal Altruism

There are many kinds of altruism. Mothers help their children; siblings help each other; friends of different families may help each other; and strangers may work together to support the church, the club, the nation, or some other large group that embodies their ideals. Many different classifications of altruisms are possible: one is given in Figure 22-1.[9]

The various behaviors in the figure are arranged in the order of their inclusiveness. At the bottom of the list is *egoism* of the purest sort, a nonaltruistic behavior in which the individual literally cares only for himself. In its pure form egoism does not exist in human beings, who are necessarily social. (If nothing else, some adults must take care of children.)

Universalism   (Promiscuous altruism)
Patriotism
Tribalism
Cronyism   (Discriminating altruisms)
Familialism
Individualism
Egoism

Figure 22-1. One possible classification of egoism and the various forms of altruism, which are not mutually exclusive. A person normally practices several different forms of altruism, with different "others."

Immediately above egoism comes *individualism,* the most limited form of exis-
tent altruism. Following the rule "Love thy neighbor as thyself," a person tries to
be consistent in his treatment of *others* and himself. The language of "rights" is the
language of individualistic altruism. Curiously this language is mostly an invention
of the past few centuries; it tends to weaken the more inclusive forms of altruism,
which have played an important role in human society for a much longer period of
time. Individualistic "rights" are principally a creation of European civilization;
failure to recognize this fact is at the root of many international misunderstandings.
The "Economic Libertarians" of our time seem to want to make individualism the
only form of altruism. (Could a purely individualistic society long survive? An
interesting question!)

Individualism does not preclude cooperation. In recent years many interesting
examples have been found in nonhuman animals. Examples are "cleaner shrimp"
and tiny "cleaner fish" that eat the licelike parasites from the skin and open mouths
of larger fish, which refrain from devouring the cleaning staff. Since the tiny cleaner
benefits from getting a meal while the larger fish benefits from being "debugged,"
the relationship is called one of *reciprocal altruism.*

David Barash maintains that reciprocal altruism "is not altruism at all. It is selfishness pure and simple, since it takes place in the expectation that personal rewards
will exceed the costs."[10] Inasmuch as the passage quoted does not answer the question "costs to whom?" it may hide a misunderstanding of the calculus of individual
pleasure (or individual gain). The presumed calculation of what we would call rational gain and loss is done by natural selection and may involve no self-awareness on
the part of any of the participants in such transactions. Be that as it may, natural
selection demands only that this "calculation" take account of the gain and loss *to
each member.* The fact that the other member of a reciprocating pair gains or loses
is irrelevant. If (as Darwin taught us) one species cannot be selected for because of
the benefits it confers on another (except through the reflexive effects on itself), neither can a species be selected for in terms of the harm that it does to another (except
through reflexive effects). Interspecies spite is as selectively irrelevant as interspecies
benevolence.

It is doubtful if a human society strongly committed to either spite or charity as
its basic motive could long survive. Malthus (4 in Box 22-1) thought that God had
made self-love stronger than benevolence in the heart of man; in healthy human
beings self-love is also stronger than spite. Interpersonal reactions have been made
much more efficient *and much healthier* by the invention of money, which is, as Ed
Wilson has said, "only a quantification of reciprocal altruism."[11] As the common
saying has it: "You scratch my back and I'll scratch yours."

Repayment of a debt (back scratching, for instance) need not be instantaneous:
memory can act as an accountant. Money objectifies the abstraction we call "debt"
and makes the defects of a poor memory less important. When the human species
invented money, it was unable, as always, "to do merely one thing." Money makes
a "debt" transmissible to nonparticipants of the original reciprocal act. The symbols of indebtedness can be accumulated or subdivided; in a word they become
"capital."

Fantastic variations have been played on the theme of capital. The less happy
results of this variation have led some to claim that "Money is the root of all evil."
This is a misquotation of the biblical aphorism, "*The love of money* is the root of

all evil." Thus does 1 Timothy 6:10 correctly put the blame where it belongs—on human behavior. The discipline of economics is an open-ended "Theory of Harmony" on the theme of money as the coin of reciprocal altruism.

More Inclusive Forms of Altruism

Figure 22-2 is an extension of the previous figure; in it there is an attempt to represent, in a rough way, the "power" of conflicting human motives. In physics, force, power, and energy are precisely defined so that they can be reliably measured. No such ability is (yet) possible in assaying the comparative strength of human motivations. Nevertheless, in a rough way, the darkened areas shown in Figure 22-2 capture what we "intuitively" know about the power of different kinds of human associations.

"Political power" refers to the sort of power that can be mustered by large political agencies—armies, policemen, jails, and so on. A nation has much more power of this sort than does a family or a small tribe. When push comes to shove, a nation can overwhelm individuals and families. That is one reason nations continue to survive. But so do families, by means that may be less violent than those used by nations and are effective in different ways. In a first, crude way we can survey the characteristics and comparative strengths of the different forms of altruism.

"Loyalty power" is distributed as shown in the right-hand shaded area. It is greatest in small groups, because it is related to the intimacy and duration of the altruistic association. (Littermates are very loyal: "Blood is thicker than water.") The power of loyalty to the few constantly threatens to erode the political power of the many.

"Familialism" includes the members of the nuclear family in our society, but little else. In most parts of the world it includes a much larger but vaguely defined "extended family." In India, for instance, the extended family is the greatest reality of social existence. Because of the keen competition for jobs, what we decry as the sin of "nepotism" is there regarded as a virtue. Such is the situation in most poor and crowded countries. (Question: Is the virtue of antinepotism affordable only by the rich?)

"Cronyism" is a form of altruism in which discrimination is made on the basis of long association, regardless of genetic relationship. Cronyism is an adaptive

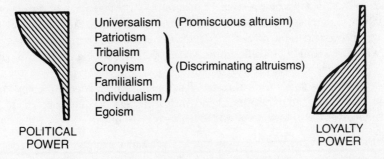

Universalism (Promiscuous altruism)
Patriotism
Tribalism
Cronyism } (Discriminating altruisms)
Familialism
Individualism
Egoism

POLITICAL POWER   LOYALTY POWER

Figure 22-2. Egoism and the various forms of altruism, showing (in an approximate way) the kinds of power they can exert, as indicated by the width of the hatched area at each level.

response to the anxiety-creating question, "How can I trust the *other?*" The extensive literature on the "prisoner's dilemma" attests to the importance of this question.[12] Because of the egocentric predicament, *ego* can never really know what goes on in the mind of *alter*. Siblings may grow up blessedly untroubled by mutual doubt, but strangers dare not risk such trust. Long periods of working together, particularly when combined with shared suffering, can create mutual trust. In battle-tested military squads, cronyism approaches brotherhood in its strength and reliability; recall the discriminative delight expressed by Shakespeare's King Harry: "We few, we happy few, we band of brothers; / For he that sheds his blood with me / Shall be my brother."[13]

Cronyism can be good, cronyism can be bad. "Whistle-blowers," who seek to serve the good of a larger group (the firm, or the nation) are, more often than not, ostracized by their fellow workers.[14] Cronyism is one of the serious limitations to the reliability of nuclear power units (Chapter 15). It was in response to this danger that Alvin Weinberg called for the creation of a "scientific priesthood," who (by hypothesis) would *always* put loyalty to the rest of society above loyalty to cronies (Box 15-3), though Weinberg admitted that his proposal sounded "eerie."

"Tribalism" is altruism operating within a tribe, a unit that defies easy definition. Tribal members need not be close kin, nor need they all know each other. They are usually of the same race, but they need not be. They share common beliefs, particularly of the sort we call religious. Almost always they speak the same language, often one that sets them apart from their competitors. Intense and widespread tribalism is the great reality that has hampered the development of modern nations in Africa, as many Africans themselves acknowledge.

Until recently tribalism has been a very minor kind of altruism in America, but the situation is changing. Activists who are now promoting "ethnicity" no doubt have various motivations, one of which seems to be a desire to undermine patriotism. "Bilingual education," initially touted as a more efficient means of achieving competence in English, has often proven, in practice, to delay such achievement. (Those who are certified as bilingual teachers do not want their students to progress too fast, lest the teachers' period of employment be shortened).[15]

In the early part of the century xenophobia (fear of foreigners and things foreign) was a common failing of Americans. Experience, especially foreign travel, as well as the efforts of anthropologists, have greatly decreased the extent of xenophobia among the general public. Unfortunately the transmigration of the radical college students of the sixties and seventies into the ranks of college faculties in the eighties has resulted in a new phobia, "Europhobia," the fear and detestation of *our* civilization, which has largely been the creation of Europeans. Europhobes are now seeking, with considerable success, to detach our civilization from its roots, replacing it with distractingly multiple ethnic myths, thus weakening the hold of patriotism.[16] The future of America is clouded.

"Patriotism" is nationwide altruism. Patriotism is often condemned by "intellectuals," who are fond of quoting eight words from Samuel Johnson. The following extract gives Dr. Johnson's words in their proper context:

> Patriotism having become one of our topicks, Johnson suddenly uttered in a strong determined tone, an apophthegm at which many will start: "Patriotism is the last refuge of a scoundrel." But let it be considered that he did not mean a real and

generous love of our country, but that pretended patriotism which so many, in all ages and countries, have made a cloak for self-interest.[17]

In other words, patriotism is only one of the many virtues that are at times falsely claimed by those who are principally interested in their own advancement. Love, generosity, piety, compassion, and many more virtues can also serve the purposes of hypocrisy. But we should not let hypocrites deprive us of useful language.

Universalism: The Promiscuous Altruism

At one extreme of the spectrum of discriminating altruisms lies *universalism,* altruism that is practiced without discrimination of kinship, shared values, acquaintanceship, propinquity in time or space, or any other characteristic. An immense literature has grown up promoting an ideal expressed well by a now forgotten poet at the end of World War I: "Let us no more be true to boasted race or clan / But to our highest dream, the brotherhood of man."[18]

This sounds lovely, but what kind of altruism does it praise? Clearly the poem is a paean to "promiscuous" altruism. Promiscuity should always be challenged. Pierre-Joseph Proudhon (1809–1865) said, "If all the world is my brother, then I have no brother."[19] The specific shortcoming of universalism is easy to identify: it promotes a pathology that was identified in the preceding chapter, namely the tragedy of the commons.

In every type of altruism there is the possibility that one of the partners to the exchange will be shortchanged. The more impersonal the relationship, the greater the probability of cheating. The language of universalism is almost invariably that of Karl Marx: "to each according to his needs." Those whose objective needs are great—the poor—benefit from exaggerating their expressed needs. The final result of universal altruism is a redistribution of wealth. When the wealth lies in the realm of information, a universal sharing of knowledge is undoubtedly a good thing. But a redistribution of the wealth of matter and energy, through gifts rather than reciprocity, produces a commons without responsibility and hence a redistribution of poverty. More or less consciously perceiving this danger, the bulk of humanity has refused to commit itself to a universalist altruism, despite some two centuries of strong propaganda in its favor. The rhetorical armamentarium of the universalists is impressive: to promote completely promiscuous altruism they have enlisted the aid of the terms *provincialism, parochialism, isolationism, nationalism, patriotism, nativism,* and of course *discrimination,* all of which are used in a pejorative way. Whether the tragic consequences of increasing promiscuity will be perceived in time is an open question.

Uneasy Coexistence of the Various Altruisms

The plurality of altruisms breeds dilemmas. The character of a culture is revealed in the language it employs to resolve these dilemmas. The twentieth century has seen a frightening growth of alienation among the self-styled "intellectuals" who have a preponderant influence on the messages of the media.[20] The novelist E. M. Forster has given the world a memorable denunciation of patriotism:

> I hate the idea of causes, and if I had to choose between betraying my country and betraying my friend, I hope I should have the guts to betray my country. Such a choice may scandalise the modern reader, and he may stretch out his patriotic hand to the telephone at once and ring for the police. It would not have shocked Dante, though. Dante places Brutus and Cassius in the lowest circle of hell because they had chosen to betray their friend Julius Caesar rather than their country Rome . . . . Love and loyalty can run counter to the claims of the state. When they do—down with the state, say I, which means that the state would down me.[21]

The extremism of this statement is understandable in the light of the time it was written. Forster wrote it in 1939, in an essay entitled "What I Believe," published just before the beginning of World War II. By this time many stories coming out of Nazi Germany told of patriotic Hitler Youth informing on their own parents when the latter were overheard making statements that belittled Der Führer or the Nazi cause. Patriotism was given absolute precedence over familialism. The world was shocked. Against this historical background Forster's condemnation of patriotism is understandable. Yet clearly there are other situations in which most of us, perhaps including Forster himself, would praise a child who informed on parents who were involved in massively criminal activities (criminal by any standard). In the conflict of patriotism and familialism, it is not a foregone conclusion which of two discriminating altruisms will (or should) win out: the answer depends on particular circumstances.

In the general case we can expect conflict between all the altruistic groups. Is there a "best" balance of altruisms for all times? Probably not. What is the best balance for our time? That is *our* problem, and a difficult one it is.

Problems of balance have been made more difficult in recent years by the rise of environmentalism and an increasing concern for the needs of posterity. The policies that govern the exploitation of environmental resources (forests, wet lands, and minerals) should aim for a *sustainable* optimum, but such policies can easily provoke opposition from citizens whose economic well-being is dependent on exploiting resources rapidly. Loggers want their wages now, even if complexly beautiful forests have to be ruined. The managers of polluting industries that endanger the atmosphere for generations to come quibble about the data so effectively as to prevent all positive action. Despairing of the slowness of normal political reform, some environmentalists have turned to violent and illegal means of sabotaging the legal actions of industry. The most harrowing of human choices is raised: should I obey the present laws of my nation, or some higher law (as I see it)?

It would be a great comfort to embrace just one of the extremes, either the unqualified individualism of Libertarians, or the seductive universalism of One Worlders. But either option would be suicidal: we must be content to make do with a changeable mixture of discriminating altruisms. This insight is older than Christianity, as is apparent in the anguished ambivalence of Hillel's cry: "If I am not for myself, who will be for me? And if I am for myself alone, what am I?"

23

The Double C–Double P Game

"Words are wise men's counters—they do but reckon by them; but they are the money of fools." So said Thomas Hobbes in the seventeenth century. Oft-repeated words, ambiguous in meaning, can easily counterfeit for the money of the mind. *Free enterprise, laissez-faire,* and *capitalism* are examples. Walter Lippmann, an esteemed commentator in the period between the two world wars, remarked on a gap between rhetoric and behavior:

> Most men have shown in their behavior that they wished to impose free capitalism on others and to escape it themselves. Employers have believed in it for their employees, and have appealed to it against factory laws and unionism. But they have not hesitated to call upon the state for protection against foreign competition. . . .
>
> There is no reason to think that business men under capitalism have had any consistent conviction of laissez-faire. Their employees have certainly not had it. They have voted for tariffs when they were told their jobs depended upon them. They have voted to close the labor market by restricting immigration. They have voted for labor laws and they have organized unions. Like their employers they have believed in laissez-faire for others.[1]

Most men believe in laissez-faire for others, while seeking to escape it themselves. A half-century after Lippmann, the economist Milton Friedman repeated the criticism: "With some notable exceptions, businessmen favor free enterprise in general but are opposed to it when it comes to themselves." This inconsistency violates the fundamental assumption of ethical theory that moral principles must be symmetrical—sauce for the goose is sauce for the gander. But it is the very nature of egoism to want sauce for the goose only: the morality Ego lives by, if he can get away with it, is asymmetrical. The discovery that social arrangements are often asymmetrical can easily lead to cynicism.

One of the myths supporting free enterprise is Emerson's story of the man who built a better mouse trap and thereby became rich as the world "beat a path to his door, though he lived in the depths of the woods." In truth, however, success more often comes by another route: an ingenious man fashions a bifurcation in the accounting system that channels the costs of his enterprise to society, while directing the profits to himself. (And a really clever man uses some of the profits to pay a publicity officer to convince the public that he acts within the grand tradition of Emerson's mouse-trap builder.)

A particular instance illustrates how the asymmetrical distribution of profits and costs works. A stockman in the western United States can raise his cattle either on private land or on government land managed by the Forest Service. In Idaho, as of 1990, the grazing fee on public land was only one-fifth what it was on private land. We can assume that a private land-owner sets his fee to cover the true cost of maintaining the carrying capacity of the land indefinitely. Obviously the government is not following this prudent rule. In direct costs, the Forest Service paid out $35 million for maintaining its grazing lands, the costs being offset by only $11 million taken in as fees. Who paid the deficit? Taxpayers, of course. Costs were commonized while the profits (from the sale of beef) were privatized to the stockmen. The formula[2] for this sort of game is simple: *Commonized Costs-Privatized Profits,* which can be abbreviated to the *CC-PP game.*

Actually the costs that stockmen impose on American taxpayers are far greater than the ones that appear explicitly on the books of the Forest Service. Stockmen, because they do not own the grazing land, put more cattle on the range than the grass can tolerate. The standing crop of fodder diminishes, soil is eroded, streams and springs dry up, and natural reforestation is interfered with. The cost of all this degradation is imposed on the general public. The stockmen are, of course, great defenders of free enterprise—for other people. For themselves, they prefer sucking at the public teat. The *CC-PP game.*

What's wrong with this game? Principally two things. Looking at it from a distributional standpoint, it can be faulted for lack of equity and justice: why should one group of citizens get rich at the expense of the rest? Unrealistically low pasturage fees encourage stockmen to transgress the carrying capacity because their sins will mostly be paid for by posterity, not by themselves. Over time, the CC-PP game yields less total income from the exploitation of the rangeland; but, since the short-term profits are greater, stockmen fight to be allowed to continue the game. When one area is ruined, they will move to another or devise another CC-PP game.

Selection: "For the Good of the Species"?

To be convincing and memorable, every intellectual explanation of the way the world works must be tied together by some simple, believable principle. The many marvelous adaptations of plants and animals to their particular ways of life were, before Darwin, explained as instances of "the greatness and goodness of God." Then Darwin put forward an alternative explanation that did not require faith in unseen beings: adaptation through differential reproduction among varied types. "Natural selection," he called it. It turned out that it was comparatively easy to convert the old explanation to the new one. "God" in all the old explanatory sentences merely had to be replaced by "natural selection." Since God, in the old system, was assumed to be well-disposed toward all of his creations, He obviously constructed the species in ways that served their own interest. In the Darwinian scheme it was at first casually assumed that natural selection also acted "for the good of the species."

Darwin himself did not make this mistake; but neither did he present the contrary view as forcefully and clearly as he might have. As a result biologists woke up a century later to realize that somehow "for the good of the species" had become embedded in popular explanations of evolution. But evolution does not—indeed, *cannot*—work that way. Natural selection, as Darwin knew and contemporary sociobiologists now emphasize, works directly for the good of the individual gene-line rather than directly for the good of the species as a whole. That is why Richard Dawkins coined the paradoxical term, "the selfish gene." Good comes to the whole species as a result of partial successes among the aggregation of germ-lines. In Aristotelian terms, the good of the species is an "accident"; it is not of the "essence."

An illustrative example is easily cited: Foster parenthood is virtually unknown in the animal kingdom. Where individual instances of adoption occur, principally among household pets, the practice does not increase in frequency with the passage of time. Adoption and foster parenthood are Aristotelian "accidents." The mother cricket who gives up her life for children makes the sacrifice only for *her* children, not for just any children. If she acted for the good of the species she would let any little cricket of the same species feast off her. But she doesn't.

At a less extreme level, we note that a ewe lets her own children suckle her, but she will reject other lambs even when they are near death by starvation. Shepherds faced with the problem of saving a lamb orphaned by the death of its mother solve the problem in an interesting way. They wrap the orphan in the skin of a lamb that has just died, then present it to the ewe who lost her lamb. Since the orphan has the right smell, the ewe will accept the changeling as her own. When the foster mother has committed herself to the new lamb the extra skin can be removed. Conceivably evolution could produce smarter ewes who would not be so easily fooled, but the situation is so rare that natural selection is unlikely to meet this challenge soon.

Foster parenthood is essentially nonexistent in the animal kingdom. What about human beings? Foster parenthood does exist, after all. The adoption of an orphaned nephew or niece has long been common: but that is a form of kin altruism, which presents no evolutionary difficulty. However, adoption of virtually unrelated children is unknown in many societies, the members of which act like other animals. They may even view nonkin foster parenthood as *unnatural.*

Technically they are right: but eyeglasses and hearing aids are also unnatural, yet we're not about to give them up. Human beings need not be bound by the simple rules that govern the evolution of crickets, spiders, and sheep. We perform many actions that are *not* written into our genes—and survive, perhaps even prosper, from our unnatural acts. The larger question is, where does the advantage lie? We can reject simple biologism, but there is a logic beyond natural selection that we must keep in mind. A century before Darwin the Swiss philosopher Helvetius said (to repeat a quotation from Box 22-1) that "the whole art of the legislator consists of forcing men, by the sentiment of self-love, to be always just to one another."

Going beyond statute law, we can say that influential people help fashion the etiquette and customs of a society. We should not expect to be able to create customs that demand unrequited altruism. To survive, an element of culture must be a form of reciprocal altruism. There must be some sort of reward, psychological or other, for every self-sacrificing element of behavior. The policy question for all of society is this: does the reward adequately compensate for the sacrifice?

To achieve population control (which is a need of the community) we must devise a community-mandated control system that confers tangible rewards to families and individuals who are asked to curtail their fertility for "the good of the species" (or of a large group like the nation).

The Ubiquity of the CC-PP Game

Several decades ago Nader's Raiders discovered that a paper company was dangerously depleting groundwater supplies. To this accusation a vice-president of the company stated: "I had my lawyers in Virginia research that, and they told us that we could suck the state of Virginia out through a hole in the ground, and there was nothing anyone could do about it."[3] Needless to say, this was not the vice-president of public relations! It is doubtful if so crudely defiant a statement would be hurled at the public today. But no doubt statements like this are still made in the intimacy of the board room by those who grow rich playing the CC-PP game. The rhetorical banners under which this game is played are many and various.

Externalities

The economist Alfred Marshall is given credit for coining the term "externality" to designate such unwanted effects as the pollution of the air by industrial smokestacks, or of water by noxious liquids flowing out of factories. All released pollutants impose costs on the community at large—cleaning costs, medical costs, esthetic costs, and so forth. Polluting enterprisers benefit from the CC-PP Game. But until very recent times, one finds little mention of the facts in economic literature. To many economists the word "external" means external not only to the account books of the enterprises but also external to ethical doubt. Externalization has been a pivotal practice in the advance of our commercial civilization, but the word "externality" is not to be found in the index of the economics histories of Schumpeter[4] and Whittaker.[5]

Farm Subsidies

Neither weather nor commodity markets are under the control of the individual farmer. Wide fluctuations can pauperize tens of thousands of farmers in a single season. There is a strong national interest in seeing to it that farmers can afford to continue farming. Hoping to solve the "farm problem," our nation instituted farm subsidies for particular crops. The farmer is paid so much per acre for growing a certain crop, or for refraining from growing any crop at all on the same land. When first instituted such a subsidy is a welcome "windfall" for the farmer, making it possible for him to continue farming.

But subsidies can be as addictive as hard drugs. Once a farm is federally certified for a particular crop, the expected bonus is capitalized into the assessed value of that farm. When the farm is sold to a new owner it will be at the new, higher valuation. The new owner then finds he cannot survive a discontinuance of the subsidy. The mortgage he pays presumes the new assessment. He becomes as economically pressed as a farmer receiving no subsidy. There may be nearly universal agreement that subsidies should be discontinued, but no one sees how to do so without a "taking" of property values from farmers. The longer the subsidy is continued the more firmly is it entrenched in the economic system. Thus it comes about that our agricultural department subsidizes tobacco farmers to grow a crop that our national health service denounces as a health hazard. By subsidizing tobacco we are subsidizing the production of lung cancer. (Later our subsidized medical services see to it that the treatment of lung cancer is also largely commonized.) It is as though the left hand knows not what the right hand is doing.

Pathological Aspects of Democracy

The mythical man from Mars would no doubt be dumfounded to learn of all this. We claim to be a democracy: why can't our legislators simply discontinue farm subsidies? The community as a whole would benefit. The detailed answer to the question uncovers an interesting property of representative democracy.

Suppose Congressman Wilson represents a wheat-growing area, Congressman Ramirez a cotton-growing area, while Congressman Thomas comes from the land of tobacco. Wilson would be willing to speak for the larger community and vote against subsidies for cotton and tobacco, provided he could get a subsidy for the wheat his constituents grow. Similarly, Ramirez would like to vote against wheat and tobacco, while Thomas is willing to vote against wheat and cotton. If each representative votes for his constituents on one crop while taking the national point of view for the other crops, they all risk being thrown out of office at the next election. But if they form a quiet conspiracy to trade supporting votes, then each congressman, when campaign time rolls around again, will be able to claim that he has represented his constituents well in Congress. Of course everyone's taxes have to increase to pay for the subsidies. It is the internalization of the *CC-PP logic* in the minds of voters that brings about a result that, in the largest sense, is unwanted by the majority. This pathological aspect of representative democracy is given various names: "pork barrel" and "log-rolling" are the commonest.

Water

Dams are very expensive, so expensive that very few would be built if they had to be paid for only by those who directly benefit from them. The costs are commonized against all taxpayers while the profits generated by the impounded water accrue to private owners of irrigable land. Every once in a while a dam collapses, causing a flood the damage from which can run into the millions of dollars. At that point some of the disaster costs are commonized as the president declares the affected area a "disaster area" and hence eligible for economic concessions.

Lumber

A large proportion of our forests are grown on publicly owned land. They are maintained and protected from fire at public expense. When a private company is given permission to harvest the lumber, the Forest Service builds access roads into the area. Permission to lumber is sold at a price far below the cost of the services given—and this even when the lumber produced does not benefit American home builders because the logs are shipped to a foreign land. In this instance one might modify the game formula to read: *American Commonization of Costs-Privatization (both American and foreign) of the profits.* Clear-cutting, which lumber companies favor, damages both the clear-cut land (through erosion) and the area below (through siltation of fishing streams and lakes, as well as greater flooding of residential flood plains). There are many areas in which we are destroying American property to build low-cost homes for foreigners. Would a legislative bill that *explicitly* spelled out the consequences of subsidized lumbering pass in Congress?

Disaster Relief

The cost of occasional disasters can be internalized by disaster insurance, which is written by private companies and paid for by the persons who are insured. A really big disaster, however, entails costs far beyond those covered by insurance, so a sympathetic public acquiesces in the commonization of at least part of the cost of disaster mitigation.

Some branches of the government systematically take advantage of the kindheartedness of the public. For instance, the Army Corps of Engineers is often brought in to build mammoth systems to protect a flood plain against floods. Thus is commonized the expense of a project that, more often than not, should not be undertaken at all. The ecologic-economic rule that should be followed is this: *The flood plain belongs to the river.* In the short term it is cheaper to build houses on a level flood plain rather than on the sloping hills nearby; but over the long haul, when the costs of rare disasters are factored in, it is far cheaper to build and maintain houses on the high ground, leaving the rich bottom land for the growing of crops. If home builders had to internalize the costs incurred by Army engineers, most of them would not build on a flood plain. The long-term economic insanity of such a CC-PP game is undeniable.

How does it happen that sane people can become supporters of insane economics? Rationally, the costs of any enterprise should be internalized. He who builds on a flood plain should pay not only for the immediate building costs but also for the premiums of the insurance needed for rebuilding when the rare but certain disaster occurs. He who smokes tobacco should pay insurance premiums that will take care of his extra medical treatment in the future. We fail to mandate economic sanity because our brains are addled by what Tom Sowell calls that magic word *compassion.*[6] Connections between actions and consequences are obscured as probable futures are denied. No place are the consequences of compassion more dangerous than in the allocation of medical costs. Since all extravagance reduces the carrying capacity of the national heritage, and hence the optimum population size, we need to understand the properties of our medical system.

The Medical Commons

In the medical version of the CC-PP game, "the people" are both the exploiters *and* the exploited. In socialized medicine the individual-as-patient privatizes the benefit of low-cost medical attention only to learn (sooner or later) that he must also assume the role of individual-as-taxpayer, against whom the costs are commonized.

Socialized medicine follows the Marxist rule, "to each according to his need." It takes no great insight to realize that hypochondriacs, as a class, will victimize the healthy in such a system. But since most people find little amusement in being ill the costs of hypochondria will probably not escalate dangerously. The constant tendency of medical costs to rise above 10 percent of the gross national product has a different explanation.

Our laws, with the temptations they offer to lawyers, are the principal source of the trouble. Ours is a litigious society: per capita, America has twenty times as many lawyers as Japan. On balance, individual rights receive far more legal protection in America than in most countries of the world. The interest of the general public receives less attention from the law. Malpractice suits against doctors are common: settling them costs money. Because of such suits doctors have to take out malpractice insurance: this costs money. The insurers insist that doctors protect themselves against lawsuits by calling for an excess of diagnostic tests: these cost money. (The doctor practices "defensive medicine," that is, medicine that defends *him*.) The costs of all this is internalized into the patient's bill, which, in these days, is largely paid for by "third parties"—either the patient's insurance company (out of his and/ or his employer's premiums) or the government (out of his taxes). The resulting "medical commons" threatens to turn into a runaway system.[7]

When President Johnson signed the Medicare Act (a part of our socialized medicine) he said that the extra $500 million in federal expenditure would present "no problem." In fact, Medicare now costs 150 times the original estimate.[8] (Most new political institutions cost far more than is initially estimated—as fiscal conservatives are kind enough to remind us.) One physician has warned us that "Big money breeds greed, not selfless service."[9] This is our old friend, the default principle of "Reward determines behavior." The formula "to each according to his needs" sounds lovely, but it rewards limitless greed, which tends to produce limitless losses, which no earthly institution can withstand.

Neonatology—A Notorious and Critical Case

In no area of medicine has the reward system been more hazardous to the interests of society as a whole than it is in neonatology—the medical treatment of newborn babies. All too often one hears an assertion to the effect that "It is impossible to put a price tag on life, particularly the life of innocent newborn babies. Just ask the parents: they will tell you that no cost is too great to save the life of their child." But what would the parents say if they were informed that *they* had to pay all the costs out of their own pocket? No one is rude enough to suggest this in America; and American journalists seldom comment on the ultimate costs of the "heroic" neonatal operations that make such "good copy" in the daily press. The public is just beginning to become aware of cases like the following.

> At Howard Hospital, in the District of Columbia, intensive care for babies born to drug-addicted mothers runs as high as $1,768 a day. One abandoned infant ran up a bill of $250,000 for its 245-day stay.[10]

At Stanford Hospital it is not unusual for the intensive care of a neonatal to cost $12,000 during its first week in the ICN ("Intensive Care, Neonatal"). One baby who spent nine weeks in the ICN cost $225,000.[11]

In the Sheraton Corporation's health plan, 12,000 employees spent $12.2 million in the year 1986. Three very premature babies accounted for 10 percent of the total, each one costing about $400,000. Each preemie cost about 400 times as much as the average worker covered by the plan.[12]

For perspective, we should compare American practice with that of a strikingly different society, namely China.[13] The testimony recorded in Box 23-1 should convince the reader that things are rather different on the other side of the world.

Because deaths are easy to tally, the infant mortality rates of different countries are easily compared. "Other things being equal," China's infant mortality rate should be higher than ours. But should we conclude that we are therefore better off than they? From the point of view of the community as a whole, which is the more rational way to react to the challenges of neonatology?

Some would say that the significance of the infant mortality rate must be judged against the economic situation of a country. It is often said that America is rich enough to afford the astronomical costs of neonatalogy; but those who say this do not mention the thousands of children with untreated lesser ailments that could be successfully corrected for a fraction of the cost of "heroic neonatology."

We have a low infant mortality rate; China, economically poorer, has a higher rate. Many people accept the infant mortality rate as a valid measure of the state of a civilization: should not this assumption be reexamined? *Mortality*—death—can be easily tallied, but *morbidity*—pain and suffering—is much harder to measure. Yet morbidity may be the more important measure of happiness. (Opinions differ.) Because of the egocentric predicament we cannot know for sure how much premature babies suffer during a prolonged stay in the hospital, connected as they are to numerous tubes and sensors, and probed hourly with various instruments. But many neonatologists suspect quite a bit of suffering occurs.

Box 23-1. A Chinese View of Neonatology.

In China, the financial costs of the technology of neonatal medicine are tremendous and intolerable, given our state of economic development. In addition, China is different from the United States culturally and socially. Three such factors are worth mentioning.

First, in China, lawyers have no right to intrude into medical matters . . . .

Second, the medical costs of treatment for children must be paid for by their parents . . . .

Third, China has a long tradition of Confucianism—about 2,000 years. And in recent decades we have Marxism. Both of these . . . have a holistic philosophy. By this, I mean that each individual is seen as a component of the whole society, the nation. Thus, each individual's interests should properly be subordinate to the interests of the whole society or nation . . . .

In China . . . if the physician insists on treating an infant with serious birth defects, the parents say "Yes, if you pay the cost." However, the income of the physician is roughly the same as the parents—in the $40 to $50 per month range.

Qui Renzong, 1987.

Moreover, the anxiety of the parents—even if they have no worries about financing the heroic medicine—are far from trivial. And when the preemie is finally saved, in what condition is it "saved"? Since technology is rapidly changing, no precise answer is possible, but the experience of the past has been that a considerable fraction of the "saved" preemies have a medically troubled history the rest of their lives. Defects in hearing, sight, intelligence, and the cardiovascular system are common. Even with "state of the art" neonatology, the prognosis for their future life is not good. The smaller the preemie, the worse the prognosis. More: the smaller the preemie, the greater the expense, and the greater the suffering (of all sorts) that is inflicted on both parents and children. One wonders: given their different philosophy, if the Chinese some day become as rich as Americans, will they elect to spend their wealth on the "saving" of neonatals, as we do?

The workings of the CC-PP Game minimizes the felt impact of economic losses on the parents. But note: the psychological costs cannot be commonized. Such costs must be borne almost entirely by the parents. (And the taxpaying public expects them not to complain.)

Economists remind us that every action we take entails *opportunity costs.* These measure the losses arising from the foreclosure of alternative ways in which the money might have been spent. *We are not infinitely rich*—nor will we ever be. We cannot purchase all the goods we long for. We must choose. The American Academy of Pediatrics estimated that the national cost of the intensive care of infants in 1987 was running well in excess of $3 billion per year.[14] Is that really the best way we can think of to spend $3 billion a year?

Dependent Individualism: A Policy Hybrid

Much of the rhetoric of "rights" and "compassion" is incompatible with rationality. "Rights" share with "infinity" the property of limitlessness, which rules out mathematical weighting and calculation, *thus ruling out rationality.* This became apparent recently when a judge in Wisconsin said that economic considerations were "totally inappropriate" in deciding what was expected of a publicly supported hospital. (Had it been a child who made this remark we might have asked: "Do you think money grows on trees?" What should we ask a childish judge?)

Fortunately, in another and similar case, an Iowa judge pointed to the consequences of ignoring economics. If a rural hospital in a county with a small tax base were required to do everything humanly possible for all the patients who might come to it, the end result would be bankruptcy, *following which the hospital could do nothing for anyone, rich or poor.* Unmeasured compassion can lead to immeasurable suffering.[15]

It is a tragic fact of life that social labels that begin with a definite meaning quietly mutate over time until they are finally attached to behavior that produces results that are incompatible with the ideals they are supposed to serve. Fred Siegel has pointed out:

> Our conventional view of American history places the conflict between the welfare
> state and self-reliant individualism at the core of post-Depression American poli-

tics. But in actuality, individualism and the welfare state have been marching arm-in-arm over the past three decades. The welfare state is no longer driven by New Deal sentiments of social solidarity. Instead it is the mechanism that, prosperity aside, has freed the individual from the social burdens once borne by family and church and fraternal, work, and community organizations . . . . As the foundations of the welfare state have shifted from, roughly speaking, the ideal of social solidarity to self-interest, the welfare state has in effect stolen the individualist clothes of its critics . . . .

Most Americans . . . are *dependent individualists*—like the rugged farmers who live off crop insurance and the dashing motorcyclists free to ride without a helmet and with the right to have others pay the tab when they're banged up.[16]

In the terms used here, farmers living on crop insurance and bare-headed motorcyclists depending on the largesse of a compassionate society are all, whatever the rhetoric they use, playing the CC-PP game, with themselves, individually, in the favored seat. They are no different from businessmen who find ways of getting the government to assume a significant part of their operating expenses while they jealously protect their profits in the name of free enterprise and rugged individualism.

The remedy requires changes in the law: these will be difficult to achieve for two reasons. First, universal sympathy with those who suffer from medical disorders leads to a wish to spare them pain even if it does cost money. Second, literally the majority of state legislators are lawyers by training; lawyers constitute something of a tribe, and we should not be surprised to find that here, as in so many instances, tribal loyalty is given preference over loyalty to the nation as a whole.

A final word: In recent years the curriculum of many American high schools has been enriched by the addition of courses in economics (which used to be found only in colleges). It is easy to mount a good defense for the change. But, as one who is ignorant of what is going on in high schools, I wonder what is included in these economics course? I daresay they praise the free enterprise system. Fine! But I wonder: do any of these courses give even an inkling of the ubiquity and importance of the CC-PP game? If not, they are shortchanging our youth—and the next generation of voters.

24

Birth Control versus Population Control

In 1956 an association of lay Catholics in Europe announced an international essay contest, the object of which was to find a solution to overpopulation in the under-developed nations. The solution, they said, would "have to comply with the requirements of Catholic principles and at the same time must be effective from a positive point of view." In words plainer than the proposers were willing to use: the solution must not resort to abortion, sterilization, or contraception. A substantial prize awaited the winner.

Four years later the committee announced that no entry had been found worthy of the prize: the contest was now closed.[1] "After a number of entries had been elim-inated because they did not satisfy the material conditions laid down in the rules, five manuscripts remained to be judged. Four of these had to be considered as not dealing with the question as formulated." The fifth entry, the committee decided, presented "no real solution."[2]

From this failure the committee extracted the following moral: what was required was *team research*. "When the fundamental problems of modern science require highly coordinated team work based on carefully planned programmes, it cannot be expected that the fundamental world-wide problems of those branches of science dealing with human beings and society would be solved by individual endeavours."

The committee's statement sounds very open-minded; but is their analysis sound? Suppose a contest had the following objective: To find two different odd integers lying between the numbers 7 and 9. What good would it do to appoint a multidisciplinary committee to work on that problem? None. The very method of stating the problem ensures that it has no solution in the real world.

Our knowledge of human behavior is not as securely based as our knowledge of mathematics, but the gap between the two is not overwhelming. Natural selection rewards the kind of human behavior that mocks the ideals of the Roman Catholic Church. In a community that cherishes the lives of *all* fetuses and children, how can functional sterility, whether partial (continence) or total (celibacy) be selected for? More than thirty years have passed since this call for an interdisciplinary com-mittee to work on a Catholic solution, but the committee has apparently never been formed. Who would serve on it? Don Quixote, perhaps; who else?

Crisis versus Crunch: "The Happiness of Frightful News" versus Boredom

Population and the environment have both received considerable attention in the latter half of the twentieth century. However much we may regret spectacular environmental disasters, we love to gossip about them. In *Emma,* Jane Austen perceptively comments that "all the youth and servants in the place were soon in the happiness of frightful news."[3] During the 1950s, trying to bestow something of this happily frightful quality on problems of population, Hugh Moore, a retired industrialist who bankrolled many Planned Parenthood efforts, coined the term, *the population bomb.* Paul Ehrlich borrowed it for the title of his popular book, published in 1968, just six years after Rachel Carson's *Silent Spring.* The title of Ehrlich's book does get one's attention, but the image of a bomb is arguably too vivid. It suggests a sudden, critical, explosive event—an event that is (for better or worse) soon over. But the growth of population is chronic, slow (by the standards of news media), and (apparently) never-stopping. Population growth is not a crisis but a *crunch.*

More than any other generation ours is one whose attitudes are determined by the media, which automatically concentrate on a crisis but tire easily when dealing with a crunch. Few years in the twentieth century were as crowded with world-shaking events as the year 1989. Suppose you had been the managing editor of a newspaper during the latter half of that year. Imagine the decisions you would have been called upon to make during that time of multiple crises: how much space would you have allotted to the following competing stories coming across your desk?

Yesterday the Berlin Wall came down, *and world population increased by a quarter of a million.*

Yesterday Lithuania declared its independence from the U.S.S.R., *and world population increased by a quarter of a million.*

Yesterday an earthquake in Romania claimed tens of thousands of lives, *and world population increased by a quarter of a million.*

Yesterday the Philippines suffered a terrible earthquake, *and . . .*

It sounds like a broken record. What we call "news" consists of crises—sharply time-focused occurrences that are easy to report. Chronic, time-extended happenings don't have much of a chance when competing for time or space in the evening broadcast or the morning newspaper. The formula for journalistic decisions is simple:

$$\text{Crisis versus Crunch} \rightarrow \text{Crisis wins out}$$

The world didn't pay much attention to global population growth when it amounted to 100,000 per day; it doesn't pay much attention now that the increase is more than a quarter of a million per day. Will the world pay any more attention when the increase is a million per day? Probably not: a repeated, predictable increase in population, no matter how great, *just doesn't seem to be news.*

Poverty, Disasters, and the Population Crunch

On 4 February 1976, at 3:05 A.M., an earthquake struck Guatemala, killing 22,778 and injuring 76,504, according to the accepted statistics. The quake measured 7.5 on the Richter scale: this would be reckoned a strong quake, but not a devastating one had it occurred in the United States. But in Guatemala nearly 100,000 people were killed or injured; the dead alone amounted to 0.37 percent of the population of 6.2 million, or 13 percent of the yearly population growth (at 2.8 percent per year). Why was the loss so great?

A detailed study of a village of 1,577 Indians was revealing.[4] The greatest mortality was suffered by people who lived in adobe *casitas* ("little houses") roofed with heavy wooden timbers. More than 85 percent of the population was so housed. People in shacks made of cornstalks or mud-chinked slats fared much better. (Expensive reinforced concrete homes were best, but there were few of these in this village.)

The cost of adobe homes is low in money but high in "sweat equity" for those who do their own work. Cornstalks and slats are cheaper in both money and labor. Because of these differences, mortality in the village, and throughout most of Guatemala, was complexly correlated with socioeconomic status.

So what should we say killed those 22,778 Guatemalans? The earthquake? But most of them would have survived had they lived in reinforced concrete houses. Since concrete costs money, should we attribute the deaths to poverty? But the poorest people of all, living in cornstock or slat shacks, survived best. Why didn't more people live in the simple abodes? Because increasing population had nearly exhausted the resources of the biotic environment—photosynthetic products like trees and cornstocks. Should we then attribute the earthquake deaths to overpopulation? No newspaper, no radio broadcast, and no television show did so. An unspoken taboo decrees that *no one ever dies of overpopulation* (see Box 24-1).[5]

It is interesting to note that the association of economic status with mortality rate in 1976 was the reverse of what it had been in the great Guatemalan quake of 1918. Earlier, with a much smaller population, the ratio of photosynthetic products to human population was much more favorable, and the poor could easily find cornstalks and the like to use in making their shanties. The "colonials," the richer element of the population, could afford to hire poor people to make adobe houses for them (concrete was not yet in fashion). In the 1918 eathquake the rich suffered greater mortality than the poor. In spite of this fact, and perhaps because few saw the relation of housing to earthquake mortality, by 1925 the prestige and comfort of living in a cooler adobe house motivated ever more poor people to invest sweat equity in producing houses like those of the colonials. For this they ultimately suffered.

The moral of the story is more than parochial, as another example shows. Every year there are many earthquakes in Anatolia (the eastern part of Turkey), causing a heavy loss of life. Most of the quakes are a modest 3 to 5 on the Richter scale. The traveler in Anatolia easily sees the reason for the high mortality. In Homeric times the land was covered with trees, but now the landscape is almost bare. Lumber is one of the safest materials to use in constructing a house in earthquake country. Lacking lumber, the Anatolians of today build their houses of stone blocks. When an earthquake comes, down come the blocks, killing many people. One could say

---

Box 24-1. Nobody Ever Dies of Overpopulation.

I was in Calcutta when the cyclone struck East Bengal in November 1970. Early dispatches spoke of 15,000 dead, but the estimates rapidly escalated to 2,000,000 and then dropped back to 500,000. A nice round number: it will do as well as any, for we will never know. The nameless ones who died, "unimportant" people far beyond the fringes of the social power structure, left no trace of their existence. Pakistani parents repaired the population loss in just 40 days, and the world turned its attention to other matters.

What killed those unfortunate people? The cyclone, newspapers said. But one can just as logically say that overpopulation killed them. The Gangetic delta is barely above sea level. Every year several thousand people are killed in quite ordinary storms. If Pakistan were not overcrowded, no sane man would bring his family to such a place. Ecologically speaking, a delta belongs to the river and the sea; man obtrudes there at his peril.

Were we to identify overpopulation as the cause of a half-million deaths, we would threaten ourselves with a question to which we do not know the answer: *How can we control population without recourse to repugnant measures?* Fearfully we close our minds to an inventory of possibilities. Instead, we say that a cyclone caused the deaths, thus relieving ourselves of responsibility for this and future catastrophes. "Fate" is *so* comforting.

What will we say when the power shuts down some fine summer on our eastern seaboard and several thousand people die of heat prostration? Will we blame the weather? Or the power companies for not building enough generators? Or the econuts for insisting on pollution controls?

One thing is certain: we won't blame the deaths on overpopulation. No one ever dies of overpopulation. It is unthinkable.

"Nobody Ever Dies of Overpopulation," 1971.

---

that the people die of stupid architecture, or of a shortage of wood, or of poverty, or of overpopulation, because their numbers have overwhelmed the carrying capacity—the photosynthetic-productive ability—of their environment. But our media decree otherwise; and so the public reads, perhaps without questioning, headlines that say: EARTHQUAKE KILLS HUNDREDS IN ANATOLIA.

No one ever dies of overpopulation: subconsciously accepting this conclusion amounts to laying a taboo on discussions of population.

The Apparent Decline of Concern about Population

The first paragraph of this book pointed out that while world population increased by 47 percent between 1970 and 1990, the serious discussion of population became something of a "no-no" in the United States. In 1991 the United Nations' prospectuses for the 1992 World Conference on Environment and Development never mentioned the word "population."

Of course an optimist could point out that the *rate* of world population growth had slowed somewhat during those two decades: from 2 percent per year to 1.8 percent. At which point an ecological realist might retort that the *absolute increase* of population rose from 73 million per year in 1970 to 96 million per year in 1990. (The arithmetic puzzle is easily explained: a slightly smaller rate was operating on a much larger base.)

Why did discussion of population become so unpopular? Accounting for the changes that take place in history is almost bound to produce controversy. It certainly does in this instance. The best we can offer are some part-answers. To begin with, while critical troubles may elicit critical action, chronic troubles are likely to elicit apathy.

Then there is the opposition of economists to population theory generally, an opposition that grew a great deal during the 1980s, when the nation was administered by an executive and a party that were "true believers" in the moral desirability of perpetual growth. Also deserving of mention is the embarrassing fact that population experts seldom propose acceptable solutions to the problems they describe. "What's the use of worrying about a sickness nobody can cure?" And, since all historical events have multiple causation, if overpopulation is only one factor among the many that contribute to a historical disaster, and if we can't control population growth anyway, why mention it?

For a good feel of the public pulse, read the full page institutional ads in *The Wall Street Journal.* Computerland (a retail computer outlet) published a revealing one in 1985.[6] After praising the popular musicians who had put out the "We Are the World" record, which garnered $45 million for the relief of hunger in Africa, the ad writers acknowledged that the "Sub-Sahara regions are deforested and severely over-farmed." A biologist would immediately infer that the region was overpopulated; but that is not the way of the commercial world. Instead, the ad said: "Food production everywhere is primitive and inefficient." What should be done was obvious: "Ending hunger is a matter of helping these suffering countries develop strong, self-sufficient economies that can support their people."

Self-sufficiency can be developed either by reducing the demand—population—or by increasing the supply. That physical realities might limit the possibility of increasing the supply is never even hinted at. We must conclude that this possibility is unthinkable. "Answers needed to eliminate the causes of hunger," said the ad writer, "can only be created through . . . an innovative way of establishing grain reserves in critical areas." How, one might ask, can *reserves* of grain be created by a nation in which the yearly demand is greater than the yearly supply? One knows the presumed answer in advance: reserves are to be created by the transfer of grain from the rest of the world. For more than two decades distributing imported grain has been the policy of Oxfam, Food First, and several other charitable organizations. Following each well-intentioned intervention the recipient population has continued to grow, thus increasing the need when the next disaster strikes.

At no place in the carefully crafted ad is there even a hint of the fundamental idea of carrying capacity or of overpopulation. Why not? Simple: the flavor, the thrust of the publicity is to encourage further efforts to increase supplies, *and supplies can always be sold by someone at a profit.* There is no reason to think that the people who paid for the ad expect to benefit *directly* from increased sales of their products. But they no doubt think (and probably correctly) that anything they can do to make the wheels of commerce turn faster will benefit themselves sooner or later. The ad does more than hint at this possibility: "As hunger and poverty are eliminated from sections of the globe, new markets will open for a wide range of goods and services." Sooner or later, the company that finances such an ad hopes to get its seed corn back. More babies in Africa will mean more computers sold by our merchants: so reasons the merchant mind.

Many people profit from an increase in supply. A decrease in demand benefits almost no one directly, though the well-being of the land and the interests of posterity require that demand and supply be brought into balance with each other. In a limited world—the only world we know—demand must ultimately be controlled. Unfortunately the human love affair with short-range "compassion" supports efforts to increase supply but discourages attempts to reduce demand.

Compassion Breeds Taboo

Additional evidence that taboo has pressed against discussions of population during the latter half of the twentieth century is found in the writings of C. P. Snow, an insightful commentator on the role of scientific knowledge in our civilization. Speaking of his own book, *The Two Cultures,* published in 1959, this scientist-administrator acknowledged ten years later that this influential little tract had been marred by

> a curious and culpable omission. It is that for which I can acknowledge the guilt now. I was talking about world crises: and I made only the slightest references to the growth of population. That wasn't out of ignorance. I knew the facts. It wasn't out of carelessness. It was deliberate. I didn't want this major problem to dominate the discussion. Partly because it seemed to me then to make social hope even more difficult: partly because I didn't want to hurt other people's religious sensibilities. The religious sensibilities of people whom I knew, respected and often loved; and of others whom I didn't know. I now believe that I was dead wrong, and seriously wrong on both counts. First, any social hope that is going to be of any use against the darkness ahead will have to be based upon a knowledge of the worst: the worst of the practical facts, the worst in ourselves. It will have to be a harsh and difficult hope. We have never needed it more. Second, the situation is so grave that sensibilities of any kind, any of ours, any of those we respect but disagree with, have to take their chance. We are dealing with the species-life. That responsibility has to take first place.[7]

Snow's final position may be fairly summarized in two statements:(1) The taboo against discussing population is powerful; (2) The survival of our species demands that the taboo be broken.

With that I agree. Moreover, the saving of at least some of nature's marvelous diversity for our descendents to enjoy requires that we take overpopulation seriously. Fortunately the population taboo is less than absolute—otherwise this book could never have been published. But it has been powerful ever since Malthus. In fact, the taboo was perceived even before Malthus.

Malthus Inherits a Taboo

Sir James Steuart's comments on population have already been recorded in Chapter 1. When Malthus was only a year old Steuart admitted that he could not see how anyone could propose a restraint upon marriage "without shocking the spirit of the times." After that honest admission he struggled no more against the taboo on population discussions.

A few years later a Belgian abbé, Theodore Augustin Mann, approached a little closer to the taboo. In 1781, just seventeen years before Malthus's *Essay,* Mann asked: "Is it possible for a population to remain in equilibrium with the food supply, when it is increased to the greatest possible extent?" To this his answer was: "This equilibrium is evidently impossible among a people with good morals, because population naturally increases in an indefinite progression, while the means of subsistence are limited by the soil."[8] One presumes that Abbé Mann, like Malthus later, subsumed under the heading of "bad morals" such practices as infanticide, abortion, and contraception. Given such an ethical framework, it is not surprising that many thinkers avoided altogether the touchy subject of population.

But there is still one more taboo that has interfered with productive thinking about population for nearly two centuries, a taboo that even now is observed by the vast majority of population professionals. Until this taboo is thoroughly set aside, no significant improvements in population policy are possible.

A Darwin Grandson Repays a Family Debt

In the world of scientific autobiographies one of the most quoted passages is the following account by Charles Darwin:

> In October 1838, that is, fifteen months after I had begun my systematic enquiry, I happened to read for amusement Malthus on *Population,* and being well prepared to appreciate the struggle for existence which everywhere goes on from long-continued observation of the habits of animals and plants, it at once struck me that under these circumstances favourable variations would tend to be preserved, and unfavourable ones to be destroyed. The result of this would be the formation of new species. Here, then, I had at last got a theory by which to work. . . . [9]

Even the phrase "the struggle for existence" comes from Malthus. Accepting, as all biologists do, that the world available to every species of plant and animal is a limited world, and knowing in his bones that all reproduction is intrinsically exponential, Darwin realized (and observed) that the majority of the individuals conceived in each generation must die "without issue." At this point in the theory two possibilities present themselves: either mortality (or nonreproduction) is strictly at random, or it is not. Without ever verbalizing the point, Malthus unconsciously developed his theory on the assumption of random mortality. This limitation of thought has been the implicit rule in demography ever since. The novelty that Darwin introduced was his explicit recognition of nonrandom mortality. (Box 24-2[10] records Darwin's admirably succinct description of *natural selection.* The inescapability of natural selection is one of the great default positions of biology.)

Natural selection is a particular instance of a broad generalization that must have been embraced by productive thinkers for thousands of years, but which even now is seldom made explicit, namely that *rewards determine consequences.* When it comes to human behavior, if society rewards thievery it will generate thieves; if it

---

Box 24-2. Charles Darwin: The Meaning of Natural Selection.

It is good to try in our imagination to give any form some advantage over another. Probably in no single instance should we know what to do, so as to succeed. It will convince us of our ignorance on the mutual relations of all organic beings; a conviction as necessary, as it seems to be difficult to acquire. All that we can do, is to keep steadily in mind that each organic being is striving to increase at a geometrical ratio; that each at some period of its life, during some season of the year, during each generation or at intervals, has to struggle for life, and to suffer great destruction.

   Can it, then, be thought improbable that variations useful in some way to each being in the great and complex battle of life, should sometimes occur in the course of thousands of generations? If such do occur, can we doubt (remembering that many more individuals are born than can possibly survive) that individuals having any advantage, however slight, over others, would have the best chance of survival and of procreating their kind? On the other hand, we may feel sure that any variation in the least degree injurious would be rigidly destroyed. This preservation of favourable variations, I call Natural Selection.

The Origin of Species, 1859.

---

rewards self-sacrifice it will beget heroes; if it rewards invention it will breed inventors. Such consequences are not universally true, only statistically so; but effective policy can be built on statistical truths.

   Much has been made of the public shock that was aroused by Darwin's support of evolution in the *Origin;* but evolution was already an old idea in 1859. The real novelty of Darwin's book was the introduction of the idea of natural selection, which tells us that the rewards of survival and reproduction determine which genetic variants will endure over time. For a very short while after 1859 natural selection received some professional attention, but by the time Darwin died in 1882 public controversy was largely concentrated on the topic of evolution-as-history, the familiar and more acceptable shocker.

   Early in the twentieth century a few biologists even proclaimed the death of natural selection. Their reasons revolved around technical points that need not be explored here. Beginning about 1930 the doubters' case was brilliantly refuted by R. A. Fisher, J. B. S. Haldane, and Sewall Wright. Never since then has any significant criticism of natural selection come from professional biologists. Inescapable natural selection is as well established as the economists' dogma "There's no such thing as a free lunch."

   Several experiences widely known to the public helped bring about a more general acceptance of the idea of natural selection after 1930. No sooner was penicillin produced in quantity than it became apparent that its use provoked the evolutionary appearance of penicillin-resistant bacteria. When DDT was developed as an insecticide, it was soon found that it selected for DDT-resistant mosquitoes. From many such experiences biologists deduced the generalization that *every biocide selects for its own failure.* Religious fundamentalists who grow livid at the mention of Charles Darwin and historical evolution have (significantly) never gone to court to try to get schools to teach the falsity of natural selection *in medical situations.*

   It was in this atmosphere that the many centennial celebrations of the publication of *The Origin of Species* were planned. The most ambitious of these took place at the University of Chicago, where the invited speakers included a grandson of Charles Darwin, one Charles Galton Darwin. This Darwin made his mark in physics, but he also had a few things to say about the social implications of his grandfather's work. One of the points he made in Chicago should have set population studies on a new track. It did not. Why not?

Before we can answer this question several steps must be taken. We need first to enlarge upon the climate of opinion in which C. G. Darwin's contribution made its appearance. Second, we need to understand why his paper should have been something of a bomb exploding in the population community. And third, we will try to explain why the bomb was a historical fizzle.

Public support for contraception grew greatly during the twentieth century. The growth was no doubt facilitated by the succession of euphemisms that it brought forth. "Birth control," coined by Margaret Sanger in 1914, was the first of these. In the 1930s it became apparent that this term was viewed as an obscenity by many people; so the term "planned parenthood" was coined. Support for the movement was broadened when Planned Parenthood clinics enriched their birth control services with the treatment of infertility. The two-pronged approach gave credibility to the contention of Planned Parenthood organizations that they were in the business of *helping women to have the children they wanted when they wanted them,* thus blunting the criticism of those who saw birth control as an exclusively negative practice, the work of people who hated babies.

From the beginning there had been some ambivalence about the primary goal of the birth control movement. Was it to free women of unwanted pregnancies? Or was it to slow the rate of population growth? Of course each prevented birth slows the rate of population growth by a certain amount; but can population control be achieved by doing no more than universalizing the knowledge of birth control? Are the terms "birth control" and "population control" synonymous?

The Planned Parenthood people never explicitly asserted this equivalence, but neither did they fight against it. In fact, an international arm of the organization is named "Planned Parenthood—World Population." Millions of dollars have been given to that organization to help women live more fulfilling lives; some of the millions were no doubt given in the belief that purely voluntary birth control would eventually produce population control.

This was the illusion that Charles Galton Darwin shattered in 1959 (Box 24-3)[11]. A bactericide selects for its own failure; an insecticide selects for its failure; and so also—for the same Darwinian reason—does *purely voluntary* control of reproduction select for failure as a means of population control. These examples are but separate instances of the general truth that every deterrent of reproduction selects for its failure. For every living system that man attempts to control, escape from control becomes the payoff.

Fertility's escape from repressive control comes about in this way. Mutation is an unstoppable process. The vast majority of new mutant forms are worse than the "normal" (usual) genes that they compete with in any particular environment. But change the environment (by adding to it either penicillin, or DDT, or the voluntary use of spermicides) and you change the selective criteria. Genes or characteristics that are more resistant to the new selecting agent will have an advantage in competing with what we previously viewed as the "normal" genes or characteristics.

Box 24-3. C. G. Darwin Reveals the Joker in Voluntary Population Control.

If I may be permitted so to put it, by the invention of contraception, the species *Homo sapiens* has discovered that he can become the new variety *"Homo contracipiens,"* and may take advantage of this to produce a much reduced fraction of the next generation. We have found out how to cheat nature. However, it would seem likely that in the very long run nature cannot be cheated, and it is easy to see the revenge it might take. Some people do have a wish for children before they are conceived, though for most of them it has not the strong compulsion of the two instincts. There will be a tendency for such people to have rather more children than the rest, and these children will inherit the wish to an enhanced extent, and these will contribute a still greater proportion of the population. Thus the direct wish for children is likely to become stronger in more and more of the race and in the end it could attain the quality of an instinct as strong as the other two. It may well be that it would take hundreds of generations for the progenitive instinct to develop in this way, but if it should do so, nature would have taken its revenge, and the variety *Homo contracipiens* would become extinct and would be replaced by the variety *Homo progenitivus.*

All this, of course, will happen only if the practice of birth control becomes so prevalent that, through it, population numbers should actually tend to decrease.

"Can Man Control His Numbers?" 1960.

The Darwin of our time underlined the truism that if family formation is purely a matter of voluntary choice, the adults who—for whatever reason—possess the stronger desire to have children will produce more children on the average than will the adults who use contraceptives because they are, at best, lukewarm about parenthood. If genes are at all involved in the differences between these two groups of adults, the proportion of individuals who deserve the name of *Homo progenitivus* will increase generation by generation. *Homo contracipiens* will eventually come close to disappearing entirely. Thus it comes about that population control, if based *only* on voluntary birth control, will ultimately fail.

In 1838 biology incurred a debt to the social sciences when Charles Darwin borrowed from Malthus the idea of overpopulation. From the resulting struggle for existence, Darwin deduced the idea of a nonrandom survival of offspring. This in turn led to the concept of evolutionary change. A hundred years after this fundamental theory of biology was presented to the world by Charles Darwin, his grandson repaid biology's debt to social studies by showing that purely voluntary population control could not, in the end, succeed. The Planned Parenthood troops should have recognized this as a major threat to their campaign, which was built on the individualistic idea of the right of each woman to have *however many children she might want,* whenever she wanted them. In effect, C. G. Darwin said, "Birth control is not necessarily population control."

Why Was the Second Darwinian Bomb a Fizzle?

Social scientists criticized C. G. Darwin's proposition for its "biologism"—the illegitimate application (as they saw it) of technical biology to social problems. The burden of proof issue was raised when critics asked for the evidence that mother love was inherited. To a biologist this is not a radical assumption. Observing non-human species in which rigorous genetic experiments are possible, genes for behavioral and psychological differences can be amply demonstrated. Moreover there is the practical evidence from animal breeders: dog breeders, for instance, have managed to stabilize some surprizing forms of behavior in the different breeds, such as "pointing" in pointers. In many species of economically important animals "good mothers" have been so well selected for that it is hard to find "bad mothers" to carry out a genetic analysis of this variation in behavior. Scholars who have had little experience with biology dismiss these examples: they cling to the doctrine of "human exemptionism," described in Chapter 16. Since the psychic hunger for this supportive doctrine is so great, it is fortunate that the argument about the possible genetic inheritance of behavior in the human species need not be joined.

The excerpt in Box 24-3 clearly assumes the genetic inheritance of behavioral characteristics. But this is not a necessary assumption. The same result follows if behavior *has absolutely no genetic component.* In the general case we must assume two sorts of inheritance in human beings: genetic and educational. The second includes not only the influence of schools but also all of the multitudinous influences of the home. Also influential is the community outside the school and home. No one—whether biologist or sociologist—disputes the reality of influences by education ("education" being understood in the broadest sense). Empirically it has been established that the daughters of mothers who had more children than the norm for their generation have more children than the norm for *their*—the daughters'—generation.[12] That's all that is required for C. G. Darwin's argument to hold. The issue of genes versus education—nature vs. nurture—can be ignored. Both forms of "heredity" are effective.

How to Publish a Heresy Without Attracting Attention

Part of the unofficial mythos that supports science is the belief that truth will prevail, no matter what. If you have a heretical idea, publish it, supporting it with data and arguments as needed, and it will be noticed. If your theory is true it will soon be accepted by the establishment; heterodoxy will metamorphose into orthodoxy.

The slow progress of C. G. Darwin's thesis makes one doubt the myth. We search for reasons why so important an idea, presented in public, should have been so generally ignored. No historical explanation is beyond doubt, but several plausible factors can be pointed out in this instance. The first of them stems from overpopulation itself.

The standard myth of "publish and be noticed" presumes a small enough body of publications. The truth is now quite otherwise. The population of scientists and scholars has grown so large, and the outpouring of professional publications is so torrential, that active researchers have to ration their reading severely. The periodicals a scientist combs over systematically are very few—two dozen would be a large number. Hoping not to miss important announcements in the outlying journals, a researcher may consult abstracting journals. Indulging in even this activity becomes increasingly onerous. More useful are connections to the "grapevine" of like-minded workers, communicating by phone and computer. Ceremonial symposia, like the one on Charles Darwin in Chicago, will for the most part be ignored by active researchers; the resulting publications are even likely to be ignored by the abstract journals. Overpopulation of people in general has produced an overpopulation of researchers and reports, producing an information overload, which has led to the erection of protective bulwarks against the torrent of publications. The defense strategies include a disposition to ignore what a researcher says when he strays outside his recognized field of expertise—for example, C. G. Darwin, the physicist, speaking about the biology of populations.

Post-Darwinian Policy: A Step Yet to Come

To say that birth control is not the same thing as population control is not to condemn the promotion of voluntary birth control. Ignorance of contraceptive methods is global and enormous. The work of planned parenthood organizations is *necessary but not sufficient* to achieve population control. That fact is quite enough justification for supporting such organizations generously. Their efforts are "buying time" during which we can be looking for ways to achieve population control.

The improvement of birth control methods is largely a technological problem. A perfect system of birth control is one that permits women to have the number of children they want, when they want them. But numerous national surveys of women's expressed desires shows that the average woman wants a family that is greater than the number needed to produce zero population growth in her community. This means that the problem of population control requires approaches that go beyond technology. We need to devise acceptable ways of influencing the desires of women in the light of community needs. This problem has not yet been solved, but some interesting proposals have been made, as the next chapter discloses.

25

Population Control: Natural versus Human

Were we able to talk with other animals, it is extremely unlikely that we should hear them debating the problem of population control. They don't need to debate: nature solves the problem for them. And what is the problem? Simply this: to keep a successful species from being too successful. To keep it from eating itself out of house and home. And the solution? Simply predation and disease, which play the role that human beings might label "providence."

As far as the written record reveals, no one recognized the self-elimination of a species as a potential problem for animals until the danger had become suspected among human beings. One of the earliest descriptions of this population problem for other animals was given by the Reverend Joseph Townsend, an English geologist. His key contribution was published in 1786, twelve years before Malthus's celebrated essay (Box 25-1).[1]

Townsend was dependent upon others for the outline of his story, and there is some question as to whether the details are historically correct. But the thrust of the story must be true: a single species (goats, in this case) exploiting a resource (plants) cannot, by itself, maintain a stable equilibrium at a comfortable level of living. The animals will either die after eating up all the food, or their numbers will fluctuate painfully. (Details differ, depending on the species and the environment.)[2] Stability and prosperity require that the gift of exponential growth be opposed by some sort of countervailing force (predatory dogs, in Townsend's example). However deplorable predators may be for individuals who happen to be captured and eaten, for the prey population as a whole predators are (over time) a blessing.

With millions of different species of animals there are many different particular explanations of how they manage to persist for thousands or millions of years. The species we are most interested in is, of course, *Homo sapiens*. A meditation on Townsend's account led to a challenging set of questions. "If all this great earth be no more than the Island of Juan Fernandes, and if we are the goats, how can we live "the good life" without a functional equivalent of the dogs? Must we create and sustain our own dogs? Can we do so, consciously? And if we can, what manner of beast will they be?"[3]

Those words point to the task of the remainder of this book, and one of humanity's major problems for as far into the future as we can see. The human species having, by its cleverness, apparently removed providence from its control system,

---

Box 25-1.   Joseph Townsend: The Goats of Juan Fernando Island.

In the South Seas there is an island, which from the first discoverer is called Juan Fernandes. In this sequestered spot, John Fernando placed a colony of goats, consisting of one male, attended by his female. This happy couple finding pasture in abundance, could readily obey the first commandment, to increase and multiply, till in process of time they had replenished their little island . . . .

[T]hey were [at first] strangers to misery and want, and seemed to glory in their numbers: but [later] they began to suffer hunger; yet continuing for a time to increase their numbers, had they been endued with reason, they must have apprehended the extremity of famine. In this situation the weakest first gave way, and plenty was again restored. Thus they fluctuated between happiness and misery, and either suffered want or rejoiced in abundance, according as their numbers were diminished or increased; never at a stay, yet nearly balancing at all times their quantity of food. This degree of equipoise was from time to time destroyed, either by epidemical diseases or by the arrival of some vessel in distress. On such occasions their numbers were considerably reduced; but to compensate for this alarm, and to comfort them for the loss of their companions, the survivors never failed immediately to meet returning plenty. They were no longer in fear of famine: they ceased to regard each other with an evil eye; all had abundance, all were contented, all were happy. Thus, what might have been considered as misfortunes, proved a source of comfort; and, to them at least, partial evil was universal good.

When the Spaniards found that the English privateers resorted to this island for provisions, they resolved on the total extirpation of the goats, and for this purpose they put on shore a greyhound dog and bitch. These in their turn increased and multiplied, in proportion to the quantity of food they met with; but in consequence, as the Spaniards had foreseen, the breed of goats diminished. Had they been totally destroyed, the dogs likewise must have perished. But as many of the goats retired to the craggy rocks, where the dogs could never follow them, descending only for short intervals to feed with fear and circumspection in the vallies, few of these, besides the careless and the rash, became a prey; and none but the most watchful, strong, and active of the dogs could get a sufficiency of food. Thus a new kind of balance was established. The weakest of both species were among the first to pay the debt of nature; the most active and vigorous preserved their lives.

A Dissertation on the Poor Laws, 1786.

---

faces a daunting problem: can we replace nature's admittedly ruthless methods with more gentle methods of our own?

Asking this question makes us aware of the essential ambiguity of the term *population control*. Clearly the size of a population may be controlled in either of two ways: by nature, without our intervention, or by ourselves (with nature kept at bay). When we speak of a policy of "population control," we clearly have in mind the second sort of control. Considering the manifold difficulties of emplacing population policy, we may sometimes wish that nature still took care of this function for us. Nonetheless we struggle on with this problem because we recognize that if a society never controls the size of the population, nature ultimately will. Nature's two great tools for population control are starvation and disease. Those are not the sort of controls that *caring* people have in mind when they call for "population control," but they have worked in the past. If we do not mend our ways, they will regain control in the future.

Population Control by Starvation

Until about two centuries ago food shortages were a significant factor in the control of human populations in the Western world (as they still are in many poor countries). The letter of Carl Linnaeus quoted in Chapter 21 shows how unthinkingly the wealthy once accepted the legitimacy of starvation. Until recently, inadequate transportation ruled out the possibility of rapidly importing food from thousands of miles away. As for the distribution of the severely limited local supplies, few thought that they should be equally divided among all the supplicants. For men and women of earlier times, the Bible was a living counselor: Christ himself had said, "Ye have the poor always with you" (Matthew 26:11). In such a world rich people surrounded by the poor could eat in good conscience (though the thinner-skinned might be somewhat ill at ease). Life was tough, but the laws of civilization had to be upheld. It was not until the end of the nineteenth century that radical thinkers began to awaken the rich to new obligations. Anatole France ironically praised "the majestic egalitarianism of the law, which forbids rich and poor alike to sleep under bridges, to beg in the streets, and to steal bread."

With the ever more rapid development of science and technology after Linnaeus's time, the ratio of supply to demand changed in a favorable direction. It became easier to prevent deaths from famine. Private philanthropy had always existed, but more and more people decided it was really the obligation of the state as a whole to prevent individual suffering. The welfare state gradually evolved during the nineteenth and twentieth centuries, and it was no longer necessary for kindhearted mothers to kill their starving children.

Though a stable population control system can be imagined that involves the death of the children of feckless parents, such a scheme is revolting to most people now. After all, the child is not responsible for his birth: why punish him for the poor judgment of his parents?

Population Control by Disease

For thousands of years human populations have been severely decimated from time to time by epidemic diseases caused by bacteria or viruses. In the fourteenth century the bacteria of the Black Plague wiped out something like a third of the European population within two years.

In the last two centuries we have gained a great deal of control over disease organisms. At first progress came about through what might well be called superstition, though we now call it "sanitation." For various and somewhat obscure reasons cleanliness started to be fashionable and popular. In the beginning, sanitation may have had no better intellectual basis than carrying a rabbit's foot. But morbidity and mortality rates went down.

Then in the nineteenth century the germ theory of disease was developed. Considering the near invisibility of most of the putative culprits (and the complete invisibility then of some of them, such as the yellow fever virus), it is a wonder that the germ theory was adopted as rapidly as it was. Florence Nightingale thought the theory was pure nonsense. She staked her reputation on sanitation.

The needless conflict between sanitationists (such as Nightingale) and bacteriologists like Pasteur is now forgotten. The two positions have melded into one. At the intellectual level we ascribe disease to microbes. On the practical side we recognize that cleanliness pretty well enables us to control the distribution and multiplication of the tiny agents we seldom see. By the middle of the twentieth century we thought we had conquered disease germs.

Continued evolution then presented us with the HIV virus and the resultant disease, AIDS. Confidence in human omnipotence was undermined. Will AIDS be conquered? Will evolution present us with other, and worse, diseases? Will disease once more be a major controller of human populations? The jury is still out.

It should be noted that the death toll from widespread disease is never known very exactly. When people are dropping dead like flies, who is going to devote the short remainder of his or her life to counting corpses? It is far more likely that those who are fortunate enough to escape the worst of an epidemic will flee the scene, perhaps to amuse themselves exchanging salacious tales, as the fortunate nobility did in Boccaccio's *Decameron.*

There is a more fundamental difficulty involved in dealing with the deaths that are *associated with* diseases. This concerns our assumptions about causation. If a starving child catches the measles and dies, what was "the cause" of his death—measles or starvation? We know that the death rate of almost all disease is much greater in a malnourished population than it is in one that is well nourished. Why, then, chalk up the deaths to the disease?

By long tradition medical personnel are under pressure to list the *proximate*—the last—factor as "the cause" of death. In "normal" periods—noncrisis times—starvation is almost never listed as the cause of death, though it may play an important causative role among chronically undernourished people. Under conditions of great food shortage, however, the habitual assignment of causation changes, and starvation is listed as the simple cause. Doctors, if they survive, have better things to do with their time than look for associated disease organisms. As for lay reporters, few of them seek assignments in a country gripped by starvation, and so the numbers affected may go uncounted.

Luxury, Simplicity, and Population Control

The real point of population control—a point that critics often miss—is not to reduce population *per se,* but to reduce misery among the living. Realizing this, Charles Galton Darwin pointed out a way to reduce misery (Box 25-2).[4] If people would *define* misery as an absence of luxury, and if they would let their fertility be governed by this new standard, it would be possible for them to enjoy luxuries indefinitely, generation after generation, as the population set point was moved to a low position. C. G. Darwin called his scheme the "bribe" of the motor car, using the motor car metaphorically to stand for all sorts of luxuries. In a culture in which women have the power of decision, rich women tend to invest their wealth in goods other than numerous offspring. So the bribe can work—*in the short run.*

Box 25-2. C. G. Darwin: The "Bribe of the Motor-Car."

It is indisputable that a considerable fraction of the population find it both easy and convenient to contribute less than their share to the next generation, and this fraction is specially the one enjoying the highest prosperity.

It is convenient to have a short phrase to describe this state of affairs in which prosperity produces childlessness, and I shall characterize it by saying that the prospect of owning a motor-car is a sufficient bribe to sterilize most people. I do not apologize for calling it sterility, for though the term is often used to imply a physical incapacity that is held in contempt, it is, biologically speaking, immaterial whether the incapacity is forced or voluntary. In my phrase the motor-car is of course only metaphorical, as a symbol of the sort of level of prosperity that tends to be associated with small families or childlessness; and it is being found that as prosperity spreads downwards in the social scale, so the families tend to become smaller there too. It would be difficult to say which is cause and which effect, for children are an economic disadvantage, so that their presence lowers their parents' prospects, and on the other hand the ease and comfort of existing prosperity discourages the creation of children.

"Can Man Control His Numbers?" 1952.

But what about the long run, as one generation succeeds another? The answer to this depends on other particulars. First, suppose that the species is composed of two well-separated populations (nations perhaps), one of which has reacted to the bribe of the motor car, the other not. The luxury-loving population remains prosperous while the population that has rejected the bribe remains poor *but becomes more numerous.* If—and it's a big *if*—the difference in numbers does *not* lead to demands for a redistribution of land or wealth, then the luxury-loving population can continue to enjoy its luxuries. These can include freedom from crowding, access to wilderness and uncrowded beaches, development of the arts—whatever a society agrees to define as *essential luxuries* (which it refuses to call an oxymoron!).

A problem may develop when people of differing opinions about luxuries live within the same sovereignty. The rich and *relatively* less fertile become a smaller and smaller proportion of the population as one generation succeeds another. Given even a slight feeling of community obligation to take care of the needy, a redistribution of wealth will take place as the rich-and-infertile yield some of their prosperity to the poor-but-fertile. (Consider the Beatitude "Blessed are the meek: for they shall inherit the earth." Is this a prediction or a threat? One wonders.)

A basic default position of economics is called Gresham's law: "Bad money drives out good." (When both good money and counterfeit money circulate in a community, the average person tries to pass the counterfeit on while he squirrels away the good money.)

Laissez-faire reproduction in a welfare state produces a *Greshamite law of population:*

Under competition, low living standards drive out high.

Those who invest in children will, in the long run, replace those who invest in material luxuries.

The Greshamite law of population lies at the base of a serious controversy. Early in the modern environmental movement the economist E. F. Schumacher brought

out a little book, *Small is Beautiful,* which was very influential in encouraging people to elect the simple life over a life of luxuries.[5] Taken together, the works of Schumacher and C. G. Darwin call for a decision in values. Since the resource limits of
the world are fixed (though not completely known), the greater the per capita
demand on these resources, the smaller the maximum population that can be supported by our resources. Jeremy Bentham and John Stuart Mill popularized the
ideal of "the greatest good for the greatest number," which is nonsense, since two
variables cannot be maximized at the same time. Which do we want: a world with
the maximum number of people in it, or one in which the per capita share of
resources is maximized? Put in terms of the Darwinian metaphor, should we just
drift toward a world population of, say, 30 billion people, and a world in which
everyone walks or rides a bicycle and is often hungry; or should we strive for a lesser
population (perhaps half a billion) in which a large minority can enjoy motor cars
and plenty of gourmet food? Going beyond simple technology, do we want a world
with a bountiful supply of unspoiled wilderness for the spiritual renewal of a few,
or a world filled wall-to-wall with people in which all wild areas are "developed" for
agriculture, industry, and housing? The arguments over values have scarcely begun.

Rights and the Welfare State

The drive toward technological innovation has seldom if ever been informed by the
wisdom of the first law of ecology, "We can never do merely one thing." We pay
people to invent one thing; we pay other people to manufacture one thing; and then
we pay promoters to persuade the general public to use that thing without considering the consequences of introducing it into a complex web of existing relations.

Beset by a shortage, people pray that the supply will be increased. Though no
ecologist, Oscar Wilde warned of the danger of such petitions: "When the gods wish
to punish us they answer our prayers." For millennia well-meaning people have
prayed for the ability to produce a surplus of food. Technology has now given us
this capability. While this change was taking place, another sort of desire was being
met by the development of the welfare state: the desire for greater personal security.
What Wilde punishment now faces us because we have accepted these two gifts?
The following newspaper account throws some light on this question.

Considerable newspaper space was devoted to an account of the first birth in the
year 1991 in the California town that serves the Vandenberg Air Force Base.[6] An
eleventh child joined six brothers and four sisters, ranging in age from one to sixteen. The mother was thirty-eight years old; the father, a technical sergeant, was
forty-one. Supporting their large brood on a salary of $23,000 a year might be
impossible were it not for the extensive welfare benefits enjoyed by members of the
armed forces. Housing is essentially free; to accommodate the growing family the
government joined together two four-bedroom houses. Their medical expenses
were almost completely taken care of by Uncle Sam: the most the family ever paid
for child delivery was $50, when twins were born. (Obstetrical charges to civilians
vary greatly around the nation, but as of 1990 they were seldom less than $1,000
per birth.)

"Will there be more children?" the reporter asked.

"We'll let the Lord decide," replied the father, "It's another joy in the house."

The couple, members of the Church of Jesus Christ of Latter-day Saints, are a telling example of what C. G. Darwin had in mind when he coined the term *Homo progenitivus*. A nation that generously supports such a "cultural subspecies" cannot realistically expect to control the size of its population.

A Suicidal Right

The essentials of the account given above are repeated in only a fraction of the American population, and so might seem to require no general treatment. The story, however, raises general problems in the relation of rights to responsibilities in a world in which "global" thinking is fashionable. Many people approve of the United Nations's statement on the rights of the family: "The Universal Declaration of Human Rights describes the family as the natural and fundamental unit of society. It follows that any choice and decision with regard to the size of the family must irrevocably rest with the family itself, and cannot be made by anyone else."[7]

This statement, like many position papers, explicitly discusses rights *but says nothing whatever about matching responsibilities.* The Universal Declaration surely implies that the ultimate responsibility for keeping children alive rests with the larger community—the nation, or the whole world—while the right to have children is passionately—"irrevocably"—asserted to reside in the nuclear family.

But no stable system is possible when rights and responsibilities are thus separated. The United Nations has given its blessing to a CC-PP game: the costs of raising a child are to be commonized, while the profits—the psychological gains of parenthood—are assigned to the parents. The United Nations did not invent this game, of course: it was anticipated by the philosophers of the welfare state, who did not understand how suicidal the game could be in a world in which the population controls of starvation and disease have been largely neutralized.

The United Nations' definition of universal human rights does not meet the challenge of Charles Frankel's definition of responsibility: *A decision is responsible when the man or group that makes it has to answer for it to those who are directly or indirectly affected by it.*[8]

There may be another source of the suicidal policy of the United Nations: the human preference for symmetry in rhetorical statements. From Margaret Sanger's time onward, the championing of women's right to practice birth control has led organizations like Planned Parenthood to put forward the symmetrical right of a woman *to have or not to have.* Except possibly in a very small nation (which the United States certainly is not) the nonbirth of a child does not threaten society. By contrast, each birth threatens to impose unasked-for burdens on society. The growth of social welfare has created an asymmetry in the distribution of responsibility. So long as reproduction in society is strictly laissez-faire, little burden is placed on society by the birth of a child. But the growth of the welfare state has shifted more and more of the burdens from the parents to the state. The United Nations's statement takes no cognizance of this change. If Frankel's criterion of responsibility is to be met, the assertion of reproductive rights needs to be made asymmetrical, thus: *Every woman has the unqualified right to refrain from having children; but the privilege of bearing a child must take into account the interests of society, which shoulders so many of the costs of child-rearing.*

1989: The End of an Illusion?

"From each according to his ability, to each according to his needs"—few words have inspired so much idealism or produced as much suffering as these, written by Marx in 1875. A decisive argument against this principle had been given by Lloyd more than forty years earlier, but it was soon forgotten. In the following century the Marxist creed became the gospel of the Soviet Union and numerous other socialist nations. A Marxist economy is one that offers each participant a chance to privatize his needs while commonizing his abilities. It is only human for each individual to overestimate the former and underestimate the latter. Then, as a member of a group, the citizen is tempted to maximize his personal well-being by neglecting his societal duties. Thus it comes about that group productivity is not maximized. Worse, envy among the citizen-servants of society erodes the spirit of altruism. To keep a nation of "freeloaders" in check, dictatorial powers are invoked. Marx's lovely words turn out to be little more than window dressing for brutal and inefficient command-and-control governments. Thus do the unfortunate subjects of totalitarian regimes discover once more the wisdom of the ancient question, *Quis custodiet ipsos custodes?*—"Who shall watch the watchers themselves?"

The excesses of the French Revolution played an important role in stimulating Malthus to write *An Essay on the Principle of Population.* In 1989, exactly two centuries after the storming of the Bastille, Marxist fellow travelers throughout the world had their faith severely challenged by the cataclysmic fall of a gaggle of socialist governments. A most remarkable two centuries!

Persuasion: The Diseconomies of Scale

"To each according to his needs" implies an unmanaged commons, a free lunch for those who can attach themselves to a community of idealists who are too stupid to see the operational meaning of the words. Must such a community always fail? Not quite always. Success critically depends on the size of the community. We see the scale effect in operation among the Hutterite communities of northwestern United States and Canada. In Box 25-3 is included a passage from an illuminating account of Hutterite experience by Kari Bullock and John Baden.[9]

A Hutterite commune consists typically of 60 to 150 people. The lower limit is determined by economies of scale. (Hutterites use a great deal of farm machinery, and expensive machinery always creates economies of scale.) At the upper limit, diseconomies of scale are in command: social psychology overrides technology.

Hutterites show their awareness of this reality in their saying, "All colonies have their drones." As a colony grows in size, the propensity of the individual to claim a share of production "according to his needs" increases, while his eagerness to work "according to his ability" diminishes. The effectiveness of the overseers (preachers or bosses) also diminishes. Then, as shirking increases, those less inclined to "goof

---

Box 25-3. The Hutterites: Ideals under the Battering of the Scale Effect.

There is a common saying among Hutterites: "All colonies [especially other colonies] have their drones." Further, it is recognized that the number of drones increases more than proportionately with an increase in colony size. Given that all goods are in the common pool, individual economic incentives are minimal, material differentials are outlawed, and everyone has equal rights to the resources but the allocation of resources is not individually defined, then a rational, maximizing person would operate to maximize his pleasure, including leisure. He might engage in such self-seeking activities as trips to town or to a neighboring ranch to "check on" or "pick up" something allegedly relevant to his assigned task. In such circumstances, a necessary tool is more likely to "need" immediate replacement when the boss or preacher is absent or otherwise engaged.

In a relatively small colony, the proportional contribution of each member is greater. Likewise, surveillance by each of the others is more complete and an informal accounting of contributions is feasible. In a Hutterite colony, there are no elaborate formal controls over a person's contribution. Thus, in general, the incentive and surveillance structures of a small or medium-size colony are more effective than those of a large colony, and shirking is lessened.

Kari Bullock and John Baden, "Communes and the Logic of the Commons, 1977.

---

off" begin to envy the brotherhood of drones, whom they presently join. Shirking becomes a growth industry, so to speak: the larger the group, the larger the proportion of those who do not pull their weight. (In the Soviet Union, during the latter days of doctrinaire communism, a Russian worker explained the system to an American reporter in these words: "First *we* pretend to work, and then *they* pretend to pay us.")

A commons like that of the Hutterites is often called an "unmanaged commons." But this description underestimates the power of persuasion: of an appeal to conscience—of shame. Unfortunately for the system, shame proves to be strongly subject to a *dis*economy of scale. Above a certain population size the "control button" of shame is ineffective. We can call this limiting size the *Hutterite limit*.

Generations of experience taught the Hutterites that this limit is approximately 150 people per operational unit. When the numbers become too great in a colony, more and more workers become drones. As the unit approaches this limit it is deliberately split into two daughter colonies, which then function well with no more coercive control than shame.

During the middle decades of both the nineteenth and twentieth centuries, many idealistic communities were set up as unmanaged commons in the United States. A few of them grew beyond the Hutterite limit and survived as long as a charismatic personality held them together. An example was the Oneida Community of upper New York state under the leadership of John Humphrey Noyes.[10] But though it was unmanaged in the sense that it did not rely on harsh laws, the Oneida community was certainly guided and controlled by the persuasive personality of one man. The community disintegrated soon after that control came to an end. Other communities, not blessed with sufficiently charismatic leadership, fell apart after transgressing the Hutterite limit.

As for whole nations of people (far beyond the Hutterite limit), it is undeniable that the Marxist motto is mischievous. It leads to a poorly managed commons, which is but a way station on the path to totalitarian control. "To each according to his needs" is the beguiling bait that persuades the poor fish of the world to swim into the totalitarian net.

China: The Failed Experiment

In the accounts of Hutterite colonies there is no discussion of population control, because the Hutterite religion is totally pronatalist. In the recent past the average number of children per Hutterite woman has been around ten. (How much longer such a reproductive pace can be maintained in a world of diminishing farm lands is an interesting question.) Enthusiastically accepting both modern medicine and modern agriculture, and rejecting anything like the clerical celibacy of the Catholic church, Hutterites have produced the fastest growing, self-supporting community in the history of humankind. (The exiled Bikinians described in Chapter 9, with their annual growth rate of 5.4 percent, are *not* self-supporting.) But though the Hutterites emphatically do not seek to control their population, their political system throws light on a method of population control that has been repeatedly recommended, namely control by conscience.

Western civilization is at a serious disadvantage when it comes to population control. Because of the growth of the philosophy of individualism during the past three centuries, together with its powerful rhetoric of "rights," it is difficult for Westerners to conceive an *acceptable* method of population control that would have a chance of working. The United Nations organization has painted the Europeanized world into a corner with its Universal Declaration of Human Rights. All Planned Parenthood organizations operate within this framework. (They are probably wise to do so; otherwise their admirable work in liberating women could scarcely be carried on.) The private organization Zero Population Growth, Inc., with its slogan "Stop at Two!" also relies on appeals to conscience.

The Hutterite experience shows that the scale effect rules all appeals to conscience. Since shame is affected by scale, how could a large population like a nation conceivably achieve population control at a comfortable set point without resorting to unacceptable coercion? A recently failed experiment in China suggests some possibilities.

Three decades after the experiment in applied Marxism was begun in Russia, it was repeated in Asia. The People's Republic of China was officially born on 1 October 1949. One of the many problems of this, the most populous nation in the world, was that of matching population size to resources. The biting of this bullet was delayed for many years because China, like Russia before it, was in the grip of the Marxist superstition that overpopulation is impossible in a socialist country. After some vacillation, and as the national population approached a billion, the communist party abandoned the superstition, acknowledging that China was already overpopulated, an acknowledgment that had been made by no other national government up to that time. More: the government committed itself to working toward an interim policy of one child per family; this, if achieved, would actually result in a negative population growth—an "unthinkable" posture for most governments. Presumably, after negative growth had reduced the excess of people, the permitted family size would be moved upward, nearer to the two children per family needed for ZPG. The world watched the Chinese experiment with interest.

Reports coming out of a country as large and as diversified as China are never satisfactory, but it looked for awhile as though China might achieve her new goal. In some of the major cities the program seemed to be carried forward along the following lines. Decision making was decentralized. Almost every able-bodied woman in a Chinese city was a member of a "production group," which was charged with making its own decisions. Each group was told by the central government what their allotment of rice would be for the year. This allotment would *not* be readjusted in accordance with the Marxist ideal of "to each according to their need." Rather, it was a flat allotment that made no allowance for increased fertility. It was up to the members of a production group to decide among themselves which women would be allowed to become pregnant during the coming year. As far as could be told from the reports to the world outside, the number of women in a production group was less than 150—less than the Hutterite limit. So the group should have been able to control the reproductive behavior of its members.

Was the policy ever successful? The answer is not clear. The size and the diversity of the country, coupled with the limited language ability of foreign reporters, made it difficult to generalize the results (which the Chinese government did not publicize adequately in any case). Details of the plans seemed to change with great rapidity.

Significantly, the government explicitly exempted some tribal and distant groups from the control policy. Farmers, claiming a need for many sons to help with the work, demanded and received special dispensations. And, as always, people found ways of cheating the system.

After awhile it looked as though China had reinvented the wheel—the wheel of demographic replacement found in many previous societies in which the people of the cities do not reproduce themselves, their places being taken by fresh bodies moving in from the agricultural boondocks. In the long run, does such a replacement system produce stability? Maybe. But a biologist is struck by the peculiarities of selection such a system establishes. Though we have little certain knowledge of the kinds of unconscious selection taking place, farm life surely must select for somewhat different characteristics than city life. If cities do not reproduce themselves, what is the long-term effect of migration from the farms to the cities being followed by the functional sterilization of those who have made the change? We don't know; but we do know that no previous civilization has lasted forever. We wonder if this kind of replacement may not contribute to the instability of civilizations.

Learning what really went on in China has not been made easier by the antipathy of many of our own people to things Chinese. Lip service to the idea of national sovereignty has often been negated by an uncritical devotion to the idea of "universal human rights" which—not surprisingly—turn out to be identical with the Western version of human rights. In the nineteenth century Europeans thoughtlessly supported programs aimed at Christianizing the whole world. In the twentieth century we just as thoughtlessly have demanded a universal devotion to the Western version of rights, to which we arrogantly attach the adjective "universal."[11]

It is very difficult for a Westerner to realize that our version of individualism is only some three centuries old, dating as it does from John Locke (1632–1704). The commitment to "radical individualism" (as philosophers call it) is confined to a minority of the world's five billion people. Socialistic fellow travelers have, in recent years, produced a large literature extolling the virtues of *community,* a somewhat mystical concept. Community has very real virtues, which may be more readily observed in small towns than in big cities. But big-city propagandists for community do not generally realize the price of togetherness: individual desires must play second fiddle to community standards.

It is equally difficult for the Chinese to understand Western individualism. The women in a Chinese production group, sitting as a committee of the whole (as we would say), deciding who may become pregnant in the next twelve months and who may not, preserve their sense of community through the implicit threat of shame, a psychological weapon abhorred by Western individualists. Were they to speak the same language, both Chinese and Americans might agree that "coercion" is the weapon used by the production group to control its individual members; but they would give this word utterly different emotional weight.

What if a Chinese member of a production group becomes pregnant after she has been specifically denied permission? So far as we can tell, this is not a difficult problem for the Chinese: she is simply told that she must abort her unlicensed embryo.

It should be pointed out that Westerners do not hesitate to license car drivers, even demanding evidence of driving ability before granting the license. Being a good parent surely demands more abilities than being a good driver, but Westerners bridle at the thought of requiring licenses for parenthood.

The U.S. reaction to reports of compulsory abortion in China has had some strange consequences. Before China adopted the new population policy, America had generously supported the work of Planned Parenthood organizations in foreign countries, including China. Some of the funds even came from our government, channeled through AID (Agency for International Development). Only a minority of our population (about 20 percent) is opposed to abortion, but this minority is very vocal. During the Reagan administration it became politically powerful. When Chinese abortions became known here a powerful and effective demand developed for cutting off government funds for the promotion of birth limitation abroad. Planned Parenthood officials promised that U.S. government funds would be used only for the promotion of contraception, never for abortion. But the administration did not trust the Planned Parenthood people, and *all* government funds for promoting birth limitation abroad were cut off. This produced a paradox, which can be simply summarized.

1. American interests are well served by reducing the growth rate of overpopulated foreign countries; both "liberals" and "conservatives" agree to this (though sometimes for different reasons).
2. Widespread experience indicates that reducing access to contraception results in more babies being conceived.
3. Therefore when, in the cause of antiabortion, America interferes with contraceptive services elsewhere, the abortion rate escalates.

The recent American antiabortion policy has clearly been counterproductive. The mythical and wholly rational man from Mars would no doubt be highly amused by the outcome. Smiles come less easily to well-informed rationalists on earth, particularly when they happen to be women.

Rationalism Through Rewards

"Rationalism" is a tricky concept to nail down in words. We need not try. It is enough to agree that, on the whole, behavior is determined by rewards. A rational political policy uses rewards to get the behavior desired. In 1758 Helvetius laid an important foundation stone of political science in his book *De l'Esprit* when he said: "It is solely through good laws that one can form virtuous men. Thus the whole art of the legislator consists of forcing men, by the sentiment of self-love, to be always just to one another."[12]

Thus did Helvetius set to one side the appeals that can be disparaged as "moralistic"—demands that we do the right thing as a matter of duty. It is easy to see how Helvetius' view fed into the idea of laissez-faire. It also anticipated by two centuries the sociobiologists' recognition that actions that benefit a group will be selected for only if there is a payoff for the individual who carries out the action.

The condemnation of laissez-faire in the romantic literature of the nineteenth century helped to launch the command-and-control nations of the twentieth. By now we should be convinced that Helvetius is our best guide to policy. Educational theory generally favors rewards over punishments. Punishment often proves counterproductive because it motivates the subject to find a way of evading punishment while doing the wrong thing. An old saying covers this situation: "Honey catches more flies than vinegar."

Population Control: Rewarding the Individual for Benefiting the Group

How is society to encourage the optimum rate of reproduction? Under American conditions of public health, coupled with a small amount of celibacy, a state of Zero Population Growth requires about 2.1 children per family. Obviously no family can have exactly 2.1 children. Society must seek to make living conditions such that the *average* works out to the desired family size.

When population control was first broached as a topic for discussion, there was a tendency to presume a command-and-control government—a non-Helvetian government—in which bureaucrats would *tell* people how many children they might have, while police and the courts stood ready to punish disobedience. But what if the allotment was two children per family, and a couple produced one child followed by twins? Should one of the twins be killed? Or should the extra child be forcibly put out for adoption by childless couples? Such questions were often raised but seldom answered.

Laissez-faire population control looks more promising because it would present fewer political problems. Would it automatically produce an average family size that is optimal for society? A priori this seems unlikely because there is no firm connection between the needs of society and the desires of individual women (or couples) for children.

If pure laissez-faire won't work, what about biased laissez-faire? Can society *lean on* its reproducers so that they bias their behavior in a socially desirable direction? It has long been recognized that young women are at the heart of the problem. Their innate fecundity is highest at an age when their appreciation of the full burden of parenthood is low—at about sixteen to eighteen years of age. A very young woman (misleadingly called a "girl") often sees motherhood as a way of escaping the dominance of her own parents. In a welfare state motherhood may even offer attractive financial rewards to the young female who is ill prepared to enter the job market. Statistical studies suggest that much "excess" fertility might be eliminated if fertile young women could be persuaded to postpone having their families for awhile. As they get older they get wiser. The longer the postponement, the smaller the completed size of family.

In the 1950s the ecologist Raymond B. Cowles suggested a program of fertility reduction through economic motivation. The plan focused on young women. In the United States more than 99 percent of all births take place in hospitals, so it would be easy to monitor births. Suppose, said Cowles, we pay adolescent females *not* to have children for awhile. For illustration: suppose we pay each young woman, from her fourteenth year to perhaps her twentieth year, x number of dollars at the end of each year she completes without producing a child. (The period might start earlier, or it might extend later.) The size of the payment would depend on the particular conditions prevailing in society. The reward might be increased if the subject enrolled in a meaningful education program. The system could be very flexible.

At first glance this looks like an expensive system. But the expense would be offset by savings resulting from costs not incurred by the children who would otherwise have been born. In the 1980s careful studies made by the Urban Institute showed that a middle class American family had to spend about $100,000 of its own money to raise each child to the age of 18—without any college education.[13] In the long run, infertility-reward programs should be cost effective. But because the benefits accrue only in the long run, and because all novel proposals are at first viewed with suspicion, Cowles' proposal has never acquired strong political support. It has been independently reinvented several times.

The most promising laissez-faire scheme of population control worked out so far is one proposed by Kenneth Boulding.[14] (See Box 25-4.) Each girl baby would be given a fixed (and possibly fractional) number of "baby rights" at the time of her birth. These rights could be traded on a sort of stock exchange. Lovers of children would become buyers of rights; those who preferred to live without kids would be sellers. Some people criticize Boulding's baby rights exchange market as a latter-day slave market. Others denounce it as "sexist," because only women can have, or acquire, baby rights. But then, nature is sexist!

To keep discussion on a rational plane, we should ask this question: does not the truly prudent couple measure their prospective ability to raise a child against their probable prosperity? Boulding's scheme would encourage prudence, of which there is little enough in the world. We note however that the word "prudence" sel-

---

Box 25-4. Kenneth Boulding: A Rational Scheme of Voluntary Population Control.

I have only one positive suggestion to make, a proposal which now seems so farfetched that I find it creates only amusement when I propose it. I think in all seriousness, however, that a system of marketable licenses to have children is the only one which will combine the minimum of social control necessary to the solution to this problem with a maximum of individual liberty and ethical choice. Each girl on approaching maturity would be presented with a certificate which will entitle its owner to have, say, 2.2 children, or whatever number would ensure a reproductive rate of one. The unit of these certificates might be the "deci-child," and accumulation of ten of these units by purchase, inheritance, or gift would permit a woman in maturity to have one legal child. We would then set up a market in these units in which the rich and the philoprogenitive would purchase them from the poor, the nuns, the maiden aunts, and so on. The men perhaps could be left out of these arrangements, as it is only the fertility of woman which is strictly relevant to population control. However, it may be found socially desirable to have them in the plan, in which case all children both male and female would receive, say, eleven or twelve deci-child certificates at birth or at maturity, and a woman could then accumulate these through marriage.

This plan would have the additional advantage of developing a long-run tendency toward equality in income, for the rich would have many children and become poor and the poor would have few children and become rich. The price of the certificate would of course reflect the general desire in a society to have children. Where the desire is very high the price would be bid up; where it was low the price would also be low. Perhaps the ideal situation would be found when the price was naturally zero, in which case those who wanted children would have them without extra cost. If the price were very high the system would probably have to be supplemented by some sort of grants to enable the deserving but impecunious to have children, while cutting off the desires of the less deserving through taxation. The sheer unfamiliarity of a scheme of this kind makes it seem absurd at the moment. The fact that it seems absurd, however, is merely a reflection of the total unwillingness of mankind to face up to what is perhaps its most serious long-run problem.

The Meaning of the Twentieth Century, 1964.

---

dom surfaces in polite conversation in our time. It is not exactly a dirty word, but we act as if it very nearly is. (Why? Is prudence unworthy of the commercial-and-welfare state? There's a mystery here!)

The differential effects of Boulding's system would be in a direction favorable to a healthy society. Those who loved children more would choose children over money; those who loved money more would have fewer children to be infected by their materialistic ideals. Boulding pointed out that the operation of his sytem would further a cause dear to the hearts of liberals, namely the redistribution of wealth. Other things being equal, rich parents who insisted on having many offspring would start their children off in life with fortunes that were closer to the mean of the population.

Since Boulding published his proposal in 1964, the new drive toward "women's lib" has gained greatly in power. Ever more women set their sights on what used to be masculine roles in business and government. Motherhood and careers outside the home both make heavy demands on women's time and attention. To some extent both careers can be pursued if employing institutions create new services for their employees, for instance, all day nurseries to take care of children. But the exigencies of competition among careerists may still pressure women to have fewer children so they can advance faster in their employing organizations. Money, power, and love of children may act as competing selective forces.

Are there genes for love of money? Genes for love of power? Genes for delight in parenthood, or a craving for interpersonal competition? It is all too easy to get snarled in inconclusive debates along these lines. There is not much hope of soon producing the statistical data needed to settle such questions. Yet common sense tells us that the questions cannot be dismissed for lack of resolution. What innate qualities are required for a woman to work her way through the political labyrinth that leads to the presidency of her country? What qualities does it take for a woman to be delighted in becoming a full-time mother of many children? It seems most unlikely that such contrasting careers would select for the same attributes.

Different modes of life select for different personal qualities. We can only assume that these qualities are determined both by inheritable elements (genes) and non-genetic environmental influences—education, in the broadest sense. It is a basic truth of evolution that even the slightest heritability leads to natural selection in the long run. The two goals of "career" and "home" (just to give them simple names) must surely favor different types of women. Those who choose the second goal would be expected to produce more children than would career women. In the absence of as-yet unspecified community controls, the competing life styles would select for the slow replacement of careerists by homebodies. The ideals of "women's lib" would appear to be self-defeating in the long run, unless counteracted by other social controls. This possibility has not yet been taken seriously by the proponents of the new reform.

Persuasion versus Coercion

Novel proposals like Cowles' and Boulding's make us realize that the word "coercion" is not completely transparent. The definition in the *Oxford English Dictionary* is typical: "the application of force to control the action of a voluntary agent." But what is "force"? Is persuasion a force? And when is an action "voluntary"? Has the OED committed an oxymoron?

In the middle of the seventeenth century Hobbes made a clear distinction between persuasion and coercion when he spoke of the importance of "winning men to obedience, not by coercion and punishing, but by persuasion." Two centuries later John Stuart Mill reintroduced the old ambiguity when he spoke of "the moral coercion of public opinion."

In the light of what sociobiology has taught us, we now see that Helvetius put us on the right track when he said that the "art of the legislator consists of forcing men, by the sentiment of self-love" to do the right thing. The wise legislator writes laws that will, in fact, achieve the desired end by rewarding individuals for actions that benefit the group (of which the individuals are members). This does not mean that each individual will find pleasure or profit in obeying every such law, but he should recognize that he is, in the long run, better off with such laws since they apply to all individuals. (Perhaps I don't want to be deprived of the pleasure of robbing a bank, but I don't see how to coerce my neighbor not to rob unless I coerce myself as well.) In a democracy, *mutual coercion, mutually agreed upon* is the formula for all restrictive laws.[15]

Are We Ready for a Solution to Overpopulation?

An essential component of educational theory is the concept of "readiness." Teachers at the elementary level know that much harm can be done by trying to teach reading to a child before he is "ready." The developmental-psychological basis of readiness is obscure, but skillful teachers are sure that it exists. They don't fight it; they pace their efforts by a child's demonstrated "reading readiness."

An analogous phenomenon occurs in science, only in this case "readiness" refers to the subject matter rather than to the practitioners of science. When Kelvin, a first-rate scientist, tried to determine the age of the earth, he failed because the knowledge necessary for good estimates—the knowledge of radioactive decay—had not yet been attained. The problem of the age of the earth was simply not "solution-ready" until, in 1905, Einstein announced that $E = mc^2$. (Kelvin died two years later, at age eighty-three.)

What about the overpopulation problem—is it "solution-ready" I think it is, in some nations. Peaceful reform depends on sovereign power, and the largest element that has sovereign power is the nation. Therefore population policy must be policy for a nation, not for the whole world, because there is no world sovereignty to back up a global policy. We can, and should, seek to persuade other nations to take steps to control their population growth; but our primary focus should be on the population growth within our own borders. This means that overpopulation can be avoided only if borders are secure; otherwise poor and overpopulated nations will export their excess to richer and less populated nations. It is time to turn our attention to this problem.

26

The Necessity of Immigration Control

Every American schoolchild knows about the Statue of Liberty and the accompanying poem, "Give me your tired, your poor, / Your huddled masses yearning to be free . . .". Implicitly, our children are doubly deceived. In the first place the official name of the statue is *"Liberty Enlightening the World"*—that is, bringing light to the world, educating it: not inviting the whole world to come in. In the second place there is the implication that the poetry on the base expresses official policy. It does not. Emma Lazarus's words were added to the base seventeen years after the statue was erected, and without the blessing of Congress, much less of the multitudes of Americans who might be asked to make room for all the huddled masses.

It is only human to want to share with the needy, but the sharing impulse must be curbed to some extent, for the goods of this world are limited. Whenever either matter or energy is redistributed, the consequence is a zero-sum game: that which one person (or group) gains is lost by others. Information, however, is different: sharing it can lead to a plus-sum game. When I give you a bit of information I do not thereby lose it. Indeed, after absorbing this information you may send it back to me in improved form. We both gain. The lady in New York Harbor promises only to enlighten the world, not to feed and clothe it. She proposes to make other people more independent, not less.

Only America has a statue that is presumed to welcome immigrants; other nations know better. Their traditions are exclusionary. Or so it seemed until 1989, when political troubles in eastern Europe led to massive movements of people, thus forcing a reassessment of policies. From now on, more and more people throughout the world will be asking Cain's question: "Am I my brother's keeper?" They will have to remember that the singular *brother* has expanded to become hundreds of millions of brothers and sisters—*who are continuing to increase.*

In the face of exponential growth, a zero-sum game can end fatally in a commons. Yet the opposite extreme, complete isolationism, has its dangers too. In his poem "Mending Wall," Robert Frost identified the dilemma: "Before I built a wall I'd ask to know / What I was walling in or walling out . . ." Japan's history furnishes a telling illustration of the danger of complete isolation.

During the Tokugawa period, from 1624 to 1867, the rulers of Japan almost completely closed their doors to the rest of the world. As a result, their technology fell more than two centuries behind. When the isolation was ended, it took Japan almost a century to catch up with other countries.

The citizens of every country should know something of contrasting cultures in order that they may usefully doubt their own. But how are they to learn of other cultures? The best way is for individuals to live among other people for awhile, during their youthful and psychologically open years. This way is necessarily expensive, and the receiving society cannot accept many alien visitors without endangering the special qualities of its own way of life. For the most part our natural and healthy curiosity must be satisfied by short visits, by reading books, and by television.

Some people recommend that we import immigrants from different cultures, but the merits of this procedure are dubious. For one thing, most immigrants come from the poorest strata of the societies that failed to hold them, so they know little about the best elements of their culture. Here, as in their own country, most immigrants are an underclass and tend to aggregate with their own kind in ghettos. The theoretical merits of diversity are seldom realized under the common modes of immigration. Useful diversity is more efficiently attained by transporting images, ideas, and dreams between geographically fixed populations rather than uprooting and moving human bodies. Pure information can be moved more cheaply than information wrapped in human bodies.

Is There a "World Population Problem"?

Globalizing problems is fashionable in our time, so it is no surprise that many voices speak of the "world population problem." But is there truly such a problem? As long ago as 1949 the leading French demographer Alfred Sauvy (1898–1990) wrote: "For the time being, there exists no world government, nor are there institutions that would come close to such a construct. [The necessary coordination of efforts] falls far short of the degree of solidarity that would be needed to make the expression 'world population' acquire real meaning."[1]

Globalization became a particularly seductive idea once the world was awash in atomic bombs. An all-out war would be suicidal for civilization, if not for the human race itself. Isn't it logical, then (people said), to try to create a global sovereignty to control nuclear weapons? Bertrand Russell cast doubt on the practicality of a comprehensive world sovereignty in the same year that Sauvy made his speech. "A world state," Russell wrote, if it were firmly established, would have no enemies to fear, and would therefore be in danger of breaking down through lack of cohesive force."[2] We have already seen that the dream of solving population problems by fleeing to other solar systems is ruled out by human nature (Chapter 2), as is the dream of unlimited and safe nuclear power (Chapter 15). Russell's denial of the possibility of an effective world government similarly rests on human nature, and is unlikely to be set aside by any imaginable technological achievement. Cooperation between mercurial human beings is always precarious. The external enemies required to sustain global cooperation are, by definition, lacking in a united world.

The instability of large organizations is amply illustrated by the history of religions. For example, the schismatic act of Martin Luther in distancing himself from the Roman Catholic Church proved to be endlessly contagious in the Protestant world. Schisms have also occurred among Moslems and Buddhists.

In the political arena it looks as though 1989 will prove to have been a watershed. No longer do we hear voices calling for an all-powerful world government. Size generates instabilities that good intentions are powerless to dispel. The Soviet Union, with 5.5 percent of the world's population, was probably too large to hold together. China, with 21 percent of the population, must also be too large. (Is the United States, with its 4.7 percent, immune to political schisms? Dare Americans ask?) In any event, it looks as if the future is going to fall under the spell of the famous Chinese curse: "May you live in interesting times!"

Calling a ubiquitous problem a "world problem" is useful *only if there is a plausible worldwide solution.* The point can be simply illustrated. All over the world there are potholes in the road: potholes are ubiquitous. But who would propose creating a "Global Pothole Authority" to undertake the repair of the roads? We know what would happen: costs of administration would escalate and few potholes would be fixed. Potholes are created by local action, and they are best corrected by local action. Likewise, the production of human beings is the result of very localized human actions; corrective action must also be local. Globalizing the "population problem" would only insure that it would never be solved. The general rule must be this: *Never globalize a problem if it can possibly be dealt with locally.*[3]

Controllable Borders: An Epicurean Necessity

Since the continued existence of many sovereign units—call them "nations," or what you will—is certain, we need to look at what takes place at the borders. Specifically, what about immigration? Should it be forbidden, encouraged, or mandated? Why?

For a long time it has been politically risky in America even to raise the issue of immigration. Anyone who openly doubts its benefits is likely to be accused of being a racist, an isolationist, a restrictionist, a nativist, a xenophobe, or a bigot. There surely can be few adult, educated Americans who have not heard it said that we should not interfere with free immigration because "We are a nation of immigrants." The implication of the attack is clear: a restrictionist is almost criminally selfish. Our first response to the incantation should be this request: "Cite a single nation that is *not* a nation of immigrants!"

Perhaps some nation in mid-Africa can claim to be composed only of indigenous peoples, but all other nations are made up entirely of immigrants and the descendents of immigrants. Over the centuries wave after wave of immigration has swept across the heavily populated countries of Europe, but this is no reason for their governments to keep their doors open forever. Following the collapse of the Soviet Union and the rising disorders in eastern Europe, the more fortunate nations of that turbulent continent are now engaged in the painful process of recognizing the necessity of restricting immigration. It is time that we rethink the problem of our own borders.

The most basic principle is the Epicurean one: the world's wealth is limited. Arguments for perpetual, unhindered immigration presume a world without limits. Epicurus seems to be unknown to idealists and ambitious developers. We will not advance beyond our growth-intoxicated world until we have given up our belief in free lunches, in perpetual motion machines, and in the creation of infinite wealth by compound interest. That everyone is made better off by immigration is also an anti-Epicurean fantasy.

The gut reactions of the man in the street are often sound. An opinion poll taken by the Roper Organization in 1990 showed that 77 percent of the general public believed that immigration should not be increased, while 45 percent wanted to see it actually reduced.[4] Only 9 percent of the people polled favored an actual increase in immigration.

The popular view is not an isolationist position: even a reduced *rate* of immigration implies some continued immigration. But, as ancient wisdom has it: "There can be too much of a good thing." The figure of 45 percent favoring a reduction in rate is slightly less than a majority, but even so it is remarkably high in a nation where so many politicians thoughtlessly continue to chant, "We are a nation of immigrants."

Despite the Roper findings, congressional acts passed in 1986 and 1990 had the effect of actually increasing the rate of immigration. It does seem odd that the legislature of a democracy can get away with passing laws so contrary to the will of the majority. Are there some hidden springs of feeling that the polls fail to tap?

The Nation as a Lifeboat

Box 26-1 lists five concepts that are notably absent in conventional economics texts. So long as they are under an apparent taboo, they are powerless to influence thinking. Diseconomies of scale have been a central part of the natural sciences since Galileo; under the name of "diminishing returns" they have, however, been belittled by mainstream economists ever since Malthus. The concept of carrying capacity (Chapter 20) is needed to fashion the conservation laws of ecology and its subscience economics, but it is notably absent in textbooks of economics. Chapter 8 of the present book deals with the Epicurean idea of limits, which is so scandalously ignored in the mythology associated with money-at-interest. The many economic systems derive their wealth from nonhuman ecological systems—oceanic fisheries, wetland complexes, tundra, grasslands, forests, and the agricultural systems that displace the natural systems. All of these systems are incredibly complex and lamentably susceptible to irreversible damage when the carrying capacity is transgressed. But of all this, economics has been extraordinarily ignorant—until quite

---

Box 26-1. Psychoanalytic Denials of Economics.

The following five concepts have been denied, denigrated, or ignored in much of the academic education of economists during the twentieth century.

Diseconomies of scale
Carrying capacity
Resource limits
Basic ecological systems
Human values

recently. This is forgivable because the ecological base of this knowledge had to be laid first.

Finally, when we come to human values we enter a realm of considerable ambivalence for most social scientists. For historical reasons many economists blush to be caught out with a statement that is *not* "value free." This was not the case with Adam Smith, who began with ethics and moved on to economics when the subject matter dictated. Economics shows signs of returning to a Smithic position.

When as simple an idea as *limits* meets intellectual resistance, it generally helps to employ a metaphor. Ecologists have found the metaphor of a lifeboat useful in enforcing the discipline of Epicurean thinking.[5] The image disturbs many kind-hearted people, but its basic meaning—a limited universe within which practical decisions must be made—is correct, because a limited world is the only world we will ever experience.

Imagine that a ship has foundered, and some of the passengers have escaped in a lifeboat. A rescue team has been dispatched in a helicopter to assess the situation. The designated spokesman on board the whirlybird is a trained economist, who radios back his conclusions: "Things look pretty good. We're close enough now to read the lettering on the gunwale: 'Cap. = 64.' I would estimate there are about 85 people in the boat already, and more are climbing aboard all the time. With a continuation of such a healthy growth in the passenger population we have nothing to worry about!"

Admittedly, the five concepts listed in Box 26-1 are difficult to give numerical meaning to, but is that any excuse for ignoring these factors, or asserting that one or more of them is "meaningless"? Implicitly, arguments for an indefinite continuation of immigration presume a limitless world into which the migrants can move.

Worldviews: Cosmopolitan versus Parochial

The politically effective arguments for immigration are less rational than sentimental. In *Ideology and Immigration* Katharine Betts argues that attitudes toward immigration are largely determined by two alternative worldviews: the *cosmopolitan* view and the *parochial* view.[6] The first name comes from the Greek *kosmopolites,* citizen of the world; the second from the Latin *parochia,* parish—which is necessarily only a small part of the world.

"I am a citizen of the world," proudly proclaimed Zeno of Cytium in the third century B.C. The assertion comes naturally to philosphers (like Zeno), to scientists, to scholars of many sorts, and to artists, all of whom often have more in common with their counterparts on the other side of the world than they do with their immediate neighbors. The majority of the populace, however, are neither scholars nor artists: their daily concerns are mostly parochial.

In the twentieth century, impressed by the progress in travel and communication, the Canadian wordsmith Marshall McLuhan asserted that the world has become a "global village." Anyone who has ever lived in a true village (say a community of a few hundred individuals) immediately recognizes this paradoxical term as an oxymoron. There is no way that village qualities—both good and bad—can persist in an assemblage of a million human beings. But few of the world's opinion makers have ever lived in a village, and so the oxymoron survives and continues to lead idealistic people astray.

Much rhetorical skill has been expended in the praise of cosmopolitanism. Two very effective modern statements are found in Box 26-2, the first by a politician,[7] the second by a poet.[8] The latter particularly calls for comment. Why is it so easy to see the earth "as it truly is"—as astronauts see it—floating blue and beautiful "in the eternal silence" of space? Because from the astronaut's vantage point one cannot see the ambushes and street fighting going on in Belfast or Beirut, Srinigar or Sarajevo. Disorder is eminently parochial and cannot be wished out of existence by myopic space poetry.

Yet poetry is potent. Since publicists for cosmopolitanism are usually referred to as "intellectuals," should not the rest of us accept their guidance? Before we relinquish our independence to such a group we should ask: What makes intellectuals tick?

Albert Einstein, who was certainly an intellectual by any standard, analyzed himself in words that will bear repeating: "My passionate sense of social justice and social responsibility has always contrasted oddly with my pronounced lack of need for direct contact with other human beings and human communities. I am truly a 'lone traveler' and have never belonged to my country, my home, my friends, or even my immediate family with my whole heart."[9]

Such self-confessed limitations are perhaps the imperatives of Einstein's occupation, which was probing into the deepest mysteries of the nonhuman world. Carl Jung, whose contrasting vocation was plumbing the depths of the human spirit, expressed a similar dissociation from the parochial: "The more uncertain I have felt about myself, the more there has grown up in me a feeling of kinship with all things." The productions of science and art come close to being universal in nature; to a large extent they are independent of the parish in which they originate. In following his vocation the "intellectual" finds that a cosmopolitan bias pays.

There is a marked contrast between the attitudes expressed by the ordinary cit-

---

Box 26-2. Poetry of the Cosmopolitan Spirit.

We travel together, passengers on a little space ship, dependent on its vulnerable resources of air and soil; all committed for our safety to its security and peace; preserved from annihilation only by the work, the care and, I will say, the love we give our fragile craft. We cannot maintain it half fortunate and half miserable, half confident, half despairing, half slave to the ancient enemies of man, half free in a liberation of resources undreamed of until this day. No craft, no crew, can travel safely with such contradictions. On their resolution depends the survival of us all.

Adlai Stevenson, 1965.

To see the earth as it truly is, small and blue and beautiful in the eternal silence where it floats, is to see ourselves as riders on the earth together, brothers on that bright loneliness in the eternal cold—brothers who know now they are truly brothers.

Archibald MacLeish, 1968.

izen and the stance taken by most of the *literati*. As the last decade of the twentieth century began, the attitude that dominated the media was one of warm approval of free immigration. (Even when increased immigration causes an escalation in social chaos, a news commentator benefits from the results, because chaos gives him more raw material to work with. Peace is so dull!)

The ordinary citizen (who should *not* be called a "nonintellectual"), living very much *in* the world (in his own parish, his own family, his own clique), exhibits a strictly limited tolerance of threats to the social order. The bulk of the citizenry clusters at the parochial end of the cosmopolitan-parochial continuum. Unfortunately for the resolution of issues like immigration, most of the organs that disseminate knowledge—press, radio, and television—are under the control of specialists who congregate at the cosmopolitan pole. Political sanity demands a judicious and changeable mixture of parochialism and cosmopolitanism.

It is only human to be lazy at times and seek an answer that is intellectually at one pole or another of a spectrum. In the distant past parochialism was the commonest choice. Now the publicly acceptable choice is more likely to be the unrelieved cosmopolitanism of "One World." But scale effects intervene in reality, which is a complex of many problems. Potholes are parochial problems; as is poverty, for which "charity begins at home" is the proper default position. But atmospheric ozone, greenhouse effects, and the preservation of a multitude of wide-ranging species of animals logically seems to call for cosmopolitanism. For this approach we lack potent political tools. The exciting and beautiful diversity of the biological world is gravely at risk, and we do not yet know what to do about it.

Emigration and the Conservation of Poverty

Many people welcome immigrants from poor nations because they anticipate that this generous action will reduce poverty in the sending nation. The argument presumes that the resources/population ratio in the poor nation would become greater following out-migration. As far as concerns straight numeracy the argument is sound: but the ecolate question must be asked: "And then what?"

What effect does the departure of emigrants have on the fertility of those who stay behind in the old country? As we saw in Chapter 16, anti-Malthusians predict that the increase in well-being that follows a decrease in population density will result in lower fertility. Malthusians predict the opposite: an increase in well-being will increase fertility.

Decisive empirical findings do not exist, so common sense must be our guide. The Malthusian demostat is the basic default position (Fig. 11-2). Like all broad practical positions this assumes "other things being equal." If they can be made unequal—if for instance, the residual population in an emigrant-generating country can be persuaded to follow the advice of Charles Galton Darwin and invest the funds freed by emigration in luxuries rather than in babies—if that improbable event can be brought about, massive emigration will improve the situation of the generating country. But changes in standards, in ideals, are likely to take more than a generation to achieve. In the meantime a typical poverty-ridden population doubles every twenty-five years or less.

Not to be forgotten are the remittance payments sent home by emigrants. Indians, Pakistanis, and Africans work in the oil fields of the Arabian peninsula, sending much of their wages home to their families. Emigrant men generally manage to visit home a time or two during the year, thus seeing to it that more babies justify their remittances. Mexicans migrating to the United States generally follow the same pattern. The end result is that some of the wealth produced in rich countries finances population expansion in poor countries. Since most poor countries are already suffering from deforestation, soil exhaustion, and other consequences of overpopulation, the end result of the emigration-and-remittance system is a further degradation of natural resources. A generous immigration policy in rich countries prolongs the reign of poverty in poor.

The Brain Drain

Opportunities for ambitious scientists and engineers are much greater in the United States than they are in poor countries. Many physicians in America were born in India or Sri Lanka; they were trained partly in their homeland, partly here. They stay here because both pay and working conditions are better. Their presence may help prevent a "doctor shortage" here. This is arguable; what is not arguable is that the transfer of talents leaves the sending country worse off.

A similar process is taking place on an even greater scale in engineering. Our specialized schools are now swarming with "Third World" students who came here for their training; most will not return to their homes, which need them desperately.

The Troublemaker Drain

When 125,000 Cubans were pushed out of their homeland by their government in the 1980 "Mariel boatlift," it was subsequently learned that 23,000 of them had been released from Cuban prisons and mental institutions.[10] All but 110 of the 23,000 were eventually released into American communities. A total of 7,500 subsequently violated parole or other local laws and landed in American jails. In making the Mariel boatlift possible, Castro saw to it that this small army included not only a generous supply of common criminals, but also many political prisoners—people who were a threat to the Castro regime. From the dictator's point of view the exodus must surely have been a good thing; but was it good for the Cuban people generally?

How one answers depends on one's political position. It is certain that the differential removal of soreheads by emigration strengthens the position of a government. Reform becomes more difficult. From a global point of view, however, it can be said that a country that is governed by evil men needs troublemakers to straighten it out.

Putting together the brain drain and the troublemaker drain, we can say that selective emigration promotes the conservation of incompetence—incompetence to change the status quo in the home country. Conventional charity can be counterproductive.

What Does the Receiving Country Gain from Immigration?

Does migration from poor to rich benefit the receiving country? The answer undoubtedly changes during the developmental history of a country. A priori, one would expect a nation early in its development to gain from immigration. Later in development a nation that is essentially "full" must lose if it takes in more immigrants. This view of development-as-progressive-change is missing from the thinking of most "developers," who are looking for the quick buck. They assume that "more is better"—*always*. Developers are shielded from disillusionment because they do not live in the houses they build or work in the factories they call into being. The defenders of immigration-as-development seldom live cheek by jowl with the newcomers.

In his *Friends or Strangers* the economist George J. Borjas points to a real gain from immigration.[11] That which is a "brain drain" from the point of the sending country is a *brain gain* to the receiver. Borjas wants to maximize America's brain gain. This emphasis leads to the following analysis of the economic competition of the United States with such countries as Canada and Australia, which also welcome immigrants.

> The existence of an immigration market implies that countries compete for the physical and human capital of immigrants, that the particular sorting of persons and countries depends on how the offers to potential migrants differ among the competing countries, and that there will be winners and losers in this competition .... How competitive is the United States in the immigration market? And how can immigration policy be changed to increase our competitiveness?[12]

Unfortunately Borjas finds strong evidence that the aggregate skills composition of immigrants entering the United States has deteriorated in the past two or three decades. If so, poor countries are now lightening their load of incompetence—at our expense.

The conclusions of traditional economic analysis are generally based only on what can be precisely measured, while ignoring that for which adequate measurements have not yet been devised. Immigrants can increase the gross national product of a country by boosting the costs of welfare and policing, because all such expenditures are added to the GNP. Not figured into this product is environmental damage that—in the absence of corrective measures (which incur real costs)—follows *any* population increase, whatever its cause: loss of topsoil, deforestation, and degradation of air and water quality.

The Erosion of Human Capital

The Bible is no longer a living document for many Americans. The change entails a real loss for public discourse. It used to be that a glancing reference to the Tower of Babel (in the eleventh chapter of Genesis) was enough to settle a dispute. Now such a reference must be explained.

Apparently the Lord of the Old Testament was fearful of the growing abilities of the human beings he had created. Viewing what they had done already, he concluded that "nothing that they resolve to do will be impossible for them" because "they all have the same language." Why an omnipotent deity should fear the abilities of mere mortals is not explained; in any case the Lord ended up by making his people speak many mutually incomprehensible languages. The tower was left unfinished and the disunited people dispersed themselves over the face of the earth. The justification for having a common language could hardly be made plainer.

By any reasonable definition of the "kinds" of languages, over five thousand different languages are spoken on earth today. Many are spoken by very small and diminishing groups. In another century only a few hundred living tongues may remain. That will still be a lot. Since the *Lau* decision of the Supreme Court in 1974, the Office of Civil Rights has acted as if the presence of a single foreign language-speaking student in a school requires the school to duplicate (in some way) the instruction in the language of that student.[13] By 1980 more than eighty languages were spoken in Los Angeles County. The number has grown since. In Hollywood, 95 percent of the new entrants to the elementary schools spoke no English. In Hollywood High the English-speaking students were native speakers of sixty different foreign tongues. When a parents' night was held, the speeches were translated into the major foreign languages only—Korean, Armenian and Spanish. Translated, a three-minute English speech took up twenty-five minutes of time.[14] Presumably paying homage to all sixty languages in this way would have taken over 8 hours for all the three-minute speeches. The democratic ideal of parent participation cannot survive such reality.

What is called "bilingual education" is a particular technique, which requires that half the time the educational material should be given in English, half in the relevant foreign language. The original intention was to move the student into English as fast as possible. The intention was noble—but my! how Topsy has growed! Bilingual education teachers now have a vested interest in keeping their students from advancing in language competence. The first year, 1968, federal support was $7.5 million. By 1990 it was 100 times as much. Many of the teachers regard the preservation of foreign ethnicity as their primary goal—a far cry from the assimilationist ideal that governed the treatment of immigrants in previous generations.

The corruption of the bilingual ideal has been amply described by many disillusioned bilingual teachers, notably Rosalie Pedalino Porter in her *Forked Tongue: The Politics of Bilingual Education*.[15] A most telling criticism of the education that is all too often thrust on needy children in the public schools comes from the Mexican foreman of a south Texas ranch: "My children learn Spanish in school so they can grow up to be busboys and waiters. I teach them English at home so they can grow up to be doctors and lawyers."[16]

There are many ways to look at the tragedy of bilingual education. Perhaps the best way to keep emotions under control is to follow the economists' example and think of "human capital," by which is meant trained, productive human beings. From a public point of view, a major object of education is to increase the human capital of the community, so that tomorrow's work may be done more expeditiously. When compared with native-speaking students, students who speak a foreign language require a greater investment of time and money to be trained to the same level of competence.

Is There Such a Thing as a "Labor Shortage"?

One of the most powerful arguments for encouraging immigration rests on the assertion that slowing population growth necessarily produces a labor shortage. This in turn results in higher wages for laborers, as employers compete with each other for workers. Higher wages produce higher consumer prices, and everybody suffers. So goes the argument.

Officially, every businessman in a market economy is in favor of competition—until his own ox is gored. William E. Simon, a successful investor and an able secretary of the Treasury, once commented on this all-too-human inconsistency: "During my tenure at Treasury I watched with incredulity as businessmen ran to the government in every crisis, whining for handouts or protection from the very competition that has made this [market] system so productive."[17]

The doctrinaire free marketer, reasoning within a cosmopolitan framework, may argue for borders completely open to workers from the entire world. But this is unacceptable because it would create an unmanaged commons that would surely produce tragic results for American workers. Our workers are paid at a rate that permits much more than the bare subsistence that many millions of foreign workers can only hope for. A century ago laborers were acutely aware that the improved prospects of immigrants were gained at the expense of laborers already here; the natives vigorously opposed immigration.

Then came the welfare state, and the true cost of immigration was lost sight of. Unemployment benefits softened the blow of losing a job. Employers became involved in the CC-PP game, with P (the profits) going to employers while C (the costs) were commonized first among the workers (see Chapter 23.) Ultimately the costs of supporting those thrown out of work were assumed by society as a whole. On the rhetorical side, the new dispensation was sold as noble cosmopolitanism, while realistic parochials who complained of immigration were attacked for being prejudiced, narrow-minded, selfish, bigoted, and (lately) racist. Over time, labor lost the battle to restrict immigration. Bit by bit, more and more costs associated with immigration were commonized: the costs of educating immigrant children, the costs of an immigrant wife's bearing more children, and even the costs of supporting foreigners in the home country through remittance payments from family members working in America.

A difference in wage levels is the great driving force of migration between nations: other things being equal, the poorer the country, the more emigrants it generates. Moving into a rich country, immigrants accept lower wages and do more unpleasant work than long-time residents. This is all to the good, said a prosperous witness before a Congressional committee in 1990. He admitted that a situation in which there are more jobs than workers might sound like a happy one to native workers:

> [However] it reflects imbalances for which there can also be penalties. One such penalty is deteriorating service, and an increase in underqualified, rude, and weakly committed employees. Another may be the advent of wage inflation, which could damage not only the U.S. but also other nations in both the Western and developing worlds. Many of these dislocations could be avoided by immigration, a superb smoother of economic and demographic swings.[18]

We should note that the witness was a successful journalist, an occupational group that never needs to fear losing their jobs to foreign language-speaking immigrants.

An economy that is truly laissez-faire is capable of prodigies of adaptation. Fluctuating wages signal the need for changes in the allocation of work, and if this communicative function is not interfered with, the necessary responses soon take place. Adjustments may be painful to both employers and employees, but a wealth of experience proves that well-meaning attempts to bypass all such pain by totally controlling the economy from a political center are most likely to increase suffering in the long run. We must never forget the tragic conclusion of the seventy-year experiment in centralized control in the Soviet Union.

Must an Older Population Be Dependent on Immigrants?

The birth rate is now slowly and irregularly trending downward in our country. If immigration were to be stopped, the average age of our people would necessarily become greater. Calling attention to this demographic fact, some journalists have become doomsayers, asking: "Who will do the work in America if immigration is no longer permitted?" The cries of these Chicken Littles are not needed because many elements are available in our society for adjusting to the so-called "labor shortage."

First: The work week can be extended. At the end of the nineteenth century a forty-eight-hour week (eight hours a day, six days a week) was common. Early in the twentieth century it fell to forty-four hours (with half-day Saturdays), and later to forty. There is nothing sacred about any of these numbers.

Second: Retirement can be postponed. Many older people would rather work than retire. They may, however, want to work a shorter day or a shorter week.

Third: Many people (such as housewives, a few of whom still exist) who are not now officially employed would jump at the chance of part-time *paid* employment outside the home. Part-time employment creates organizational problems for managers, but the problems are not insuperable.

Fourth: Question: How many of the 11 million students now enrolled in American colleges and universities are there because they have a passion for learning? Robert Maynard Hutchins, president of the University of Chicago for many years, asserted that most college education is a disguised form of baby-sitting: labor laws and union practices restrict productive employment of minors, and parents don't know what to do with full-grown offspring who stay home. Offered meaningful employment at fair wages, it is highly probable that the majority of college students would leave school. It would be a daring prophet who would maintain that the true education of such young people would be prevented if they abandoned school to work for a year or two beginning at age sixteen. (For many, age fourteen would not be too early: but this is too radical an idea to be proposed at the present time.)

Fifth: The efficiency of work is always susceptible of improvement. This conclusion follows from one of the great default positions of social psychology, namely "Parkinson's law": *Work expands so as to fill the time available for its completion.*[19] If you can make the necessary arrangements, some time you should sit quietly to one side in a working establishment while you keep track of the time spent working, compared with the time spent "goofing off," particularly after mid-day. In many establishments the *work* week is considerably less than 40 hours. Perhaps this is as it should be: our ancestors, the hunter-gatherers, did well enough on only a 20-hour work week.[20] That arrangement prevailed for more than a million years. The last few hundred years of experience with longer work weeks may not have been enough for *Homo sapiens* to evolve the genes needed to accept wholeheartedly the greater load.

Of course some people actually work more than 20 hours and enjoy it. Given the spur of accepted necessity (coupled with suitable rewards) our workers might find that they could truly work something like 40 hours a week. (Whether the greater productivity would be ecologically tolerable is another question. After all: the more work performed, the more garbage generated.)

Sixth: Society could employ many of those who are now unemployed. In the United States it has been donkey's years since the army of the unemployed was less than five million. The official figure for the unemployed is always criminally under-stated. Young people who have never held down a job are not included in the cat-egory of "unemployed." Workers who have given up trying to find employment are not counted either. The true number of the unemployed may well be twice the cer-tified number.

That the army of the unemployed numbers so many millions strikes some crit-ics as wasteful, but it may not be entirely so. Every well-functioning system has some loose joints in it. When change is called for, the looseness of the joints makes for adaptability in the system. Unhindered, a truly laissez-faire system can take advantage of loose jointedness.

Taking account of all the reservoirs of labor available, we must conclude that such a thing as a true "labor shortage" is a great rarity indeed. What we face, time after time, is a *management shortage.* It is human to be lazy; even managers are human. Complaining of a shortage is easier than thinking. (In this case, as in so many others, refusing to think may be dangerous to our future.)

Beyond Our Abilities

A prime danger to continued national survival is uncontrolled immigration, which unquestionably increases unemployment. Long continued unemployment pro-duces social disorder. If it were true (as some journalists maintain) that immigration actually increased employment, then we would do well to invite all the world's two billion wretchedly poor to come into our country. No advocate of immigration has yet had the nerve to suggest that we do this, so we should take with a bucket of salt all claims that immigration has no adverse effect on employment.

Our desire to help the wretched of the world does our hearts credit, but not our heads: two thousand million people in the world are dreadfully poor by U.S. stan-dards. That is eight times the population of our country. In our softer moments we wish we could share our wealth with all the world's poor. But suppose we asked every American family to take in its share of these wretched people: how big would each family's load be? Assuming four members to an American family, each family would have to take in thirty-two permanent guests. And since new poor are generated at a rate of about 50 million a year, approximately one more guest would have to be added to each household each year just to keep up with population growth elsewhere. (And presumably the two billion taken in would produce more children in our own homes.)

Unfortunately some of our most idealistic people are unable to think in numerate terms, and so cannot see the ecolate danger of creating a commons. Some deeply religious Catholics and Quakers proudly flout the laws of our country to help bring in immigrants illegally. They justify their actions by referring to a higher law than any that Congress can pass. After the earthly lawbreakers have done their work, the expenses of taking care of the illegal immigrants and their children fall upon taxpayers in general, most of whom never agreed to the religion-driven philanthropy.

"Diversity" as a Problem for Population Control

The waves of immigration into the United States during the first decades of the twentieth century were bearable because both residents and immigrants agreed that the newcomers should adopt the language and the ways of the residents as rapidly as possible. The process was called "assimilation." Today, however, assimilation is out of favor: *diversity* is the magic word. "Ethnic pride" causes some minorities to resist assimilation. We can all rejoice when ethnic pride results in the descendents of immigrants becoming genuinely bicultural. But in recent years self-appointed leaders of immigrants have interpreted ethnic pride to mean *ethnic intolerance—* of the ways of the majority. This new development bodes ill for future peace in America.

Many of the resident intellectuals, overanxious to avoid all appearances of bigotry, support the radical ethnics in their resistance to assimilation. Cosmopolitans terrified of "ethnocentrism" embrace what can only be called "ethnofugalism"—a flight from the ethnic center of their own upbringing. Those who promote limitless diversity seem not to have noticed the disorder and violence associated with massive diversity in Africa and the Balkans. The faster the rate of immigration and the more diverse the reluctantly conjoined cultures, the greater is the threat of balkanization. And balkanized territories, under whatever name, are not noted for their devotion to political equality. Lawrence Auster has made some telling points:

> "Iceland's population of 240,000 is a notably homogeneous society," writes the *New York Times.* "Like these other well-off homogeneous nations [i.e., Scandinavia and Japan] Iceland's wealth is evenly distributed and its society is remarkably egalitarian." Even liberals seem to recognize the correlation between homogeneity and equality—for every country, that is, except the United States, where we have conceived the fantastic notion that we can achieve equality *and* unlimited diversity at the same time. A far more likely result is a devolution of society into permanent class divisions based on ethnicity.[21]

Such a devolution calls to mind the situation in caste-bound India. Despite laws to the contrary, the caste system still dominates that nation of nearly 900 million people, though many educated Indians regard the system as a major misfortune.

Do our enthusiasts of ethnic diversity consider the possibility that caste formation may be an unavoidable result of unlimited diversity? Of all the problems facing a multicultural nation none is more resistant to solution than population control. Every method proposed in a multiethnic society elicits a knee-jerk cry of "*genocide!*"

It cannot be too often repeated that an extravagantly multicultural nation is poorly positioned to compete with nations that have not succumbed to the siren call for more "diversity." Think of Japan. In facing the real dangers of overpopulation following World War II, Japan showed that she could achieve a unanimity of purpose that is hard to imagine in a multicultural nation. Whatever measures may be required to tame population growth, their difficulty will increase strictly in proportion to the amount of diversity in the population. In a multicultural nation patriotism withers under the onslaught of internal competition between ethnic groups. The nation is then less favorably positioned to deal with external competition. Everyone within the multiethnic nation suffers.

An Unsolved Problem of Representative Democracy

Earlier in the chapter it was pointed out that the majority of the American people are opposed to increasing the rate of immigration (and almost half want to decrease it). Despite these findings Congress has repeatedly encouraged more immigration. Those who suppose that democracy means the rule of the majority find this inconsistency puzzling, yet examples are legion. The majority of the people are in favor of gun control, but for decades Congress has resisted passing the needed legislation. The majority of the people think women should be able to choose abortion over mandatory motherhood, yet Congress resists passing the needed legislation. How come?

The paradoxical behavior of a democracy derives from the essential properties of a *representational democracy*. In a republic the electorate does not directly vote on legislation; it elects only its legislators, who are then presumed to carry out the will of the people. *Presumed* . . . and the presumption often fails—for understandable reasons.

Katharine Betts has thrown light on this problem (Box 26-3).[22] Like the United States, Australia is a nation in which the majority of the electorate wants to minimize immigration. Also as in the United States, the cosmopolitans have, in recent years, been gaining in political power over the parochials.

In a representative democracy, a legislator counts noses in the boondocks less carefully than he measures nearby pressures. Who are the constituents that he is least able to ignore, and what do they want in the way of immigration?

First, there is the businessman who wants to keep his labor costs low. The profits—deriving from the lower wages paid to immigrant workers—come to the businessman, who can therefore afford to spend a significant amount of money lobbying legislators. By contrast, the costs of immigration directly impinging on each taxpayer don't amount to much; consequently, few citizens feel they can afford to spend much time or money lobbying legislators. *In a representative democracy squawks count for more than noses.*

Box 26-3. Katharine Betts: A Paradox of Representative Democracy.

Politicians do not invariably respond to majority interests. There may be more political advantage to be gained from taking up a focused and articulate minority interest than from supporting a diffuse and inarticulate majority interest. And there is a logical reason for this. Any given claim on resources that is successful and based on membership of a small category will result in a higher return for an individual than a similar claim made on the basis of membership of a large category, because in the latter case the benefit will have to be more widely shared. So it is in the interests of individuals to make claims on politicians as members of an ethnic minority rather than as, for example, members of the working class or as citizens of the nation. From the politician's point of view voters who receive a relatively large benefit are more likely to express their gratitude at the polls than voters who receive a relatively small benefit.

Idealogy and Immigration, 1988.

To the pressure of employers another pressure has been added in recent years—the pressure of ethnic groups. Now that diversity and multiculturalism have become fashionable (and assimilation has become suspect), politicians among the ethnic groups believe that accentuating ethnicity is a golden road to personal power. They may be right.

The rank and file of each ethnic group often understand both sides of the question: they would like to bring in more of their own kind (especially relatives), but they recognize that newcomers will also compete with them for jobs. They don't like the thought of increased competition. But ethnic politicians often manage to swing the group toward the support of more immigration. Curiously, they are helped in this by some of the great foundations, such as the Ford Foundation, which is one of the major bankrollers of ethnic power groups. (One wonders what Henry Ford would have thought of the way his money is now being used to help dissolve the unity of the country that made him rich.)

Finally there is another dissolving force that seems even stranger: labor unions. A hundred years ago organized labor was against immigration because workers saw it as a threat to their jobs. As indeed it was. Now some laboring groups, such as garment workers, are actually agitating for more immigration. Whatever the increase may do to job prospects for the rank and file of the union, the union executives perceive an ultimate increase in union membership as increasing the security and power of *their* positions. Between the executives and the rank and file there is a dangerous mismatch in goals.

One wonders if activist ethnic politicians have asked themselves the ecologist's question, *And then what?* What if they succeed? What if Latino politicians succeed in *ethnicizing* the law (if there is such a word)? How will they feel when activists from *other* ethnic groups—Russians, Armenians, Sikhs, Bangladeshi, Indo-Chinese or whatever—make *their* "nonnegotiable" demands? Sauce for the goose is sauce for the gander. Bilingual and bicultural goals will be replaced by multilingual and multicultural ones. The biblical Tower of Babel will become a reality. Ethnic activists will find that they are fighting less against an old majority than against a multitude of new minorities, each striving for its own aggrandizement—and to hell with the nation as a whole! But when the nation as a whole suffers, individuals suffer. At the very least, there will be an appalling waste of time in a multicultural nation that has become multilingual by force of law.

Population versus Liberty

The greater the size of the population, the more numerous are the freedoms that must be sacrificed—a point that the English engineer Jack Parsons has eloquently made in a uniquely excellent book, *Population versus Liberty*.[23] His compelling argument has many facets: I will develop only a few, and in the American context.

Consider some of the diseconomies of scale that have afflicted our national government as the population has grown. In 1933, President Franklin D. Roosevelt had a White House staff of thirty-seven. In 1981, President Ronald Reagan had a staff of seventeen hundred. During that near-half century the population grew by 70 percent, but the White House staff grew by 4,500 percent! Of course the federal government had taken on more functions in the meantime, but not that many more. Most of the growth in staff was caused by diseconomies of scale.

Then there is Congress. We cherish a simple mental image of a constituent talking to his congressperson or Senator. But the number of these representatives is fixed, while the populace of constituents continues to grow. So if you want to speak to your congressperson you may be disappointed. The average member of Congress has more than thirty-seven staff members: it is with one of these that you will probably communicate. Given such a large staff a naive constituent might suppose a congressperson would get a great deal of legislating done. Not so, said a senior staff member in 1987: "The 535 members of the U. S. Congress accomplished very little this year, and it took 20,000 staffers to help them do it."[24]

Will we be governed better if babies are born faster? Or more immigrants come into our nonexpansible country? Long ago Aristotle knew that bigger is *not* better when it comes to the governance of a country (Box 26-4).[25] Anyone who encourages more population growth, through immigration or any other means, is promoting the curtailment of liberty, whether he knows it or not.

The most basic theoretical point to be made is that the exchange of opinion within a group suffers from a diseconomy of scale. Notice that Christ had only twelve disciples—not twenty, not a hundred—and certainly not 535! The number of possible relations between n elements of a system is roughly proportional to n^2. The load that this imposes on the spirit of democracy can be put in several ways. (1) If the group becomes 10 times bigger, the time taken for universal communi-

---

Box 26-4. Aristotle on the Possibility of a Highly Populous, Well-Governed State.

Experience shows that it is difficult, if not impossible, for a very populous state to secure a general habit of obedience to law. Observation tells us that none of the states which have a reputation for being well governed are without some limit of population. But the point can also be established on the strength of philosophical grounds. Law is a system of order; and a general habit of obedience to law must therefore involve a general system of orderliness. Order, however, is the one thing which is impossible for an excessive number.

cation will increase by a factor of 100, if individual communications are the same length. Or (2), you can cut the messages short, restricting the remarks of each person to one-tenth the time. Or (3), ninety of the members can become silent partners. When villages were small, a New England town meeting might safely allow an equal voice to all. That's democracy. But when New England villages swelled to small cities, representative democracy had to be substituted for pure democracy. And when the numbers to be unified by some sort of communication grow very large, the representative machinery groans and creaks. We invent more and more short-cuts; some of them do not deserve the name of democracy.

Journalism: On the Bias Created by Job Security

It takes no great intellect to foresee the logical consequences of a promiscuous policy of immigration; but taboo throttles discussion. Why don't the "intellectuals" who man the media sound the alarm?

The explanation is simple: the media masters have no fear for their rice bowls. The threat of job displacement is all but nonexistent for "intellectuals" because they deal in words. For the most part it takes two generations to master the subtleties of another language. Joseph Conrad (Polish) and Vladimir Nabokov (Russian) are about the only exceptions that come to mind. Of course these two were masters at a high level, but the homely idiomatic level at which the wordsmiths of press, radio, and television operate is beyond the reach of most first generation immigrants. Native wordsmiths do not have to worry that new immigrants will take their jobs. But farm workers and unskilled laborers do have to worry.

The masters of the media act as the gatekeepers of a culture. Unfortunately they are far from being an unbiased sample of the general population. The danger of this misrepresentation can hardly be overemphasized. Being shielded from job competition, some wordsmiths are bamboozled into accepting the theory that the entry of immigrants has no effect on the job market.

The standard apology for immigration should be reworded thus: "We are a nation of *assimilated* eximmigrants." It will be devastating if today's professional cosmopolitans succeed in selling the public a different alternative: "We are a multicultural nation of immigrants committed to pursuing pluralistic goals." If present trends continue, the national motto will have to be changed from *E pluribus unum*—"one out of many," to *E uno in plura*—"From one into many." From unity to unlimited diversity. Is that any way to survive in a world in which other nations still esteem, as the American people once did, the blessings of unity?

"Diversity is the opposite of unity, and unity is a prime requirement for national survival in the short run. In the long run, beliefs must be susceptible to change, but massive immigration is a dangerous way to bring about change in ideas and practices. To nurture both unity and progress a double policy should be embraced: *Great diversity worldwide; limited diversity within each nation.*"[26]

27

Recapitulation and a Look Ahead

The cosmopolitan approach is required for some worldwide problems, such as ozone depletion, acid rain, and the exhaustion of oceanic fisheries. By contrast, potholes and population call for a parochial orientation. But if local "laissez-faire" in population matters is interpreted to mean *no borders,* a suicidal commons results. To survive, rich nations must refuse immigration to people who are poor because their governments are unable or unwilling to stop population growth.

With its borders secured, how is a nation to control its own population growth? In one sense population control is inevitable; in another problematical. If the citizens of a nation pay absolutely no attention to their numbers, population will eventually be controlled by "nature"—by disease, starvation, and the social disorders that follow from too many people fighting for limited resources. But when well-wishers call for "population control" they mean something gentler than nature's ultimate response. Can we now predict what form successful human measures will take?

I don't think we can, because the question demands that we successfully predict human history. Who, in the year 1700, could have predicted the Constitution of the United States? Who, in 1900, could have predicted Chernobyl? What happens in history is the result of the interaction of (first) the dependable "Laws of Nature" with (second) the apparent capriciousness of *human* nature. As concerns the first component, Francis Bacon should be our guide: "Nature to be commanded must be obeyed." Coming to the second factor we turn to the inventor of the holograph, the Nobelist Dennis Gabor: "The future cannot be predicted, but futures can be invented." Ignorance of this insight leads the public to take too seriously the *projections* of demographers (who rightly insist that they cannot predict the future). Demographers merely project curves—present trends—into the unknown future, all the while knowing—as Rene Dubos said—that trend is not destiny.

This book has been one long dissertation on the laws of nature that must be obeyed, namely: the properties of exponential growth; limits generally; the properties of usury; the significance of human unreliability; and the consequences of reproductive competition (including natural selection). But within these limitations lie many possibilities of population control. Some controls are kinder than others. We would like to evaluate the various possibilities through thought alone, without making dangerous social experiments; but the predictive power of thought is limited. Humanity will have to experiment. Many possibilities call for many experiments.

Some social experiments may have very bad outcomes indeed. For this reason Kenneth Boulding wisely said: "There are catastrophes from which there is recovery, especially small catastrophes. What worries me is the irrevocable catastrophe. That is why I am worried about the globalization of the world. If you have only one system, then if anything goes wrong, everything goes wrong."

The wisdom is very old: Don't put all your eggs in one basket. Given many sovereign nations it is possible for humanity to carry out many experiments in population control. Each nation can observe the successes and failures of the others. Experiments that have a good outcome can be copied and perhaps improved upon; unsuccessful experiments can be noted and not repeated. Such learning by trial and error is perilous if the borderless world created by unrestricted migration converts the entire globe into a single huge experiment. As long as the intelligence of the human species is less than perfect—which is forever—segmented parochialism is superior to unified cosmopolitanism in disclosing and capitalizing on the diverse possibilities of human nature. The formula for survival and progress is simple:

Unity within each sovereignty; diversity among sovereignties.

The Peril of "Universal Human Rights"

Tolerance of other ways of doing things should certainly be part of the recipe for getting along with other nations. But must we tolerate unlimited tolerance? As concerns population control, should we tolerate coerced abortion or institutionalized infanticide in another nation? Questions like this perplex populationists. Are some moral principles so general that all nations must follow them?

The idealists who were most active in founding the United Nations thought so. In 1948 the General Assembly "unanimously" adopted the "Universal Declaration of Human Rights." Included were such things as the right to a fair trial; freedom of thought, conscience, and religion; and the right to work and enjoy social security, education, and the arts. One should not impute too much force to the word "unanimously." Only one-third of the world's nations belonged to the United Nations at that time; in the vote on the declaration, abstentions were registered by Saudi Arabia, the Union of South Africa, and a Soviet bloc of countries.

However one may judge the soundness of the rights, anyone with an anthropologist's knowledge of the variation of mores around the world cannot but notice the suspicious identity of the U.N. list with what the "best people" in the European civilizations would select. Were the selecting criteria universal? Or was some sort of moral imperialism at work? Such questions are seldom asked.

In any case the existence of the Universal Declaration has not prevented friction between nations when it comes to methods of population control. Since 1980, because of news reports that the Chinese government coerces women to have abortions, the American government has refused to allocate money to promote birth control in China. Our administration feared that Planned Parenthood money would be diverted to pay for abortions, which were strongly disapproved of by the particular Republicans who came to power in the United States in 1980.

The Concept of Ethnocentrism: a Major Intellectual and Moral Advance

Can the general idea of universal rights be reconciled with the intolerance of certain forms of birth control shown by our government? Abortion prohibitionists assume that the right to life is a right that adheres to any organized mass of living human cells, from the earliest embryonic stage onward. The supporters of reproductive choice say that the earliest stages in human development should not be defined as "human" when it comes to the allocation of rights.

The drafters of the U.N. document took no account of a major advance in anthropology and ethnology made at the beginning of the century, namely the idea of *ethnocentrism*. A moral judgment that is tied to the values of a particular ethnic group is said to be "ethnocentric." This word, quite opposite in thrust from the word *universal*, was coined in 1900 but was only given wide circulation in 1907, with the publication of William Graham Sumner's popular *Folkways*. The *Oxford English Dictionary* of 1933 did not include the term, but its 1972 supplement did. So the lack of reference to the idea in the 1948 U.N. document, though unfortunate, is not surprising.

The notion of rights that are unique and universal makes for intolerance, whereas sensitivity to the idea of ethnocentrism promotes tolerance. This is not to say that we should be tolerant of all the practices of every other ethnic group; but given the perils of war, we should hesitate to express intolerance publicly. As concerns population we should be intolerant of national refusals to control growth, because the overpeopling of one nation threatens others. (In 1991 the president of Mexico, in scarcely veiled language, threatened the United States with more unwanted immigrants if we did not make generous economic concessions to his nation.)

Though we should not be indifferent to another country's refusal to use effective birth control, *exactly which methods* are used is surely of secondary importance. It would be an unbalanced nation indeed that went to war over condoms or abortion. When it comes to methods, MYOB—"mind your own business"—is the prudent formula for untroubled international relations. Abortion has been an approved method of birth control among the Chinese for over two thousand years. As for "coercion," this word has a different meaning among people who have not embraced the post-Lockean radical individualism of the European world. The Chinese have no enthusiasm for radical Western individualism; they can justifiably say to us: "MYOB." We, of course, are free to try to persuade them they are wrong; but *persuade* should be the operational word.

Obstacles to Population Control in the United States

Birth control does not equal population control. Mistakenly equating these two interferes with productive thinking about population. A perfect system of birth control permits a woman to have the number of children she wants when she wants them; but if she wants too many for the common good, she will have too many, and population control goes out the window. Of course women vary in this regard (as in others); but the Darwinian principle of selection (see Box 24-3.) insures that, in a regime committed to reproductive laissez-faire, the demographic future will be determined by those who reject birth control.

Like it or not, the issue of coercion must be faced. The dictionary tells us that coercion is "the application of force to control the action of a voluntary agent." This definition is burdened with two seriously undefined terms: *force* and *voluntary*. If a government offers $50,000 to anyone who informs of a crime, is it coercing someone to squeal? If a mother says to her child, "You will break my heart if you take to drugs" (or alcohol, or dancing), is she coercing him? If a seductive young woman purrs, "Pretty please!", is that coercion? And when is action truly voluntary?

Perhaps the realm of personal relations is too complex for analysis. What about government? The OED says that coercion is "government by force, as opposed to that which rests upon the will of the community governed." If the majority of Americans approve of legislation that forbids smoking on scheduled air flights, are smokers being illegitimately coerced?

A democracy is governed by restrictive laws that can be legitimately described as exerting *mutual coercion, mutually agreed upon*. Unanimity is not required (otherwise no rules could be established); but some restrictions require a larger measure of agreement than others to gain adherrence. Only Robinson Crusoe could live a totally noncoercive life, and even he was coerced by the laws of nature.

The present generation has become pathologically sensitive to the word "coercion." The underlying issue is too large to be explored further at this point. Suffice it to say that, as population increases, governmental coercion necessarily plays a larger and larger role in human life. As a paradigmatic example of this principle, recall what happened to our freedom to move in automobiles as the population increased. First came rules of precedence at street corners. Then came stop signs. Then signal lights. Then the prohibition of travel by certain defined modes at certain places at certain times. As traffic gridlock took over in midtown Manhattan, people sometimes asked, "Shall we walk, or do we have time to take a taxi?"

Loss of freedom is an inevitable consequence of unlimited population growth in a limited space. Governmental coercion of some sort is needed to prevent logjams. Knee-jerk reactions to government regulations may make us feel good, but they don't cut the mustard. When we come to that great knee-jerker, "population control," we should not titillate ourselves with visions of a policeman under every matrimonial bed. There are more effective and less obnoxious ways to distribute rewards and punishments.

Already we allow our government to coerce us in the direction of *having* children. In calculating our income tax we are allowed to deduct a certain amount for each child. If this deduction has any coercive effect, it is in the direction of encouraging the production of more children. When a large enough majority of a democracy becomes convinced of the need for population control they will no doubt agree to a cancellation (or at least a lessening) of this deduction after, say, one child is born. Such an advance will be politically difficult to achieve. When it comes to family allowances, children have society over a barrel. We want to insure that the family has enough money to feed and educate its children adequately; on the other hand, a generous allowance to the caretakers—the parents—risks sending them a message to have more children in order to earn a larger allowance. To take care of children without "spoiling" their parents, we must look for ways of accurately directing public funds toward the children rather than to the parents. Publicly supported schools are correctly targeted.

Beyond this sort of public subsidy we should look for means of rewarding parents who produce fewer than the average number of children. Perhaps the relatively infertile might be rewarded with prestigious subsidized vacations. While the parents are away their few children must be adequately cared for, of course. If the much-praised American inventiveness can be directed into new channels we should be able to come up with reward systems that encourage the production of small families. Since errors will no doubt be made we should carefully observe populational measures taken by other nations. Vicariously sharing in their learning experiences should minimize the cost and pain of our own experiments.

From Limits to No-Limits—and Back to Limits Again

When the history of civilization is rewritten in the twenty-first century, it is likely that it will be summarized as consisting first of a revolution from limits to an apparently unlimited world, followed by a counterrevolution back to limits. Two great processes contributed to the first revolution: the opening of new lands for human occupancy followed by the liberating discoveries of science and technology. The second, and slower, revolution began, roughly, with Galileo and Newton.

When a given area of the earth becomes infected with *Homo sapiens,* should the result be called "progress" or not? A history of civilization written from the point of view of an observer staying in one place for several centuries would read something like this: "First there is a forest, in which men have only a marginal existence. Then the forest is cleared and the land is devoted to agriculture that supports many more people. Then as the soil erodes away (and, in some cases, irrigation systems fall into ruin), fewer and fewer people can be supported by returns from the land. Finally the area becomes a desert, or a near desert, more unsuitable for human life than the original forest."

Is that progress? Many people think not. But most histories are written by people living near the "cutting edge" of "development." Only in this favorable and temporary zone is prosperity great enough to support historians.

The cutting edge of civilization is no longer restricted to a discrete geographical area. The cutting edges of science and technology are widespread. But the pattern of *discover—exploit—ruin—move on* is so ingrained in human minds that there are still voices calling for continuing the old pattern out into space. Robert Heinlein, a leading science fiction writer, once said: "We've just about used up this planet; time to go find another one." Timothy Leary, a charismatic guru of the drug culture of the seventies, has said that "pollution is nature's code to tell the species it is time to migrate into space." The physicist Freeman J. Dyson has turned the argument on its head, asserting that the principal reason for space travel "is garbage disposal; we need to transfer industrial processes into space so that the earth may remain a green and pleasant place for our grandchildren to live in."

Those who hold that the acceptance of limits is an essential part of esthetics are repelled by such messy surrenders to "progress." Though it is true that we cannot make accurate estimates of future costs, all that we now know indicates that space travel will always be very expensive. It is possible that we may some day be able to send an inoculum of our species to some distant planet, but it is beyond belief that we will ever be able to export human bodies as fast as we can produce more babies here on earth (Chapter 2). As of 1991 more than a quarter of a million people would have had to be shot off the earth *each day* just to keep earth's population constant at 5.3 billion. Extraterrestrial solutions to our garbage problems are not practical either; we must look for mundane solutions. The time-honored practice of *pollute and move on* is no longer acceptable.

The Carson Revolution: A Cause for Optimism

An old medical theory held that recovery from a life-threatening disease required that the body first pass through a "crisis." How true this theory is can be debated; but when it comes to the "physiology of the body politic," the theory is on sound ground. The philosophy of "Don't fix it if it ain't broke" is the usual way of dismissing what may turn out to be bad news. The pain of political malfunction generally has to become very bad—almost lethally bad—before we consent to reform. "Better to endure the evils we know than risk the unknown"—this attitude slows all reform, all progress.

But now and then, deciding that enough is enough, people risk reform. Such a moment came in the middle of the twentieth century, when we began the process of rejecting the wilderness-to-desert evolution in favor of sustainable ecology. An eloquent statement of the ecological crisis was given by game manager Aldo Leopold in *A Sand County Almanac.* Published posthumously in 1949, this passage accurately mirrors the pessimistic attitude of the most knowledgeable ecologists at mid-century:

> One of the penalties of an ecological education is that one lives alone in a world of wounds. Much of the damage inflicted on land is quite invisible to laymen. An ecologist must either harden his shell and make believe that the consequences of science are none of his business, or he must be the doctor who sees the marks of death in a community that believes itself well and does not want to be told otherwise.

Very soon another path-breaking book opened the way to a new optimism. The book was Rachel Carson's *Silent Spring,* published in 1962. It was a runaway success; and it cast doubt on that sacred cow, progress-through-technology. Technology was not totally condemned by Carson. Rather, this rational question was raised: what is the balance of good and evil that follows from embracing technology?

On the basis of an extensive survey of the effects of a wide range of insecticides and other chemicals applied to various crops, Rachel Carson built up a strong case for the immense harm being done by modern agriculture. The facts had been previously gathered piecemeal by many researchers, but reported in a fragmentary way. Carson brought the evidence together in one place, described it with great skill, and managed to get her argument published in a very influential magazine, *The New Yorker.* The book that followed was an immediate best-seller.

The multibillion dollar chemical industry reacted forcefully, of course, and a raft of critical notices soon appeared. When the dust had cleared it was obvious that the errors of the book were piddling in comparison with its virtues. *Silent Spring* is now regarded as one of the classics of ecology. Alternative forms of agriculture are now being investigated more seriously.

By the Bowels of Christ, Have We Been Mistaken?

By the middle of the twentieth century technological progress had become a sort of religion. "You can't stop progress," was the standard defense, and any technology that brought money to the businessman's door was regarded as progress. "Grow or die" and "We can't go back" were two common shibboleths of the Church of Technological Progress. To such as these Rachel Carson said much the sort of thing Oliver Cromwell wrote to the General Assembly of the Church of Scotland in 1650: "I beseech you, in the bowels of Christ, think it possible you may be mistaken."

For many decades before Carson, technological change had been automatically accepted whenever change made the change agents richer, even if considerable losses were commonized over the rest of society. The time gap between Leopold and Carson was only thirteen years. At the beginning of this period reform seemed impossible. At the end, hope blossomed. The interests of posterity, long neglected, now moved to the front of public attention.

Led by ecologists, the public began to wonder if it might not be better to stop "progress" after all—purely technological progress, that is. Perhaps long-standing assumptions, especially "value judgments," could be changed after all. In historical perspective, the change came suddenly. No one in the year Leopold died foresaw the Carsonian revolution. But pessimistic assertions like Leopold's may have helped stir the soil in which the seed of *Silent Spring* was sown.

Public opinion was thoroughly aroused by a medical disaster just before the publication of Carson's work. In response to the tragic birth of thalidomide-deformed babies, and after many years of legislative turmoil, the Kefauver-Harris amendments to the Food, Drug and Cosmetics Act were passed in 1962. For centuries Anglo-Saxon law had been committed to the assumption, "innocent until proven guilty." This was the default position of the criminal law, and it was thoughtlessly carried over into other areas. The thalidomide tragedy convinced people that the default position for new medical substances should be the reverse, that the proponent of any novelty should bear the heavy burden of proving innocence. Though criminal law has been left untouched, the laws bearing on medical novelties are now governed by the assumption, "guilty until proven innocent."

This shocking reversal in the law came about just before Carson's book was published. Thus was the way prepared for a similar reversal in the attitude toward ecological innovations (insecticides, dam building, and the like). Just seven years later the National Environmental Policy Act (NEPA) of 1969 extended the "guilty until proven innocent" revolution.

More surprisingly, here and there attempts are now being made to undo ecological mischief done earlier. Southern Florida furnishes an example. The water relations in the Everglades are too complex to be described here, but suffice it to say that overly simplistic ideas led to an "improvement" of the Kissimmee River in order to get more water to Miami. Some hundred miles of picturesque, winding river were altered into fifty-three miles of boringly straight ditch at a cost of $32 million. (By coincidence, this creation of the Army Corps of Engineers began in the *annus mirabilis* of 1962.) As a result of this "development" the wildlife of the region, a major attraction of Florida, was devastated. The population of winter wildfowl dropped by 90 percent, and nesting bald eagles by 70 percent. After a quarter of a century of squabbling, an agreement was reached to *undo* "development." The remedial work will extend well into the twenty-first century; the cost is estimated at $422 million. (This figure will, no doubt, prove to be an underestimate.)

There are at least two ways to look at this imbroglio. From one point of view it is a disgraceful example of waste in public enterprise: $422 million to correct a $32 million mistake. On the other hand, to use Cromwell's words, "in the bowels of Christ" we have considered that we may have made a mistake. Fraudulent "progress" *can* be stopped. We *can* turn back when we have the humility to admit that we have made a mistake.

Out of this messy history comes an immensely optimistic conclusion. Suppose someone had asked, in the year 1949, "How long will it take for society to decide that the destructive actions of 'developers'—both private and governmental—must be checked? How long will it be before we are willing to undo the harm?" The probable and pessimistic answer would have been "centuries—if ever!" Yet only thirteen years brought the beginnings of significant cracks in the dike built by the power of money.

People who sing "you can't stop progress!" have been called optimists; in the light of a deeper understanding we now see them as pessimists. John Q. Public is much more amenable to argument based on facts than he is generally given credit for. The furniture of the mind can be changed. Change often appears suddenly; it is seldom predictable by the statistician's "projection" of a curve.

All this has a bearing on the difficulties that stand in the way of population control. The techniques of birth control have been much improved since the time of Sir James Steuart and Robert Malthus. The theory and practice of population control seem to have stood still. Those who understand the issues best are apt to be pessimists. Projecting present trends they suppose that the intellectual changes needed for population control will take centuries to achieve. But Aldo Leopold failed to foresee the rapidity of changes that took place in political-ecological thinking after his death. Is it not possible that we stand on the threshold of a similarly rapid evolution of political ideas about population control? The future, as Gabor said, *can* be invented. What kind of population control might be worth inventing?

Unconscious Near-Success in the United States

Unnoticed by most Americans there was, during the 1980s, a movement in the direction of a stabilized population. The progress was not obvious because the overall growth rate during the decade was 0.7 percent per year, which means that our population was doubling once a century. That's a long way from ZPG (zero population growth). Yet the following technical analysis justifies an optimistic view of this decade.

For a population to remain constant in size, each woman should (on the average) produce two children: one to replace herself, one to replace her mate (who is unable to bear babies). More exactly: the average has to be somewhat greater than 2.0 children per woman—say 2.1 or 2.2, the extra fraction allowing for loss from accidents and for those offspring who become celibate or sterile. Whatever the exact figure for a given society at a given time, that number is called the *replacement number*. For a short time during the 1980s the total fertility rate of American women was *less* than 2.0. Yet the population was still doubling at the rate of once a century. How come?

Two factors were involved. First, because of the "baby boom" after World War II, there was a bulge in the proportion of women in the fertile years (arbitrarily taken as between fifteen and forty-five). Second, immigration was high and getting higher; and the immigrant women brought with them the fertile habits of their places of origin (principally the villages of Mexico).

The first source of extra fertility would correct itself in the course of time, as the baby boomers were replaced by non-baby boomers. Altering the second factor—immigration—depends on the will of the U.S. public, which so far has been ambivalent. Congress passed some restrictive laws but then did not adequately fund their enforcement. The administration dragged its feet too.

Without immigration the nation would ultimately have reached (first) ZPG, and (second) NPG—negative population growth—*if the trend had continued.* Trends can change; but the fact that this trend persisted even for a little while gives us hope for the future. It indicates that fertility can be low enough, even in the absence of legal coercion, to produce ZPG. How is this to be explained?

Housing Shortage as a Contraceptive

A hint comes from eastern Europe. From time to time during the twentieth century, one eastern European country after another has, for a period of years, enjoyed—if that is the correct word—negative population growth. In every case the cause was the same: a housing shortage. Young people who wanted to start their own families could not find apartments. The parents of one of a pair might generously take in the couple, but it was with the definite understanding that grandchildren would *not* start making their appearance until the young couple had removed themselves into housing of their own. This experience led to the saying that "The most effective contraceptive is a housing shortage."

Though true in parts of Europe, this does not apply to such countries as India, where living outdoors is possible in the mild winters and where traditions are different. For both religious and social reasons a Hindu family is unwilling to stop producing children until it has had two sons (one and a spare). This means (on the average) four children in the family. Northern Europeans, however, are under less social compulsion: among them, a lack of adequate housing has an understandably chilling effect on family formation.

Anti-Malthusians say, "Look: there is a negative correlation between prosperity and fertility. Where prosperity is great (for example, Europe), fertility is low; where poverty prevails (as in India), fertility is high. Therefore the solution to overpopulation is obvious. All we have to do is make poor people rich, and the population problem will solve itself."

One of the first things a student learns in statistics is that correlation is *not* causation. To find causes we must go behind the figures. Malthusians say that overpopulation *causes* poverty, rather than the reverse. Who is right? We get some insight by translating the problem to our own country.

Compare the situation of a middle-income family in Manhattan with that of a similar family in a small town in Utah. An income that would be more than adequate for raising several children in Utah might not be enough to have any at all in Manhattan. Think of all the good things in life that a family can enjoy in Utah— fishing, hunting, hiking, horseback riding, or just getting away from other human beings. Think of how casual parents can be about turning small children loose to explore the world around them in Utah, as compared with the situation facing families in Manhattan. Notice that crowded and crime-ridden Central Park is a poor substitute for the natural beauty that is so widespread in Utah.

Now ask, how much income would it take for a family to live really well in New York City? The direct cost would be much greater than in Utah, and the amount of time taken to travel hundreds of miles, several times a year, to find suitable recreation would be prohibitive. Imagine the horror of trying to raise a family of six children in Manhattan if one earned no more than $90,000 a year! Conventional economics may tell us that a New Yorker who gets $90,000 a year is three times as well off as a Utahan who earns but $30,000. In truth, in terms of *real* income, the reverse is more nearly true.

Anti-Malthusians maintain that money prosperity partially sterilizes people. Malthusians, focusing on real wealth, come to the opposite conclusion: fertility is *directly* proportional to well-being, *when wealth is correctly measured.*

The Malthusian Demostat: A Universal Principle

Natural selection, to use E. T. Whittaker's words, has its origin in "a conviction of the mind" that things could not be otherwise. If I fantasize myself as a god who has decided to bring the world into being I find I cannot imagine a persisting, living world without heredity and mutation; and since the world is necessarily limited, competition is inescapable. From the interaction of these deductions, natural selection necessarily follows. Natural selection is one of the great default positions of the natural sciences. (Social sciences are built on a comparable default position: "Behavior is determined by real rewards.")

Though accidents and natural selection are inescapable, survival is possible because every living species has built into it the power of exponential increase. (Any genetic variant that lacked this power would soon become extinct.) Each population can be kept from "eating itself out of house and home" only by contrary forces, which can be lumped under the single term "misery." The other force is called "felicity." They act together to produce the Malthusian demostat, as seen in the figure here repeated from Chapter 16. *The Malthusian demostat is the major default position of demography.*

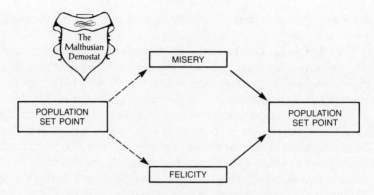

A final look at the Malthusian Demostat.

In the interests of simplicity Malthus's "misery" has been adopted as the comprehensive term for all forms of negative (corrective) feedback operating against overpopulation. There is clearly a relationship between Malthus's "misery" and the Buddha's "sorrow." Neither can be wished out of existence; instead, the struggle against them endures.

As concerns population, how can a human community lessen the misery or sorrow threatened by exponential growth? We need first to survey the many ways that population growth can be suppressed. The following seem to be the principal variants.

- Famine
- Fatal crowd diseases
- Sterilizing diseases promoted by sexual promiscuity
- Civic disorders promoted by overpopulation
- International wars
- Housing shortages
- A highly materialistic ethos (high standard of living)
- Prudence in preparing for future troubles

The position of the set point can be moved up or down by secular changes, such as occurred during the scientific-industrial revolution. Unaware of the upward shift that was taking place in his lifetime, Malthus made particular predictions that exposed him to ridicule when they were not fulfilled. Malthusian theory is often said to have been "discredited," a useful word for dismissing a theory without examining it. Unnoticed is the fact that tieing the set point to a single measure (such as the amount of food producible) lowers the share per capita for other goods. A world tied to food as the limiting factor will inevitably be inadequately supplied with wilderness, quietness, and a sense of community.

The "misery" caused by rising levels of pollution, noise, and traffic congestion should be perceived as signs of overpopulation, but the widespread taboo of population discussions results in public pressure to increase the search for "technological fixes" of these "miseries." The ultimate futility of this approach is most apparent in traffic control. Hoping to diminish traffic jams, we build ever more multilane roads; as a result more traffic is attracted to them and traffic congestion gets steadily worse.

Anti-Malthusians cling to the hope that population control can be painlessly achieved, without altering any beliefs or values sanctified by time. The Christian apologist Tertullian, a Malthusian sixteen centuries before Malthus, regarded misery (in whatever form) as a "blessing," since it corrects overpopulation before it can do even more harm. Obviously none of today's politicians would dare endorse Tertullian's view.

Since misery is partly a matter of subjective perception, the Malthusian demostat suggests the possibility of controlling population by public opinion. This is the approach Charles Galton Darwin took in suggesting the "bribe" of the motorcar. If people develop a tradition of including certain luxuries in their standard of living, then the availability of those luxuries can be a limiting factor for population size. A population, when it depends on such energy-expensive components as motorcars, will equilibrate at a smaller size, which means that the per capita share of *other* goods will be higher. Since making the motorcar a prime desideratum is a matter of choice, human "will" becomes of importance in determining both the size and the well-being of the population. To a significant extent, the Malthusian demostat is a matter of human definition. Giving greater weight to luxuries causes the set point of population to equilibrate at a smaller population. This means that the good things of life are present in greater abundance.

How Beautiful Is Austerity?

Thanks to electronics and satellites it is now possible to see pitiful, potbellied children starving to death "in real time" on the other side of the earth. It is not surprising that some people find it difficult to enjoy a TV dinner while looking at people starving to death on a television screen. It is all too human to want to share with the needy.

The impulse to share does credit to the heart. So suppose that we adopt a more austere way of life and then ship the food that is thus freed to starving people in an already overpopulated country. What happens then? Malthusian and anti-Malthusian reasoning generate different answers. Anti-Malthusians expect that increasing the food supply to malnourished people will lower their fertilty; Malthusians expect the opposite result. Biology and most of the evidence from human experience supports the Malthusians. Embracing austerity to help the starving is a dubious policy. At best, it increases the need for food in the recipient country when it suffers its next climatic disaster.

Luxury has always had a bad press. On several occasions Malthus defended a modest degree of luxury. In the second edition of his essay he took note of the argument that the great consumption of "corn" (grain) in the making of alcoholic spirits in China was a major cause of the frequent famines in that unhappy country. Not so, said Malthus, who turned the argument upside down:

> The consumption of corn in any other way but that of necessary food, checks the
> population before it arrives at the utmost limit of subsistence; and as the grain may

be withdrawn from this particular use in the time of scarcity, a public granary is
thus opened, richer, probably, than could have been formed by any other
means. . . . China, without her distilleries, would certainly be more populous, but
on a failure of the seasons, would have still less resource than she has at present,
and as far as the magnitude of the cause would operate, would in consequence be
more subject to famines, and those famines would be more severe.

Using the word "luxury" in a metaphorical sense, to include not only out-and-
out luxuries but also such sensible measures as "safety factors," we can say that
population size and the amount of luxury are trade-offs: maximizing the one minimizes the other. Malthus, though he never dealt systematically with this problem,
is reported to have held that "there should be no more people in a country than
could enjoy daily a glass of wine and a piece of beef for their dinner."

Beef and the wine are to be understood symbolically. In our own time people
who decry the ingestion of alcohol and meat are likely to insist on salad made with
lettuce—which is almost entirely water, transported at considerable cost in energy
for a distance of one to three thousand miles. When to use the word "luxury" and
when the word "austerity" is a matter of taste.

The policy ideal, commonly identified with Jeremy Bentham, of "the greatest
happiness of the greatest number," is, strictly speaking, an unachievable goal. A
society can maximize one or the other, but not both at the same time. Those who
would settle a controversy by opting for the maximum number of human lives are,
whether they realize it or not, opting for maximizing human misery as well.

Some environmentalists maintain that the austerest life is the most moral one,
perceiving populationists as selfish people who don't want to share with the needy.
This perception no doubt made many environmentalists passively agree to the
omission of population from the observances of Earth Day 1990.

What Is the Proper Arena for "Doing Good"?

Anyone who tries to comprehend the spirit of our times is soon impressed with the
popularity of guilt-mongering—making other people feel guilty about something.
(Actually, many of the guilt-mongers even seem to enjoy taking their own medicine.) In the first half of the twentieth century anthropologists taught people to be
ashamed of ethnocentrism. So successful were they that some guilt-mongers have
now gone to the extreme of becoming *ethnofugalists:* they see virtue only in people
other than their own kind. Often the greater the *otherness,* the greater the asserted
virtue and beauty.

Like compulsive and universal altruism, ethnofugalism tends to destabilize a
society. (When everyone prefers minding the business of others to minding his own,
no business will be well tended.) Wise men have long recognized this danger, as is
apparent in a statement made by Adam Smith in 1759: "The administration of the
great system of the universe . . . the care of the universal happiness of all rational
and sensible beings, is the business of God, and not of man. To man is allotted a
much humbler department, but one much more suitable to the weakness of his
powers, and to the narrowness of his comprehension—the care of his own happiness, of that of his family, his friends, his country,"

A commentator of our time is likely to cry out: "But look how things have changed since Smith's time! Think of what technology has done to time and space. The humility of the eighteenth century is no longer called for!"

Yes and no. In the speed of transmission of information there is indeed a great contrast between the two periods. In 1759, learning what was taking place on the other side of the world may have taken two or three months; now, thanks to satellites, we can learn what is happening literally in a fraction of a second. But because we can see what is happening elsewhere does not mean that we can, or should, intervene. The transport of human bodies and artifacts half way around the world is not instantaneous, and it is still expensive, both in money and in energy. If we devote more of our resources to the alleviation of poverty ten thousand miles away, we can devote less to helping those who are in need in our own community.

Every act of charity should be followed by a post-audit to determine both the good and the harm that it has done. This is difficult enough to do well in our own community; it is *very* difficult to do from a distance of ten thousand miles. (Is that why so many kind-hearted people favor distant philanthropy? Because distance shields them from knowledge of the harm they have done?)

Two ancient concepts have not been significantly altered by the progress of technology:

Sovereignty: In trying to maximize peace we clearly must support the idea of national sovereignty. Each nation should be free to govern its own affairs. (The record of American intervention in the affairs of other nations during the twentieth century certainly does not justify optimism about our ability to help other nations by our interventions.)

Responsibility: Frankelian responsibility must go with sovereignty. When the rulers of an overpeopled country—whether they be individual leaders or the *demos* of a democracy—ask us for food, or ask that we open our doors to their emigrants, they thereby abandon their responsibility. Worse, such irresponsible rulers ensure the continuance of the pathological system that caused overpopulation in the first place.

The "bottom line" of our relations with other sovereign nations is this: the safest aid to give is information only—particularly information about birth control. (Inexpensive materials for this purpose can also be safely given.) It is in the interest of every country that all countries control their populations.

Promoters of "ethnic power" love to scold rich countries for urging a lower birth rate on poor countries; the ethnics call this "genocide." But if a country is poor and powerless because it already has too many children for its resources, it will become even poorer and more powerless if it breeds more. If ethnic pronatalists have their way, poor countries will be ruined.

The Importance of Women

Advice is most convincing when those who give it have taken it themselves. On that ground, reproductive advice giving by such a country as the United States can be criticized somewhat. The American birth control movement is about a century old. Margaret Sanger stated its goal: "Every child a wanted child." The goal has still not been completely achieved in the United States. We need to do better.

Birth control clinics should be subsidized generously because it is far cheaper to prevent the birth of an unwanted child than it is to take care of it later. In many parts of the country it is still difficult for a poor woman to obtain an abortion or other birth control services that rich women get so easily. An abortion can be had for less than a thousand dollars. Contraception services are even cheaper. Empirical studies show that raising a child to age eighteen, at what we regard as a medium American standard of living (but without a college education) costs parents and taxpayers well in excess of $100,000. The failure of the rich and powerful to promote equality of treatment in birth control might lead the mythical and objective "man from Mars" to think that the rich simply love to pay taxes!

A most optimistic harbinger of the future is the women's liberation movement. The world over, there is no question but that the greatest progress in reducing birth rates is occurring in societies in which women have been the most liberated from male domination. Without question, many of the pronatalist attitudes inherited from the past have had their source in machismo, in the aggressive desires of males to dominate family activities and decisions. It is easy for the sex that never bears children to see procreation as a noble and heroic act. From time immemorial the child-bearing sex has been compelled, by force or trickery, to propagate far beyond the bounds of the heart's desire. Worse, the voices of some women have been infected with the rhetoric of pronatalism that comes so easily to the irresponsible sex.

Reducing the power of pronatalism in other sovereign nations will not be easy now that our species has largely given up conquest and colonialism. It is the women in other cultures who are most in need of contact with the outside world. But how can the needed contacts be established with cultures in which the principal gatekeepers are men? Ideas are infectious, however, and there are signs that the idea that women are as worthy as men is leaping over the walls of the seraglios.

Progress is occuring, but pinpoint prediction is hazardous. Female literacy is a great aid. Though ironclad proof is lacking, it seems highly probable that completely liberated women will (after some delay perhaps) willingly choose an average number of offspring that will make a stable population achievable. Opinion polls do not prove this, but then the dream of liberated womanhood is very new.

Focusing on the Furnishings of the Mind

Birth control is not population control. Improvements in the technology of birth control will make population control easier, but perfect methods of birth control are not enough. How much these methods are used is determined by the furnishings of the mind.

The ideas that are necessary for population control are easily accessible to the ordinary mind. They are widely known, but people are not as acutely aware of them as they must be if population control is ever to be achieved. If talented teachers can find striking ways of fitting the following generalizations into primary and secondary education, the advance of population control will be greatly furthered.

Exponential growth: This is just a fancy term for growth by compound interest, which people understand from their banking experience. Most economic literature fails however to emphasize the following important point: no positive rate of exponential growth of a population can safely be regarded as "small." A bank that offered only 1 percent interest on deposits would be ridiculed, but in a population 1 percent growth per year is so very, very great that it was not achieved worldwide until the year 1950. (More important: such a rate cannot long be maintained.)

Our world is finite: Television space operas, like the fairy tales they displaced, leave children with expectations of limitless worlds. We need to disillusion children. They need to grow up feeling in their bones that they cannot escape earth's problems by fleeing to the stars.

There will never be a perpetual motion machine: Time after time a proposed method of escape from limits turns out to be a fraudulent but cleverly disguised perpetual motion machine. Students need to be trained to detect such fraud.

Diseconomies of scale are the rule: Whatever may be the relative frequencies of economies and diseconomies of scale, human beings naturally recognize and exploit the economies first. Increasingly, society is left with diseconomies. As a result, in ever more instances, more (of almost anything) is worse. This expectation contradicts the "bigger is better" philosophy of the recent past.

Carrying capacity is measured in terms of (number of people) multiplied by (the physical quality of life): The maximum number of people can be supported only if the per capita share of physical wealth (energy, space, food, luxuries) is kept to the minimum. (Of course some aspects of the "quality of life" call for little or no substantive expenditures: friendliness, for example.)

Population size is demostatically controlled: It takes negative feedback to keep the potential of exponential growth from destroying a population. A community has a choice of negative feedbacks; but if it refuses to choose, nature will step in with the painful negative feedbacks of famine, disease and social chaos.

Zero population growth is the NORM for every population: Ignoring minor fluctuations, more than 99 percent of the existence of every species is passed in an essentially ZPG condition. The rapid growth of the human population during the past two centuries is very exceptional. It must soon come to an end. The experience will probably never be repeated.

ZPG *can be exciting:* The conservation rules of science apply to matter and energy, the joint product of which can be neither destroyed nor created. Conservation does *not* rule "information," which can be either destroyed or created. Economic growth and population growth must finally come to a halt: but there is no perceivable limit to progress in the arts—including the art of living together!

Without the control of immigration, no country can succeed in controlling its population size: The Marxist philosophy, "From each according to his ability, to each according to his needs," defines an unmanaged commons, which ends in ruin.

One of the most reliable things in the world is human unreliability: It is for this reason that complex technologies with tremendous potential for harm (such as nuclear reactors) must probably be abandoned.

So long as demand increases exponentially, solving a material shortage is impossible: People are repeatedly surprised when building more roads merely makes traffic jams worse. They are also surprised when giving food to a starving population today increases the number of the starving in future years.

Every "shortage" of supply is equally a "longage" of demand: Focusing on shortages encourages greed (and makes a favored few people rich). Focusing on longages encourages temperance in making demands. The problem of balancing supply and demand is not in the stars, and the solution is not in technology: it is in our heads.

Every complex function is subject to spontaneous decay and loss of the sort that physicists call "entropy": Knowledge is one of the most valuable complex functions, and the evidence of its entropic degeneration are everywhere. Some 2,500 years ago the Greeks inscribed this advice on the temple at Delphi: *Nothing in excess.* Somewhat later Epicurus said, "If you live according to nature you will never be poor; if you live according to opinion you will never be rich."

In 1971 the U.S. Council of Economic Advisors, apparently ignorant of both classical literature and modern science, solemnly proclaimed that, "If it is agreed that economic output is a good thing it follows by definition that there is not enough of it." The advisors wisely started their statement with an "if," but it looks like they forgot the "if" before they reached the conclusion of the sentence. The council evidently believed that wealth is not subject to the ancient doctrine that "There can be too much of a good thing."

Probably every one of these economists had a Ph.D. degree. Yet a well-educated teenager could have set them straight. Food is a good thing, but it is all too easy to have too much of it. The fat-soluble vitamins are good things, but he who eats a generous slab of polar bear liver dies of the excess. Oxygen is a good thing; but breathe 100 percent oxygen for a few hours and you're dead.

Ours is a society that finds it difficult to keep a firm hold on the concept of temperance. When the Women's Christian Temperance Union was formed to reduce the drinking of alcohol the word "temperance" was soon corrupted to mean total abstinence. Prohibition laws polarized much of society into heavy drinkers and teetotalers. Discussions of population control risk a similar polarization. Already a pronatalist has condemned the idea of population control by entitling a book *The War Against Population,* a title that implies that only a thorough misanthrope could hope that the human population might be less than the maximum possible—that is to say, the most miserable possible.

Pure pronatalism and pure misanthropy are both suicidal in their thrust. With population, as with most goods in life, a golden mean is to be sought. An understanding of numbers and ratios is essential, but the level of mathematical ability required is within reach of most of humankind.

The preceding italicized principles represent so many pieces of mental furniture that must be installed in the minds of men and women if nature is to be kept from controlling population by her own more brutal means. The resistance to positioning this furniture in the minds of citizens is very great among many interested parties. All advertizers will fight against the change, as will those who believe in science fiction, as well as all people who are "conservative" in the sense of wanting to conserve the present social and political arrangements forever. Opposition will also be expressed by some Marxists, some Christians, some idealistic atheists, some capitalists, some socialists and some ethnofugalists. Radical changes are called for in universal education. These will be supported by ecological conservatives, whose aim is to preserve as much wealth as possible for our children and grandchildren. The educational challenge is formidable.

Temperance must be the guiding ideal. There is no all-powerful world government to achieve universal population control; and there is no reason to expect one to develop. Population control must be coextensive with sovereignty. The existence of many sovereignties calls for the parochial control of population. Here and there throughout the world one sees hints that temperance in balancing population size and the quality of life is being achieved. Let us hope that ours is one of the countries that manages to find—and accept—effective means of controlling its population.

Notes and References

Chapter 2

The most useful sources of further information on problems connected with interstellar migration may be found in the following publications.

Dyson, Freeman J. 1978. "Pilgrim Fathers, Mormon Pioneers, and Space Colonists: An Economic Comparison." *Proceedings of the American Philosophical Society* 122:63–68.

Finney, Ben R. and Eric M. Jones, eds. 1985. *Interstellar Migration and the Human Experience.* Berkeley: University of California Press.

Hardin, Garrett, 1959. "Interstellar Migration and the Population Problem." *Journal of Heredity* 50:68–70. This paper is reprinted, with added comments, in Hardin 1969.

———. 1969. *Population, Evolution, and Birth Control,* 2d ed. San Francisco: W. H. Freeman.

———. 1978. *Stalking the Wild Taboo,* 2d ed. Los Altos, CA: William Kaufmann.

———. 1985. *Filters against Folly: How to Survive Despite Economists, Ecologists, and the Merely Eloquent.* New York: Viking-Penguin.

Chapter 3

1. Will Durant, *The Age of Faith* (New York: Simon & Schuster, 1950), 207.

2. *Encyclopaedia Britannica.* 1974; vol. 6, p. 567. The man's name was John L. O'Sullivan.

3. Edward M. Hart, "The Shape of Things to Come." *Next* (Nov./Dec. 1980): 66.

4. "Malthus" undoubtedly was originally "Malthouse," named perhaps for a tavern keeper or brewer. Rapidly pronounced, English fashion, it became "Malt-hus," without a diphthong *th.* But, in the United States, everyone sounds the diphthong. This information comes from John Maynard Keynes' charming account of Malthus in his excellent collection, *Essays and Sketches in Biography* (New York: Meridian Books, 1956).

5. William Wordsworth, The Prelude, book 11, lines 9–10 and 14–16. Wordsworth's title for this book is "French Revolution as it appeared to Enthusiasts at its Commencement." By its roots, an "enthusiast" is one who has a god inside, i.e., one who is "possessed." In Wordsworth's day this label was not a compliment.

6. Alexander Gray, *The Socialist Tradition,* (New York: Longmans, Green, 1946). Gray's unfailingly wise and witty treatment of the personalities involved is at its best in chapter 5, devoted to Godwin.

7. The quotations in Box 3-1 are taken from William Godwin, *Enquiry Concerning Political Justice,* 3d ed. (1798; reprint, New York: Penguin Books, 1985). The relevant pages are as follows: "Property," 711; "Promises," 218, 219; "Cooperation," 758; "Gratitude," 171; "Obedience," 228, 229; "War," 522; "Work," 745, 746; "Utopia," 776, 777.

8. *Political Justice,* 1st ed., 430. See also Gray, above, 125.

9. C. Kegan Paul, *William Godwin,* vol. 2 (London: Henry S. King & Co., 1876), 141.

10. Graham Wallas, *The Life of Francis Place* (London: Longmans Green, 1898), 60.

11. Keith Michael Baker, *Condorcet: From Natural Philosophy to Social Mathematics,* (Chicago: University of Chicago Press, 1975), 10. The French phrase, literally translated, is, "the title and profession of a savant." But though the word *savant* has been affiliated into English it is not commonly used. "Scientist" would be an acceptable translation, but this English word was not coined until 1840 (by William Whewell); and some of the French still have not adopted it, using the more awkward *homme de science.*

12. Frank E. Manuel, *The Prophets of Paris* (Cambridge, MA: Harvard University Press, 1962), (58–60).

13. Antoine-Nicolas de Condorcet, *Sketch for an Historical Picture of the Progress of the Human Mind,* translated by June Barraclough (1795, reprint, New York: Noonday Press, 1955). (Introduction by Stuart Hampshire.)

14. Thomas S. Kuhn, *The Structure of Scientific Revolutions* (Chicago: University of Chicago Press, 1962). For criticisms of this analysis, together with a rejoinder by Kuhn, *Criticism and the Growth of Knowledge* ed. Imre Lakatos and Alan Musgrave (Cambridge: Cambridge University Press, 1970).

15. J. B. Bury, *The Idea of Progress* (1932; reprint, New York: Dover, 1955).

16. Frederick J. Teggart, ed., *The Idea of Progress: A Collection of Readings* (Berkeley: University of California Press, 1949). Throughout this section I have drawn on the original translation (1795) of Condorcet's work (included in Teggert, 321–58).

Chapter 4

1. Garrett Hardin, *Population, Evolution and Birth Control,* 2d ed. (San Francisco: W. H. Freeman, 1969).

2. Garrett Hardin, "Population Skeletons in the Environmental Closet," *Bulletin of the Atomic Scientists,* 1972, no. 6:37–41. An account of the acrimonious controversy between environmentalist Barry Commoner and populationist Paul R. Ehrlich. Their positions have not noticeably changed in the intervening years.

3. Ruth Coffey, personal communication.

4. Michelle Perrot, "Malthusianism and Socialism," in *Malthus Past and Present,* ed. J. Dupaguier, A. Fauve-Chamoux, and E. Grebenik (New York: Academic Press, 1983), 258.

5. William Petersen, "Marx versus Malthus: The Men and the Symbols," *Population Review* 1 (1957): 26–27).

6. T. R. Malthus, *An Essay on the Principle of Population.* 3d ed., vol. 2 (London: J. Johnson, 1806), 515.

7. Ibid., 507 (italics added).

8. Ibid., 509.

9. Vincent J. Knapp, "Major Dietary Changes in Nineteenth-Century Europe," *Perspectives in Biology and Medicine* 31 (1988): 190.

10. John P. Wiley, Jr., "Phenomena, comment and notes," *The Smithsonian* (1986): 26–31.

11. For glimpses of science fiction futures that never came to pass, see Joseph J. Corn and Brian Horrigan, *Yesterday's Tomorrows: Past Visions of the American Future* (New York: Summit Books, 1984).

12. *The Wall Street Journal,* 11 January 1988, 25.

13. The escalating cost of liability insurance bears a great deal of the blame for the downturn in the manufacturing of private airplanes. The Piper Aircraft company estimates that manufacturers' liability insurance adds $75,000 to the cost of each new plane they build. For some of their smaller aircraft, insurance costs more than the manufacturing process. And of

course the operator of the plane has to pay additional liability insurance. See Philip H. Abelson, "Product Liability in a Litigious Society," *Science* 240 (1988): 1589. One of the elements that enters into this escalation of liability costs is population, because, by diminishing the amount of population-free space, it increases the probability of expensive accidents. This is not to deny the importance of public attitudes toward liability and the propensity of juries to make extravagant awards; but the increase in population density is one of the factors that make private airplane ownership ever less feasible.

14. Provincial Elections Act, RSBC 1960, chap. 306, para. 166.

15. I am indebted to Dr. and Mrs. Colin W. Clark for this information.

16. Paul Demeny, "World Population Trends," *Current History* 88 (1989): 17.

17. Joseph S. Davis, "Our Changed Population Outlook and Its Significance," *American Economic Review* 42 (1952):304–25.

18. Michael S. Teitelbaum comments on Ben Wattenberg's *The Birth Dearth* in, *Population and Environment* 10 (1988): 70–72.

19. Nathan Keyfitz, "Introduction: Population and Biology," in *Biology and Demography,* ed. Nathan Keyfitz (Liege: Ordina Editions, 1984), 1.

20. Isaiah Berlin, *The Hedgehog and the Fox: An Essay on Tolstoy's View of History* (London: Weidenfeld & Nicholson, 1953).

21. Richard P. Feynman, *QED: The Strange Theory of Light and Matter* (Princeton, NJ: Princeton University Press, 1985), 7.

22. Paul Demeny, *Population Notes,* no. 55 (7 September 1984), 1(New York: The Population Council). This paper was later published in *European Journal of Population,* 1, (2).

23. Paul R. Ehrlich, "An Ecologist Standing Up Among Seated Social Scientists," *CoEvolution Quarterly* 31 (1981): 24–35.

Chapter 5

1. Willard Van Orman Quine, (1957). "The Scope and Language of Science, *British Journal of the Philosophy of Science* 8 (1957):1–17.

2. John Rader Platt, *The Excitement of Science* (Boston: Houghton & Mifflin, 1962) 2.

3. Michael Polanyi, *The Tacit Dimension* (Garden City, NY: Doubleday, 1966), 64–65.

4. Ken Alder, "The Search for Perpetual Motion." *American Heritage of Invention and Technology* (1986): 58–63.

5. Arthur Stanley Eddington, *The Nature of the Physical World* (New York: Macmillan, 1928), 74.

6. Constance Holden, "Science in Court," *Science* 243 (1989): 1658–59.

7. Arthur W.J.G. Ord-Hume, *Perpetual Motion: The History of an Obsession* (London: Allen & Unwin, 1977). Readers of this interesting book will agree that the subtitle is justified.

8. E. T. Whittaker, "Some Disputed Questions in the Philosophy of the Physical Sciences," *Proceedings of the Royal Society of Edinburgh* 61 (1942): 168.

9. I am indebted to Tracy Fernandez for this insight.

10. Frank J. Galland, ed., *Dictionary of Computing: Data Communications, Hardware and Software Basics, Digital Electronics* (New York: John Wiley & Sons, 1982). I have modified the form given in this dictionary to free it of the more idiosyncratic references to computers themselves.

11. Anthony Ralston, ed., *Encyclopedia of Computer Science and Engineering,* 2d ed. (New York: Van Nostrand Reinhold, 1983).

12. John Silber, "The Alienation of the Humanities," *Academic Questions,* 1989, no. 3: 15.

13. Cyril Bailey, ed., *Epicurus: The Extant Remains* (Oxford: Clarendon Press, 1926), 21. The quotation is from the letter, "To Herodotus."

14. Derek J. de Solla Price, *Science Since Babylon* (New Haven, CT: Yale University Press, 1961), 34–35).

15. George Gilder, *Wealth and Poverty* (New York: Basic Books, 1981), 232).

16. Constance Holden, *Science* 236 (1987): 769.

17. Allen V. Kneese, "The Economics of Natural Resources," *Population and Development Review* 14 (1988 suppl.): 302.

18. Daniel A. Underwood and Paul G. King, "On the Ideological Foundations of Environmental Policy," *Ecological Economics* 1 (1989): 324.

Chapter 6

1. Thomas Sowell, *Compassion versus Guilt, and Other Essays* (New York: William Morrow. 1987). Sowell trained as an economist, turns out one of the better newspaper columns—clear, pungent, provocative. To ecologists some of his essays seem to combine short-term wisdom with long-term blindness. Economists think otherwise. In any case, his essay "Oil Prices" should repay rereading and group discussion every five years.

2. Kenneth Eaton, *The Wall Street Journal,* 29 November 1977, 1.

3. That the female of the species is often the one to make the significant choice in mating was strongly argued by Charles Darwin in 1871 in *The Descent of Man, and Selection in Relation to Sex.* For most of a century many influential biologists, to their discredit, scoffed at Darwin's interpretation. Then in the second half of the twentieth century, sociobiologists revived the doctrine and established it firmly. For a fascinating introduction to the field see chap. 14, "Female Choice," in Robert Trivers, *Social Evolution* (Menlo Park, CA: Benjamin/Cummings, 1985).

4. Kenneth Eaton, *The Wall Street Journal,* 29 November 1977, 1.

5. Barbara W. Tuchman, *The March of Folly (New York: Knopf, 1984), 295.*

Chapter 7

1. W. P. Webb, *The Great Frontier* (Boston: Houghton Mifflin, 1952).

2. William R. Catton, Jr., and Riley E. Dunlap, "A New Ecological Paradigm for Post-Exuberant Sociology," *American Behavioral Scientist* 24 (1980): 15–47.

3. Henry George, *Progress and Poverty* (1879; reprint, New York: Schalkenberg, 1962), 141–42).

4. Robert P. McIntosh, "Ecology: A Clarification," *Science* 188 (1975): 1258. A review of the history of the term "ecology." On the basis of a handwritten manuscript, the first use was at one time credited to Thoreau, but a second and more careful examination convincingly showed that Thoreau had written "geology," not "ecology." The first use by Haeckel was in either 1866 or 1869. The 1933 edition of the *Oxford English Dictionary* did not include the term, and the 1972 printing of the *A–G Supplement* mistakenly credited it to Thoreau. It is worth noting that University of Michigan biologists have informally divided their subject into "skin-in biology" and "skin-out biology." The former comprises such subsciences as physiology and molecular genetics; the latter is simply ecology.

5. Paul P. Christensen, "Historical Roots for Ecological Economics—Biophysical versus Allocative Approaches," *Ecological Economics* 1 (1989): 21.

6. Kenneth E. Boulding, "The Economics of the Coming Spaceship Earth," in *Environmental Quality in a Growing Economy,* ed. Henry Jarrett (Baltimore: Johns Hopkins Press, 1966).

7. Kenneth E. Boulding, in *Pollution, Resources, and the Environment,* ed. Alain C. Enthoven and A. Myrick Freeman, III, (New York: W. W. Norton, 1973), 21.

8. Theodore H. White, *In Search of History* (New York: Warner Brothers, 1978), 578.

Chapter 8

1. The ready availability of "electronic slide-rules" in financial and scientific models makes it easy for the reader to check the figures that follow. If *ln* = the natural logarithm, and *i* = the annual rate of interest stated as a decimal fraction, then the compound interest formula can be given as:

$$ln(\text{value}) = ln(\text{deposit}) + [(\text{time}) \times ln(1 + i)].$$

Once the logarithm of the value is found, one takes the antilogarithm (e^x, on the calculator) of this figure, which gives us what we want.

2. Edward R. Tufte, *The Visual Display of Quantitative Information* (Cheshire, CT: Graphics Press, 1983). This handsome volume is by far the best manual on the art of converting figures into graphs.

3. The distinction between numeracy and literacy is made at the end of the second chapter of this book. For more details see: Garrett Hardin, *Filters Against Folly: How to Survive Despite Economists, Ecologists, and the Merely Eloquent* (New York: Viking, 1985; Penguin edition, 1986).

4. The division of academia into two cultures was made in 1959 by C. P. Snow (1905–1980), a British physicist turned administrator. (See his *Two Cultures and the Scientific Revolution* [Cambridge: Cambridge University Press, 1959].) His analysis was vigorously attacked by the literary critic F. R. Leavis. As a broad-brush description, most scientists think Snow's distinction is close to the truth. In any case, Snow could claim some knowledge of both cultures, since he was also a successful novelist. In the present work, the discrimination of three investigative filters is derived from Snow's two cultures.

5. This is a plea, of course, for more graphing in public education; but I am not unaware of the fact that reforms can easily miscarry. Consider, for instance, the words of Alfred North Whitehead, referring to the English situation at the time of World War I: "A few years ago there was an outcry that school algebra was in need of reform, but there was a general agreement that graphs would put everything right. So all sorts of things were extruded, and graphs were introduced. So far as I can see, with no sort of idea behind them, but just graphs. Now every examination paper has one or two questions on graphs. Personally, I am an enthusiastic adherent of graphs. But I wonder whether as yet we have gained very much." *The Organisation of Thought* (London: Williams and Norgate, 1917), 15. The moral may be simply stated: Pedagogues can spoil any good idea.

6. John Maynard Keynes, *The Economic Consequences of the Peace* (London: Macmillan, 1919), 153.

7. Ibid., 3.

8. Garrett Hardin, *Nature and Man's Fate.* (New York: Rinehart, 1959), 307.

9. Joseph Fletcher, *Situation Ethics: The New Morality* (Philadelphia: Westminster Press, 1966).

10. Benjamin Nelson, *The Idea of Usury: From Tribal Brotherhood to Universal Otherhood,* 2d ed. (Chicago: University of Chicago Press, 1969).

11. P. T. Bauer, "Remembrance of Studies Past: Retracing First Steps, in *Pioneers in Development,* ed. Gerald M. Meier and Dudley Seers, (New York: Oxford University Press, 1984), 28, 29).

12. *The Correspondence of Charles Darwin,* vol. 1. (Cambridge: Cambridge University Press, 1985), 233.

13. Garrett Hardin, "Running on 'Empty,'" *BioScience* 36 (1986): 2.

14. See, for instance, *The Ecologist* (U.K.), 15, 16, and 17 (1985–1987).

15. Robert Repetto, "Wasting Assets," *Technology Review,* January 1991, 39–44.

16. To see what a barrow is, look at a reproduction of Breughel's painting of "The Wedding Feast," the original of which is in Vienna's Kunsthistorisches Museum. In this scene, food is being brought into the room by two men, one at either end of the barrow. The date of the painting is 1568, long after the invention of the wheelbarrow, but barrows without wheels were then, and are now still, improvised on occasion.

17. Martin Mayer, *The Greatest-Ever Bank Robbery: The Collapse of the Saving and Loan Industry* (New York: Scribner's, 1990), 299–300.

18. Herman E. Daly, "The Economic Thought of Frederick Soddy," *History of Political Economy* 12 (1980): 469–88.

19. *Wall Street Journal,* 5 March 1975, 1.

20. Frederick Soddy, *Wealth, Virtual Wealth, and Debt* (London: Allen & Unwin, 69).

21. James R. Newman, ed., *The World of Mathematics* vol. 1 (New York: Simon & Schuster, 1956), 514. The passage quoted there is from E. T. Bell, *Mathematics—Queen and Servant of Science.*

22. Laurence J. Kotlikoff, "The Deficit is Not a Well-Defined Measure of Fiscal Policy." *Science* 241 (1988): 791–95.

23. Will and Ariel Durant, *The Age of Reason Begins* (New York: Simon & Schuster, 1961), 275.

24. Lionel Casson, "Biting the Bullet in Ancient Rome," *Horizon* 18 (1976): 18–21.

25. Aristotle, *Politics,* book 1, chap. 10.

26. James Simon, *A Dictionary of Economic Quotations,* 2d ed. (London: Croom Helm, 1984). The original is in Oresme's *The Origin, Nature, Law and Alterations of Money.*

27. John Maynard Keynes, *Essays in Persuasion* (New York: Norton, 1963), 371–72.

28. It is noteworthy that the 1988 Nobel prize in economics was awarded to Maurice Allais of France, who, in 1947, set forth a theory that postulated that the optimum rate of interest in a truly stationary economy is zero. See *Science* 242 (1988):511.

Chapter 9

1. Baron de Montesquieu, *Persian Letters,* letter 113, 1721.

2. Colin McEverdy and Richard Jones, *Atlas of World Population History* (New York: Penguin Books, 1978). This book is a good source for population data of the world and of particular regions. The figures used in the text have been read off the graphs of this atlas.

3. William Godwin, *Of Population* (1820; reprint, New York: Augustus M. Kelley, 1964), 508.

4. The first edition of Malthus's *Essay* is available in many different printings. It is highly recommended to those who have the time to dip into it. It is only about a third as large as subsequent editions, which deserve to be called treatises rather than essays; and which are not nearly as interesting.

5. Alfred North Whitehead, *The Organisation of Thought* (1917; reprint, Westport, CT: Greenwood Press, 1974), 127.

6. Those who enjoy using an "electronic slide rule" may like to play with the basic mathematics of population growth.

Malthus's "geometrical" series has now been replaced by the term "exponential growth," the equation for which is shown below. The equation assumes no environmental resistance to population growth.

$$y = ke^{bt}$$

where: y = population size after time t has elapsed

t = time

k = size of population at $t = 0$

e = base of natural logarithms (2.718 . . .)

b = "biotic potential"

The superscript bt is said to be an exponent of the term to the left. The population growth curve is an *exponential* function. The equation for money placed at compound interest (if compounded "instantaneously") is also an exponential function. In fact, it is the same function, with the letters suitably redefined.

Don't worry about that e: it's a crazy sort of number that never ends (2.718 . . . et cetera, et cetera). The number e is a legitimate, if surprising, player in the game.

As for b, keep in mind that the faster the population grows, the greater b is. If $b = 0$, there is zero population growth. If b is a negative number, the population is shrinking.

To carry out the computations it is useful to take the natural logarithms (ln) of the equation given above:

$$ln\ y\ =\ ln\ k\ +\ bt$$

A peculiar but useful fact comes out of population mathematics. As a quite good approximation, if you divide the number 70 by the annual percentage rate of growth, you get the doubling time (in years) of population growth. Kenya, with an annual growth rate of 4 percent, is doubling its population in 17.5 years (unless the rate changes). But notice that even the Kenyans' rate of increase is dwarfed by that of the unhappy Bikinians (see note 8 below), which is 5.4 percent per year, or 35 percent greater.

Also: dividing 70 by the doubling time gives you the growth rate. If the early population of America doubled every 25 years, as Malthus supposed, its annual growth rate was 2.8 percent.

7. Charles Darwin, *The Origin of Species*, chap. 3 (1859). (Many editions and printings.)

8. William S. Ellis, "A Way of Life Lost: Bikini," *National Geographic* 169 (1986): 813–34.

9. Gen. 1: 22.

10. As Alfred L. Malobre did in *The Wall Street Journal* of 15 March 1976.

11. Population Reference Bureau, *Population Today* 16 (July/August 1988): 10.

12. Jonathan Lieberson, "Too Many People?," *New York Review of Books,* 26 June 1986, 37.

13. An awkward problem encountered in writing a book that deals with a variable population is to make statements that will not be significantly wrong by the time the book is printed and read. The figures given here were true as of mid-1988. Obviously they will become less and less accurate as time passes. It is important that their inaccuracy not invalidate the points made. The northern European countries listed are all growing more slowly than the world as a whole: at 0.2 percent per year for northern Europe versus more than 1.7 percent for the rest of the world. So, if present trends continue, the changes in the numbers will make the argumentative point developed here even stronger with the passage of time. The position taken is, then, a conservative one.

14. George J. Stigler, *Essays in the History of Economics* (Chicago: University of Chicago Press, 1965), 16–17.

15. The material in Box 9-3 originally appeared in Huxley's *Tomorrow and Tomorrow and Tomorrow,* but it has been taken directly from Aldous Huxley, *Collected Essays* (New York: Bantam Books, 1960), 242.

Chapter 10

1. John Maynard Keynes, *Essays in Biography* (1933; reprint, New York: Meridian Books, 1956). See particularly pp. 23–25 and 36.

2. Helmut Schoeck, *Envy: A Theory of Social Behavior* (New York: Harcourt, Brace & World, 1969). The author makes a convincing case for a taboo enveloping the subject of envy, which is why there are so few writings on this subject. The word *envy* is one of the least often heard four-letter words in the English language. The alarums and excursions of the academic community cannot be understood without an acute awareness of the extent to which academicians are driven by envy. (But then, so are most ambitious men and women.)

3. Francis Bacon, *Of the Dignity and Advancement of Learning,* Ellis and Spedding ed. (1623; reprint, Freeport, New York: Books for Libraries Press, 1970), 548 (italics added to the most significant part).

4. Garrett Hardin, "Meaninglessness of the Word Protoplasm," *Scientific Monthly* 82 (1956): 112–120. The word *panchreston* is included in the *Oxford English Dictionary,* but as a simple synonym for "panacea" (which needs no synonym). A folksy equivalent of panchreston is "waterproof hypothesis." In science, panchresta can survive only so long as they are not recognized for what they are. More religiously inclined people welcome, rather than object to, panchresta.

5. T. R. Malthus, *An Essay on the Principle of Population . . . A New Edition, Very Much Enlarged* (London: J. Johnson, 1803), (472) (italics added to the key portions). The significance of this passage was called to my attention by Edwin Cannan, *A History of the Theories of Production and Distribution in English Political Economy from 1776 to 1848,* 3d ed. (London: P. S. King, 1924).

6. John W. Osborne, *The Silent Revolution* (New York: Scribner's, 1970), 67.

7. John Sparrow, *Too Much of a Good Thing* (Chicago: University of Chicago Press, 1977). This wise little book of only ninety-two pages is the work of a lawyer. Its message is much needed in our time, but it is seldom alluded to. No one in the business of selling *anything* wants to give this idea "a leg up"—and most of us are trying to sell *something.* Academics are trying to sell ideas, if nothing else.

8. Garrett Hardin, *Filters Against Folly* (New York: Viking, 1985). See particularly chap. 17.

Chapter 11

1. *Eccles. 12:12 (Goodspeed Bible).*

2. Rose E. Frisch, "Demographic Implications of the Biological Determinants of Female Fecundity," *Social Biology* 22 (1975): 17–22.

3. Tertullian, "On the Soul," in *Apologetical Works and Minucius Felix Octavius* (Washington, D.C.: Catholic University of America Press, 1950), 250.

4. E. P. Hutchinson, *The Population Debate* (Boston: Houghton Mifflin, 1967), 124.

5. For an example of the extreme illogicality to which an unacknowledged "unthinkable" can lead, dip into Allan Chase, *The Legacy of Malthus: The Social Costs of the New Scientific Racism* (New York: Alfred A. Knopf, 1976). This is surely the most fantastic analysis of population ever published by a legitimate press.

6. T. R. Malthus, *An Essay on the Principle of Population,* 3d ed. (London: J. Johnson, 1806), 509.

7. T. R. Malthus, *A Letter to Samuel Whitbread, Esq. M.P.,* 2d ed. (London: J. Johnson, 1807) in *The Pamphlets of Thomas Robert Malthus* (New York: Kelley, 1970), 38.

8. A statement made by M. Rupert Cutler when he was assistant secretary of agriculture

in the Carter administration. This sentence is frequently quoted in environmental publications, but it would be most surprising if it were ever printed in a realtors' journal.

Chapter 12

1. Raymond Swing, *Good Evening* (New York: Harcourt, Brace & World, 1964), 137.

2. William Godwin, *Of Population: An Enquiry Concerning the Power of Increase in the Numbers of Mankind, Being an Answer to Mr. Malthus's Essay on That Subject* (1820; reprint, New York: Augustus M. Kelley, 1964), 327–28.

3. James Bonar, *Malthus and His Work,* (1885; reprint, New York: Augustus M. Kelley, 1966), 371.

4. This graph owes much to the article "The human population," by Edward S. Deevey, Jr., in *Scientific American,* September 1960. Deevey uses a logarithmic scale for both axes. A little reflection, however, leads to the conclusion that logarithmic time is a very strange notion indeed. That is why I have preferred to put time on an arithmetic scale, with interruptions.

5. Edward T. Hall, *The Hidden Dimension* (New York: Doubleday, 1966), 100.

6. James Q. Wilson and Richard J. Herrnstein, *Crime and Human Nature.* (New York: Simon & Schuster, 1985). See entries under "time discounting." See also Seymour L. Halleck, *Psychiatry and the Dilemmas of Crime,* (New York: Hoeber, Harper & Row, 1967). (See entries under "gratification.")

7. Oscar Lewis, *The Children of Sanchez* (New York: Random House, 1961).

8. John Stuart Mill, *Principles of Political Economy.* (1848). The relevant passages are reprinted in the "Archives" section of *Population and Development Review* 12(February 1986): 317–22.

9. Richard E.W. Adams and Woodruff D. Smith, "Apocalyptic Visions: The Maya Collapse and Medieval Europe," *Archaeology,* Sept. 1977, 292–301.

10. Will Durant, *The Reformation* (New York: Simon & Schuster, 1957), 190.

11. Douglas Anderson, *Wall Street Journal,* 15 December 1986, 30.

Chapter 13

1. Garrett Hardin, *Exploring New Ethics for Survival: The Voyage of the Spaceship Beagle.* (New York: Viking, 1972), 66.

2. The empirical data together with methods of dealing with them can be found in the following excellent treatise: John Harte, *Consider a Spherical Cow: A Course in Environmental Problem Solving* (Los Altos, CA: William Kaufmann, 1985).

3. World Resources Institute, *World Resources 1987* (New York: Basic Books, 1987), 268.

4. This passage, taken from the "Second Day," is shortened without indicating the elisions. The accompanying figure is labeled Fig. 27.

5. Thomas Sowell, *A Conflict of Visions* (New York: William Morrow, 1987).

6. Shortly after the end of World War II, an iconoclastic biologist, the Californian Joel Hedgpeth, announced the founding of a Society for the Prevention of Progress. At its founding Professor Hedgpeth was president, treasurer, secretary, and sole member. The society followed its own advice and made no progress whatever—but it furnished amusement to many, not the least to Hedgpeth himself. He was almost two decades ahead of the environmental movement of the sixties.

7. P. H. Harman, *Energy, Force, and Matter* (Cambridge: Cambridge University Press, 1982), 67.

Chapter 14

1. W. Stanley Jevons, *The Coal Question,* 2d ed. (London: Macmillan, 1866), 331. The first edition was published in 1865.

2. Ibid., 176.

3. Ibid., 174.

4. Ibid., 239.

5. Ibid., 242–43.

6. Donella H. Meadows, Dennis L. Meadows, J. Randers, and W. W. Behrens III, *The Limits to Growth* (New York: Universe Books, 1972).

7. The work most often cited as a refutation of *The Limits to Growth* is the following, assembled by faculty at the University of Sussex: *Models of Doom: A Critique of The Limits to Growth,* ed. by H.S.D. Cole, et al. (New York: Universe Books, 1973). This has led to the work of Meadows, et al. being most often referred to as "discredited," though, curiously, the final chapter of the Sussex book—a response by Meadows et al.—is a successful refutation of the refuters. (How few who praise the opening pages of a book ever get around to reading the conclusion of it!)

8. Jevons, op. cit., v–vi.

9. Ibid., 242.

10. M. King Hubbert, "The World's Evolving Energy System." *American Journal of Physics* 49 (1981): 1007–29. This is the source of the data, the conversion factors being found ibid., 242.

11. John Harte, *Consider a Spherical Cow: A Course in Environmental Problem Solving* (Los Altos, CA: William Kaufmann, 1985), 240.

12. M. King Hubbert, "Energy from Fossil Fuels," *Science* 109 (1949): 103–9. (Also published in *Centennial,* a collection of papers from the Centennial Celebration of the American Association for the Advancement of Science (Washington, D.C.: American Association of the Advancement of Science, 1950).

13. Stephen Goodwin, "Hubbert's Curve," *Country Journal,* 1980, no. 11: 56–61.

14. Hubbert (1981), op. cit., 1007.

15. John Maynard Keynes, *Essays and Sketches in Biography* (New York: Meridian Books, 1956), 132.

Chapter 15

1. Mario Bunge and William R. Shea, eds., *Rutherford and Physics at the Turn of the Century* (London: Dawson, 1979), 120.

2. Robert A. Millikan, "Alleged Sins of Science," *Scribner's Magazine,* 87(1930): 119–30.

3. Joseph J. Corn, ed., *Imagining Tomorrow* (Cambridge, MA: MIT Press, 1987), 60–61.

4. Ibid., 73.

5. Ibid., 58.

6. Richard T. Sylves, *The Nuclear Oracles* (Ames, IA: Iowa State University Press, 1987), 189, 193.

7. Otto R. Frisch, "Somebody Turned the Sun on With a Switch," *Science and Public Affairs* 30(1974):17.

8. Philip M. Morse, (1950) "Pure and Applied Research," *American Scientist* 38 (1950): 257.

9. Eliot Marshall, "Hanford's Radioactive Tumbleweed," *Science* 236 (1987) 1616.

10. Daniel Ford, *The Cult of the Atom* (New York: Simon & Schuster, 1982), 50.

11. Aristotle, *Politics,* book 2, chap. 3 (New York: Viking, 1971), 27.

12. Early on, technological optimists proposed that we load nuclear wastes into rockets which we would shoot off to the sun. This was a splendid idea except for one small difficulty: our rockets are not 100 percent reliable, nor are they ever likely to be. When the control machinery of a rocket malfunctions early in its trajectory the ground crew gives an order for its self-destruction. At that point the contents of the rocket are blown into fragments and distributed widely in the stratosphere—from which they will eventually fall back to earth. Oh, well, back to the drawing board!

13. What it means for conscientious and honest people to try to work in such a lab is revealed in the following report: Deborah Blum, "Weird Science: Livermore's X-ray Laser Flap," *Bulletin of the Atomic Scientists,* 44(1988): 7–13.

14. A sound and thorough discussion of the Rasmussen Report and its logic may be found in K. S. Shrader-Frechette, *Nuclear Power and Public Policy* (Boston: D. Reidel, 1983).

15. Bruce L. Welch, "Deception on Nuclear Power Risks: A Call for Action," *Bulletin of the Atomic Scientists,* 1980, 50–54.

16. Richard C. Bell and Rory O'Connor, 1982). *Nukespeak* (San Francisco: Sierra Club Books, 1982). (See Stephen Hilgartner, et al., 127.)

17. Alvin M. Weinberg, "Social Institutions and Nuclear Energy," *Science* 177 (1972): 33–34.

18. Wilson Clark, *Energy for Survival* (Garden City, NY: Anchor, 1974), 276.

19. Adam Smith, *The Wealth of Nations* (1776; reprint, New York: Modern Library, 1937), 734.

20. Samuel C. Florman, *The Civilized Engineer* (New York: St. Martin's Press, 1987), 146.

21. Garrett Hardin, "How Diversity Should Be Nurtured," *The Social Contract* 1 (1991): 137–39. This journal, as well as another quarterly, *Academic Questions,* have much to say about the recent degradation of higher education into an instrument designed to fragment society.

Chapter 16

1. William Godwin, *Enquiry Concerning Political Justice,* 3d ed. (1798; reprint, New York: Penguin Books, 1985), 776–77.

2. Sterility that is not universal *can* be selected for. Consider the honey bee. The queen produces scads of infertile daughters (worker bees) for every fertile daughter (queen bee) that she produces, and this scheme clearly has selective value. But universal sterility . . . ? It's not in the cards.

3. Gen. 1:26, (Goodspeed Bible, 1923).

4. William Witte, article on J.C.F. Schiller, *Encyclopaedia Britannica* 16 (1974): 342.

5. J. DuPaquier et al., *Malthus Past and Present* (New York: Academic Press, 1983), 228.

6. William R. Catton, Jr. and Riley R. Dunlap, "A New Ecological Paradigm for Post-Exuberant Sociology, *American Behavioral Scientist* 24 (1980): 15–47, 17–18. These authors use the term *exemptionalism,* which I have shortened to *exemptionism.*

7. Riley E. Dunlap, "Ecological "News" and Competing Paradigms," *Technological Forecasting and Social Change* 23 (1983): 204n. For evidence on the economic position, Dunlap cites D. Hamrin, *Managing Growth in the 1980s: Toward a New Economics* (New York: Praeger, 1980).

8. Kenneth E. Boulding, *The Image* (Ann Arbor: University of Michigan Press, 1956), 117–19. Boulding's "image" is related to, but not completely congruent with, the "vision" of reality so successfully advanced by Thomas Sowell thirty-one years later in *A Conflict of Visions.* Sowell seems not to have read Boulding's book.

9. Adam Smith, *The Wealth of Nations* (1776; reprint, New York: Modern Library, 1937), 79.

10. For a wide-ranging survey of "rational" adaptations of breeding to environmental factors see David Lack, *Ecological Adaptations for Breeding in Birds* (London: Methuen, (1968). For a particularly striking instance of "wisdom in nature," see J. Koskimies, 1950. "The Life of the Swift, *Micropus apus* (L.), in Relation to the Weather," *Annales Academiae Scientiarum Fennicae, Series A, IV. Biologica* 12 (1950): 1–151.

11. Thomas Rowe Edmonds, *An Enquiry into the Principles of Population, exhibiting a System of Regulations for the Poor; designed immediately to lessen, and finally to remove, the evils which have hitherto pressed upon the Labouring Classes of Society* (London: published anonymously, 1832).

12. Thomas Doubleday, *The True Law of Population* (London: Simpkin, Marshall & Co., 1842).

13. Rose E. Frisch, "Population, Food Intake, and Fertility," *Science* 199 (1978): 22–30.

14. Ancel Keys, et al. *The Biology of Human Starvation* (Minneapolis: University of Minnesota Press, 1950).

15. Josué de Castro, *The Geography of Hunger* (Boston: Little, Brown, 1952), 71.

16. Kingsley Davis, review of *The Geography of Hunger,* by Josué de Castro, *American Sociological Review* 17 (1952): 500–501.

17. Henry Pratt Fairchild, review of *The Geography of Hunger,* by Josué de Castro, *Social Forces* 31 (1952): 82–84.

18. A. Sauvy, review of *The Geography of Hunger,* by Josué de Castro, *Pacific Affairs* 25 (1952): 298–99.

19. Marston Bates, *The Prevalence of People,* (New York: Scribner's, 1955).

20. Lester R. Brown, "In the Human Interest," *A Strategy to Stabilize World Population* (New York: W. W. Norton, 1974), 119.

21. D.E.C. Eversley, *Social Theories of Fertility and the Malthusian Debate* (Oxford: Clarendon Press, 1959), 201. Italics added.

22. Carl E. Taylor, "Ethics for an International Health Profession," *Science,* 153 (1966): 719.

23. A. J. Coale, "The Demographic Transition," *International Population Conference of the International Union for the Scientific Study of Population,* (Liège, Belgium, 1973), 61.

24. S. Preston, *The Effects of Infant and Child Mortality on Fertility* (New York: Academic Press, 1978).

25. A.K.M.A. Chowdhury, "The Effect of Child Mortality Experience on Subsequent Fertility: In Pakistan and Bangladesh," *Population Studies,* 30 (1976): 249–261.

26. Karen L. Michaelson, ed., *And the Poor Get Children: Radical Perspectives on Population Dynamics,* report by Barbara Aswad (New York: Monthly Review Press, 1981), 91.

27. Denis Fair, "Sub-Saharan Africa and the Population Issue," *Africa Insight* 15 (1985): 252–55, 253.

28. Anne R. Pebley, Hernan Delgado, and Elena Brinemann, *Studies in Family Planning,* 1979, 129–36.

29. Oscar Harkavy, *The Ford Foundation's Work in Population* (New York: Ford Foundation, 1985), 18–19.

30. Alan Gregg, "A Medical Aspect of the Population Problem," *Science* 121 (1955): 681–82.

31. Garrett Hardin, "Gregg's Law," *BioScience* 25 (1975): 294.

32. David Ewing Duncan, "Africa: The Long Good-bye," *The Atlantic* 266 (1990): 20–24.

33. William James, *Pragmatism: A New Name for Some Old Ways of Thinking,* lecture 1 (1907; reprint, Cambridge, MA: Harvard University Press, 1975).

34. Ibid., 11.

Chapter 17

1. Etienne van de Walle, review of, *Population and Development Review* 13 (1987): 547–50.

2. William Petersen, *Population,* 2d ed (New York: Macmillan, 1969), 11.

3. Michael S. Teitelbaum, "Relevance of Demographic Transition Theory for Developing Countries," *Science* 188 (1975): 420.

4. Michael S. Teitelbaum and Jay M. Winter, *The Fear of Population Decline* (Orlando, Florida: Academic Press, 1985), 14.

5. Forty per thousand is the same as 4 percent. For no particularly good reason, demographers long ago standardized on presenting birth and death rates as numbers *per mil* rather than as numbers *per centum.* Perforce, we follow the crowd.

6. Tim Dyson and Mike Murphy, "The Onset of Fertility Transition," *Population and Development Review* 11 (1985): 430, 432.

7. Karl R. Popper, *The Poverty of Historicism* (London: Routledge & Kegan Paul, 1957).

8. Robert C. Tucker, ed., *The Marx-Engels Reader* (New York: Norton, 1972), 603.

9. John Silber, *Straight Shooting* (New York: Harper & Row, 1989), 57.

10. Dennis Gabor, *Inventing the Future* (London: Secker & Warburg, 1963), 185.

11. W. W. Rostow, "The Take-off into Self-Sustained Growth," *Economic Journal* 66 (1956): 25–48.

12. Van de Walle, op. cit. This conclusion is undergirded by the work of Ansley Coale, Coale and Watkins; and many others.

13. Ester Boserup, "Economic and Demographic Interrelationships in Sub-Saharan Africa," *Population and Development Review* 11 (1985): 395.

14. Thomas J. Goliber, "Africa's Expanding Population: Old Problems, New Policies," *Population Bulletin,* 1989, no. 3.

Chapter 18

1. John Maynard Keynes, *General Theory of Employment, Interest, and Money* (London: Macmillan, 1936), 383.

2. Darrell Huff, *How to Lie with Statistics* (New York: Norton, 1954).

3. Harold J. Barnett, Gerald M. van Muiswinkel, Mordecai Shecter, and John G. Myers, "Global Trends in Non-Fuel Minerals," in Julian L. Simon and Herman Kahn, *The Resourceful Earth,* (Oxford: Basil Blackwell, 1984). Quotations 1, 6, 7, and 8 come respectively from pages 317, 317, 317, and 321.

4. Harold J. Barnett and Chandler Morse, *Scarcity and Growth: The Economics of Resource Scarcity* (Baltimore: Johns Hopkins University Press, for Resources for the Future, 1963), 199.

5. Ibid., 317.

6. World Commission on Environment and Development, *Our Common Future* (New York: Oxford University Press, 1987), 8.

7. Herman E. Daly, "Toward Some Operational Principles of Sustainable Development," *Ecological Economics,* 2 (1990):1–6. It is worth noting that Jessica Tuchman Mathews has referred to "sustainable development" as this "still elusive term." (*Preserving the Global Environment* [New York: Norton, 1991], 16.) This is more tactful than Daly's "oxymoron." Most commentaters are more tactful still and use the term as if it had a defensible meaning, though they never say what it is. With the coinage of "sustainable development," the defenders of the unsteady-state have won a few more years' moratorium from the painful process of thinking.

8. Kenneth E. Boulding. In a personal communication Professor Boulding acknowl-

edges that he is the author of this aphorism, but he cannot recall the occasion on which he first voiced it.

9. Paul R. Ehrlich, "An Ecologist Standing Up Among Seated Social Scientists," *CoEvolution Quarterly* 31 (1981): 28.

10. Herman E. Daly, *Steady-State Economics* (San Francisco: W. H. Freeman, 1977). It is worth noting that the epithet comes from the Roman satirist Juvenal: *rara avis in terris nigroque simillima cycno,* "a rare bird upon the earth and very like a black swan."

11. J. H. Fremlin, "How Many People Can the World Support?", *New Scientist* 415 (1964): 285–87.

12. Daniel A. Underwood and Paul G. King, "On the Ideological Foundations of Environmental Policy, *Ecological Economics* 1(1989): 326.

13. Ibid., 329.

Chapter 19

1. Piercy Ravenstone, *A Few Doubts . . . on . . . Population and Political Economy* (1821; reprint, New York: Augustus M. Kelley, 1966), 45.

2. Garrett Hardin, "The Cybernetics of Competition," *Perspectives in Biology and Medicine* 7 (1963): 58–84.

3. "Why Government Often Makes Matters Worse," *Fortune,* February 1974, 56.

4. Francis Thompson, "The Mistress of Vision," *The Works of Francis Thompson,* vol. 2. (London: Burns & Oates, 1897), 9.

5. John Muir, *My First Summer in the Sierra* (1911; reprint, Sellanraa, Dunwoody, Georgia: Norman S. Berg, 1972), 211.

6. Barry Commoner, *The Closing Circle* (New York: Knopf, 1971), 33.

7. John Passmore, *Man's Responsibility for Nature* (New York: Scribner's, 1974), 194.

8. Beverly Taylor, *Francis Thompson* (Boston: Twayne, 1897), 4.

9. Robert K. Merton, "The Unanticipated Consequences of Purposive Social Action," *American Sociological Review* 1 (1936): 894–904.

10. Robert A. Leone, *Who Profits. Winners, Losers, and Government Regulation* (New York: Basic Books, 1986), 3.

11. Daniel L. McKinley, 1969. Personal communication.

12. Garrett Hardin, "Guilty Until Proven Innocent," chap. 7 in *Exploring New Ethics for Survival* (New York: Viking, 1972).

13. Paul Ehrlich and John Holdren, "The Impact of Population Growth, *Science* 171 (1971): 1212–17.

14. Paul R. Ehrlich and Anne H. Ehrlich, *Healing the Planet* (Reading, MA: Addison-Wesley 1991), 7.

15. Mark Sagoff, "The Philosopher As Teacher?", *Metaphilosophy* 11 (1980): 315.

16. James S. Coleman, "On the Self-Suppression of Academic Freedom," *Academic Questions,* 4 (1991): 21.

Chapter 20

1. Herman E. Daly, review, *Population and Development Review* 12 (1986): 582–85.

2. National Research Council, *Population Growth and Economic Development: Policy Questions,* Working Group on Population Growth and Economic Development, Committee on Population, (Washington, D.C.: National Academy Press, 1986).

3. The references for the statements in the box are as follows: (1), (2) William Petersen,

"Marxism and the Population Question: Theory and Practice," *Population and Development Review* 14(1988 suppl.): 77–101. (3), Bernard Berelson, "The World's Second Problem, *Phelps-Stokes Intercollegiate Assembly* (Phelps-Stokes Fund, 1965). (4)Herman E. Daly, *Steady-State Economics* (San Francisco: W. H. Freeman, 1977), 164. (5) Peter T. Bauer, *Dissent on Development* (Cambridge, MA: Harvard University Press, 1976), 64 (6) Edward Goldsmith, "Developing the Third World," *The Ecologist* 7(1977): 338–39. (7) Julian Simon and Herman Kahn, *The Resourceful Earth* (Oxford: Basil Blackwell, 1984), 45. (8) Constance Holden, news report, *Science,* 1987, 236: 769. (9) Gro Harlem Brundtland, "How to Secure our Common Future, *Scientific American* 261 (1989): 190.

4. Donald Mann, "Reflections on Sustainable Development," *Human Survival,* 15 (1989): 2.

5. Herman E. Daly, review, *Population and Development Review* 12 (1986): 584.

6. Garrett Hardin, "Carrying Capacity as an Ethical Concept," *Soundings* 59 (1976): 120–37.

7. E.F. Schumacher, Plowboy interview, *Mother Earth News,* November 1976, page 15.

8. Henry Miller, *The Colossus of Maroussi* (New York: New Directions, 1941), 153.

9. Henry Davis has remarked that this passage is extremely involved and probably corrupt. I have used the Jowett translation, making numerous elisions in order to maintain the thread of thought. To aid in the reading I have omitted ellipses (. . .).

10. David Sheridan, *Desertification of the United States* (Washington, DC: Superintendent of Documents, 1981), 121.

11. David R. Klein, "The Introduction, Increase, and Crash of Reindeer on St. Matthew's Island, *Journal of Wildlife Management* 32 (1968): 350–67.

For a retelling and interpretation of this work, and much else in the present chapter, see my "Sentiment, Guilt, and Reason in the Management of Wild Herds," *The Cato Journal* 2 (1982): 823–33. This has been reprinted in *CoEvolution Quarterly* 40 (Winter 1983); and in *Free Inquiry* 5(Winter 1984–1985): 32–36. The spread of these journals from conservative right to liberal left shows that the ideas of biological conservation should not be labeled as either liberal or conservative (in the political sense).

12. Joseph Townsend, *A Dissertation on the Poor Laws, by a Well-Wisher to Mankind* (1786; reprint, Berkeley: University of California Press, 1971).

13. Susan L. Flader, *Thinking Like a Mountain* (Columbia: University of Missouri Press, 1974). This is the source of most of the material bearing on Leopold; see particularly pages 93–94 and 153–54.

14. Hugh Iltis, 1992, personal communication.

15. Flader, *Thinking Like a Mountain,* 202.

16. Curt Meine, *Aldo Leopold* (Madison: University of Wisconsin Press, 1988), 462. Italics added.

17. UPI news report, *Santa Barbara News-Press,* 11 March 1981, C13.

18. This "Calorie" is the nutritionist's unit and is a thousand times as large as the physicist's "calorie," which is written with a small c. The nutritionist's Calorie is also called a "kilocalorie," and abbreviated "kCal."

19. Roger Revelle, "Food and Population," *Scientific American* 231 (1974): 161–70.

20. Deut. 8:3. (Goodspeed Bible).

21. Patricia James, *Population Malthus* (London: Routledge & Kegan Paul, 1979), 363.

22. William R. Catton, Jr., "The World's Most Polymorphic Species: Carrying Capacity Transgressed in Two Ways, *BioScience* 37 (1987): 416.

23. Garrett Hardin, "Wilderness, a Probe into 'Cultural Carrying Capacity,'" *Population and Environment* 10 (1988): 5–13.

24. Garrett Hardin, "Cultural Carrying Capacity: A Biological Approach to Human Problems, *BioScience* 36 (1986): 599–606.

Chapter 21

1. Paul Hollander, *Political Pilgrims* (New York: Oxford University Press, 1981), 417n.

2. Karl Marx, "Critique of the Gotha Program" (1875) in *The Marx-Engels Reader*, ed. Robert C. Tucker (New York: Norton, 1972), 388.

3. Eric Hoffer, *The True Believer* (New York: Harper, 1951).

4. William Forster Lloyd, *Two Lectures on the Checks to Population* (1833; reprint, New York: Augustus M. Kelley, 1968), 19–20, 30–31.

5. Garrett Hardin, "The Tragedy of the Commons," *Science* 162 (1968): 1243–48.

6. Lloyd, *Two Lectures*, 21.

7. Charles Frankel, *The Case for Modern Man* (New York: Harper, 1955), 203.

8. Lloyd, *Two Lectures*, 21–23.

9. Knut Hagberg, *Carl Linnaeus* (New York: Dutton, 1953), 118.

10. William L. Langer, "Europe's Initial Population Explosion, *American Historical Review* 69 (1963): 1–17.

11. E. P. Hutchinson, *The Population Debate* (Boston: Houghton Mifflin, 1967), 25–26.

12. James Alfred Field, *Essays on Population* (Chicago: University of Chicago Press, 1931), 111.

13. Ronald Hamowy, *The Scottish Enlightenment and the Theory of Spontaneous Order* (Carbondale, IL: Southern Illinois University Press, 1987), 6.

14. Adam Smith, *The Wealth of Nations*, ed. Edwin Cannan (1776; reprint, NY: Modern Library, 1937), 423.

15. Richard M. Romano, "William Forster Lloyd—A Non-Ricardian?," *History of Political Economy*, 9 (1977): 412–41.

16. United Nations, *The Determinants and Consequences of Population Trends* (New York: United Nations, 1953), 32.

Chapter 22

1. I have been told that Ralph Barton Perry (1876–1957) is responsible for the term "egocentric predicament," but I have not yet been able to verify this.

2. Ernest Jones, *The Life and Work of Sigmund Freud*, vol. 2 (New York: Basic Books, (1955) 389.

3. UPI report, *Santa Barbara News-Press*, 26 October 1978, 1.

4. References for the statements in the box follow. (2) David Harris, article on Helvetius, *Encyclopaedia Britannica* 6 (1974):891–92. (3) Adam Smith, *The Theory of Moral Sentiments* (1759; reprint, Indianapolis: Liberty Classics, 1969), 152. (4) Thomas Robert Malthus, *An Essay on the Principle of Population*, 3d ed., vol. 2, app. (1806; reprint, London: J. Johnson, 522. (5) Peter Singer, *The Expanding Circle* (New York: Farrar, Straus & Giroux, 1981), xiii. (6) (7) Herman Feifel, *The Meaning of Death*, 117. (8) Fyodor Dostoyevsky, *The Brothers Karamazov*. vol. 1 (1880; reprint, Baltimore: Penguin Books, 1890, 62. (9) C. S. Lewis, *The Screwtape Letters* (1942; reprint, London: Fontana Books, 1955), 134–35. (10) Graham Hancock, *Lords of Poverty* (New York: Atlantic Monthly Press, 1989), 71.

5. Joseph Fabry, "The Golden Rule of the Ecosystem," *The Churchman* 190 (1976): 6–8.

6. Charles Darwin, *The Origin of Species by Means of Natural Selection*, 6th ed. (1859; reprint, New York: Macmillan, 1927), 197–98. (italics added).

7. Richard D. Alexander, "The Evolution of Genitalia and Mating Behavior in Crickets (Gryllidae) and Other Orthoptera," *Miscellaneous Publications of the Museum of Zoology, University of Michigan* 133 (1967): 1–62.

8. Richard Dawkins, *The Selfish Gene* (New York: Oxford University Press, 1976).

9. Garrett Hardin, "Discriminating Altruisms," *Zygon* 17 (1982): 163–86. The present chapter leans heavily on this paper.

10. David P. Barash, *The Whisperings Within* (New York: Harper & Row, 1979), 155.

11. Edward O. Wilson, *Sociobiology* (Cambridge, MA: Harvard University Press, 1975), 553.

12. Anatol Rapaport and A. M. Chammah, *The Prisoner's Dilemma* (Ann Arbor: University of Michigan Press, 1965).

13. William Shakespeare, *King Henry V,* act 4, sc. 3.

14. Alan F. Westin, ed., *Whistle-Blowing: Loyalty and Dissent in the Corporation* (New York: McGraw-Hill, 1981).

15. Rosalie Pedalino Porter, *Forked Tongue: The Politics of Bilingual Education* (New York: Basic Books, 1990).

16. Roger Kimball, *Tenured Radicals: How Politics Has Corrupted Our Higher Education* (New York: Harper & Row, 1990).

17. James Boswell, Life of Samuel Johnson (New York: Viking-Penguin, 1979, 182) (italics added).

18. Thomas Curtis Clark, "The New Loyalty," in *The New Patriotism,* ed. Thomas Curtis Clark and Esther Gillespie (Indianapolis: Bobbs-Merrill, 1927).

19. Alexander Gray, *The Socialist Tradition* (London: Longmans, Green, 1946), 159.

20. Paul Hollander, *Political Pilgrims* (New York: Oxford University Press, 1981).

21. E. M. Forster, *Two Cheers for Democracy* (New York: Harcourt, Brace & World, 1951), 68.

Chapter 23

1. Walter Lippmann, *The Method of Freedom* (New York: Macmillan, 1934), 25–26.

2. Garrett Hardin, *Filters Against Folly: How to Survive Despite Economists, Ecologists, and the Merely Eloquent,* chap. 10 (New York: Viking-Penguin, 1985).

3. Peter Passell and Leonard Ross, "Effluence and Affluence: Or, Growth Is Not a Dirty Word," *Columbia Forum* 2 (1973): 32.

4. Joseph A. Schumpeter, *History of Economic Analysis* (New York: Oxford University Press, 1954).

5. Edmund Whittaker, *A History of Economic Ideas* (London: Longmans, Green, 1940).

6. Thomas Sowell, *Compassion versus Guilt* (New York: William Morrow, 1987), 38.

7. Howard H. Hiatt, 1975. "Protecting the Medical Commons: Who is Responsible?" *New England Journal of Medicine* 293 (1975): 235–41. See also his book, *America's Health in the Balance* (New York: Harper & Row, 1987).

8. Peter G. Peterson, *Atlantic Monthly* (October 1987): 43–69.

9. Mildred T. Stahlman, "Future Ethical Issues in Neonatality," *Seminars in Perinatalogy* 9(1987): 201–90.

10. News report by Cathy Trost, *Wall Street Journal,* 18 July 1989, A7.

11. Roberta Friedman, "Miracle Babies," *The Stanford Magazine,* 1988, no. 4: 47–51.

12. News report, *Wall Street Journal,* 30 December 1987, A15.

13. Qui Renzong, "Economics and Medical Decision-Making: A Chinese Perspective," *Seminars in Perinatology* 9(1987): 262–63.

14. *Los Angeles Times,* 8 November 1987, 1, 3.

15. Fred Siegel, "Nothing in Moderation," *Atlantic Monthly* 265(1990): 110.

16. Fred Siegel, "Dependent Individualism: A Welfare State Without an Ethical Core?" *Dissent* (Fall 1988) 437, 443.

Chapter 24

1. J.A.M.H. Damoiseaux, "Result of the International Contest on Population Problems in Underdeveloped Areas," *Social Compass* 7 (1960): 267–72.

2. I have always regretted that I was not a mouse in the woodwork when my entry was received and reacted to. My answer to the problem posed was that an acceptable Catholic "solution" would prove counterproductive, that it would in fact create runaway population growth. I sent copies to both the award committee and the Vatican. Curiously, I received replies from neither quarter. I later published my little paper under the modest title "A Second Sermon on the Mount" in *Perspectives in Biology and Medicine* 6 (1963): 366–71. It has been republished on pages 60–66 of my book, *Stalking the Wild Taboo,* 2d ed. (Los Altos, CA: William Kaufmann, 1978). So far as I know, it has been reprinted nowhere else.

3. Jane Austen, *Emma,* vol. 3, chap. 3) (1816).

4. Roger Glass, et al., "Earthquake Injuries Related to Housing in a Guatemalan Village," *Science* 197 (1977): 638–43.

5. Garrett Hardin, "Nobody Ever Dies of Overpopulation," *Science* 171 (1971): 527. This has been slightly shortened for Box 24-1. What was then the East Bengal region of Pakistan has since become Bangladesh.

6. *Wall Street Journal,* 19 June 1985, 32.

7. C. P. Snow, *The State of Siege* (New York: Scribner's, 1969), 19–20.

8. H. M. Robertson, "Reflexions on Malthus and His Predecessors," *South African Journal of Economics* 10 (1982): 304.

9. Nora Barlow, *The Autobiography of Charles Darwin* (1876; reprint, London: Collins, 1958), 120.

10. This is a selection, without ellipses, from the last paragraph of chap. 3 and the first paragraph of chap. 4 of Charles Darwin's *The Origin of Species.*

11. Charles Galton Darwin, "Can Man Control His Numbers?" in *Evolution After Darwin,* vol. 2, ed. Sol Tax (Chicago: University of Chicago Press, 1960), 460.

12. Jeffrey M. Wise and Spencer J. Condie, "Intergenerational Fertility Throughout Four Generations," *Social Biology* 22 (1975): 144–50.

Chapter 25

1. Joseph Townsend, *A Dissertation on the Poor Laws, By a Well-Wisher to Mankind* (1786; reprint, Berkeley: University of California Press, 1971, 36–38.

2. Daniel B. Botkin, *Discordant Harmonies* (New York: Oxford University Press, 1990). This book contains a meaningful analysis of the conditions necessary for stability.

3. Garrett Hardin, *Population, Evolution and Birth Control: A Collage of Controversial Ideas,* 2d ed. (San Francisco: W. H. Freeman, 1969), 28.

4. Charles Galton Darwin, "Can Man Control His Numbers?", in *Evolution After Darwin,* vol. 2, ed. Sol Tax (Chicago: University of Chicago Press, 1960), 464.

5. E. F. Schumacher, *Small is Beautiful* (New York: Harper Torchbooks, 1973).

6. Nora K. Wallace, "Lompoc's First Baby Joins Big Crowd—6 Brothers, 4 Sisters," *Santa Barbara News-Press,* 4 January 1991, A1, A6.

7. News report, *Planned Parenthood News,* 1968, no. 168: 3.

8. Charles Frankel, *The Case for Modern Man* (New York: Harper, 1955, 203).

9. Kari Bullock and John Baden, "Communes and the Logic of the Commons," *Managing the Commons,* ed. Garrett Hardin and John Baden, (San Francisco: W. H. Freeman, 1977).

10. Constance Noyes Robertson, *Oneida Community: An Autobiography, 1851–1876.* (Syracuse, NY: Syracuse University Press, 1970).

11. Garrett Hardin, 1991, review of *Coercive Birth Control in China,* by John S. Aird, *Population and Environment,* 1991, no. 4: 417–18.

12. *Encyclopaedia Britannica,* 1974, vol. 6, p. 891.

13. I am informed by Professor Hugh Iltis that a Wisconsin study completed in 1991 found that society invested an average of $14,000 per year for twenty years in each child raised, making a total of $280,000. Inflation being the norm in our welfare state, this figure can only go up with the passage of time.

14. Kenneth E. Boulding, *The Meaning of the Twentieth Century* (New York: Harper & Row, 1964), 135–36.

15. Garrett Hardin, "The Tragedy of the Commons," *Science* 162 (1968): 1243–48.

Chapter 26

1. Alfred Sauvy, "The 'False Problem' of World Population." (reprinted) *Population and Development Review* (1949), reprint, 16 (1990): 760.

2. Bertrand Russell, *Authority and the Individual* (London: Allen & Unwin, 1949), 17.

3. Garrett Hardin, *Filters Against Folly. How to Survive Despite Economists, Ecologists, and the Merely Eloquent,* chap. 13 (New York: Viking-Penguin, 1985).

4. News report, *Immigration Report* (Federation for American Immigration Reform), 1990, no. 6: 1.

5. Garrett Hardin, "Living on a Lifeboat," *BioScience* 24 (1974):561–68.

6. Katharine Betts, *Ideology and Immigration: Australia 1976 to 1982* (Melbourne: Melbourne University Press, 1988).

7. Adlai Stevenson, speech given in Geneva, July 1965, shortly before he died on Bastille Day. Often quoted, seldom referenced.

8. Archibald MacLeish, *New York Times,* 25 December 1968.

9. Banesh Hoffman, *Albert Einstein, Creator and Rebel* (New York: New American Library, 1972), 253.

10. News report, *Members' Corner* (Federation for American Immigration Reform), May 1990, 2.

11. George J. Borjas, *Friends or Strangers: The Impact of Immigrants on the U.S. Economy* (New York: Basic Books, 1990), 24.

12. Ibid., 9.

13. Linda Chavez, *Out of the Barrio: Toward a New Politics of Hispanic Assimilation,* (New York: Basic Books, 1991), 14ff.

14. News report, *Wall Street Journal,* 25 September 1980, 1.

15. Rosalie Pedalino Porter, *Forked Tongue: The Politics of Bilingual Education* (New York: Basic Books, 1990).

16. John Silber, *Straight Shooting* (New York: Harper & Row, 1989), 25.

17. William E. Simon, *A Time For Truth.* (New York: McGraw-Hill, 1978), 195–96.

18. Ben Wattenberg, testifying before the House Judiciary Subcommittee on Immigration, 1 March 1990.

19. C. Northcote Parkinson, *Parkinson's Law: And Other Studies in Administration* (Cambridge, MA: Houghton Mifflin, 1957). This 113-page book is undoubtedly a major contribution to social and political science. Unfortunately it is seldom recognized as such by the academic community. Why? Several possible explanations can be advanced. It is easily understood. The argument is developed in humorous vein, with amusing cartoons by Robert C. Osborn. The author is identified as the "Raffles Professor of History"; to those who are unfamiliar with the history of southeast Asia the whimsical word "Raffles" may sound fictitious, thus suggesting that the whole argument is a put-on. A pity.

20. Richard B. Lee and Irven DeVore, eds., *Man the Hunter* (Chicago: Aldine, 1968).

21. Lawrence Auster, *The Path to National Suicide: An Essay on Immigration and Multiculturalism* (Monterey, VA: The American Immigration Control Foundation, 1990), 60–61.

22. Katharine Betts, *Idealogy and Immigration* (Melbourne: Melbourne University Press, 1988), 154.

23. Jack Parsons, *Population versus Liberty* (London: Pemberton Books, 1971). See particularly Part III.

24. *Newsweek,* 4 January 1988, 24.

25. Ernest Barker, trans., *The Politics of Aristotle* (New York: Oxford University Press, 1946), 291.

26. Garrett Hardin, How diversity should be nurtured. *The Social Contract* 1(1991): 139.

Index

333